• T R O P H

Intervention Teacher's Guide

Grade 1

Orlando Boston Dallas Chicago San Diego

Visit *The Learning Site!*
www.harcourtschool.com

Printed in the United States of America

ISBN 0-15-326512-4

15 16 048 10 09 08 07

Table of Contents

Introduction

Research has shown the importance of building a strong foundation early in the process of learning to read. Most children will acquire the foundational skills needed for success in learning to read. These requisite skills that include phonemic awareness, letter names and sounds, letter-sound associations, word blending and word building, and recognition of high-frequency words all contribute to success in learning to read.

However, research also shows us that children enter school with a wide range of previous experiences with forms and functions of print. Also, there are enormous individual differences in learning rates and learning needs that will affect children's progression in learning to read. Many children will have difficulty learning to read unless extensive additional instruction and practice is provided.

Intervention that addresses the learning needs of these children is paramount to effective prevention of difficulty in learning to read. Intervention that is offered early and targeted to children who need it most will facilitate success in learning to read. Intervention requires additional engaged academic time and support through strategic and systematic instruction in the foundational and requisite reading skills.

The *Trophies* Intervention Kit provides additional intensive systematic teaching and practice to help children to learn the skills and strategies important for proficient reading. Aligned with and correlated to the instructional goals and objectives of *Trophies* Grade 1 program, the Intervention Kit optimizes the learning opportunities and outcomes for children at risk. The additional targeted teaching and practice will help children build a strong foundation in the fundamental skills for successfully learning to read.

Components

Teacher's Guide

A collection of day-by-day lessons directly aligned with and correlated to the lessons in the Trophies Teacher's Editions.
Each day's plan includes:

Warm-up An optional activity to review and reinforce the phonemic awareness skills of sound isolation, blending, substitution, and deletion and rhyming.

Phonics Instruction and activities to **Reteach** the phonics skills taught in the core program that day.

High-frequency Words Suggestions to **Preteach**, **Reteach**, and provide cumulative review and reinforcement of the high-frequency words taught, increasing the exposure to and experiences with words children should be learning.

Read Daily suggestions for reading or rereading one title in the Trophies Grade 1 Below-level Reader Collection. Instructional strategies include echo reading, choral reading, directed reading, and rereading for fluency.

Phonics Instruction and activities to **Preteach** the next day's phonics skills.

Below-level Readers Collection, Grade 1

A set of books written to controlled vocabulary and progressive phonics elements to reinforce high-frequency words, phonic elements, and comprehension strategies.

Assessment

A book of tests for frequent, ongoing evaluation of knowledge and skills being taught and a Recording Form to record children's progress.

Picture Cards

A set of four-color illustrations to support phonemic awareness, phonics instruction, and sentence building.

Alphabet Masters

A book of reproducible illustrations and letter forms to support instruction of letter names, letter forms and formation, and letter-sound associations.

Word Builder and Word Builder Cards

A teacher can use the Word Builder and the consonant and vowel cards as an instructional tool to demonstrate blending and word building. The child can use the Word Builder and the cards to develop blending and word building skills.

Write-On/Wipe-Off Board with Phonemic Awareness Disks

This instructional tool helps make the abstract concept of phonemes more concrete. One side of the board has Elkonin boxes so children can track phonemes in two and three phoneme words or syllables in two- and three-syllable words. The other side provides a model of the uppercase and lowercase alphabet, space for writing or drawing with dry-erase markers, and write-on lines to practice letter formation and handwriting.

Practice Book

A write-in, consumable text to provide direct application and practice of phonic elements and high-frequency words. It includes a set of individual picture and letter cards for the child to practice sound matching, decoding, and sentence building.

Tactile Letter Cards

A set of cards with textured uppercase and lowercase letters to support recognition of letter names and letter forms and to practice word blending and word building.

Magnetic Letters

A set of three-dimensional uppercase and lowercase magnetic letters for hands-on practice with letter names, letter forms, word blending, and word building.

Game Boards

A set of five board games with word card game pieces to practice and apply decoding skills in a game format.

Resources

Select from the following activities to support and extend class-room activities to help children adjust to the climate, culture, and experience of school.

Classroom Routines

Working Together Gather children together in the small group area. Explain that they will often work together in small groups. Talk about various small group activities and behaviors. Emphasize the following:

Sometimes children share ideas and talk about things such as stories, games they like to play, things they have done during the day, and many other things.

Ask what happens if everyone talks at once. Set or review guidelines with children, such as raising one's hand to speak and listening politely as others speak.

Working Independently Ask children to think of some activities that they have done on their own. Help them recall activities such as drawing a picture, listening to a story at the Listening Center, looking at books, and so on.

Talk About Behavior Discuss the following:
Is it important to be quiet when everyone is working on their own? Why? How do you feel when it is noisy and you are trying to listen to a story?

When you are drawing or painting a picture, have you ever had to share crayons or paints with others? How do you feel when someone won't share a color you need?

Help children understand that it is important to be considerate of others. Set or review classroom guidelines such as being quiet when others are trying to work and sharing common classroom items.

The Alphabet

Uppercase Letters Make and display the chart shown below. Explain that you have written all the uppercase letters of the alphabet. Point to each letter as you rhythmically chant the letter names. Take care to enunciate the names clearly—especially the names in the line "L-M-N-O-P." Repeat several times, encouraging children to join in on the letter names they know.

A B C D E F G H I J K L M N O P
Q R S T U V W X Y Z

Repeat this activity with lowercase letters.

Phonemic Awareness

Rhyme Recognition Tell children that they are going to learn something about how words sound. Remind them that it is important to listen carefully and follow your directions. Use the following procedure.

Ask children to listen as you say three words: *ham-Sam-lamb*. Point out that the words all end with the same sounds— /am/.

Explain that *ham*, *Sam*, and *lamb* are called rhyming words; ham, Sam, and lamb rhyme. Have children say each word after you.

Have children listen to and then say these rhyming words: *red-fed-head, boat-coat-goat, sun-fun-run*.

Listen for Rhyming Words Tell children to listen carefully as you say two words: *sheep-keep*. Have them repeat each word. Ask if *sheep* and *keep* rhyme. Direct children to raise both hands to show that the words rhyme; model as necessary. Then have children say *calf-dog*. Ask if *calf* and *dog* rhyme. Direct children to keep their hands down to show that the words do not rhyme. Continue with the following:

goose-loose	**dog-pink**	**kick-chick**	**pup-cup**
kid-bell	**hen-men**	**cat-that**	**duck-luck**
nine-goat	**kitty-city**		

Follow One-Word Directions Tell children that you are going to say a word and they should do what the word means. Say: Smile. Emphasize that you said one word. Have children clap as they repeat the word and smile again. Continue with these directions: Clap. Laugh.

Follow Two-Word Directions Follow a similar procedure for these two-word directions: *Stand up. Sit down. Look up. Look down.*

Count Words in Directions Give children the following directions. Then have them repeat the directions and clap for each word: *Touch your toes. Pat your tummy. Wiggle your nose. Sit up straight and tall.*

Warm-Up: Phonemic Awareness

Onset and Rime Tell children that you are going to say some words, but you are going to say them in parts. Have children listen to see if they can figure out the word. Demonstrate by saying: **/b/-at—What word did I say?** (*bat*)

/r/-ack	**/s/-ad**	**/m/-ap**	**/f/-at**
/s/-ack	**/p/-at**	**/m/-ad**	**/r/-ag**

MATERIALS

Word Cards for down, got, up

Word Builder

Word Builder Cards a, c, h, m, n, p, t

Alphabet Masters Aa

A Hat

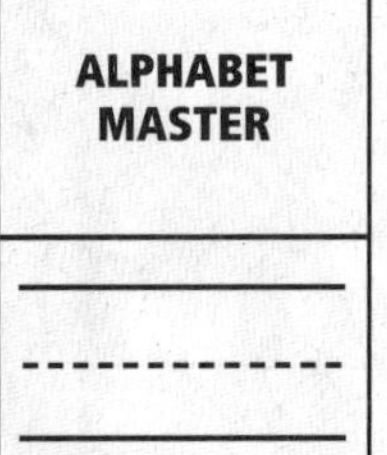

Phonics: Short Vowel /a/a

RETEACH **Blending** Display Alphabet Master *Aa*. **This letter is *a*. The letter *a* can stand for the /a/ sound, the short sound of the letter *a* in words such as *add*, *at*, and *ant*.** Point to the Alphabet Master and say /a/. Tell children that the /a/ sound appears in the middle of such words as *had*, *man*, and *rat*. Have children repeat the sound as you touch the letter several times.

Use the Word Builder Cards and a pocket chart to model blending words.

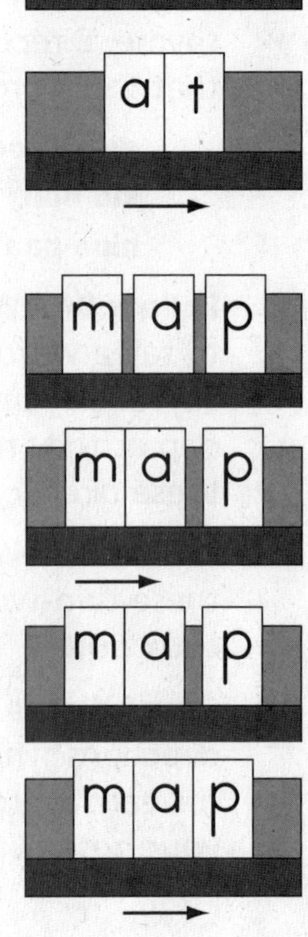

Place the Word Builder Cards *a* and *t* in the Word Builder. Point to the *a* and say /a/. Point to the *t* and say /t/.

Slide the *t* next to the *a*. Move your hand under the letters and blend the sounds, elongating them /aatt/. Have children repeat after you. Then say the word naturally—*at*. Have children do the same.

Place the Word Builder Cards *m*, *a*, and *p* in the Word Builder. Point to the *m* and say /m/. Point to the *a* and say /a/.

Slide the *a* next to the *m*. Move your hand under the letters and blend the sounds, elongating them /mmaa/. Have children repeat after you.

Point to the letter *p* and say /p/. Have children say /p/ as you point to *p*.

Slide *p* next to *ma*. Slide your hand under *map* and blend by elongating the sounds—/mmaapp/. Have children repeat. Then have children read the word *map* along with you.

High-Frequency Words

down

got

up

PRETEACH ***down, got, up*** Display the word card *down*. **This word is *down*. I walked down the stairs. Read the word with me—*down*. Spell the word with me—*d-o-w-n*. Read the word with me. What is this word?** (*down*)

Follow the same procedure for the words *got* and *up*.

got—**I got a toy on my birthday.**

up—**Look up in the sky. Can you see the bird?**

Then place the three words in a pocket chart and have volunteers read the words, as you randomly point to them.

Read: *A Hat*

Distribute copies of the book and have children put their finger on the title. Read the title aloud while children follow along. Ask them to touch the word *A*, then the word *Hat*. Have volunteers point to a word in the title and read it aloud. Echo read the book with children. Read page 2 aloud and then have children read it to you. Follow this procedure throughout the book.

Phonics: Word Building with /a/a

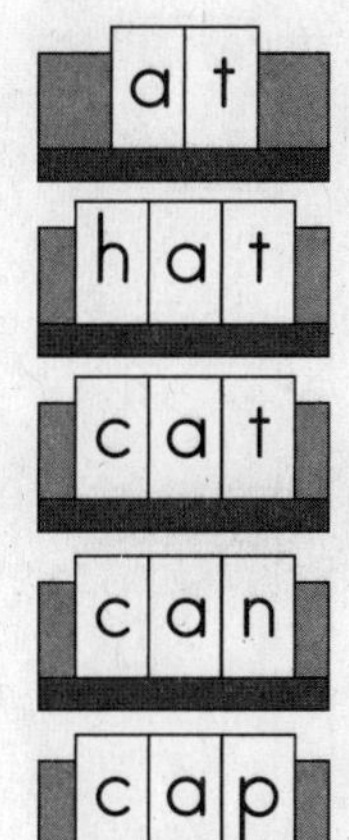

c a p

t a p

PRETEACH Place the letters *a* and *t* in a Word Builder and have children do the same. Model how to blend the word *at*. Slide your hand under the letters as you slowly elongate the sounds /aatt/. Have children do the same. Then read the word naturally—*at*. Have children do the same.

Have children blend and read new words by telling them:

Add an *h* to the front of *a* and *t*. What word did you make? *(hat)*

Change the *h* to *c*. What word did you make? *(cat)*

Change the *t* to *n*. What word did you make? *(can)*

Change the *n* to *p*. What word did you make? *(cap)*

Change the *c* to *t*. What word did you make? *(tap)*

Distribute *Intervention Practice Book* page 1 to children.

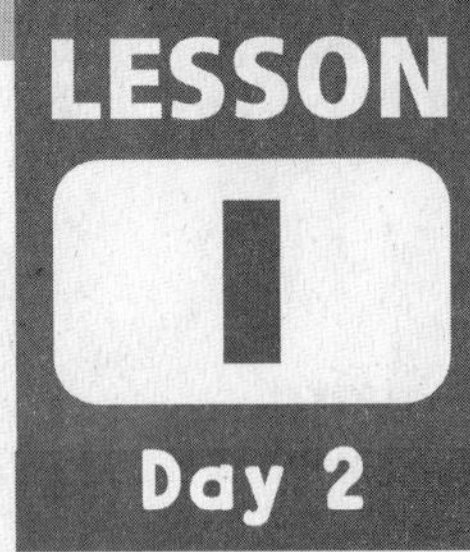

Warm-Up: Phonemic Awareness

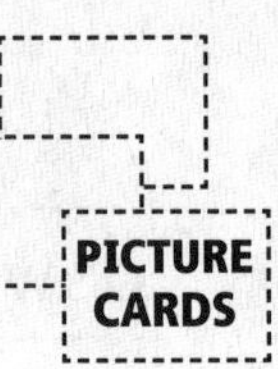

Phoneme Isolation Display the Picture Cards *bat, map,* and *nut.* Hold up the bat. Have children say the word *bat* aloud. Tell children to listen to the /a/ sound in the middle of the word *bat*. Have them say the names of the other two pictures aloud. Ask: **What other picture name has the /a/ sound?** (*map*) Continue with the Picture Cards *cat, sled, fan; bat, can, sock; hat, sled, map.*

MATERIALS

Word Builder

Word Builder Cards a, c, d, m, p, t

Picture Cards: bat, can, cat, fan, hat, map, nut, sled, sock

A Hat

Phonics: Word Building with /a/a

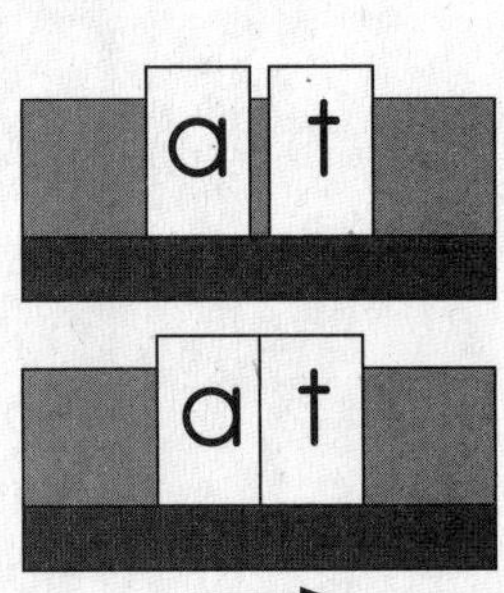

RETEACH Place the letters *a* and *t* in a Word Builder and have children do the same. Model how to blend the word *at*. Slide your hand under the letters as you slowly elongate the sounds /aatt/. Have children do the same. Then read the word naturally—*at*. Have children do the same.

Have children blend and read new words by telling them:

Add ***c*** **to the front of** ***at*****. What word did you make?** *(cat)*

Change the ***t*** **to** ***p*****. What word did you make?** *(cap)*

Change the ***c*** **to** ***t*****. What word did you make?** *(tap)*

Change the ***t*** **to** ***m*****. What word did you make?** *(map)*

Change the ***p*** **to** ***d*****. What word did you make?** *(mad)*

High-Frequency Words

RETEACH ***down, got, up*** Draw two simple sets of stairs, one with an arrow pointing up the steps and the other with an arrow pointing down the steps. Write *up* and *down* between the staircases. Have children read the words. **Which word goes with which picture? Let's read the words again.** Invite volunteers to draw lines from each word to the correct staircase and use that word in a sentence. Then write the word *got* on the board. Say the word and have children repeat it. Use the word in a sentence. **I just got a new puppy.** Have children read the word as you point to it. Then have volunteers read all the words as you point to them.

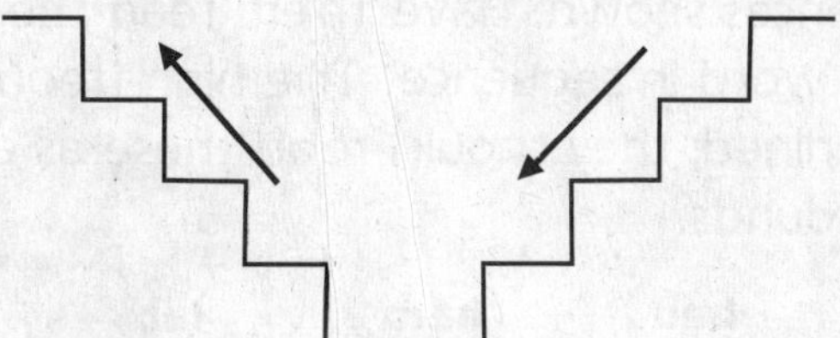

A Hat

Read: *A Hat*

Distribute copies of the book to children. Read page 2 with them. Have children find and read the words *Sam*, *ran*, and *up*. Point to the period at the end of the sentence, and tell children that this mark is called a period. **A period is used at the end of a telling sentence.** Then choral read the book with children. Let your voice fade if children start to gain control of the text.

Phonics: Reading Sentences with /a/a

PRETEACH Distribute *Intervention Practice Book* page 2 to children. Point to the first sentence and have children read it aloud. Ask them to find the word *bat*, frame it with their fingers, and circle the word. Then work with children to complete the page.

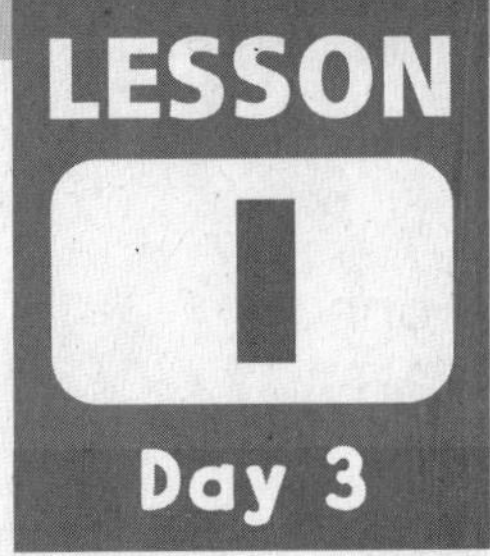

LESSON 1

Day 3

MATERIALS

Picture Cards: bed, box, bug, jet, mule, nine, smile, sock, sun, train, wagon, yarn

Word Builder

Word Builder Cards a, d, h, m, n, p, r, t

A Hat

Warm-Up: Phonemic Awareness

Phoneme Blending Tell children that they are going to play a guessing game. Then say: **I'm thinking of a word that is an animal. It is like a mouse, but it is bigger. It is a /r/-/a/-/t/. What's my word?** (*rat*) Continue with the following words: /n/-/a/-/p/ (*nap*), /f/-/a/-/n/ (*fan*), /m/-/a/-/d/ (*mad*), /t/-/a/-/k/ (*tack*), /a/-/n/-/t/ (*ant*).

Phonics: Reading Sentences with /a/a

RETEACH Help children blend and read new words and sentences shown. Have them read the sentence, blending each word in sequence. The high-frequency words are underlined; they should read these as a unit, not blending the sounds.

bad **ham** **lab** **rag**

We are sad.

The rat ran.

I see the cat.

I am mad.

High-Frequency Words

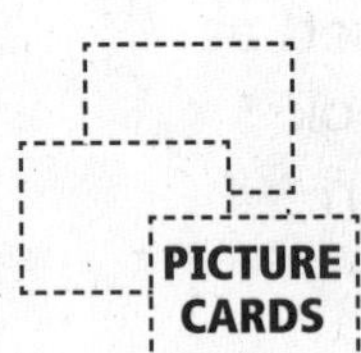

RETEACH ***down, got, up*** Write the following sentence on tag board and display it in a pocket chart along with the Picture Cards *box, jet, mule, yarn, sock, sun.* Call on children to choose a Picture Card to complete the sentence and read it aloud. Then ask: **Can you really get up on a ________?**

I got up on the ________.

Do the same for the following sentence and Picture Cards *bed, wagon, train, nine, bug, smile.*

I sat down on the ________.

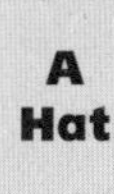

Read: *A Hat*

Distribute copies of the book and have children read aloud the title. Then guide children through the book as they read.

Pages 2–3: Have children read the pages to find out what Sam is doing.

Where is Sam? (*in a hat store*) **What is Sam doing?** (*looking for a hat*) **Is he running or walking? Find and frame the word that tells.** (*ran*)

Pages 4–5: Have children read to see where Sam is going.

Has Sam found a hat he likes yet? (*no*) **Which way is he going? Find and read the words that tell.** (*up, down*)

Pages 6–8: Have children read to find out what Sam found.

What did Sam find? (*a red hat*) **What picture tells the color? Point to it. What word tells what he found? Find and read it.** (*hat*)

Ask children to use the pictures to help summarize the book.

Phonics: Building Words

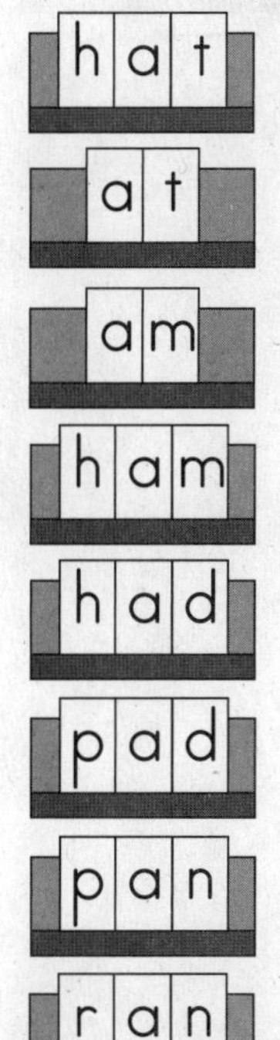

PRETEACH Put the letters *h*, *a*, *t* in a Word Builder and have children do the same. Slide your hand under the letters as you blend the sounds—/hhaatt/. Then read the word naturally—*hat*. Have children repeat after you. Then have children build and read new words.

Take the *h* away. What word did you make? *(at)*

Change *t* to *m*. What word did you make? *(am)*

Add *h* in front of *a* and *m*. What word did you make? *(ham)*

Change *m* to *d*. What word did you make? *(had)*

Change *h* to *p*. What word did you make? *(pad)*

Change *d* to *n*. What word did you make? *(pan)*

Change *p* to *r*. What word did you make? *(ran)*

MATERIALS

Picture Cards bat, cat, fan, hat, map

Write-on/Wipe-off Boards with disks

Word Cards for down, got, up, a, the

Word Builder

Word Builder Cards a, c, h, n, p, t

A Hat

Warm-Up: Phonemic Awareness

Phoneme Segmentation Have children use the three boxes on the Write-on/Wipe-off Boards. Remind children that the boxes stand for the sounds in words. Show the Picture Card *bat* and ask: **What is the first sound you hear in *bat*?** (/*b*/) Have children place a disk in the first box. Then have children name the second sound in *bat* (/*a*/) and place a disk in the second box. Then have them identify the last sound in *bat* (/*t*/) and place a disk in the third box. Point to each box in sequence as children say the word. **How many sounds do you hear in *bat*?** (*three*) Repeat this procedure with the following Picture Cards: *cat, map, hat, fan*.

Phonics: Building Words

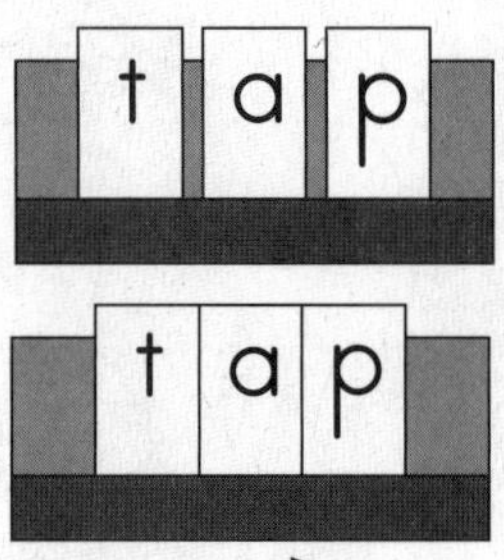

RETEACH Put the letters *t, a, p* in a Word Builder and have children do the same. Slide your hand under the letters as you blend the sounds—/ttaapp/. Then read the word naturally—*tap*. Have children repeat after you. Then have children build and read new words.

Change *t* to *c*. What word did you make? *(cap)*

Change *p* to *n*. What word did you make? *(can)*

Change *n* to *t*. What word did you make? *(cat)*

Change *c* to *h*. What word did you make? *(hat)*

Take the *h* away. What word did you make? *(at)*

Distribute *Intervention Practice Book* page 3 to children.

High-Frequency Words

down

got

up

a

the

RETEACH ***down, got, up, a, the*** Distribute word cards with the words listed above. Have partners take turns displaying the words for each other and reading them. After they read each word, have children spell it and then repeat the word. Then have them spell the word again and write it on a sheet of paper.

Read: *A Hat*

Sequence Remind children that knowing the order things happen in a story can help them understand what they read. Have children reread *A Hat*, thinking about the order in which things happen. Ask: **What did Sam do first? What did Sam do next? What did Sam do last?** Help children make a First-Next-Last chart.

First: Sam ran up.
Next: Sam ran down.

Phonics: Phonograms -ap, -at

PRETEACH Write the letters *ap* and *at* at the top of a sheet of chart paper. Have children suggest words that end with *–ap* and say what letters they would need to write the words. Then write the words underneath the heading *ap*. Use the same procedure for *at*. Then have children read each column of words. End the activity by pointing to words at random and having children read the words.

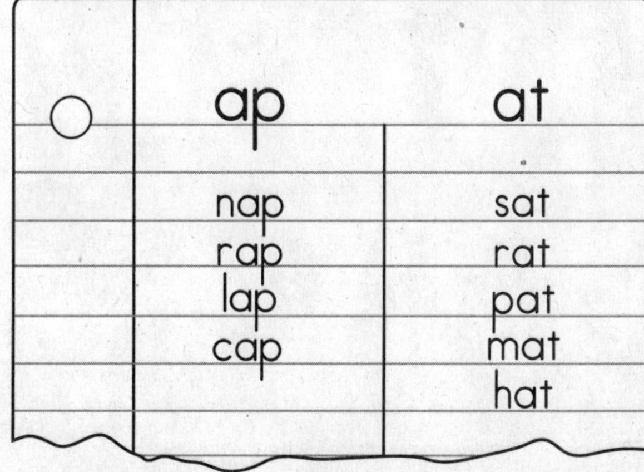

ap
at
nap
rap
lap
cap
sat
rat
pat
mat
hat

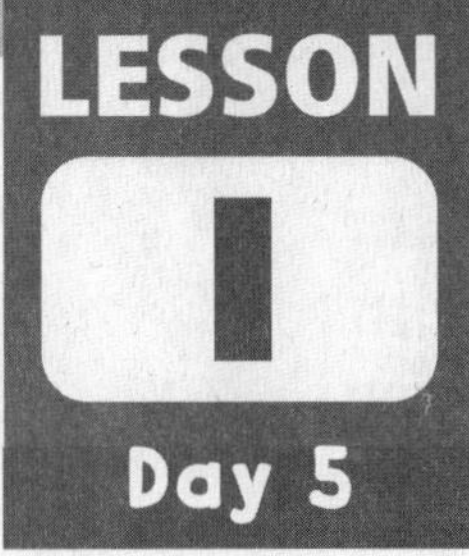

Warm-Up: Phonemic Awareness

Phoneme Blending Tell children that together you are going to play a game of "Fix It." Tell them that you are going to say some words that are all broken and they should listen to see if they can put the sounds together to figure out the word. **Listen: /p/-/a/-/t/. What word does /p/-/a/-/t/ say?** (*pat*) Continue with the following words:

/s/-/a/-/d/ *(sad)*	**/t/-/a/-/g/** *(tag)*	**/r/-/a/-/g/** *(rag)*
/l/-/a/-/p/ *(lap)*	**/h/-/a/-/t/** *(hat)*	**/m/-/a/-/n/** *(man)*

MATERIALS

Write-on/Wipe off Boards

Word Cards for you, have, my, do

Word Builder

Word Builder Cards a, b, d, g, n, p, r, s, t

Phonics: Phonograms -ap, -at

RETEACH Write the word *rat* on a Write-on/ Wipe-off Board and have children do the same. Then have them read the word. Ask: **What letter should we write if we want to change *rat* to *sat*?** (*s*) Let's do that. Continue the activity with the following words: *pat, hat,* and *bat.* Repeat the activity, using the words *map, rap,* and *tap.*

High-Frequency Words

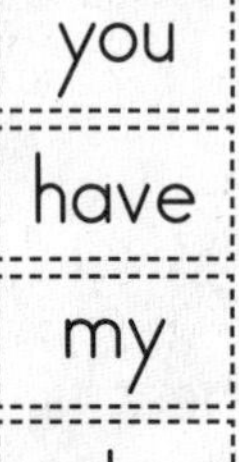

Cumulative Review *you, have, my, do* Place the words in a pocket chart. Say aloud one of the words and use it in a sentence. Have a volunteer find and point to the word. Have children clap and say the spelling of the word. Then have them write it. Have children read aloud their list of words.

Read: Self-Selected Reading

Have children select a book to read from their browsing boxes. After they have completed their reading, have them tell you what they were most successful in during the reading of the book.

Phonics: Short Vowel /a/a

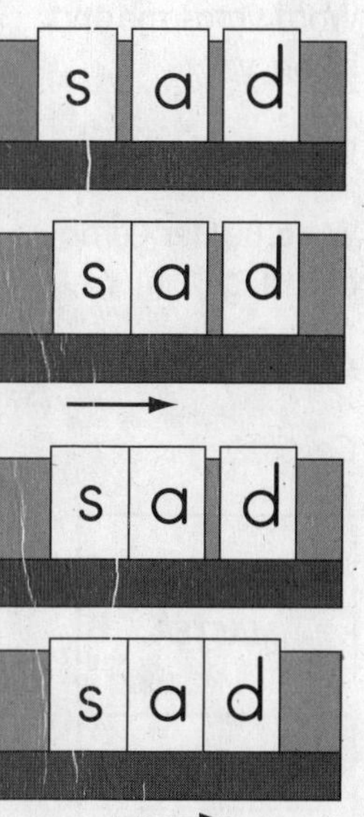

PRETEACH Use the Word Builder and Word Builder Cards to model blending words. Place the Word Builder Cards *s, a,* and *d* in the Word Builder. Point to the *s* and say /s/. Point to *a* and say /a/.

Slide the *a* next to the *s*. Move your hand under the letters and blend the sounds, elongating them /ssaa/. Have children repeat after you.

Point to the letter *d*. Say /d/. Slide the *d* next to *sa*. Slide your hand under *sad* and blend by elongating the sounds /ssaadd/. Have children repeat.

Then have children read the word *sad* along with you.

Follow the same procedure for the words *rat, pan, tap,* and *bag.*

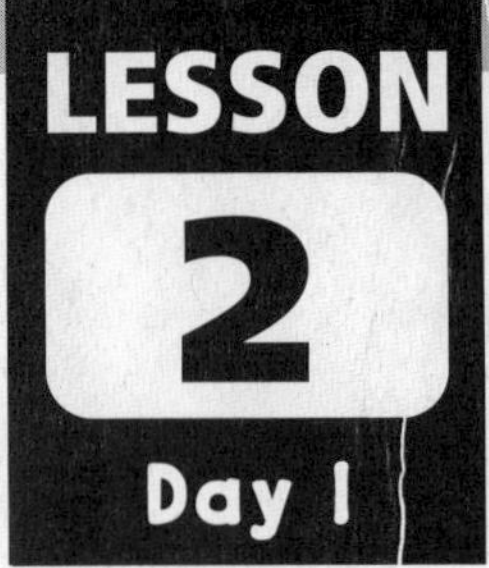

Warm-Up: Phonemic Awareness

Onset and Rime Tell children that you are going to say some words, but you are going to say them in parts. Have children listen to see if they can figure out the word. Demonstrate by saying: **/r/-an—What word did I say?** (*ran*)

/b/-ad	**/t/-ack**	**/m/-an**	**/ch/-at**
/l/-ap	**/p/-an**	**/r/-ash**	**/n/-ap**

MATERIALS

Word Cards for *and, in, oh, yes*

Word Builder

Word Builder Cards a, b, d, g, h, m, r, t

Alphabet Masters Aa

Go Cat!

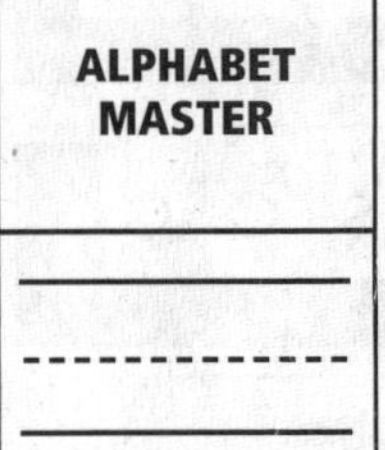

Phonics: Short Vowel /a/a

RETEACH **Blending** Display Alphabet Master *Aa*. **This letter is *a*. The letter *a* can stand for the /a/ sound, the short sound of the letter *a* in words such as *am, at,* and *and*.** Point to the Alphabet Master and say /a/. Tell children that the /a/ sound appears in the middle of such words as *pad, lab,* and *sat*. Have children repeat the sound as you touch the letter several times.

Use the Word Builder Cards and a pocket chart to model blending words.

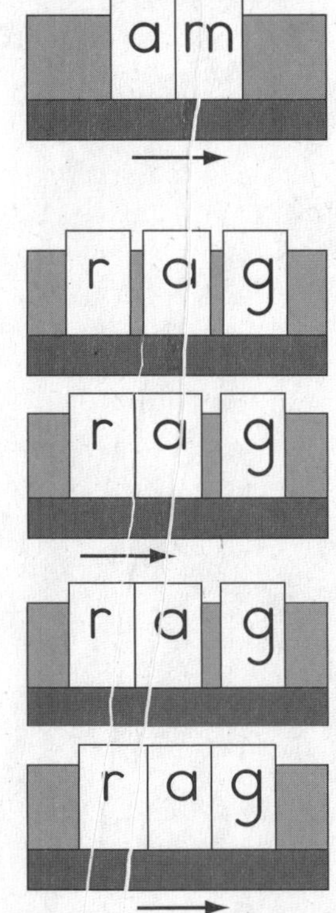

Place the Word Builder Cards *a* and *m* in the Word Builder. Point to the *a* and say /a/. Point to the *m* and say /m/.

Slide the *m* next to the *a*. Move your hand under the letters and blend the sounds, elongating them /aamm/. Have children repeat after you. Then say the word naturally—*am*. Have children do the same.

Place the Word Builder Cards *r, a,* and *g* in the Word Builder. Point to the *r* and say /r/. Point to the *a* and say /a/.

Slide the *a* next to the *r*. Move your hand under the letters and blend the sounds, elongating them /rraa/. Have children repeat after you.

Point to the letter *g* and say /g/. Have children say /g/ as you point to *g*.

Slide *g* next to *ra*. Slide your hand under *rag* and blend by elongating the sounds—/rraagg/. Have children repeat. Then have children read the word *rag* along with you.

High-Frequency Words

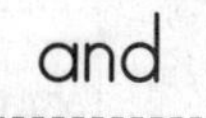

PRETEACH ***and, in, oh, yes*** Display the word card *and*. **This word is *and*. My friend and I are going to the park. Read the word with me—*and*. Spell the word with me—*a-n-d*. Read the word with me. What is this word?** (*and*)

Follow the same procedure for the words *in, oh,* and *yes.*

in—**I put the key in my pocket.**

oh—**Oh, my goodness! I lost a tooth!**

yes—**Yes, I would like to see the baseball game.**

Then place the four words in a pocket chart and have volunteers read the words, as you randomly point to them.

Read: *Go Cat!*

Distribute copies of the book and have children put their finger on the title. Read the title aloud while children follow along. Ask them to touch the word *Go*, then the word *Cat*. Have volunteers choose a word in the title to read aloud. Echo read the book with children. Read page 2 aloud and then have children read it to you. Follow this procedure throughout the book.

Phonics: Word Building with /a/a

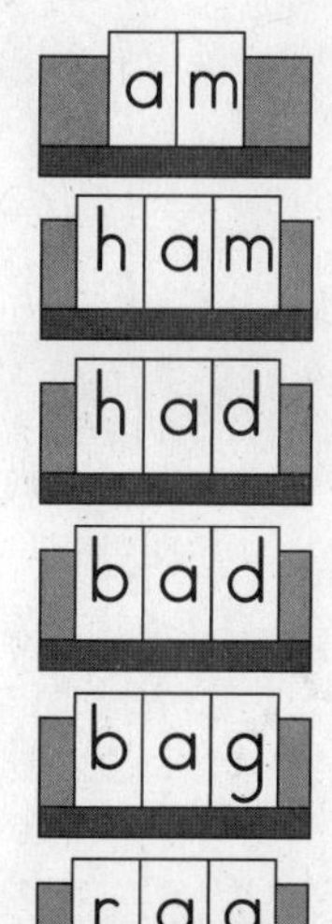

PRETEACH Place the letters *a* and *m* in a Word Builder and have children do the same. Model how to blend the word *am*. Slide your hand under the letters as you slowly elongate the sounds /aamm/. Have children do the same. Then read the word naturally—*am.* Have children do the same.

Have children blend and read new words by telling them:

Add an *h* to the front of *a* and *m*. What word did you make? *(ham)*

Change the *m* to a *d*. What word did you make? *(had)*

Change the *h* to a *b*. What word did you make? *(bad)*

Change the *d* to a *g*. What word did you make? *(bag)*

Change the *b* to an *r*. What word did you make? *(rag)*

Distribute *Intervention Practice Book* page 4 to children.

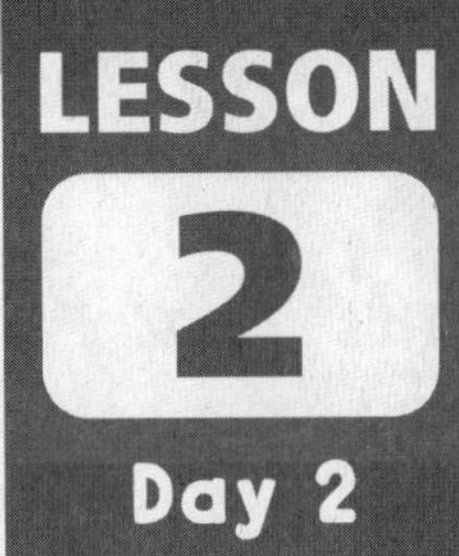

Warm-Up: Phonemic Awareness

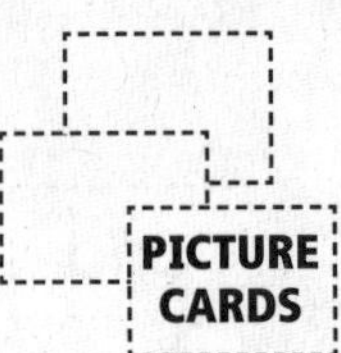

Phoneme Isolation Display the Picture Cards *cat, ax,* and *nine.* Hold up the *cat.* Have children say the word *cat* aloud. Tell children to listen to the /a/ sound in the middle of the word *cat*. Have them say the names of the other two pictures aloud. Ask: **What other picture name has the /a/ sound?** (*ax*)

Continue with the Picture Cards *hat, flag, quilt; ax, clam, goat; lamp, nine, hat.*

MATERIALS

Word Builder

Word Builder Cards a, b, d, g, h, m

Picture Cards: ax, cat, clam, flag, goat, hat, lamp, nine, quilt

Go Cat!

Phonics: Word Building with /a/a

RETEACH Place the letters *a* and *m* in a Word Builder and have children do the same. Model how to blend the word *am*. Slide your hand under the letters as you slowly elongate the sounds /aamm/. Have children do the same. Then read the word naturally—*am*. Have children do the same.

Have children blend and read new words by telling them:

Add *h* to the front of *am*. What word did you make? *(ham)*

Change the *m* to *d*. What word did you make? *(had)*

Change the *h* to *m*. What word did you make? *(mad)*

Change the *m* to *b*. What word did you make? *(bad)*

Change the *d* to *g*. What word did you make? *(bag)*

High-Frequency Words

RETEACH ***and, in, oh, yes*** Write the word *a* and have children read it. Then write the word *and* next to *a*. Have children read the word. **How are these words the same? How are they different? Let's read them again.**

a | and

Repeat the procedure with *I/in* and *on/oh.*

Read: *Go Cat!*

Go Cat!

Distribute copies of the book to children. Have them read the title aloud. Then have children find and frame the words *go* and *cat*. Point to the exclamation mark at the end of the title and tell children that this symbol is called an exclamation mark. **An exclamation mark is used to show that the speaker or writer is excited or feels strongly about something.** Then choral read the book with children. Let your voice fade if children start to gain control of the text.

Phonics: Reading Sentences with /a/a

PRETEACH Distribute *Intervention Practice Book* page 5 to children. Point to the first sentence and have children read it aloud. Ask them to find the word *Sam*, frame it with their fingers, and circle the word. Then work with children to complete the page.

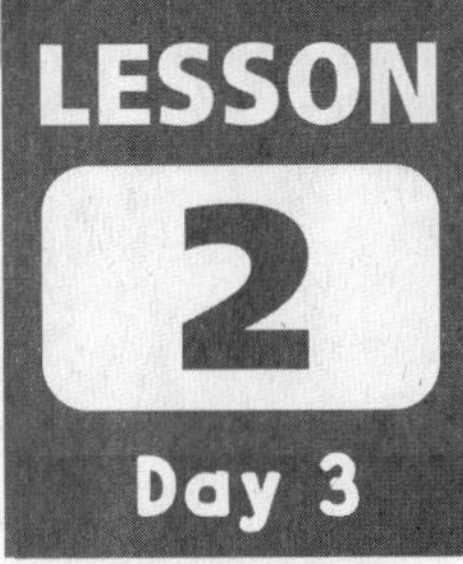

MATERIALS

Picture Cards: clock, cup, jet, map, mop, rose, ship, six, train, yarn, zebra

Word Builder

Word Builder Cards a, b, c, d, g, h, m, r, t

Go Cat!

Warm-Up: Phonemic Awareness

Onset and Rime Tell children that they are going to be detectives and find the word you are thinking about. Say: **I'm thinking of a word that you put things into. You can carry groceries in it. I'll say it in two parts. It is a /b/-ag/. What's my word?** (*bag*) Continue with the following words: /s/-/at/ (*sat*), /ch/-/at/ (*chat*), /b/-/ad/ (*bad*), /r/-/ag/ (*rag*), /l/-/ams/ (*lambs*).

Phonics: Reading Sentences with /a/a

RETEACH **phonics.** Help children blend and read new words and sentences shown. Have them read the sentence, blending each word in sequence. The high-frequency words are underlined; they should read these as a unit, not blending the sounds.

tan **wag** **bad** **lap**

You <u>have</u> <u>a</u> map.

<u>I</u> <u>like</u> ham.

<u>We</u> <u>see</u> <u>the</u> cat.

<u>I</u> sat <u>on</u> <u>the</u> hat.

High-Frequency Words

RETEACH ***and, in, oh, yes*** Write the following sentence on tagboard and display it in a pocket chart along with the Picture Cards *clock, jet, mop, ship, yarn, train.* Call on children to choose a Picture Card to complete the sentence and read it aloud. Then ask: **Can you really go in a ________?**

PICTURE CARDS

Dan and I go in a ________.

Do the same for the following sentence and Picture Cards *map, rose, six, zebra, cup.*

Oh, yes! I like to see a ________.

Read: *Go Cat!*

Distribute copies of the book and have children read aloud the title. Then guide children through the book as they read.

Pages 2–3: Have children read the pages to find what Cat did.

What did Cat do? (*ran and ran*) **Where did Cat run? Find and frame the words that tell.** (*in the bag*)

Pages 4–5: Have children read to see where Cat went next.

Where did Cat run now? (*into a hat*) **Find and read the words that tell.** (*in the hat*) **Do you think Cat likes it in the hat?**

Pages 6–8: Have children read to find what happens at the end.

Who goes into the box? (*Cat*) **What word tells you the answer? Find and read it.** (*Cat*) **Does Cat stay in the box?** (*no*) **Find and read the sentence that tells.** (*Go Cat!*)

Ask children to use the pictures to help summarize the book.

Phonics: Building Words

PRETEACH Put the letters *c*, *a*, *t* in a Word Builder and have children do the same. Slide your hand under the letters as you blend the sounds—/ccaatt/. Then read the word naturally—*cat*. Have children repeat after you. Then have children build and read new words.

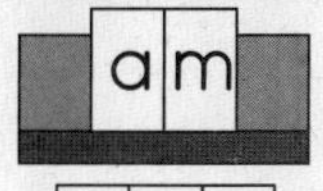

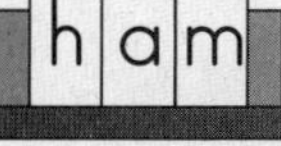

Take the *c* away. What word did you make? *(at)*

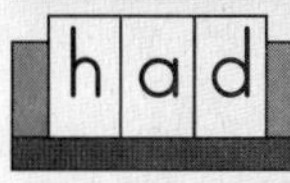

Change *t* to *m*. What word did you make? *(am)*

Add *h* in front of *a* and *m*. What word did you make? *(ham)*

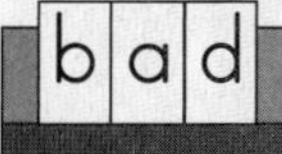

Change *m* to *d*. What word did you make? *(had)*

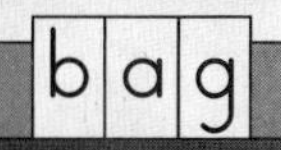

Change *h* to *b*. What word did you make? *(bad)*

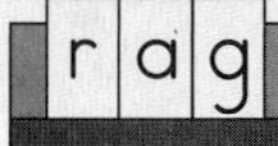

Change *d* to *g*. What word did you make? *(bag)*

Change *b* to *r*. What word did you make? *(rag)*

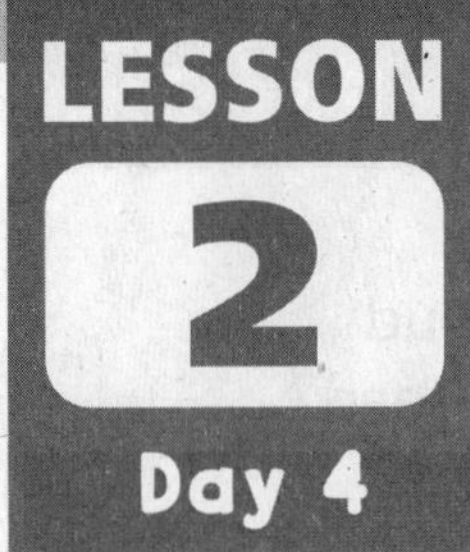

MATERIALS

Picture Cards bat, can, cat, fan, hat, map

Write-on/Wipe-off Boards with disks

Word Cards for and, in, oh, yes, up, go

Word Builder

Word Builder Cards a, b, c, d, g, h, m, t

Go Cat!

Warm-Up: Phonemic Awareness

Phoneme Segmentation Have children use the three boxes on the Write-on/Wipe-off Boards. Remind children that the boxes stand for the sounds in words. Show the Picture Card *cat* and ask: **What is the first sound you hear in cat?** (/*k*/) Have children place a disk in the first box. Then have children name the second sound in *cat* (/*a*/) and place a disk in the second box. Then have them identify the last sound in *cat* (/*t*/) and place a disk in the third box. Point to each box in sequence as children say the word. **How many sounds do you hear in *cat*?** (*three*) Repeat this procedure with the following Picture Cards: *can, hat, bat, fan, map.*

Phonics: Building Words

RETEACH Put the letters *b, a, g* in a Word Builder and have children do the same. Slide your hand under the letters as you blend the sounds—/bbaagg/. Then read the word naturally—(*bag*). Have children repeat after you. Then have children build and read new words.

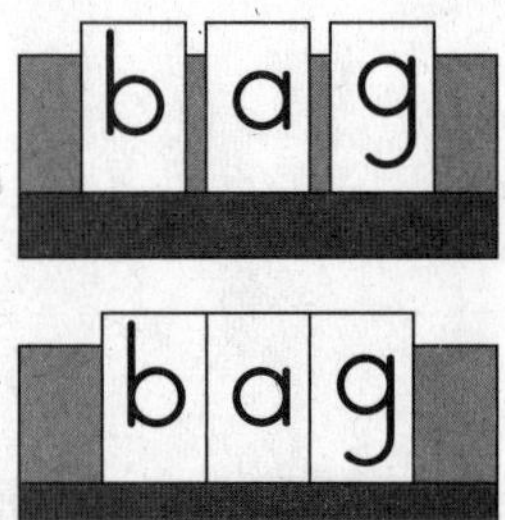

Change *g* to *d*. What word did you make? *(bad)*

Change *b* to *h*. What word did you make? *(had)*

Change *d* to *m*. What word did you make? *(ham)*

Take the *h* away. What word did you make? *(am)*

Change *m* to *t*. What word did you make? *(at)*

Add *c* in front of *a* and *t*. What word did you make? *(cat)*

Distribute *Intervention Practice book* page 6 to children.

High-Frequency Words

and
in
oh
yes
up
go

RETEACH ***and, in, oh, yes, up, go*** Distribute word cards with the words listed above. Have partners take turns displaying the words for each other and reading them. After they read each word, have children spell it and then repeat the word. Then have them spell the word again and write it on a sheet of paper.

Read: *Go Cat!*

Go Cat!

Predict Outcomes Remind children that predicting outcomes can help them understand a story. Have children reread *Go Cat!* one page at a time and predict what they think will happen next. Ask: **What do you think will happen next? What would you do if you were Cat? Where do you think Cat would like to go?** You may wish to have children write or draw one of their predictions.

Phonics: Inflection: -s

PRETEACH Write the word *cat* at the top of a sheet of chart paper. Have children read it. Then add *s* to the end of *cat*. Have children read the new word. Explain that *cats* means more than one cat. Write the following words on the chart: *bat, hat, bag, cap, map, fan.* Have children say what letter they would need to make *bat* into *bats.* Write *s* at the end of *bat.* Use the same procedure for the other words. End the activity by pointing to words at random and having volunteers read the words and use them in sentences.

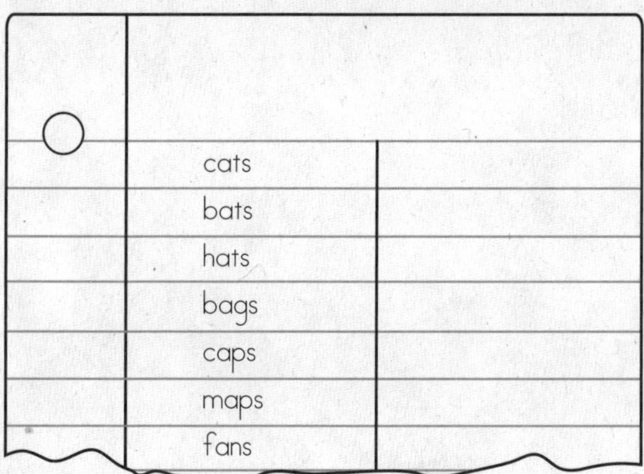

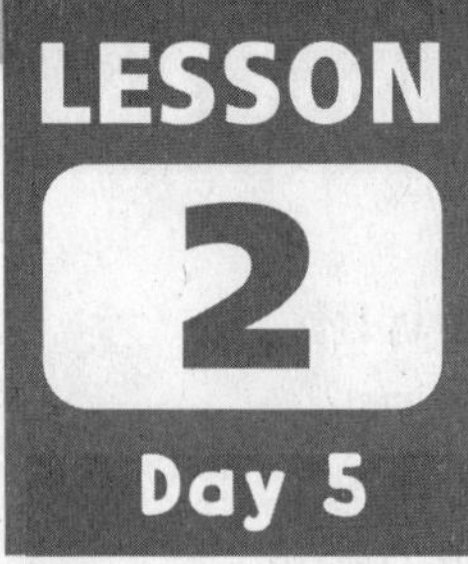

Warm-Up: Phonemic Awareness

Onset and Rime Tell children that you are going to say some word parts and they should put them together to figure out the word. **Listen: /w/-/ag/. What word did I say?** (*wag*) Continue with the following words:

/s/-/ick/ (*sick*)	**/t/-/ag/** (*tag*)	**/r/-/ack/** (*rack*)
/p/-/in/ (*pin*)	**/h/-/it/** (*hit*)	**/m/-/itt/** (*mitt*)

MATERIALS

Write-on/Wipe-off Boards

Word Cards for and, in, oh, yes, down, got, up

Word Builder

Word Builder Cards f, g, i, n, p, w

Phonics: Inflection: -s

RETEACH Write the word *cap* on a Write-on/Wipe-off Board and have children do the same. Then have them read the word. Ask: **What letter should we write if we want to change *cap* to *caps*?** (*s*) **Let's do that.** Continue the activity with the following words: *pad, hat, rag, lap, look*, and *see*.

High-Frequency Words

Cumulative Review *and, in, oh, yes, down, got, up* Place the words in a pocket chart. Say aloud one of the words and use it in a sentence. Have a volunteer find and point to the word. Have children clap and say the spelling of the word. Then have them write it. Have children read aloud their list of words.

and

in

oh

yes

down

got

up

Read: Self-Selected Reading

Have children select a book to read from their browsing boxes. After they have completed their reading, have them tell you what they were most successful in during the reading of the book.

Phonics: Short Vowel /i/i

PRETEACH Write the letter *i* on the board or on chart paper. **The letter *i* can stand for the /i/ sound in words such as *pig, tin,* and *sick.*** Point to the letter *i* and say /i/. Have children repeat the sound as you touch the letter *i* several times.

Use the Word Builder and Word Builder Cards to model blending words. Place the Word Builder Cards *p, i,* and *n* in the Word Builder. Point to the *p* and say /p/. Point to *i* and say /i/.

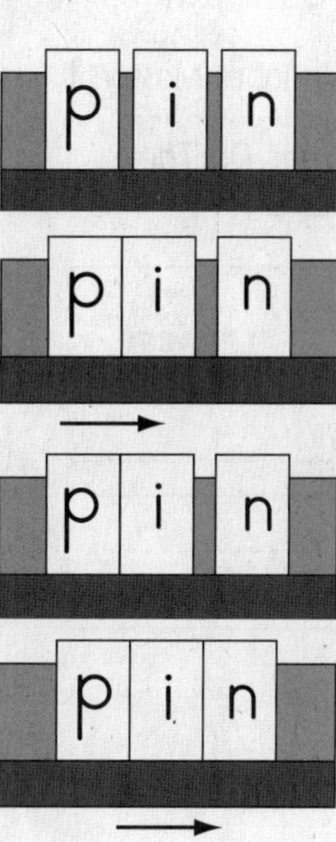

Slide the *i* next to the *p*. Move your hand under the letters and blend the sounds, elongating them /ppii/. Have children repeat after you. Point to the letter *n*. Slide the *n* next to *pi.* Slide your hand under *pin* and blend by elongating the sounds /ppiinn/. Have children repeat. Then have children read the word *pin* along with you.

Follow the same procedure for the words *win, fin, pig,* and *wig.*

INTERVENTION ASSESSMENT BOOK

pages 9–10

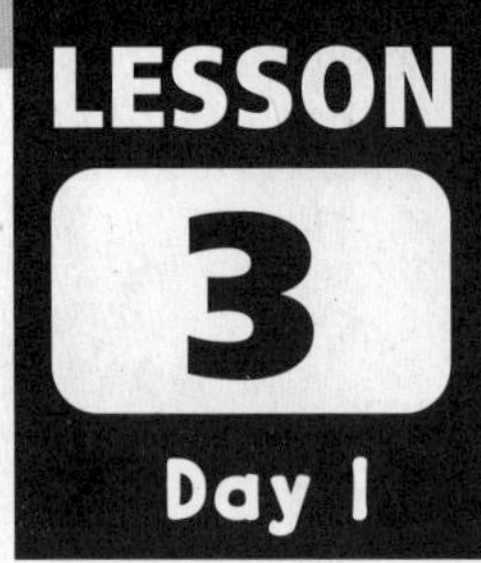

Warm-Up: Phonemic Awareness

Onset and Rime Tell children that you are going to say some words, but you are going to say them in parts. Have children listen to see if they can figure out the word. Demonstrate by saying: **/s/ -it—What word did I say?** *(sit)*

/t/-ick	**/b/-ig**	**/ch/-in**	**/h/-id**
/s/-ick	**/h/-ip**	**/d/-ish**	**/d/-ig**

MATERIALS

Word Cards for make, walk, they

Word Builder

Word Builder Cards f, g, i, n, p, w

Alphabet Masters Ii

What Do They Make?

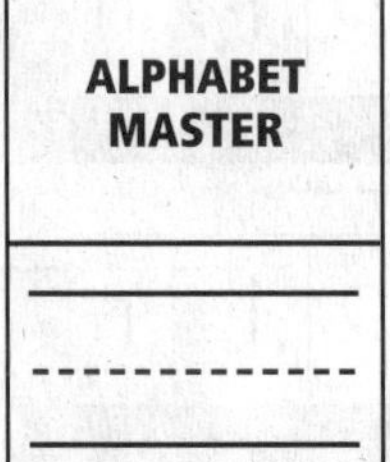

Phonics: Short Vowel /i/i

RETEACH Blending Display Alphabet Master Ii. **This letter is *i*. The letter *i* can stand for the /i/ sound, the short sound of the letter *i* in such words as *it, in,* and *if*.** Point to the Alphabet Master and say /i/. Tell children that the /i/ sound appears in the middle of words such as *sit, rib,* and *tip.* Have children repeat the sound as you touch the letter several times.

Use the Word Builder Cards and a pocket chart to model blending words.

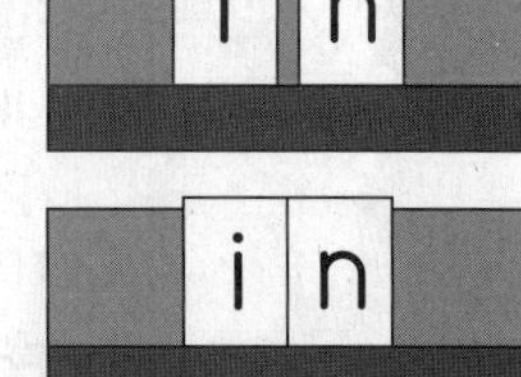

Place the Word Builder Cards *i* and *n* in the Word Builder. Point to the *i* and say /i/. Point to *n* and say /n/.

Slide the *n* next to the *i*. Move your hand under the letters and blend the sounds, elongating them /iinn/. Have children repeat after you. Then say the word naturally—*in*. Have children do the same.

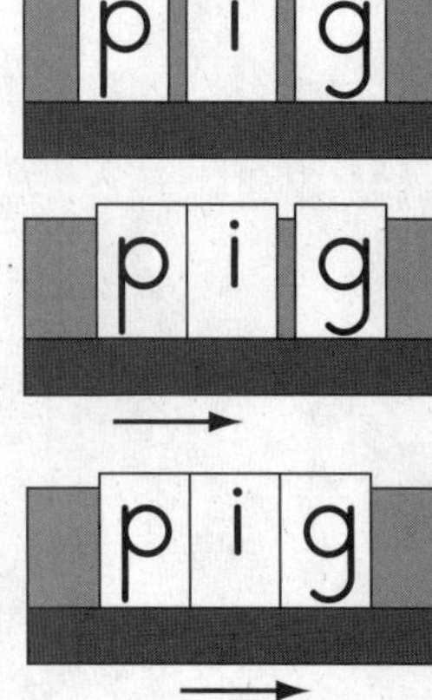

Place the Word Builder Cards *p, i,* and *g* in the Word Builder. Point to the *p* and say /p/. Point to the *i* and say /i/.

Slide the *i* next to the *p*. Move your hand under the letters and blend the sounds, elongating them /ppii/. Have children repeat after you.

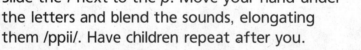

Point to the letter *g* and say /g/. Have children say /g/ as you point to *g*.

Slide *g* next to *pi*. Slide your hand under *pig* and blend by elongating the sounds—/ppiigg/. Have children repeat. Then have children read the word *pig* along with you.

High-Frequency Words

make

they

walk

PRETEACH ***make, they, walk*** Display the word card *walk*. **This word is *walk.* (Child's name) walks to the door. Read the word with me—*walk.* Spell the word with me—*w-a-l-k*. Read the word with me. What is this word?** (*walk*)

Follow the same procedure for the words *make* and *they*.

make—**Make a birthday cake.**

they—**This is (child's name) and (child's name). They are friends.**

Then place the three words in a pocket chart and have volunteers read the words, as you randomly point to them.

Read: *What Do They Make?*

What Do They Make?

Distribute copies of the book and have children put their finger on the title. Have children follow along as you read the title aloud. Then have them frame the word *they* and then the word *make.* Echo read the book with children. Read page 2 aloud and then have children read it to you. Follow this procedure throughout the book.

Phonics: Word Building with /i/i

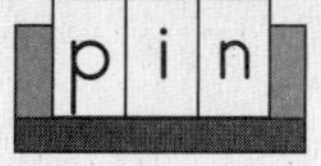

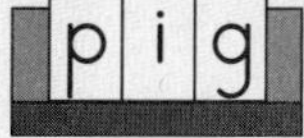

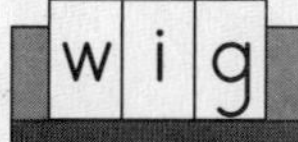

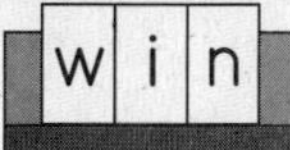

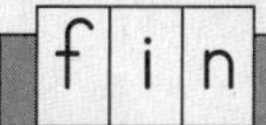

PRETEACH Place the letters *i* and *n* in a Word Builder and have children do the same. Model how to blend the word *in.* Slide your hand under the letters as you slowly elongate the sounds /iinn/. Have children do the same. Then read the word naturally—*in.* Have children do the same.

Have children blend and read new words by telling them:

Add a *p* to the front of *i* and *n*. What word did you make? *(pin)*

Change the *n* to *g*. What word did you make? *(pig)*

Change the *p* to *w*. What word did you make? *(wig)*

Change the *g* to *n*. What word did you make? *(win)*

Change the *w* to *f*. What word did you make? *(fin)*

Distribute *Intervention Practice Book* page 7 to children.

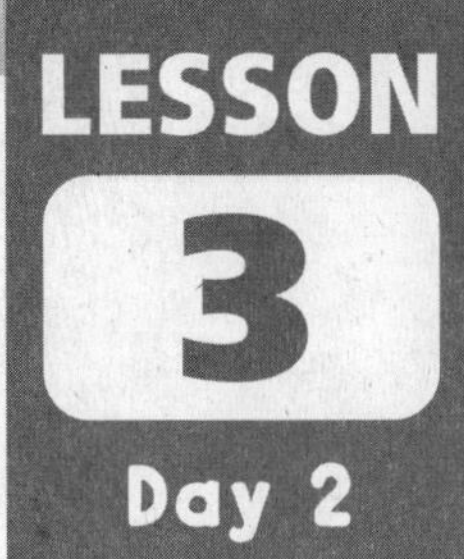

Warm-Up: Phonemic Awareness

Phoneme Isolation Display the Picture Cards *pin*, *fish*, and *cat*. Hold up the *pin*. Have children say the word *pin* aloud. Tell children to listen to the /i/ sound in the middle of the word *pin*. Have them say the names of the other two pictures aloud. Ask: **What other picture name has the /i/ sound?** (*fish*) Continue with the Picture Cards *six, fish, net; pin, ship, mop; fish, six, rake.*

PICTURE CARDS

MATERIALS

Word Builder

Word Builder Cards f, g, i, n, p, w

Picture Cards: cat, fish, mop, net, rake, pin, ship, six

What Do They Make?

Phonics: Word Building with /i/i

RETEACH Place the letters *i* and *n* in a Word Builder and have children do the same. Model how to blend the word *in*. Slide your hand under the letters as you slowly elongate the sounds /iinn/. Have children do the same. Then read the word naturally—*in*. Have children do the same.

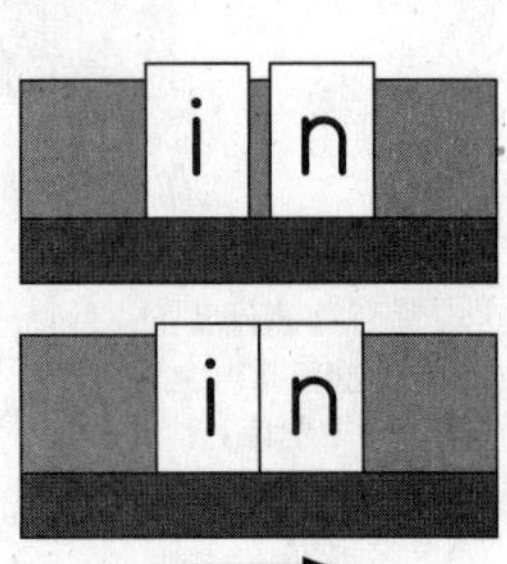

Have children blend and read new words by telling them:

Add *f* to the front of *in*. What word did you make? (*fin*)

Change the *f* to *w*. What word did you make? (*win*)

Change the *n* to *g*. What word did you make? (*wig*)

Change the *w* to *p*. What word did you make? (*pig*)

Change the *g* to *n*. What word did you make? (*pin*)

High-Frequency Words

RETEACH ***make, they, walk*** Write the word *the* and have children read it. Then write the word *they* next to *the* and have children read the word. **How are these words the same? How are they different? Let's read them again.**

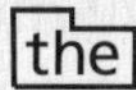 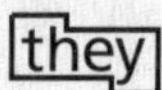

Repeat the procedure with *walk/what* and *mad/make.*

Read: *What Do They Make?*

What Do They Make?

Distribute copies of the book and ask children to read the title aloud. Then have children frame the words *they* and *make.* Point to the question mark and tell children that this is a question mark. **A question mark is used at the end of a question.** Ask children to point to the names of the people who wrote and illustrated the book. Read their names aloud. Then choral read the book with children. Let your voice fade if children start to gain control of the text.

Phonics: Reading Sentences with /i/i

PRETEACH Distribute *Intervention Practice Book* page 8 to children. Point to the first sentence and have children read it aloud. Ask them to find the word *hit*, frame it with their fingers, and circle the word. Then work with children to complete the page.

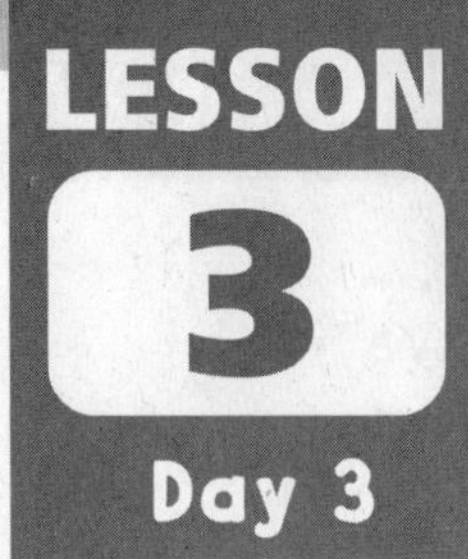

MATERIALS

Picture Cards bug, cat, desk, drum, fox, goat, lamp, mule, pig, seal, ship

Word Builder

Word Builder Cards a, h, i, n, p, t

What Do They Make?

Warm-Up: Phonemic Awareness

Phoneme Blending Tell children that they are going to play a guessing game. Then say: **I'm thinking of a word that is an animal. It is usually quite big. It is a /p/-/i/-/g/. What's my word?** *(pig)* Continue with the following words: /d/-/i/-/sh/ *(dish)*, /w/-/i/-/g/ *(wig)*, /b/-/i/-/b/ *(bib)*, /l/-/i/-/p/-/s/ *(lips)*.

Phonics: Reading Sentences with /i/i

RETEACH Help children blend and read new words and sentences shown. Have them read the sentence, blending each word in sequence. The high-frequency words are underlined; they should read these as a unit, not blending the sounds.

sit **in** **fin** **bib**

The cat will win.

I can win.

Look at the pin and can.

Pam will sit.

High-Frequency Words

RETEACH ***make, they, walk*** Write the following sentence on tag board and display it in a pocket chart along with the Picture Cards *cat, fox, pig, mule, goat, bug, seal.* Call on children to choose a Picture Card to complete the sentence and read it aloud. Then ask: **Can you really walk a __?**

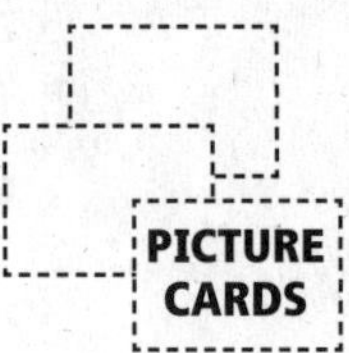

I walk the ______.

Do the same for the following sentence and Picture Cards *desk, drum, lamp, ship.*

They make a _____.

Read: *What Do They Make?*

What Do They Make?

Distribute copies of the book and have children read aloud the title. Ask what this book is about. Then guide children through the book as they read.

Pages 2–3: Have children read to find out what the ants make.

What do the ants make? *(a bicycle)* **Find and read the sentence that tells.**

What word means the same as the ants? Find and frame that word. *(they)*

Pages 4–5: Have children read to find out what else the ants make.

Why can only one ant ride the bike at a time? *(It is little.)*

What else do the ants make? *(a seesaw)* **Find and read the sentence that tells.**

Pages 6–7: Have children read to find out if the ants will all be able to use the seesaw.

Why can't the ants use the seesaw together? *(It is little.)* **Find and read the sentence that tells.**

What else did they make? *(a car)* **Do you think it will be little, too?**

Page 8: Have children read to find out if the car is little.

Is the car little? *(no)* **Find and read the sentence that tells.** *(It is big!)*

Ask children to use the pictures to help summarize the book.

Phonics: Building Words

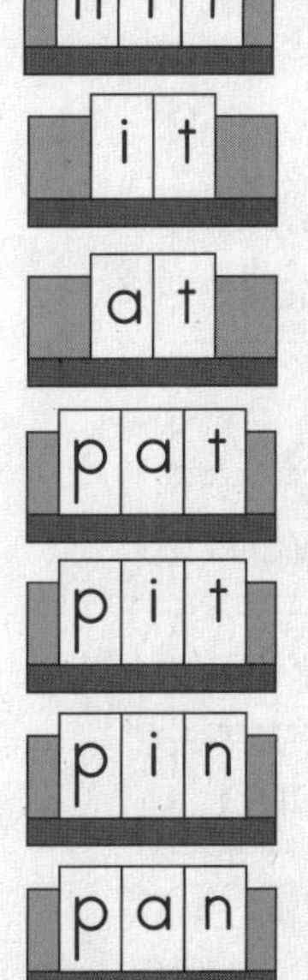

PRETEACH Put the letters *h, i, t* in a Word Builder and have children do the same. Slide your hand under the letters as you blend the sounds—/hhiitt/. Then read the word naturally—*hit.* Have children repeat after you. Then have children build and read new words.

Take the *h* away. What word did you make? *(it)*

Change the *i* to *a*. What word did you make? *(at)*

Add p in front of *a* and *t*. What word did you make? *(pat)*

Change the *a* to *i*. What word did you make? *(pit)*

Change the *t* to *n*. What word did you make? *(pin)*

Change the *i* to *a*. What word did you make? *(pan)*

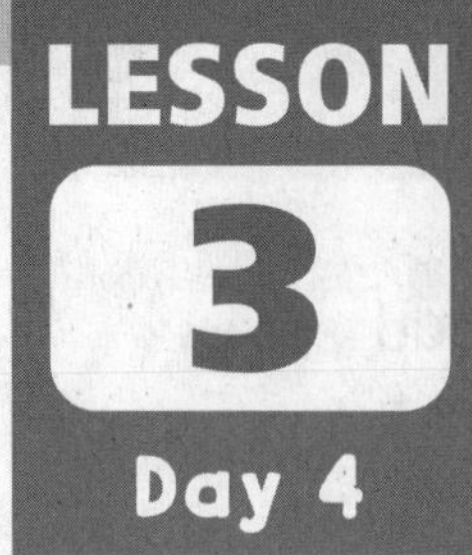

Warm-Up: Phonemic Awareness

Phoneme Segmentation Have children use the three boxes on the *Write-on/Wipe-off Boards.* Remind children that the boxes stand for the sounds in words. Show the Picture Card *pig* and ask: **What is the first sound you hear in *pig*?** (/p/) Have children place a disk in the first box. Then have children name the second sound in *pig* (/i/) and place a disk in the second box. Then have them identify the last sound in *pig* (/g/) and place a disk in the third box. Point to each box in sequence as children say the word. **How many sounds do you hear in *pig*?** (three) Repeat this procedure with the following Picture Cards : *pin, rake, goat, hat, mop.*

MATERIALS

Picture Cards pig, pin, rake, goat, hat, mop

Write-on/Wipe-off Boards with disks

Word Cards for make, they, walk, yes, and

Word Builder

Word Builder Cards a, f, i, n, p, t

What Do They Make?

Phonics: Building Words

RETEACH Put the letters *p, i, n* in a Word Builder and have children do the same. Slide your hand under the letters as you blend the sounds—/ppiinn/. Then read the word naturally—*pin.* Have children repeat after you. Then have children build and read new words.

Take away the *p*. What word did you make? *(in)*

Change the *i* to *a*. What word did you make? *(an)*

Add *f* in front of *a* and *n*. What word did you make? *(fan)*

Change the *a* to *i*. What word did you make? *(fin)*

Change the *n* to *t*. What word did you make? *(fit)*

Take away the *f*. What word did you make? *(it)*

Distribute *Intervention Practice Book* page 9 to children.

High-Frequency Words

RETEACH ***make, they, walk, yes, and*** Distribute word cards with the words listed above. Have partners take turns displaying the words for each other and reading them. After they read each word, have children spell it and then repeat the word. Then have them spell the word again and write it on a sheet of paper.

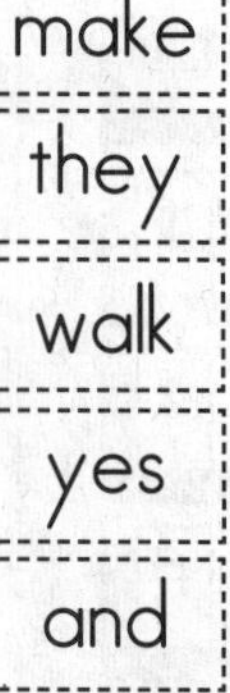

What Do They Make?

Read: *What Do They Make?*

(Focus Skill) **Details** Remind children that details can help them understand information that they read. Tell them that details can also help them picture what happens in a story. Have children reread *What Do They Make?* and then together make a list of story details.

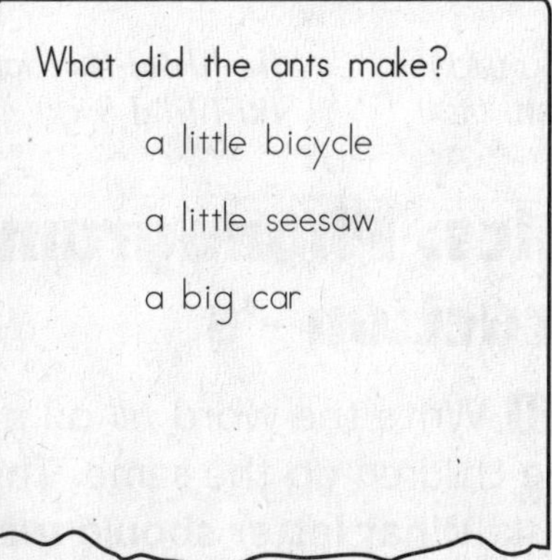

What did the ants make?
a little bicycle
a little seesaw
a big car

Phonics: Phonograms -ill, -it; Contraction -'s

PRETEACH Write the letters *ill* and *it* at the top of a sheet of chart paper. Have children suggest words that end with *–ill* and say what letters they would need to write the words. Then write the words underneath the heading *ill*. Use the same procedure for *it*. Then have children read each column of words. End the activity by pointing to words at random and having children read the words.

Write the following sentences on the board:

It is a little ant.

It's a little ant.

Have children read the first sentence aloud. Then point to *It's* and read the second sentence to children. Explain that *it's* is a contraction—a short way to say *it is*—and that a mark called an apostrophe takes the place of the *i* in the word is. Have children repeat *it is—it's* and listen to the difference.

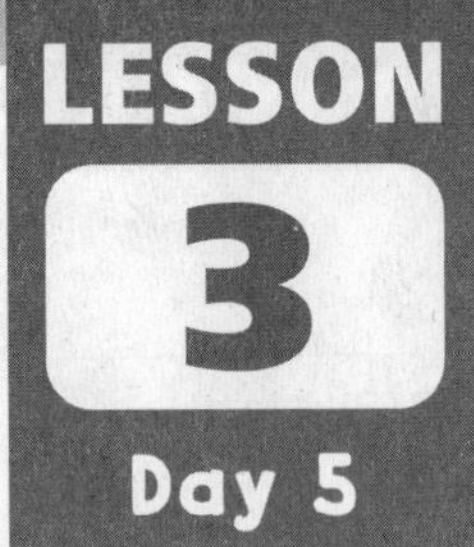

Warm-Up: Phonemic Awareness

Phoneme Blending Tell children that together you are going to play a game of "Fix It." Tell them that you are going to say some words that are all broken and they should listen to see if they can put the sounds together to figure out the word. **Listen: /p/-/i/-/n/. What word does /p/-/i/-/n/ say?** *(pin)* Continue with the following words:

/s/-/i/-/k/ *(sick)*	**/k/-/l/-/o/-/k/** *(clock)*	**/t/-/a/-/k/** *(tack)*
/f/-/i/-/sh/ *(fish)*	**/k/-/i/-/k/** *(kick)*	**/s/-/l/-/i/-/p/** *(slip)*

MATERIALS

Write-on/Wipe off Boards

Word Cards for and, in, oh, yes, make, they, walk

Word Builder

Word Builder Cards a, b, c, k, i, l, p, s, t

Phonics: Phonograms -ill, -it; Contraction -'s

RETEACH Write the word *fill* on a Write-on/ Wipe-off Board and have children do the same. Then have them read the word. Ask: **What letter should we write if we want to change *fill* to *will*?** *(w)* **Let's do that.** Continue the activity with the following words: *pill, bill*, and *hill*. Repeat the activity, using the words *sit, fit, bit, pit,* and *hit.*

Also on the Write-on/Wipe-off Boards, have children first write the words *he is*. Ask: **What do you need to do to turn *he is* into the contraction *he's*?** Have children erase the *i* in *is* and insert an apostrophe. Then have them read the contraction aloud. Repeat the activity, using *she is* and *it is.*

High-Frequency Words

Cumulative Review *and, in, oh, yes, make, they, walk* Place the words in a pocket chart. Say aloud one of the words and use it in a sentence. Have a volunteer find and point to the word. Have children clap and say the spelling of the word. Then have them write it. Have children read aloud their list of words.

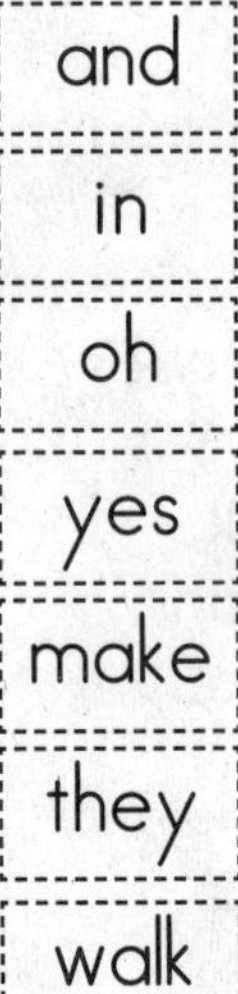

Read: Self-Selected Reading

Have children select a book to read from their browsing boxes. After they have completed their reading, have them show you a word they figured out successfully on their own.

Phonics: Digraph /k/ck

PRETEACH Write the letters *ck* on the board or on chart paper. **The letters *ck* can stand for the /k/ sound, the sound in words such as *pick, sock,* and *tack.*** Point to the letters *ck* and say /k/. Have children repeat the sound as you touch the letters *ck* several times.

Use the Word Builder and Word Builder Cards to model blending words.

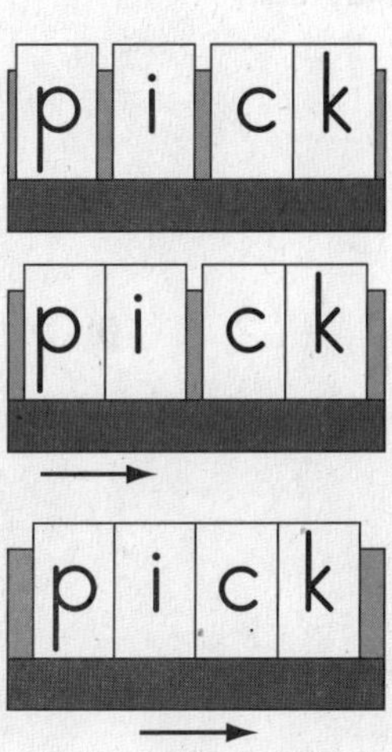

Place the Word Builder Cards *p, i, c* and *k* in the Word Builder. Point to the *p* and say /p/. Point to *i* and say /i/.

Slide the *i* next the *p.* Move your hand under the letters and blend the sounds, elongating them /ppii/. Have children repeat after you.

Point to the letters *ck*. Say /k/. Slide the ck next to *pi*. Slide your hand under *pick* and blend by elongating the sounds /ppiick/. Have children repeat.

Then have children read the word *pick* along with you.

Follow the same procedure for the words *sick, tack, back,* and *lick.*

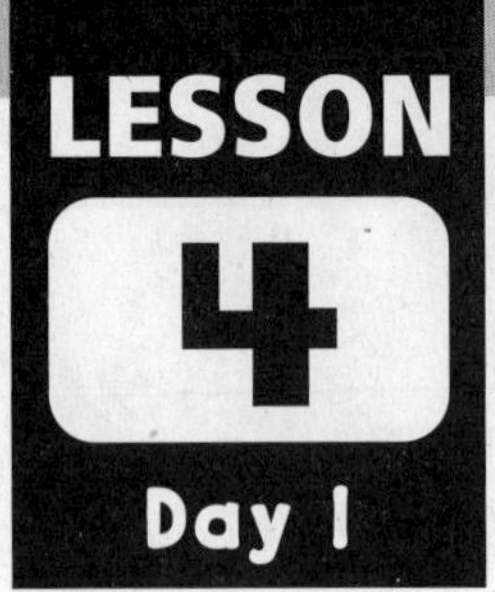

Warm-Up: Phonemic Awareness

Onset and Rime Tell children that you are going to say some words, but you are going to say them in parts. Have children listen to see if they can figure out the word. Demonstrate by saying: **/r/-ack—What word did I say?** *(rack)*

/b/-ack	**/t/-ick**	**/r/-ock**	**/ch/-ick**
/l/-ick	**/p/-ack**	**/d/-uck**	**/n/-eck**

MATERIALS

Word Cards for help, now, play, too, want

Word Builder

Word Builder Cards p, a, i, c, k, t, b, s

Play Ball!

Phonics: Digraph /k/ck

RETEACH **Blending** On a piece of chart paper write the letters *c* and *k* close together and display them for children. **These letters are *c* and *k*. When they are put in that order, the letters *c* and *k* can stand for the /k/ sound in words such as *back, lock,* and *sick*.** Underline both letters at the same time and say /k/. Tell children that the /k/ sound appears at the end of words such as *pack*, *sock*, and *check*. Have children repeat the sound as you touch the letters simultaneously several times.

Use the Word Builder Cards and a pocket chart to model blending words.

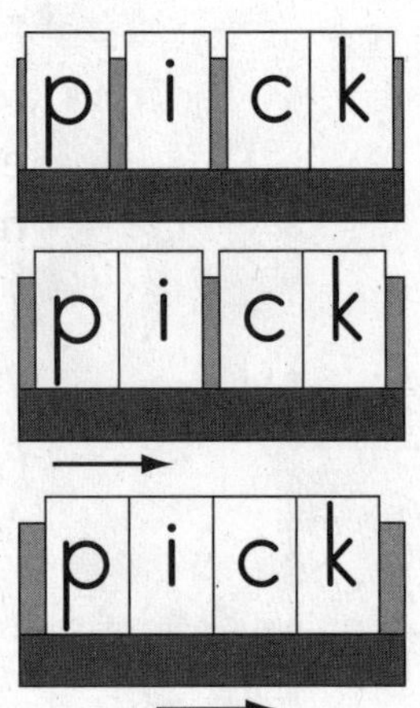

Place the Word Builder Cards *p, i, c,* and *k* in the Word Builder. Point to the *p* and say /p/. Point to the *i* and say /i/.

Slide the *i* next to the *p*. Move your hand under the letters and blend the sounds, elongating them /ppii/.

Point to the letters *ck* and say /k/. Have children say /k/ as you point to *ck*.

Slide *ck* next to *pi*. Slide your hand under pick and blend the sounds by elongating them— /ppi-ikk/. Have children do the same. Then say the word naturally—*pick*. Have children do the same.

High-Frequency Words

PRETEACH ***help, now, play, too, want*** Display the word card *help*. **This word is *help*. I will help you find your pencil. Read the word with me—*help*. Spell the word with me—*h-e-l-p*. Read the word with me. What is this word?** *(help)*

help

now

play

too

want

Follow the same procedure for the words *now*, *play*, *too*, and *want*.

now—**What are you doing now?**

play—**Let's play ball.**

too—**Please, let me play, too.**

want—**I want to play with you.**

Then place the five words in a pocket chart and have volunteers read the words, as you randomly point to them.

Play Ball!

Read: *Play Ball!*

Distribute copies of the book and have children put their finger on the title. Read the title aloud while children follow along. Ask them to touch the word *Play* and then the word *Ball*. Have volunteers choose a word in the title to read aloud. Echo read the book with children. Read page 2 aloud and then have children read it to you. Follow this procedure throughout the book.

Phonics: Word Building with /k/ck

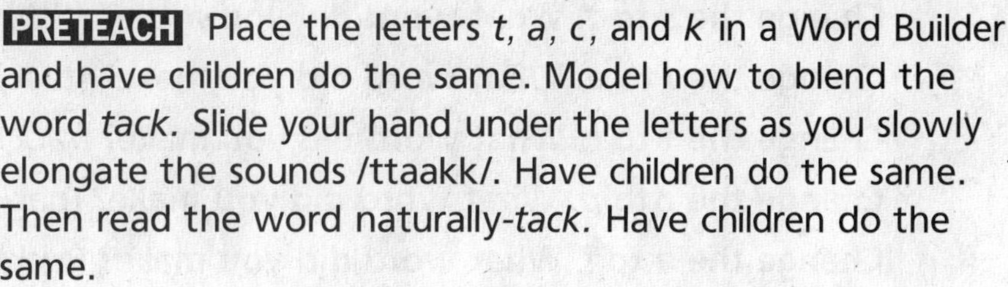

PRETEACH Place the letters *t*, *a*, *c*, and *k* in a Word Builder and have children do the same. Model how to blend the word *tack*. Slide your hand under the letters as you slowly elongate the sounds /ttaakk/. Have children do the same. Then read the word naturally-*tack*. Have children do the same.

Have children blend and read new words by telling them:

Change the *t* to a *p*. What word did you make? *(pack)*

Change the *p* to a *b*. What word did you make? *(back)*

Change the *b* to an *s*. What word did you make? *(sack)*

Change the *a* to an *i*. What word did you make? *(sick)*

Change the *s* to an *p*. What word did you make? *(pick)*

Distribute *Intervention Practice Book* page 10 to children.

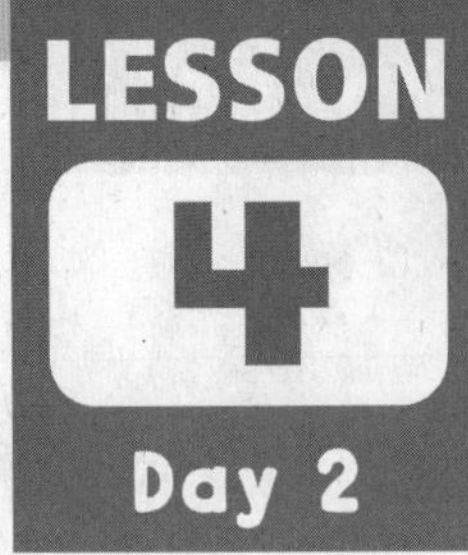

Warm-Up: Phonemic Awareness

Phoneme Isolation. Say the word *duck* aloud, and have children repeat it. Tell children to listen to the /k/ sound at the end of *duck*. Then say the words *lock* and *face*, and have children repeat both words. Ask: **Which word has the same /k/ sound you hear in *duck*?**

Continue with the words *clock, comb, lick; kick, fit, back; pack, luck, cave.*

MATERIALS

Word Builder

Word Builder Cards a, c, i, k, p, r, s, t

Play Ball!

Phonics: Word Building with /k/ck

RETEACH Place the letters *s, i, c,* and *k* in a Word Builder and have children do the same. Model how to blend the word *sick*. Slide your hand under the letters as you slowly elongate the sounds /ssiikk/. Have children do the same. Then read the word naturally—*sick*. Have children do the same.

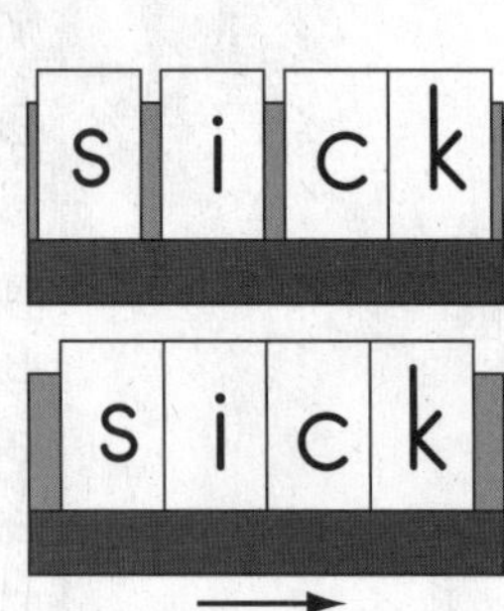

Have children blend and read new words by telling them:

Change the *s* to *t*. What word did you make? *(tick)*

Change the *i* to *a*. What word did you make? *(tack)*

Change the *t* to *r*. What word did you make? *(rack)*

Change the *r* to *p*. What word did you make? *(pack)*

Change the *a* to *i*. What word did you make? *(pick)*

High-Frequency Words

RETEACH ***help, now, play, too, want*** Write the word *help* on the board. Chant the letters with the children in the following phrase: **H-e-l-p, please come help me.** Have children read the word.

Repeat the procedure with *now:* **N-o-w, now I'll spell it for you;** *play:* **P-l-a-y, come play with me;** *too*: **T-o-o, Can I play, too?; want: w-a-n-t, I want to play.**

Read: *Play Ball!*

Play Ball!

Distribute copies of the book to children. Read pages 2 and 3 with them. Ask children to point to the word that says *Zack.* Tell children that this is a name. **The first letter in a name is written with an uppercase letter.** Then choral read the book with children. Let your voice fade if children start to gain control of the text.

Phonics: Reading Sentences with /k/ck

PRETEACH Distribute *Intervention Practice Book* page 11 to children. Point to the first sentence and have children read it aloud. Ask them to find the word *pack,* frame it with their fingers, and circle the word. Then work with children to complete the page.

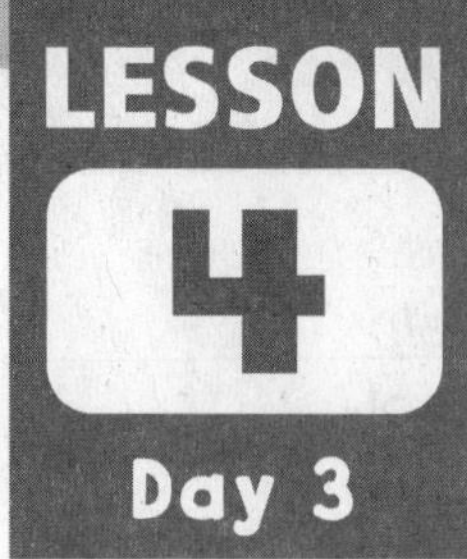

LESSON 4 Day 3

MATERIALS

Picture Cards bed, clock, drum, flag, kite, nine, rose, ship, smile, sock, train

Word Builder

Word Builder Cards a, c, i, k, n, p, s, t

Play Ball!

Warm-Up: Phonemic Awareness

Phoneme Blending. Tell children they will need to be detectives and find the word you are thinking about. Say: **I'm thinking of something that you wear on your foot. It is not a shoe. It is a /s/-/o/-/k/. What's my word?** *(sock)* Continue with the following words: /r/-/o/-/k/ *(rock)*, /ch/-/i/-/k/ *(chick)*, /p/-/a/-/k/ *(pack)*, /n/-/e/-/k/ *(neck)*, /d/-/u/-/k/-/s/ *(ducks)*.

Phonics: Reading Sentences with /k/ck

RETEACH Help children blend and read new words and sentences shown. Have them read the sentence, blending each word in sequence. The high-frequency words are underlined; they should read these as a unit, not blending the sounds.

tick **lick** **rack** **wick**

A pig is sick.

Kick the can.

Jack can play.

Pick up the tack.

High-Frequency Words

RETEACH ***help, now, play, too, want*** Write the following sentence on tag board and display it in a pocket chart along with the Picture Cards *flag, bed, clock, smile, ship, kite.* Call on children to choose a Picture Card to complete the sentence and read it aloud. Then ask: **Can you really pack a ____?**

PICTURE CARDS

Help me pack the __________ now.

Do the same for the following sentence and Picture Cards *drum, sock, nine, train, bed, rose.*

I want to play on the __________, too.

Read: *Play Ball!*

Distribute copies of the book and have children put their finger on the title. Then guide children through the book as they read.

Pages 2–3: Have children read the pages to find out what the animals can do.

What can the animals do? *(They can play.)* **Who joined the bird and the rabbit? Find and read the sentence that tells.** *(Zack is here now.)*

Pages 4–5: Have children read to see what Rick has brought.

What did Zack bring? *(a sack)*

What do the animals do with the sack? Find and read the sentence that tells. *(They pick it up.)*

What do Bird and Rabbit want to know? *(what is in the sack)*

Pages 6–8: Have children read to find out what the animals do with what is in the sack.

What was in the sack? *(bats, balls, and mitts)*

What do they do with the bats and balls? *(play with them)* **Find and read the sentence that tells.** *(Now they play ball!)*

Ask children to use the pictures to help summarize the book.

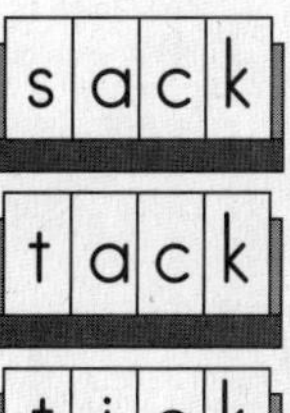

Phonics: Building Words

PRETEACH Put the letters *s*, *a*, *c*, and *k* in a Word Builder and have children do the same. Slide your hand under the letters as you blend the sounds—/ssaakk/. Then read the word naturally—*sack*. Have children repeat after you.

Then have children build and read new words.

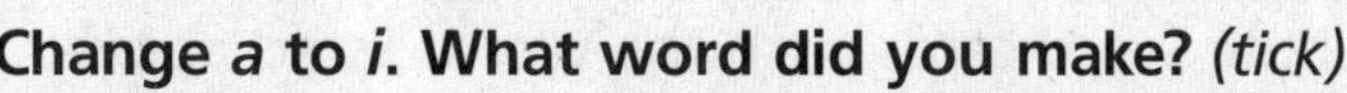

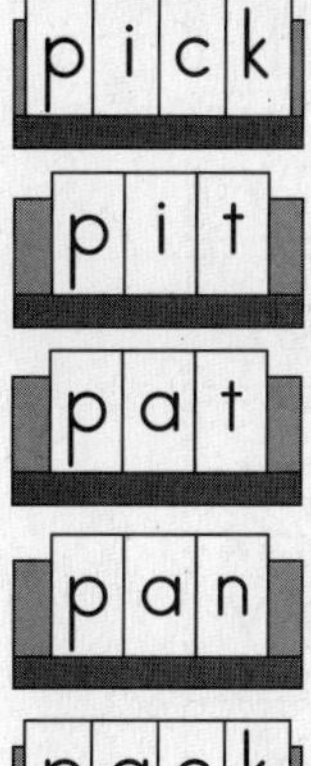

Change *s* to *t*. What word did you make? *(tack)*

Change *a* to *i*. What word did you make? *(tick)*

Change *t* to *p*. What word did you make? *(pick)*

Change *ck* to *t*. What word did you make? *(pit)*

Change *i* to *a*. What word did you make? *(pat)*

Change *t* to *n*. What word did you make? *(pan)*

Change *n* to *ck*. What word did you make? *(pack)*

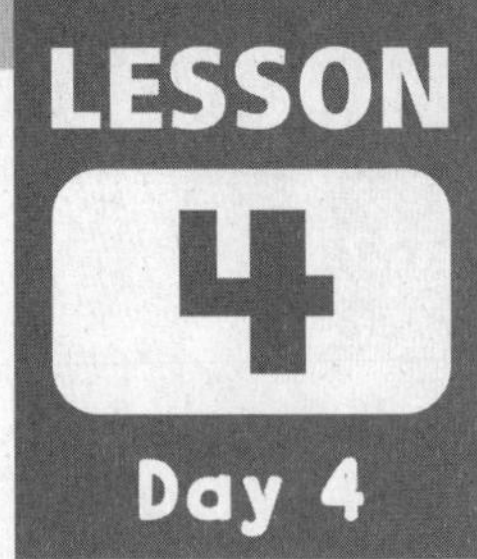

Warm-Up: Phonemic Awareness

Phoneme Segmentation Have children use the three boxes on the Write-on/Wipe-off Boards. Remind children that the boxes stand for the sounds in words. Show the Picture Card *lock* and ask: **What is the first sound you hear in *lock*?** (/l/) Have children place a disk in the first box. Then have children name the second sound in *lock* (/o/) and place a disk in the second box. Then have them identify the last sound in *lock* (/k/) and place a disk in the third box. Point to each box in sequence as children say the word. **How many sounds do you hear in *lock*?** *(three)* Repeat this procedure with the following Picture Cards: *cat, sock, hat, pin, fish.*

MATERIALS

Picture Cards cat, fish, hat, lock, pin, sock

Write-on/Wipe-off Boards with disks

Word Cards for help, now, play, too, they, walk, want

Word Builder

Word Builder Cards a, b, c, i, k, n, p, s, t

Play Ball!

Phonics: Building Words

RETEACH Put the letters *b, a, c, k* in a Word Builder and have children do the same. Slide your hand under the letters as you blend the sounds—/bbaakk/. Then read the word naturally—*back*. Have children repeat after you. Then have children build and read new words.

Change *b* to *t*. What word did you make? *(tack)*

Change *t* to *p*. What word did you make? *(pack)*

Change *ck* to *n*. What word did you make? *(pan)*

Change *a* to *i*. What word did you make? *(pin)*

Change *n* to *ck*. What word did you make? *(pick)*

Change *p* to *s*. What word did you make? *(sick)*

Change *i* to *a*. What word did you make? *(sack)*

Distribute *Intervention Practice Book* page 12 to children.

High-Frequency Words

RETEACH ***help, now, play, too, they, walk, want*** Distribute word cards with the words listed above. Have partners take turns displaying the words for each other and reading them. After they read each word, have children spell it and then repeat the word. Then have them spell the word again and write it on a sheet of paper.

Play Ball!

Read: *Play Ball!*

Focus Skill **Sequence** Remind children that the order of events is important to a story. Have children reread *Play Ball!* and then together think about the order of events in the story.

First
Next
Last

Ask: **What happened first? Who came to the park next? What did the boys do then?** Help children make a chart to show the order of events.

Phonics: Phonograms -ick, -ink; Contraction 'll (will)

PRETEACH Write the letters *ick* and *ink* at the top of a sheet of chart paper. Have children suggest words that end with *-ick* and say what letters they would need to write the words. Then write the words underneath the heading *-ick*. Use the same procedure for *-ink*. Then have children read each column of words. End the activity by pointing to words at random and having children read the words.

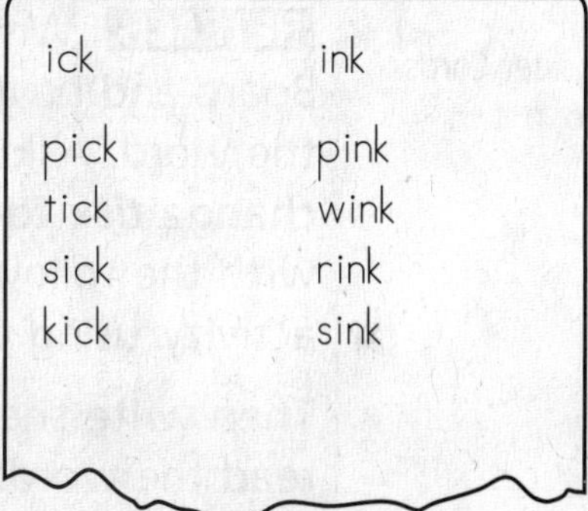

ick
ink
pick
tick
sick
kick
pink
wink
rink
sink

Write the sentence *I will* on the board and have children read it. Write the two words again, leaving out the space: *Iwill*. Say: **Sometimes two words come together like this.** Write them once more, making the *wi* quite small: *I(wi)ll.* **When they do, some of the letters are taken out and replaced with a mark we call an apostrophe.** Write *I'll* on the board. Explain that it is short for *I will*—a contraction of *I will*. Repeat with *you will* and *we will*.

I will

Iwill

I(wi)ll

I'll

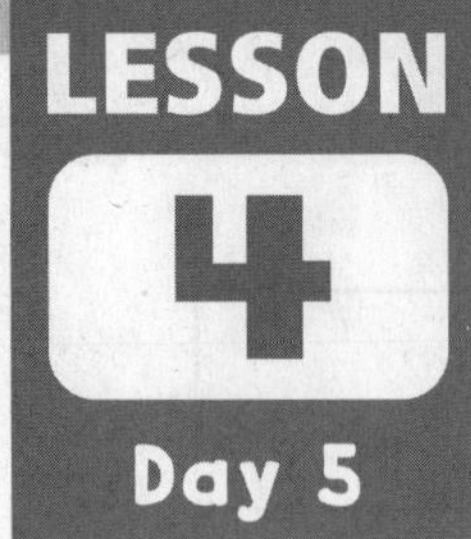

LESSON 4

Day 5

MATERIALS

Write-on/Wipe-off Boards

Word Cards for help, now, play, too, make, they, walk, want

Word Builder

Word Builder Cards d, h, n, o, p, t

Warm-Up: Phonemic Awareness

Phoneme Blending. Tell children that together you are going to play a game. Tell them to listen to three sounds and pretend that each sound is a piece of a puzzle. **See if you can put all three puzzle pieces together to make a word. Listen: /s/-/a/-/k/. What word does /s/-/a/-/k/ say?** *(sack)* Continue with the following words:

/n/-/o/-/k *(knock)* **/w/-/a/-/g/** *(wag)* **/r/-/i/-/p/** *(rip)*
/r/-/o/-/d/ *(rod)* **/t/-/a/-/p/-/s/** *(taps)* **/k/-/l/-/o/-/k/** *(clock)*

Phonics: Phonograms -ick, -ink; Contraction 'll

RETEACH Write the word *tick* on a Write-on/Wipe-off Board and have children do the same. Then have them read the word. Ask: **What letter should we write if we want to change *tick* to *sick*?** *(s)* **Let's do that.** Continue the activity with the following words: *lick*, *pick*, and *kick*. Repeat the activity, using the words *sink*, *pink*, and *wink*.

Then write the words *you will* on the board. Have children read the words. Ask: **How can we make these two words into a contraction?** (*Change* will *to* 'll) **Let's do that.** Continue the activity with *we will* and *I will*.

High-Frequency Words

Cumulative Review *help, now, play, too, make, they, walk, want* Place the words in a pocket chart. Say aloud one of the words and use it in a sentence. Have a volunteer find and point to the word. Have children clap and say the spelling of the word. Then have them write it. Have children read aloud their list of words.

help

now

play

too

make

they

walk

want

Read Self-Selected Reading

Have children select a book to read from their browsing boxes. After they have completed their reading, have them tell you what they were most successful in during the reading of the book.

Phonics: Short Vowel /o/o

PRETEACH Write the letter *o* on the board or on chart paper. **The letter *o* can stand for the /o/ sound, the sound in words such as *mop, job,* and *mom*.** Point to the letter *o* and say /o/. Have children repeat the sound as you touch the letter o several times.

Use the Word Builder and Word Builder Cards to model blending words. Place the Word Builder Cards *n, o,* and *t* in the Word Builder. Point to the *n* and say /n/. Point to *o* and say /o/.

Slide the *o* next to the *n*. Move your hand under the letters and blend the sounds, elongating them /nnoo/. Have children repeat after you.

Point to the letter *t*. Slide the *t* next to *no.* Slide your hand under *not* and blend by elongating the sounds /nnoott/. Have children repeat. Then have children read the word *not* along with you.

Follow the same procedure for the words *dot, hot, hop,* and *top.*

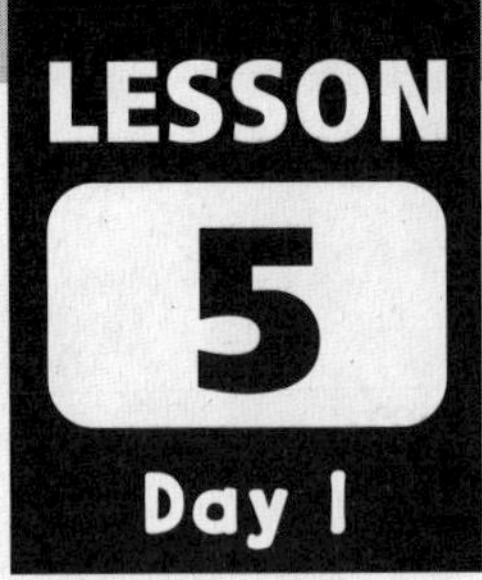

Warm-Up: Phonemic Awareness

Onset and Rime Tell children that you are going to say some words, but you are going to say them in parts. Have children listen to see if they can figure out the word. Demonstrate by saying: /l/-ot—What word did I say? (*lot*)

/n/-od	**/p/-op**	**/s/-ock**	**/r/-ob**
/sh/-op	**/r/-ock**	**/d/-ot**	**/ch/-op**

MATERIALS

Word Cards of, so, don't

Word Builder

Word Builder Cards d, h, n, o, p, p, t

Alphabet Masters Oo

The Box

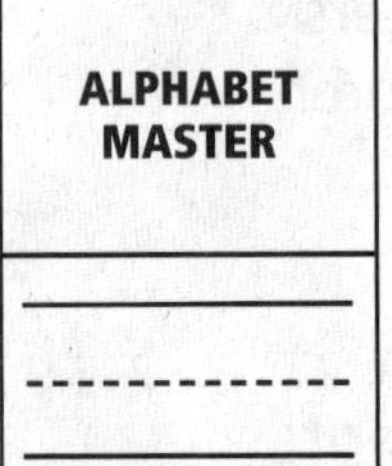

Phonics: Short Vowel /o/o

RETEACH **Blending** Display Alphabet Master *Oo*. **This letter is o. The letter *o* can stand for the /o/ sound, the short sound of the letter *o* in words such as *on, off,* and *odd*.** Point to the Alphabet Master and say /o/. Tell children that the /o/ sound appears in the middle of words such as *hop, lot,* and *pot*. Have children repeat the sound as you touch the card several times.

Use the Word Builder Cards and a pocket chart to model blending words.

Place the Word Builder Cards *o* and *n* in the Word Builder. Point to the *o* and say /o/. Point to the *n* and say /n/.

Slide the *n* next to the *o*. Move your hand under the letters and blend the sounds, elongating them /oonn/. Have children repeat after you. Then say the word naturally—*on*. Have children do the same.

Place the Word Builder cards *h, o,* and *p* in the Word Builder. Point to the *h* and say /h/. Point to the *o* and say /o/.

Slide the *o* next to the *h*. Move your hand under the letters and blend the sounds, elongating them /hhoo/. Have children repeat after you.

Point to the letter *p* and say /p/. Have children say /p/ as you point to *p*.

Slide *p* next to *ho*. Slide your hand under *hop* and blend by elongating the sounds—/hhoopp/. Have children repeat. Then have children read the word *hop* along with you.

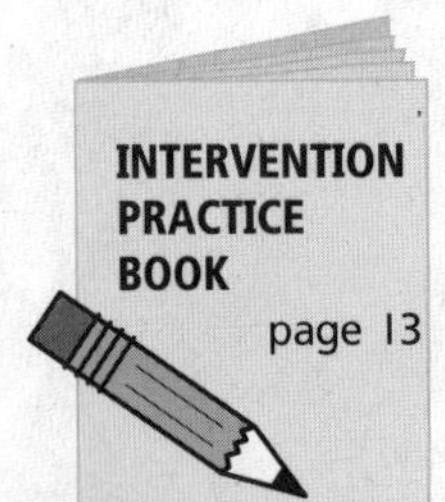

High-Frequency Words

of

so

don't

PRETEACH ***of, so, don't*** Display the word card *of*. **This word is *of*. This is one of my favorite books. Read the word with me—*of*. Spell the word with me—*o-f*. Read the word with me. What is this word?** *(of)*

Follow the same procedure for the words *so* and *don't*.

so—**I am feeling so happy today.**

don't—**I don't have any apples.**

Then place the three words in a pocket chart and have volunteers read the words, as you randomly point to them.

Read: *The Box*

The Box

Distribute copies of the book and have children put their finger on the title. Read the title aloud while children follow along. Ask them to touch the word *The*, then the word *Box*. Have volunteers choose a word in the title to read aloud. Echo read the book with children. Read page 2 aloud and then have children read it to you. Follow this procedure throughout the book.

Phonics: Word Building with /o/o

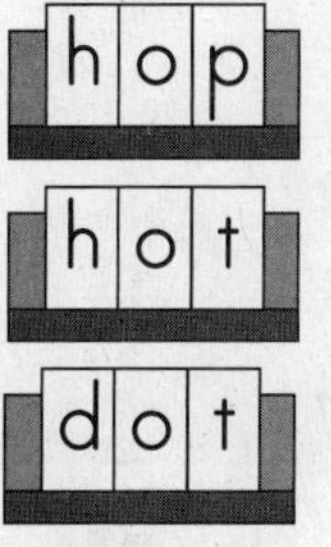

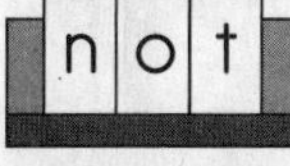

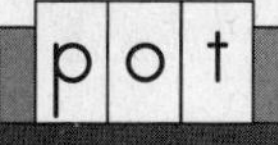

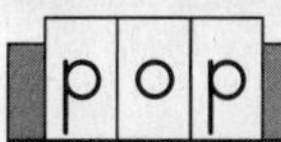

PRETEACH Place the letters *h*, *o*, and *p* in a Word Builder and have children do the same. Model how to blend the word *hop*. Slide your hand under the letters as you slowly elongate the sounds /hhoopp/. Have children do the same. Then read the word naturally—*hop*. Have children do the same.

Have children blend and read new words by telling them:

Change the *p* to *t*. What word did you make? *(hot)*

Change the *h* to *d*. What word did you make? *(dot)*

Change the *d* to *n*. What word did you make? *(not)*

Change the *n* to *p*. What word did you make? *(pot)*

Change the *t* to *p*. What word did you make? *(pop)*

Distribute *Intervention Practice Book* page 13 to children.

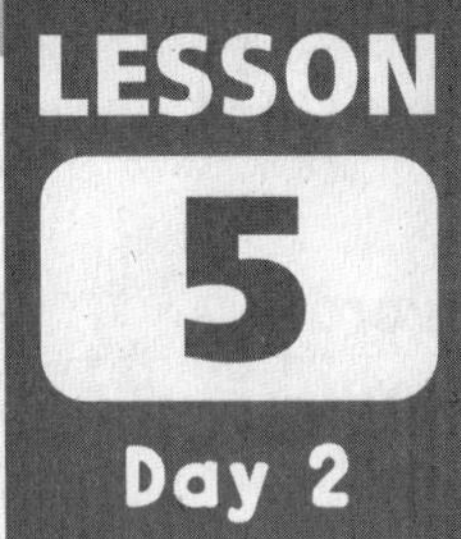

Warm-Up: Phonemic Awareness

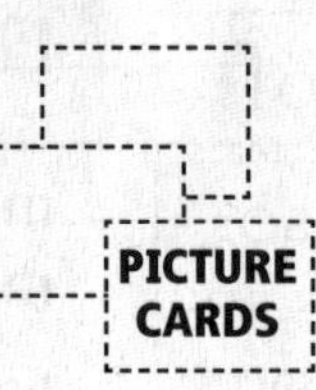

Phoneme Isolation Display the Picture Cards *clock*, *fox*, and *net*. Hold up the clock. Have children say the word *clock* aloud. Tell children to listen to the /o/ sound in the middle of the word *clock*. Have them say the names of the other two pictures aloud. Ask: **What other picture name has the /o/ sound?** *(fox)*

Continue with the Picture Cards *mop, lock, lamp; box, fish, mop; sock, mule, fox.*

MATERIALS

Word Builder

Word Builder Cards d, h, n, o, p, p, t

Picture Cards box, lock, fish, fox, lamp, lock, mop, mule, net, sock

The Box

Phonics: Word Building with /o/o

RETEACH Place the letters *h*, *o*, and *p* in a Word Builder and have children do the same. Model how to blend the word *hop*. Slide your hand under the letters as you slowly elongate the sounds /hhoopp/. Have children do the same. Then read the word naturally—*hop*. Have children do the same.

Have children blend and read new words by telling them:

Change the *h* to *p*. What word did you make? *(pop)*

Change the *p* at the end of the word to *t*. What word did you make? *(pot)*

Change the *p* to *h*. What word did you make? *(hot)*

Change the *h* to *d*. What word did you make? *(dot)*

Change the *d* to *n*. What word did you make? *(not)*

High-Frequency Words

RETEACH ***of, so, don't*** Write the word *on* and have children read it. Then write the word *of* next to *on*. Have children read the word. **How are these words the same? How are they different? Let's read them again.**

on   of

Repeat the procedure with *see/so* and *do/don't.*

Read: *The Box*

The Box

Distribute copies of the book to children. Read pages 2 and 3 with them. Have children find and read the word *Is.* Point to the uppercase letter that starts the word. Explain to children that this letter is uppercase because the word *is* begins the question. **A question and a sentence always begin with a capital letter.** Then choral read the book with children. Let your voice fade if children start to gain control of the text.

Phonics: Reading Sentences with /o/o

PRETEACH Distribute *Intervention Practice Book* page 14 to children. Point to the first sentence and have children read it aloud. Ask them to find the words *Dot* and *rock*, frame them with their fingers, and circle the words. Then work with children to complete the page.

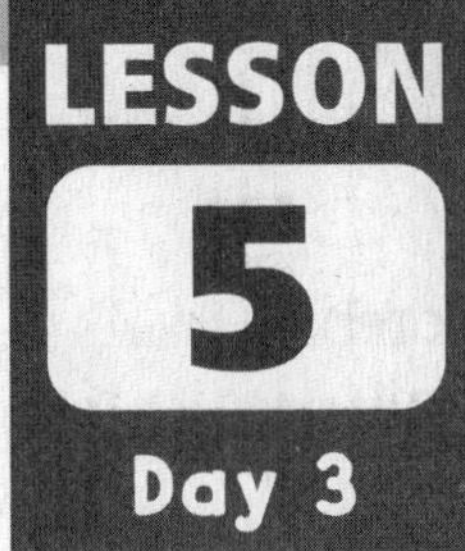

MATERIALS

Picture Cards bed, boat, gate, igloo, kite, leaf, red, six, sock, ten, thumb, train, wagon

Word Builder

Word Builder Cards c, h, i, k, l, o, s, t

The Box

Warm-Up: Phonemic Awareness

Phoneme Blending Tell children that they are going to play a guessing game. Then say: **I'm thinking of a word that means a big stone. It is a /r/-/o/-/k/. What's my word?** *(rock)* Continue with the following words: /l/-/o/-/t/ *(lot)*, /ch/-/o/-/p/ *(chop)*, /t/-/o/-/p/ *(top)*, /s/-/o/-/k/ *(sock)*, /b/-/l/-/o/-/k/ *(block)*

Phonics: Reading Sentences with /o/o

RETEACH Help children blend and read new words and sentences shown. Have them read the sentence, blending each word in sequence. The high-frequency words are underlined; they should read these as a unit, not blending the sounds.

top **got** **Tom** **lock**

<u>Look</u> in the <u>box</u>.

<u>The</u> pot is hot.

Pick up <u>the</u> sock!

Can <u>my</u> cat hop?

High-Frequency Words

RETEACH ***of, so, don't*** Write the following sentence on tagboard and display it in a pocket chart along with the Picture Cards *bed, boat, thumb, wagon, ten, sock.* Call on children to choose a Picture Card to complete the sentence and read it aloud. Then ask: **Can you really have animals in your ____?**

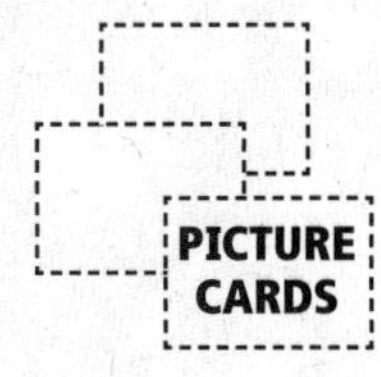

I had a lot of dogs and cats in my ____________.

Do the same for the following sentence and Picture Cards *bed, sock, kite, red, igloo, train.*

It is so hot in the ____________.

Repeat for the following sentence and Picture Cards *leaf, bed, gate, six, red, wagon.*

I don't like to hop on the ______________.

Read: *The Box*

Distribute copies of the book and have children put their finger on the title. Tell children this is a story about a girl and her grandfather. Then guide children through the book as they read.

Pages 2–3: Have children read the pages to find out who is talking.

Who is talking first? *(the girl)* **To whom is she talking?** *(her grandfather)*

What will she make? *(a box)*

What does her grandfather guess is in the box? Find and read the question that tells. *(Is it a box of cats?)*

Pages 4–5: Have children read to see what the grandfather thinks is in the box now.

Was it a box of cats? *(no)* **What does the girl tell her grandfather? Find and read the words that tell.** *(Don't look, Pa!)* **What does the grandfather guess now?** *(socks)* **Do you think the grandfather knows what is really in the box?**

Pages 6–7: Have children read to find out the grandfather's next guess.

What is the grandfather's third guess? *(tops)* **What question tells? Find and read it.** *(Is it a box of tops?)* **Was that the right answer?** *(no)*

Page 8: Have children read to find out if the girl shows her grandfather what is in the box.

Does the girl let her grandfather see what is in the box? What does she ask him? Find and read the question that tells. *(Don't you like it?)* **What do you think his answer will be?**

Ask children to use the pictures to help summarize the book.

Phonics: Building Words

PRETEACH Put the letters *l*, *o*, and *t* in a Word Builder and have children do the same. Slide your hand under the letters as you blend the sounds—/lloott/. Then read the word naturally—lot. Have children repeat after you. Then have children build and read new words.

Change the *t* to *ck*. What word did you make? *(lock)*

Change the *l* to *s*. What word did you make? *(sock)*

Change the *o* to *i*. What word did you make? *(sick)*

Change the *ck* to *t*. What word did you make? *(sit)*

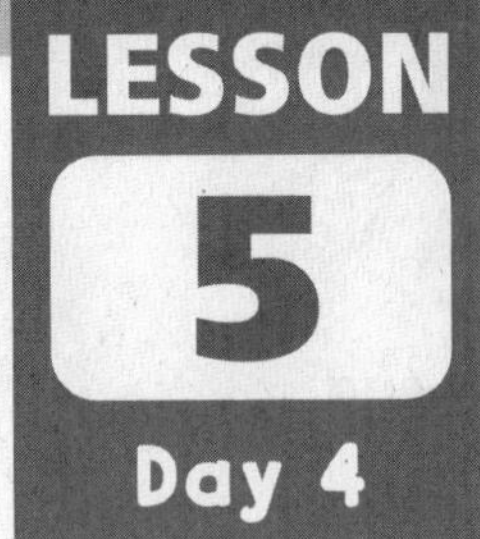

Warm-Up: Phonemic Awareness

Phoneme Segmentation Have children use the three boxes on the Write-on/Wipe-off Boards. Remind children that the boxes stand for the sounds in words. Show the Picture Card *sock* and ask: **What is the first sound you hear in *sock*?** (/s/) Have children place a disk in the first box. Then have children name the second sound in *sock* (/o/) and place a disk in the second box. Then have them identify the last sound in *sock* (/k/) and place a disk in the third box. Point to each box in sequence as children say the word. **How many sounds do you hear in *sock*?** (*three*) Repeat this procedure with the Picture Cards *hat, pin, fan, mop, lock.*

PICTURE CARDS

MATERIALS

Picture Cards fan, pin, hat, lock, mop, sock

Write-on/Wipe-off Boards with disks

Word Cards of, so, don't, now, want

Word Builder

Word Builder Cards a, b, c, h, i, k, o, p, r, s, t

The Box

Phonics: Building Words

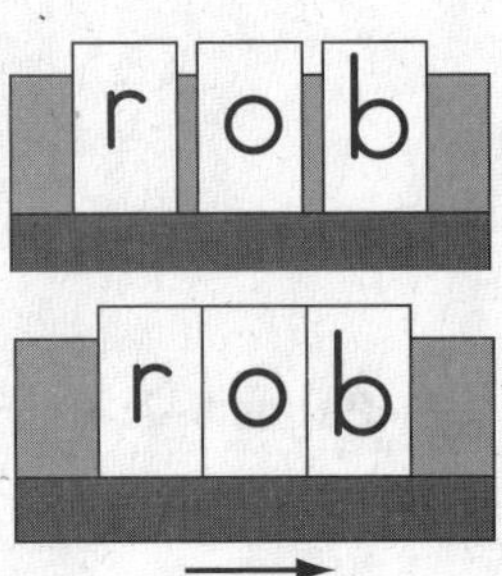

RETEACH Put the letters *r, o, b* in a Word Builder and have children do the same. Slide your hand under the letters as you blend the sounds—/rroobb/. Then read the word naturally—*rob.* Have children repeat after you. Then have children build and read new words.

Change the *b* to *ck*. What word did you make? *(rock)*

Change the *o* to *a*. What word did you make? *(rack)*

Change the *r* to *t*. What word did you make? *(tack)*

Change the *ck* to *p*. What word did you make? *(tap)*

Change the *a* to *i*. What word did you make? *(tip)*

Change the *i* to *o*. What word did you make? *(top)*

Change the *t* to *h*. What word did you make? *(hop)*

Add *s* to the end of *hop*. What word did you make? *(hops)*

Distribute *Intervention Practice Book* page 15 to children.

of

so

don't

now

want

High-Frequency Words

RETEACH ***of, so, don't, now, want*** Distribute word cards with the words listed above. Have partners take turns displaying the words for each other and reading them. After they read each word, have children spell it and then repeat the word. Then have them spell the word again and write it on a sheet of paper.

The Box

Read: *The Box*

Focus Skill **Draw Conclusions** Remind children that sometimes they must figure out things for themselves in a story. Have children reread *The Box* one page at a time. Ask: **Who is the girl making the box for? How do you know? Why does she say, "Don't look"? Why do you think she lets him look at the end?** Have children write one answer they gave.

Phonics: Inflections -ed, -ing

PRETEACH Write the word *lock* at the top of a sheet of chart paper. Have children read it. Then add *-ed* to the end of *lock*. Have children read the new word. Explain that *locked* means that the action happened in the past. Write these words on the chart: *play, want*. Have children say what letters they would need to make *play* into *played*. Write *ed* at the end of *play*. Use the same procedure for the word *want*. Repeat with the same words and the ending *–ing*. Finish the activity by pointing to words at random and having children read the words.

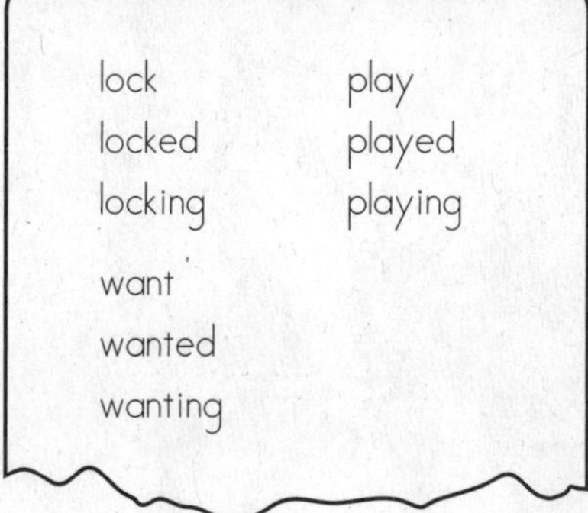

lock
locked
locking
play
played
playing
want
wanted
wanting

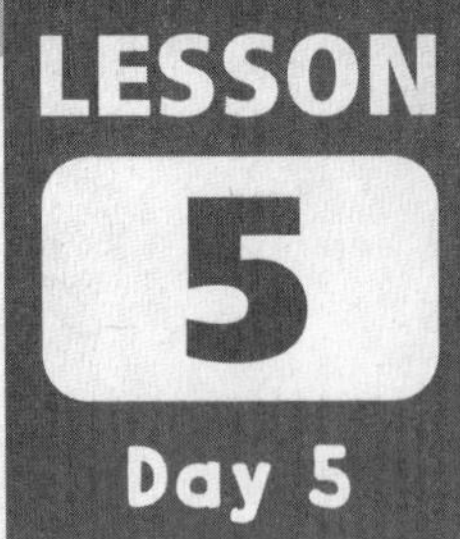

Warm-Up: Phonemic Awareness

Phoneme Blending. Tell children that together you are going to play a game of "Fix It." Tell them that you are going to say some words that are all broken and they should listen to see if they can put them together to figure out the word. **Listen: /t/-/o/-/p/. What word does /t/-/o/-/p/ say?** *(top)* Continue with the following words:

/l/-/o/-/k/ *(lock)*	**/w/-/i/-/g/** *(wig)*	**/f/-/ô/-/l/** *(fall)*
/p/-/o/-/t/ *(pot)*	**/r/-/a/-/k/** *(rack)*	**/w/-/ô/-/l/-/s/** *(walls)*

MATERIALS

Write-on/Wipe-off Boards

Word Cards of, so, don't, help, now, play, too, want

Word Builder

Word Builder Cards a, b, c, f, l, l, t, w

Phonics: Inflection -ed, -ing

RETEACH Write the word *rock* on a Write-on/ Wipe-off Board and have children do the same. Then have them read the word. Ask: **What letters should we write if we want to change *rock* to *rocked*?** *(ed)* **Let's do that. What letters should we write if we want to change *rock* to *rocking*?** *(ing)* **Let's do that.** Continue the activity with the words: *play* and *want*. Point out the different sounds for *-ed*: /t/ in *rocked*, /d/ in *played*, /ed/ in *wanted*.

High-Frequency Words

Cumulative Review *of, so, don't, help, now, play, too, want* Place the words in a pocket chart. Say aloud one of the words and use it in a sentence. Have a volunteer find and point to the word. Have children clap and say the spelling of the word. Then have them write it. Have children read aloud their list of words.

of

so

don't

help

now

play

too

want

Read: Self-Selected Reading

Have children select a book to read from their browsing boxes. After they have completed their reading, have them tell you what they were most successful in during the reading of the book.

Phonics: Vowel Variants /ô/a(all)

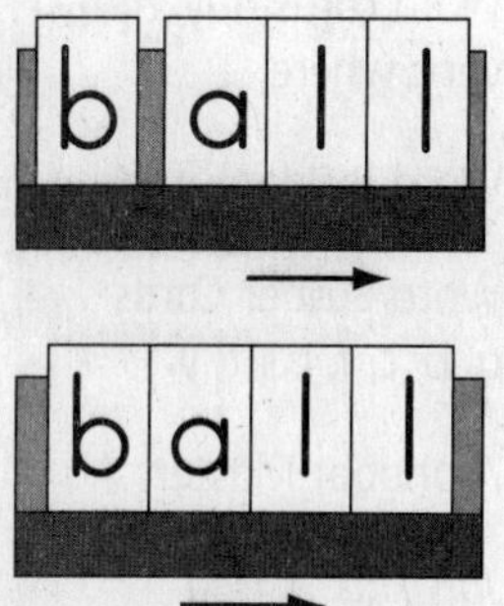

PRETEACH Use the Word Builder and Word Builder Cards to model blending words. Place the Word Builder Cards *b, a, l,* and *l* in the Word Builder. Point to the *a.* Tell children that *a* often says /ô/ when it is next to *ll.* Point to *ll.* Say /l/.

Slide the *ll* next to the *a.* Move your hand under the letters and blend the sounds, elongating them /ôôll/. Have children repeat after you.

Point to the letter *b*. Slide the *all* next to *b*. Slide your hand under *ball* and blend by elongating the sounds /bbôôll/. Have children repeat.

Then have children read the word *ball* along with you. Follow the same procedure for the words *fall*, *call*, *wall*, and *tall*.

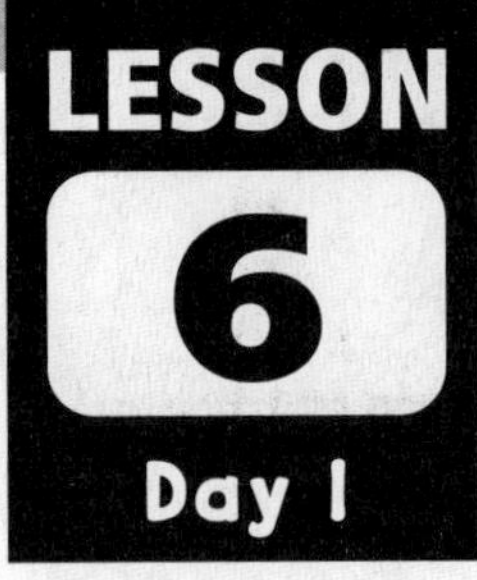

Warm-Up: Phonemic Awareness

Onset and Rime Tell children that you are going to say some words, but you are going to say them in parts. Have children listen to see if they can figure out the word. Demonstrate by saying: **/f/-all—What word did I say?** (*fall*)

/h/-all	**/m/-all**	**/k/-all**	**/w/-all**
/t/-all	**/sh/-awl**	**/b/-all**	**/kr/-awl**

MATERIALS

Word cards buy, that, very, where

Word Builder

Word Builder Cards a, b, c, f, l, l, t, w

Alphabet Masters Aa

Jan Has a Doll

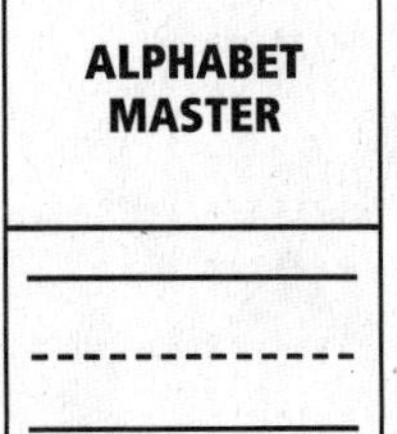

Phonics: Vowel Variant /ô/all

RETEACH **Blending** Display Alphabet Master *Aa* and write the letters *ll* on the board or on chart paper. Then place the Alphabet Master in front of *ll*. **When the letter *a* comes before *ll*, it can stand for the /ô/ sound, the sound of the vowel in words such as *ball*, *call*, and *tall*.** Have children repeat the sound as you touch the letters *all*.

Use the Word Builder Cards and a pocket chart to model blending words.

Place the Word Builder Cards *a*, *l*, and *l* in the Word Builder, with the *ll* together but separated from the *a*. Point to the *a* and say /ô/. Point to the *ll* and say /l/.

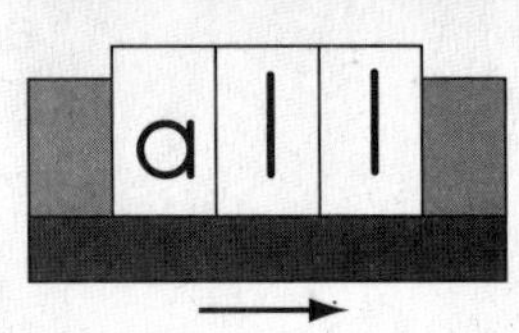

Slide the *ll* next to the *a*. Move your hand under the letters and blend the sounds, elongating them /ôôll/. Have children repeat after you. Then say the word naturally—*all*. Have children do the same.

Place the Word Builder Cards *c*, *a*, *l*, and *l* in the Word Builder. Point to the *a* and say /ô/. Point to the *ll* and say /l/.

Slide the *ll* next to the *a*. Move your hand under the letters and blend the sounds, elongating them /ôôll/. Have children repeat after you.

Point to the letter *c* and say /k/. Have children say /k/ as you point to *c*.

Slide *all* next to *c*. Slide your hand under *call* and blend by elongating the sounds—/kkôôll/. Have children repeat. Then have children read the word *call* along with you.

INTERVENTION PRACTICE BOOK page 16

High-Frequency Words

PRETEACH ***that, where, buy, very*** Display the word card *that*. **This word is *that*. That girl is very smart. Read the word with me—*that*. Spell the word with me—*t-h-a-t*. Read the word with me. What is this word?** (*that*)

that
where
buy
very

Follow the same procedure for the words *where*, *buy*, and *very*.

where—**Where are you going?**

buy—**I will buy flowers with my money.**

very—**I am very happy today.**

Then place the four words in a pocket chart and have volunteers read the words, as you randomly point to them.

Read: *Jan Has a Doll*

Jan Has a Doll

Distribute copies of the book and have children put their finger on the title. Read the title aloud while children follow along. Ask them to touch the word *Jan*, then the words *Has*, *a*, and *Doll*. On page 2, explain that the picture shows the father is making a cornhusk doll. Then echo read the book with children. Read page 2 aloud and then have children read it to you. Follow this procedure throughout the book.

Phonics: Word Building with /ô/all

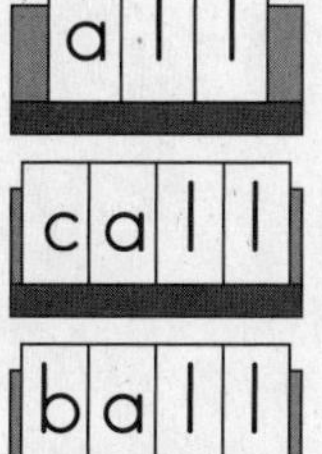

PRETEACH Place the letters *a*, *l*, and *l* in a Word Builder and have children do the same. Model how to blend the word *all*. Slide your hand under the letters as you slowly elongate the sounds /ôôll/. Have children do the same. Then read the word naturally—*all*. Have children do the same.

Have children blend and read new words by telling them:

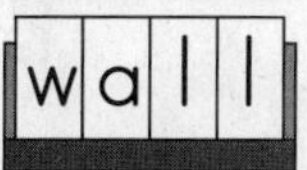

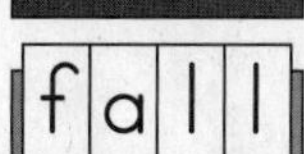

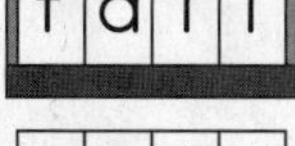

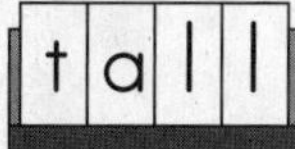

Add *c* to the front of *all*. What word did you make? *(call)*

Change *c* to *b*. What word did you make? (*ball*)

Change *b* to *w*. What word did you make? (*wall*)

Change *w* to *f*. What word did you make? (*fall*)

Change *f* to *t*. What word did you make? (*tall*)

Distribute *Intervention Practice Book* page 16 to children.

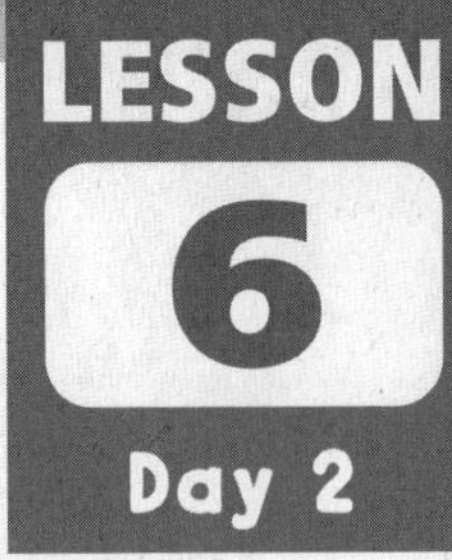

Warm-Up: Phonemic Awareness

Phoneme Isolation Say the word *wall* aloud and have children repeat it. Tell children to listen to the /ô/ sound in the middle of *wall*. Then say the words *tick* and *fall*. Ask: **Which of these words has the same ô sound you hear in *wall*?** (*fall*)

Continue with the words *tall*, *sit*, *ball*; *call*, *fox*, *mall*; *hall*, *rules*, *wall*.

MATERIALS

Word Builder

Word Builder Cards a, b, c, f, h, l, l, t, w

Jan Has a Doll

Phonics: Word Building with /ô/all

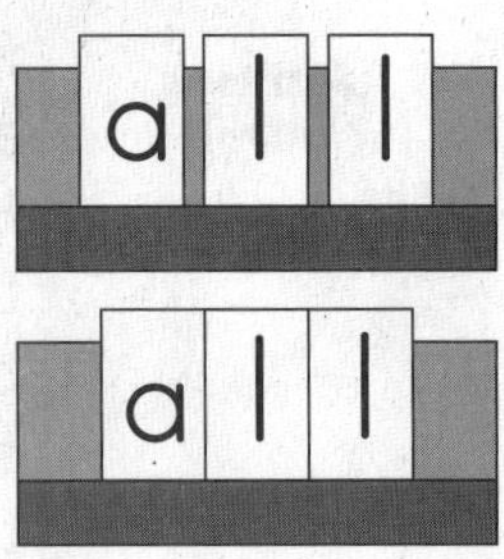

RETEACH Place the letters *a*, *l*, and *l* in a Word Builder and have children do the same. Model how to blend the word *all*. Slide your hand under the letters as you slowly elongate the sounds /ôôll/.

Have children do the same. Then read the word naturally—*all*. Have children do the same.

Have children blend and read new words by telling them:

Add an *f* in front of *all*. What word did you make? *(fall)*

Change *f* to *h*. What word did you make? *(hall)*

Change *h* to *w*. What word did you make? *(wall)*

Change *w* to *t*. What word did you make? *(tall)*

Change *t* to *b*. What word did you make? *(ball)*

Change *b* to *c*. What word did you make? *(call)*

High-Frequency Words

RETEACH ***that, where, buy, very*** Write the word *that* and have children read it. Then teach children this chant to help them remember the word and its spelling: **T-h-a-t, give that hat back to me.** Touch each letter in turn as you say its name. Have children repeat the chant as they use their index finger to write the letters of *that* in the air.

Repeat the procedure with the following chants:

B-u-y, I want to buy some pie.

W-h-e-r-e, where can my puppy be?

V-e-r-y, I am very warm and dry.

Read: *Jan Has a Doll*

Jan Has a Doll

Distribute copies of the book to children. Read page 2 with them. Have children find and read the name that tells who will get the doll. Then choral read the book with children. Let your voice fade if children start to gain control of the text.

Phonics: Reading Sentences with /ô/all

PRETEACH Distribute *Intervention Practice Book* page 17 to children. Point to the first sentence and have children read it aloud. Ask them to find the word *fall*, frame it with their fingers, and circle the word. Then work with children to complete the page.

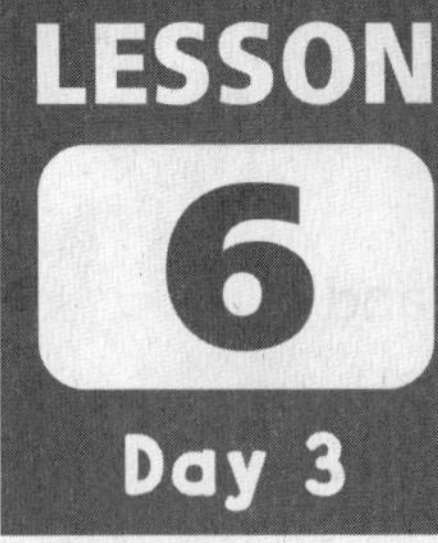
LESSON 6
Day 3

MATERIALS

Picture Cards fish, fox, hat, lamp, nine, rose, seal, smile, sock, sun, zebra

Word Builder

Word Builder Cards a, c, f, i, l, p, t, w

Jan Has a Doll

Warm-Up: Phonemic Awareness

Phoneme Blending Tell children that they are going to be builders and put together the word you are thinking. Say: **I'm thinking of a word that is something you can throw or kick. It is round. It is a /b/-/ô/-/l/. What's my word?** (*ball*) Continue with the following words: /f/-/ô/-/l/ (*fall*), /p/-/ô/-/l/ (*Paul*), /t/-/ô/-/l/ (*tall*), /w/-/ô/-/l/-/s/ (*walls*), /s/-/m/-/ô/-/l/ (*small*)

Phonics: Reading Sentences with /ô/all

RETEACH Help children blend and read new words and sentences shown. Have them read the sentence, blending each word in sequence. The high-frequency words are underlined; they should read these as a unit, not blending the sounds.

mall **hall** **calls** **falls**

Do not fall!

I will call you.

Pack a big ball.

That rock is tall.

High-Frequency Words

RETEACH ***that, where, buy, very*** Write the following sentence on tag board and display it in a pocket chart along with the Picture Cards *hat*, *sun*, *lamp*, *sock*, *rose*, *smile*. Call on children to choose a Picture Card to complete the sentence and read it aloud. Then ask: **Can you really buy a ______?**

PICTURE CARDS

I will buy that ______.

Do the same for the following sentence and Picture Cards *zebra*, *fox*, *fish*, *seal*, *sun*, *nine*.

Where is the very sick ______?

Read: *Jan Has a Doll*

Distribute copies of the book and have children put their finger on the title. Then guide children through the book as they read.

Pages 2–3: Have children read the pages to find out who the doll is for.

Who is talking first? (*the boy*) **What does the boy ask his father? Find and read his question.** (*Is that for Jan?*)

What does the father tell the boy to do? (*Go call Jan.*) **Why do they want to find Jan?** (*to give her the doll*)

Pages 4–5: Have children read to find out if Jan is found.

Who finds Jan? (*the boy*) **What does he tell Jan to do? Find and read his words.** (*Look in here. Look on the wall.*)

Pages 6–7: Have children read to see what happens when Jan finds the doll.

What does Jan want to know? Find and read her question. (*Is that for me?*)

What does Jan say about the doll? Find and read the words that tell. (*It looks like me*).

Page 8: Have children read to find out what Jan will do now.

What can the children do now? Find and frame the words that tell. (*Now we can play.*)

Ask children to use the pictures to help summarize the book.

Phonics: Building Words

PRETEACH Place the letters *f*, *a*, *l*, and *l* in a Word Builder and have children do the same. Slide your hand under the letters as you blend the sounds—/ffôôll/. Then read the word naturally—*fall*. Have children repeat after you. Then have children build and read new words.

Change *f* to *c*. What word did you make? *(call)*

Take away the *c*. What word did you make? *(all)*

Change *a* to *i*. What word did you make? *(ill)*

Add *p* in front of *ill*. What word did you make? *(pill)*

Change *p* to *w*. What word did you make? *(will)*

Change *i* to *a*. What word did you make? *(wall)*

Change *w* to *t*. What word did you make? *(tall)*

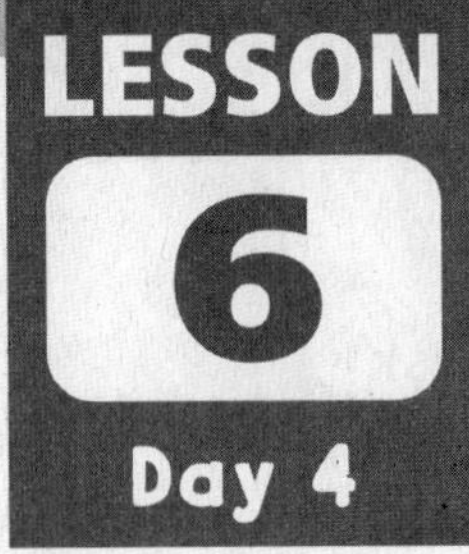

Warm-Up: Phonemic Awareness

Phoneme Segmentation Have children use the three boxes on the Write-on/Wipe-off Boards. Remind children that the boxes stand for the sounds in words. Point to a wall of your classroom and ask: **What is the first sound you hear in *wall*?** (/w/) Have children place a disk in the first box. Then have children name the second sound in *wall* (/ô/) and place a disk in the second box. Then have them identify the last sound in *wall* (/l/) and place a disk in the third box. Point to each box in sequence as children say the word. **How many sounds do you hear in *wall*?** (*three*) Repeat this procedure using a real ball and a real hall.

MATERIALS

Write-on/Wipe-off Boards with disks

Word Cards buy, of, so, that, very, where

Word Builder

Word Builder Cards a, b, c, f, h, i, l, l, m, t

Jan Has a Doll

Phonics: Building Words

RETEACH Put the letters *c*, *a*, *l*, *l* in a Word Builder and have children do the same. Slide your hand under the letters as you blend the sounds—/kkôôll/. Then read the word naturally—*call*. Have children repeat after you. Then have children build and read new words.

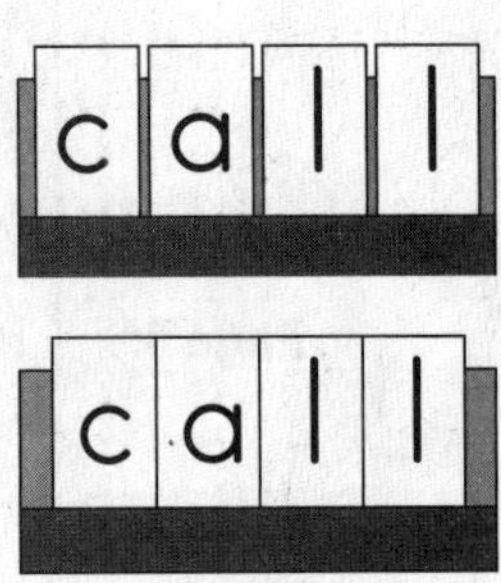

Change *c* to *f*. What word did you make? *(fall)*

Change *f* to *b*. What word did you make? *(ball)*

Change *a* to *i*. What word did you make? *(bill)*

Change *b* to *m*. What word did you make? *(mill)*

Change *i* to *a*. What word did you make? *(mall)*

Change *m* to *t*. What word did you make? *(tall)*

Change *t* to *h*. What word did you make? *(hall)*

Distribute *Intervention Practice Book* page 18 to children.

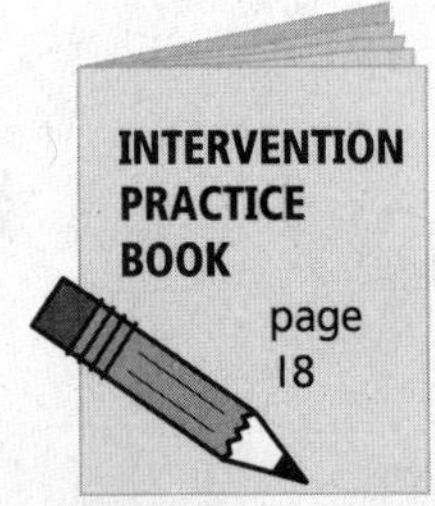

High-Frequency Words

that
where
buy
very
so
of

RETEACH ***that, where, buy, very, so, of*** Distribute word cards with the words listed above. Have partners take turns displaying the words for each other and reading them. After they read each word, have children spell it and then repeat the word. Then have them spell the word again and write it on a sheet of paper.

Read: *Jan Has a Doll*

Focus Skill **Sequence** Remind children that noticing the order in which things happen in a story can help them understand the story. Have children reread *Jan Has a Doll*. Ask: **What happens first? What happens next? What happens after Jan finds the doll? What happens at the end of the story?** Help children list the sequence of events using pictures.

Phonics: Phonograms: -all, -ill Contraction: n't

PRETEACH Write the letters *-all* and *-ill* at the top of a sheet of chart paper. Have children suggest words that end with *-all* and say what letters they would need to write the words. Then write the words underneath the heading *-all*. Use the same procedure for *-ill*. Then have children read each column of words. End the activity by pointing to words at random and having children read the words.

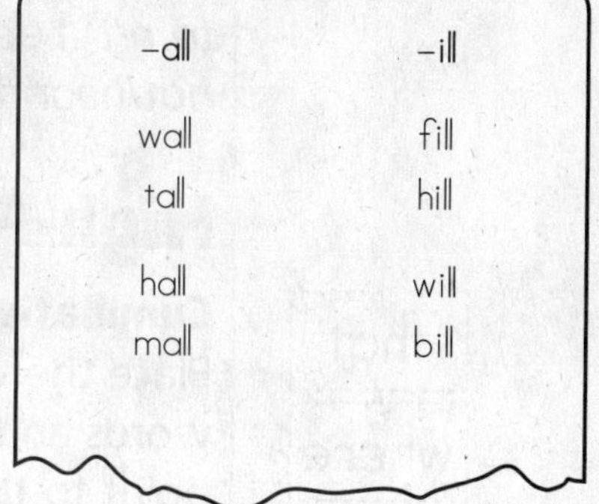

-all
wall
tall
hall
mall
-ill
fill
hill
will
bill

Write the words *did not* on the board and have children read them. Write the two words again, leaving out the space: *didnot*. Say: **Sometimes two words come together like this.** Erase the *o* and put an apostrophe in its place. **When they do, that *o* is dropped and is replaced with this mark, which we call an apostrophe. The letters *n't* are short for the word *not*.** Explain that *did not* can be written as *didn't* for short. Repeat with *is not/isn't*, *has not/hasn't*, and *had not/hadn't*.

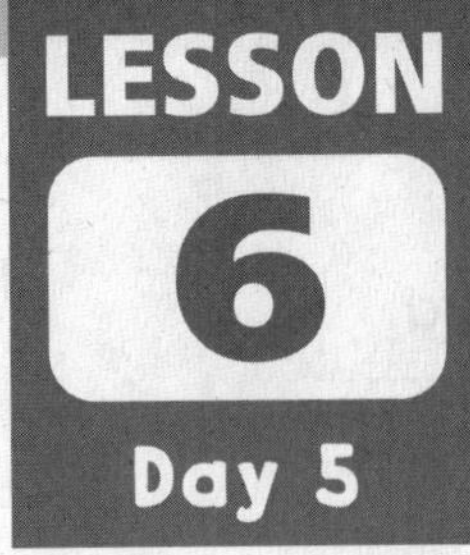

LESSON 6 Day 5

Warm-Up: Phonemic Awareness

Phoneme Blending Tell children that together you are going to play a game by putting some sounds together to make words. **Let's see if you can figure out this word. Listen: /h/-/ô/-/l/. What word does /h/-/ô/-/l/ say?** (*hall*) Continue with the following words:

/t/-/ô/-/l/ (*tall*)	**/w/-/i/-/l/** (*will*)	**/t/-/e/-/n/** (*ten*)
/p/-/a/-/s/-/t/ (*past*)	**/n/-/e/-/k/** (*neck*)	**/k/-/ô/-/l/-/s/** (*calls*)

MATERIALS

Write-on/Wipe-off Boards

Word Cards buy, don't, of, so, that, very, where

Word Builder

Word Builder Cards e, h, m, n, p, s, t

Phonics: Phonograms -all, -ill Contraction n't

RETEACH Write the word *fall* on a Write-on/Wipe-off Board and have children do the same. Then have them read the word. Ask: **What letter should we change if we want to change *fall* to *fill*?** (*a to i*) **Let's do that.** Continue the activity with the following words: *hall/hill*, *bill/ball*, and *wall/will*. Then write the words *do not* on the board. Have children read the words. Ask: **How can we make these two words into one word, the contraction *don't*?** (*change not to n't*) **Let's do that.** Continue the activity with *had not/hadn't* and *did not/didn't*.

High-Frequency Words

Cumulative Review *that, where, buy, very, of, so, don't* Place the words in a pocket chart. Say aloud one of the words and use it in a sentence. Have a volunteer find and point to the word. Have children clap and say the spelling of the word. Then have them write it. Have children read aloud their list of words.

that

where

buy

very

so

of

don't

Read: Self-Selected Reading

Have children select a book to read from their browsing boxes. After they have completed their reading, have them tell you what they were most successful in during the reading of the book.

Phonics: Short Vowel /e/e

PRETEACH Write the letter e on the board or chart paper. The letter e can stand for /e/, the short sound of the vowel e in words such as *men*, *hen*, and *bed*. Point to the letter e and say /e/. Have children repeat the sound as you touch the letter several times.

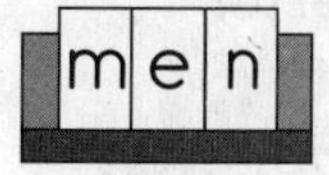

Use the Word Builder and Word Builder Cards to model blending words. Place the Word Builder Cards *m*, *e*, and *n* in the Word Builder. Point to the *m* and say /m/. Point to the e and say /e/.

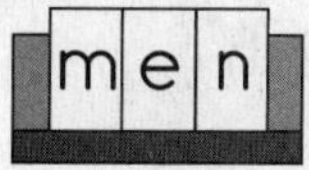

Slide the *e* next to the *m*. Move your hand under the letters and blend the sounds, elongating them /mmee/. Have children repeat after you. Point to the letter *n*. Slide the *n* next to *me*. Slide your hand under *men* and blend by elongating the sounds /mmeenn/. Have children repeat. Then have children read the word *men* along with you.

Follow the same procedure for the words *hen*, *pen*, and *set*.

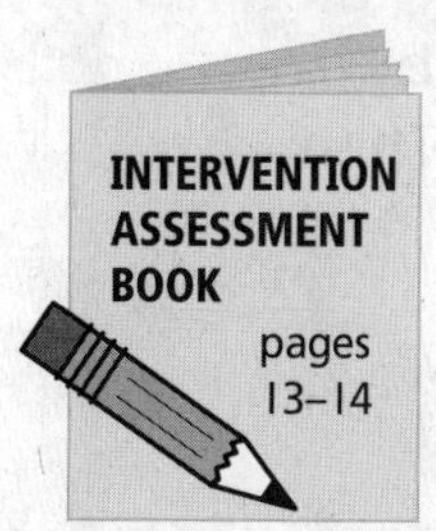

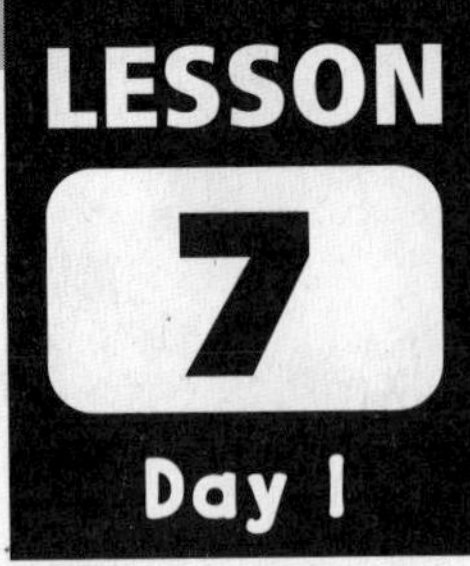

MATERIALS

Word Cards day, every, her, said, was, with

Word Builder

Word Builder Cards d, e, h, m, n, p, s, t

Alphabet Masters Ee

Apples

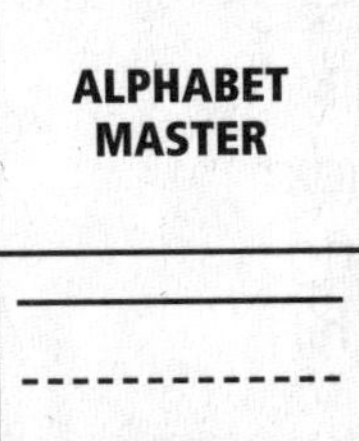

Warm-Up: Phonemic Awareness

Onset and Rime Tell children that you are going to say some words, but you are going to say them in parts. Have children listen to see if they can figure out the word. Demonstrate by saying: **/p/-et—What word did I say?** (*pet*)

/r/-ed	**/y/-es**	**/v/-et**	**/sh/-ell**
/b/-eg	**/t/-ell**	**/m/-en**	**/n/-eck**

Phonics: Short Vowel /e/e

RETEACH Blending Display Alphabet Master *Ee*. **This letter is e. The letter e can stand for the /e/ sound, the short sound of the letter e in words such as *egg*, *Ed*, and *end*.** Point to the Alphabet Master and say /e/. Tell children that the /e/ sound appears in the middle of words such as *bed*, *pet*, and *hen*. Have children repeat the sound as you touch the letter several times.

Use the Word Builder Cards and a pocket chart to model blending words.

Place the Word Builder Cards *e*, *n*, and *d* in the Word Builder. Point to the *e* and say /e/. Point to the *n* and say /n/.

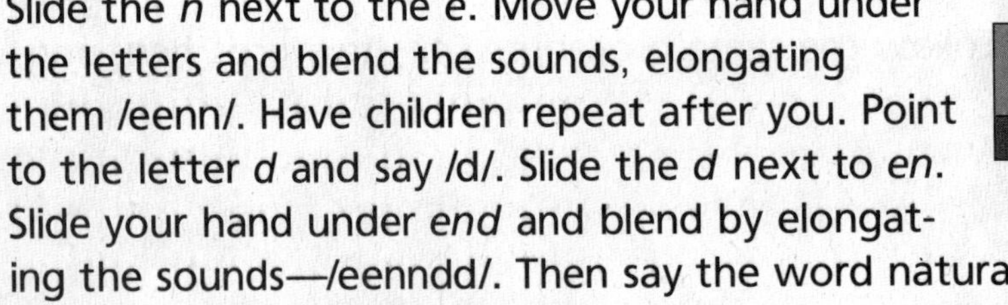

Slide the *n* next to the *e*. Move your hand under the letters and blend the sounds, elongating them /eenn/. Have children repeat after you. Point to the letter *d* and say /d/. Slide the *d* next to *en*. Slide your hand under *end* and blend by elongating the sounds—/eenndd/. Then say the word naturally—*end*. Have children do the same.

Place the Word Builder Cards *h*, *e*, and *n* in the Word Builder. Point to the *h* and say /h/. Point to the *e* and say /e/.

Slide the *e* next to the *h*. Move your hand under the letters and blend the sounds, elongating them /hhee/. Have children repeat after you.

Point to the letter *n* and say /n/. Have children say /n/ as you point to *n*.

Slide *n* next to *he*. Slide your hand under *hen* and blend by elongating the sounds—/hheenn/. Have children repeat. Then have children read the word *hen* along with you.

High-Frequency Words

said | was | with | every | day | her

PRETEACH ***was, said, with, every, day, her*** Display the word card *said*. **This word is *said*. He said his name. Read the word with me—*said*. Spell the word with me—*s-a-i-d*. Read the word with me. What is this word?** (*said*)

Follow the same procedure for the words *was*, *with*, *her*, *every*, and *day*.

was—**Yesterday was (day of week).**

with, *her*—**(Child's name) eats lunch with her friends.**

every, *day*—**Brush your teeth every day.**

Then place the six words in a pocket chart and have volunteers read the words, as you randomly point to them.

Read: *Apples*

Distribute copies of the book and ask children what they think the story will be about. Have children put their finger on the title. Have them follow along as you read the title aloud. Echo read the book with children. Read page 2 aloud and then have children read it to you. Follow this procedure throughout the book.

Phonics: Word Building with /e/e

PRETEACH Place the letters *h*, *e*, and *n* in a Word Builder and have children do the same. Model how to blend the word *hen*. Slide your hand under the letters as you slowly elongate the sounds /hheenn/. Have children do the same. Then read the word naturally—*hen*. Have children do the same.

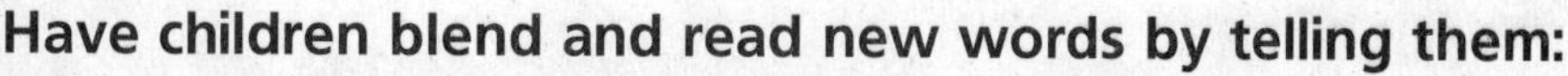

Have children blend and read new words by telling them:

Change *h* to *p*. What word did you make? *(pen)*

Change *p* to *m*. What word did you make? *(men)*

Take away *m* and add *d* after the letters *en*. What word did you make? *(end)*

Add *s* to the front of *end*. What word did you make? *(send)*

Change *nd* to *t*. What word did you make? *(set)*

Distribute *Intervention Practice Book* page 19 to children.

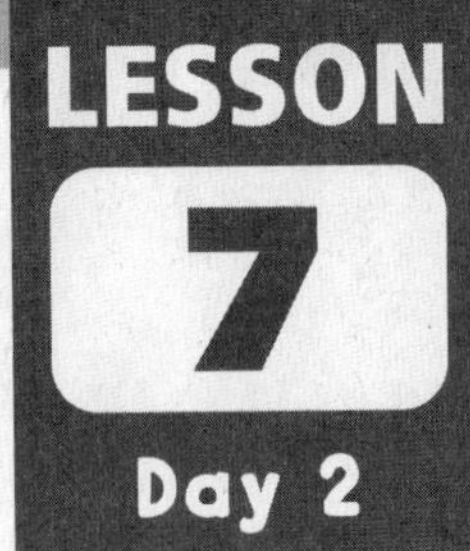

MATERIALS

Word Builder

Word Builder Cards d, e, h, m, n, p, s, t

Picture Cards bed, egg, flag, jet, net, pen, red, map, fish, lock, sled, ten

Warm-Up: Phonemic Awareness

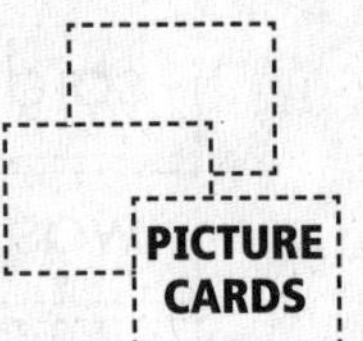

Phoneme Isolation Display the Picture Cards *jet*, *bed*, and *lock*. Hold up the jet. Have children say the word *jet* aloud. Tell children to listen to the /e/ sound in the middle of the word *jet*. Have them say the name of the other two pictures aloud. Ask: **What other picture name has the same /e/ sound you hear in *jet*?** (*bed*)

Continue with the Picture Cards *net*, *egg*, *fish*; *pen*, *red*, *map*; *ten*, *sled*, *flag*.

Phonics: Word Building with /e/e

RETEACH Place the letters *h*, *e*, and *n* in a Word Builder and have children do the same. Model how to blend the word *hen*. Slide your hand under the letters as you slowly elongate the sounds /hheenn/. Have children do the same. Then read the word naturally—*hen*. Have children do the same.

Have children blend and read new words by telling them:

Change *h* to *m*. What word did you make? *(men)*

Change *m* to *p*. What word did you make? *(pen)*

Take *p* away and add *d* after the *en*. What word did you make? *(end)*

Add *s* to the front of *end*. What word did you make? *(send)*

Change *nd* to *t*. What word did you make? *(set)*

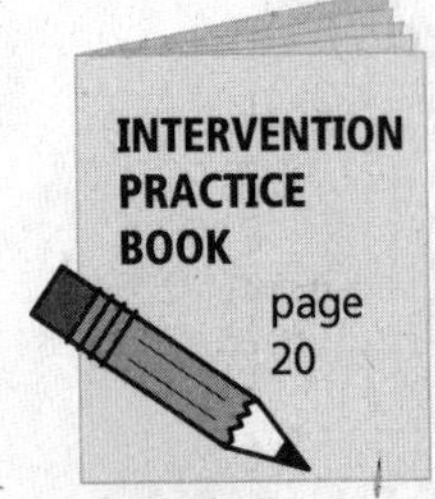

High-Frequency Words

RETEACH ***was, said, with, every, day, her*** Write the word *sad*, and have children read it. Then write the word *said* next to *sad*, and have children read the word. **How are these words the same? How are they different? Let's read them again.**

sad　　said

Repeat the procedure with *win/with*, *play/day*, *very/every*, *her/here*, and *wall/was*.

Read: *Apples*

Apples

Distribute copies of the book to children and read the title aloud. Ask children to point to the names of the people who wrote and illustrated the book. Read their names aloud. Explain that the author wrote the story and the illustrator drew the pictures. Then choral read the book with children. Let your voice fade if children start to gain control of the text.

Phonics: Reading Sentences with /e/e

PRETEACH Distribute *Intervention Practice Book* page 20 to children. Point to the first sentence and have children read it aloud. Ask them to find the word *eggs*, frame it with their fingers, and circle the word. Then work with children to complete the page.

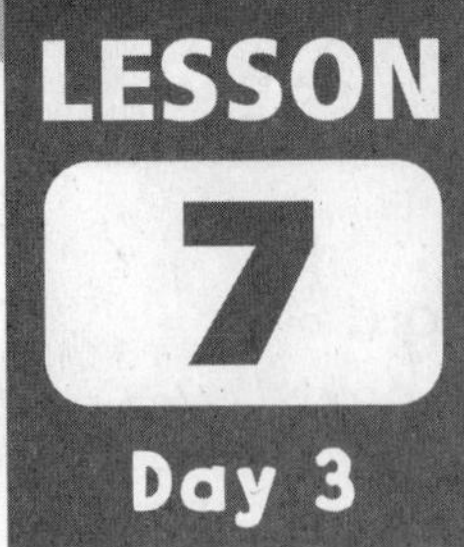

LESSON 7 Day 3

MATERIALS

Word Builder

Word Builder Cards a, e, g, m, n, o, s, t

Picture Cards bat, bug, cat, drum, egg, fish, mask, nut, pig, plum, ten, wagon

Apples

Warm-Up: Phonemic Awareness

Phoneme Blending Tell children that they are going to play a guessing game. Then say: **I'm thinking of a word that is an animal. It lays eggs. It is a /h/-/e/-/n/. What's my word?** *(hen)* Continue with the following words: /sh/-/e/-/l/ *(shell)*, /ch/-/e/-/k/ *(check)*, /m/-/e/-/s/ *(mess)*, /r/-/e/-/d/ *(red)*.

Phonics: Reading Sentences with /e/e

RETEACH Help children blend and read new words and sentences shown. Have them read the sentence, blending each word in sequence. The high-frequency words are underlined; they should read these as a unit, not blending the sounds.

men **sell** **den** **peg**

<u>The</u> mop is wet.

<u>A</u> vet will fix his leg.

<u>Where</u> can I sell eggs?

<u>See</u> <u>my</u> mess.

High-Frequency Words

RETEACH ***was, said, with, every, day, her*** Write the following sentence on tag board and display it in a pocket chart along with the Picture Cards *drum*, *fish*, *pig*, *cat*, *wagon*. Call on children to choose a Picture Card to complete the sentence and to read it aloud. Then ask: **Do you really play with a ______ every day?**

PICTURE CARDS

Ann and I play with her ______ every day.

Do the same for the following sentence and Picture Cards *egg*, *mask*, *nut*, *bug*, *plum*, *bat*.

They said it was a very big ______.

Read: *Apples*

Distribute copies of the book and have children read aloud the title. Ask children what they think this book will be about. Then guide children through the book as they read.

Pages 2–3: Have children read the pages to find out what Sam needs.

What does Sam need? (*help*) **Find and read the words that tell. What mark do you see?** (*question mark*)

Pages 4–5: Have children read the pages to find out if Ann will help Sam.

Will Ann help Sam? (*yes*) **Find and read the sentence that tells what Ann says.** (*I will help you.*)

What are Sam and Ann going to do with the bags? (*fill the bags*)

Pages 6–8: Have children read to find out if Sam needs more help.

What does Ann do first? Find and read the sentence that tells. (*Ann got the bags*) **What does Sam ask Ann?** (*Will you help me?*) **What is Ann's answer?** (*I will help you.*)

What do you think they will do with the apples?

Ask children to use the pictures to help summarize the book.

Phonics: Building Words

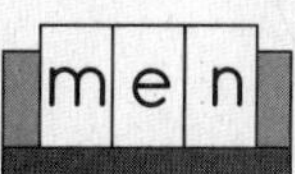

PRETEACH Place the letters *m*, *e*, and *n* in a Word Builder and have children do the same. Slide your hand under the letters as you blend the sounds—/mmeenn/. Then read the word naturally—*men*. Have children repeat after you. Then have children build and read new words.

Change *e* **to** *a*. **What word did you make?** *(man)*

Change *n* **to** *t*. **What word did you make?** *(mat)*

Change *m* **to** *s*. **What word did you make?** *(sat)*

Change *a* **to** *e*. **What word did you make?** *(set)*

Change *s* **to** *g*. **What word did you make?** *(get)*

Change *e* **to** *o*. **What word did you make?** *(got)*

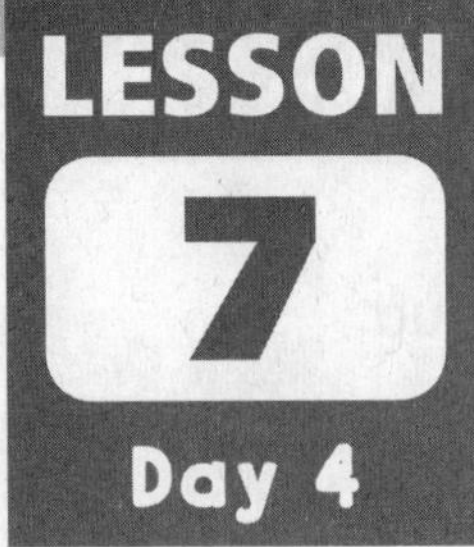

Warm-Up: Phonemic Awareness

Phoneme Segmentation Have children use the three boxes on the Write-on/Wipe-off Boards. Remind children that the boxes stand for the sounds in words. Show the Picture Card *jet* and ask: **What is the first sound you hear in *jet*?** (/j/) Have children place a disk in the first box. Then have children name the second sound in *jet* (/e/) and place a disk in the second box. Then have them identify the last sound in *jet* (/t/) and place a disk in the third box. Point to each box in sequence as children say the word. **How many sounds do you hear in *jet?*** (*three*) Repeat this procedure with the following Picture Cards: *red*, *ten*, *pen*, *leaf*, *sock*.

PICTURE CARDS

MATERIALS

Picture Cards jet, leaf, pen, red, sock, ten

Write-on/Wipe-off Boards with disks

Word Cards day, every, her, said, that, very, was, with

Word Builder

Word Builder Cards d, e, i, j, n, p, s, t

Apples

Phonics: Building Words

RETEACH Put the letters *p*, *e*, *n* in a Word Builder and have children do the same. Slide your hand under the letters as you blend the sounds—/ppeenn/. Then read the word naturally—*pen*. Have children repeat after you. Then have children build and read new words.

Change *e* to *i*. What word did you make? *(pin)*

Change *n* to *t*. What word did you make? *(pit)*

Change *i* to e. What word did you make? *(pet)*

Change *p* to *j*. What word did you make? *(jet)*

Change *j* to *s*. What word did you make? *(set)*

Change *t* to *nd*. What word did you make? *(send)*

Distribute *Intervention Practice Book* page 21 to children.

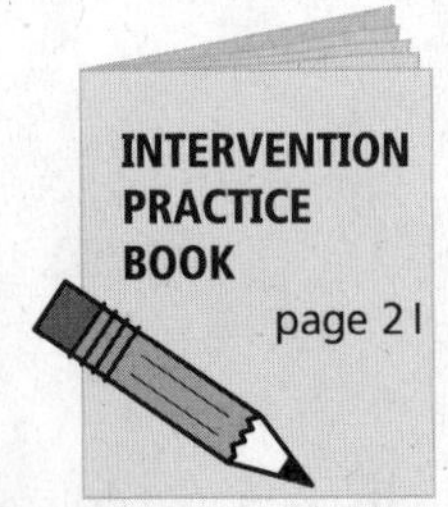

was

said

with

every

day

very

that

her

High-Frequency Words

RETEACH ***was, said, with, every, day, very, that, her***
Distribute word cards with the words listed above. Have partners take turns displaying the words for each other and reading them. After they read each word, have children spell the word and then repeat it. Then have them spell the word again and write it on a sheet of paper.

Read: *Apples*

Focus Skill **Setting** Remind children that the setting of a story includes where and when a story takes place. Tell them that knowing about the setting can help them better understand and picture what happens in a story. Have children reread *Apples* and then together make a list of clues that tell about the setting.

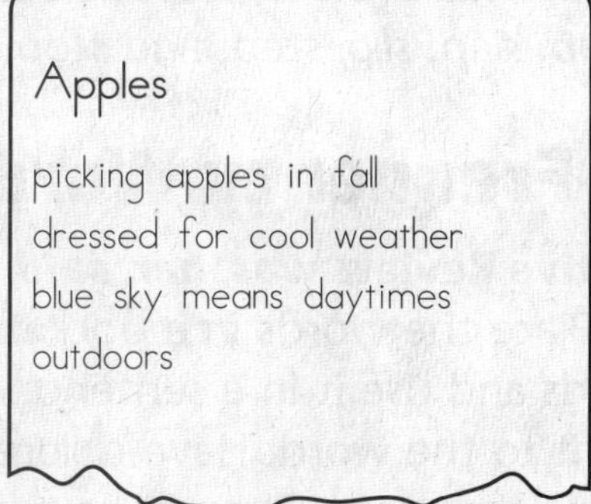

Apples
picking apples in fall
dressed for cool weather
blue sky means daytimes
outdoors

Phonics: Blends with s

PREATEACH Write the letters *sl*, *sm*, *sn*, *sp*, *st*, and *sw* at the top of a sheet of chart paper. Have children suggest words that begin with *sl*. Add word suggestions of your own, as necessary. Then write the words underneath the heading *sl*. Use the same procedure for the other blends. Then have children read each column of words. End the activity by pointing to words at random and having children read the words.

sl	sm	sn	sp	st	sw
sled	smack	snack	spell	stop	swim
slap	small	sniff	spill	step	swell
	smell	snap	spin		swish
	smog				

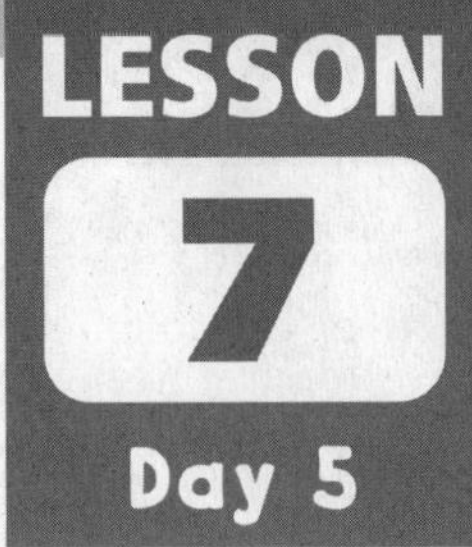

MATERIALS

Write-on/Wipe-off Boards

Word Cards day, every, her, said, that, was, where, with

Word Builder

Word Builder Cards a, e, h, i, m, n, p, s, t, t

Warm-Up: Phonemic Awareness

Phoneme Blending Tell children that together you are going to play a game of "Fix It." Tell them that you are going to say some words that are all broken and they should listen to see if they can put sounds together to figure out the word. **Listen: /m/-/e/-/n/. What word does /m/-/e/-/n/ say?** (*men*) Continue with the following words:

/w/-/i/-/th/ *(with)*	**/th/-/a/-/t/** *(that)*	**/th/-/e/-/m/** *(them)*
/ch/-/e/-/ck/ *(check)*	**/s/-/e/-/l/** *(sell)*	**/w/-/e/-/d/** *(wed)*

Phonics: Blends with s

RETEACH Write the word *smell* on a Write-on/Wipe-off Board and have children do the same. Then have them read the word. Ask: **What letter should we write if we want to change *smell* to *spell*?** (*p*) **Let's do that.** Continue the activity with the word: *swell*. Repeat the activity, using the words *snip*, *snap*, *slap*, *slip*, *step*, and *stop*.

High-Frequency Words

Cumulative Review *was, her, said, with, every, day, that, where* Place the words in a pocket chart. Say aloud one of the words and use it in a sentence. Have a volunteer find and point to the word. Have children clap and say the spelling of the word. Then have them write it. Have children read aloud their list of words.

was
her
said
with
every
day
that
where

Read: Self-Selected Reading

Have children select a book to read from their browsing boxes. After they have completed their reading, have them tell you about a word, such as a short *e* word, that they figured out on their own.

Phonics: Digraph /th/th

PRETEACH Write the letters *th* on the board or on chart paper. The letters *th* make the /th/ sound, the sound in words such as *then*, *this*, and *that*. Point to the letters *th* and say /th/. Have children repeat the sound as you touch the letters *th* several times.

Use the Word Builder and Word Builder Cards to model blending words.

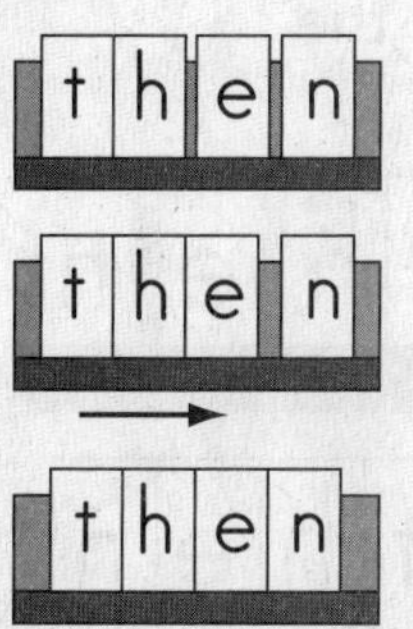

Place the Word Builder Cards *t*, *h*, *e*, and *n* in the Word Builder. Point to the *th* and say /th/. Point to *e* and say /e/.

Slide the *e* next the *th*. Move your hand under the letters and blend the sounds, elongating them /ththee/. Have children repeat after you.

Point to the *n*. Say /n/. Slide the *n* next to *the*. Slide your hand under *then* and blend by elongating the sounds /theenn/. Have children repeat.

Then have children read the word *then* along with you.

Follow the same procedure for the words *them*, *this*, *that*, and *path*.

MATERIALS

Word Cards could, friends, new, put, she, use

Word Builder

Word Builder Cards a, e, h, i, m, n, p, s, t, w

Boots for Red

Warm-Up: Phonemic Awareness

Onset and Rime Tell children that you are going to say some words, but you are going to say them in parts. Have children listen to see if they can figure out the word. Demonstrate by saying: **/th/-en—What word did I say?** (*then*)

/th/-em	**/th/-at**	**/th/-is**	**/th/-ick**
/s/-outh	**/m/-oth**	**/b/-ath**	**/w/-ith**

Phonics: Digraph /th/th

RETEACH **Blending** Write *th* on the board. **These letters are *th*. The letters *th* when grouped together make one sound, the /th/ sound, as in words such as *them*, *this*, and *that*.** Point to the letters and say /th/. Tell children that the /th/ sound appears at the end of words such as *bath*, *with*, and *path*. Have children repeat the sound as you touch the letters several times.

Use the Word Builder Cards and a pocket chart to model blending words.

Place the Word Builder Cards *t*, *h*, *e*, and *n* in the Word Builder. Point to the *th* and say /th/. Point to the *e* and say /e/.

Slide the *e* next to the *th*. Move your hand under the letters and blend the sounds, elongating them /tthhee/. Have children repeat after you. Point to the letter *n* and say /n/. Slide the *n* next to *the*. Slide your hand under *then* and blend by elongating the sounds—/tthheenn/. Then say the word naturally—*then*. Have children do the same.

Place the Word Builder Cards *p*, *a*, *t*, and *h* in the Word Builder. Point to the *p* and say /p/. Point to the *a* and say /a/.

Slide the *a* next to the *p*. Move your hand under the letters and blend the sounds, elongating them /ppaa/. Have children repeat after you.

Point to the letters *th* and say /th/. Have children say /th/ as you point to *th*.

Slide *th* next to *pa*. Slide your hand under *path* and blend by elongating the sounds—/ppaatthh/. Have children repeat. Then have children read the word *path* along with you.

High-Frequency Words

friends
put
new
she
use
could

PRETEACH ***put, friends, new, she, use, could*** Display the word card *friends*. **This word is *friends*. (Child's name) and (child's name) are friends. Read the word with me—*friends*. Spell the word with me—*f-r-i-e-n-d-s*. Read the word with me. What is this word?** (*friends*)

Follow the same procedure for the remaining words.

put—**Put your shoes away.**

new—**I have a new coat.**

she—**She is a girl.**

use—**I will use the scissors.**

could—**Could you help me?**

Then place the six words in a pocket chart and have volunteers read the words, as you randomly point to them.

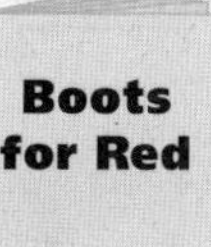

Read: *Boots for Red*

Distribute copies of the book. Have children put their finger on the title. Have them follow along as you read the title aloud. Tell children to notice pictures of boots and the word *boots* as they read. Echo read the book with children. Read page 2 aloud and then have children read it to you. Follow this procedure throughout the book.

Phonics: Word Building with /th/th

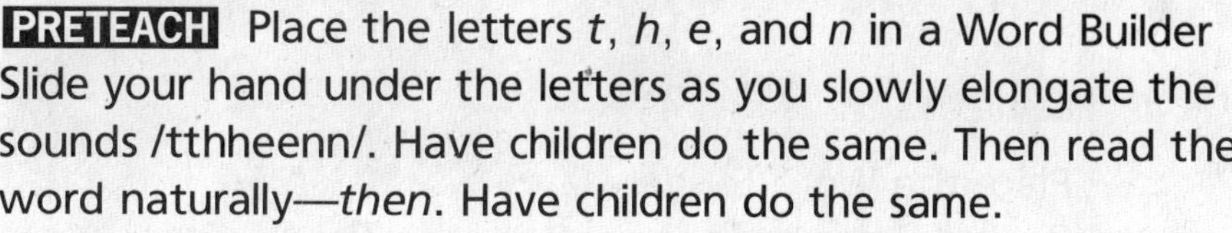

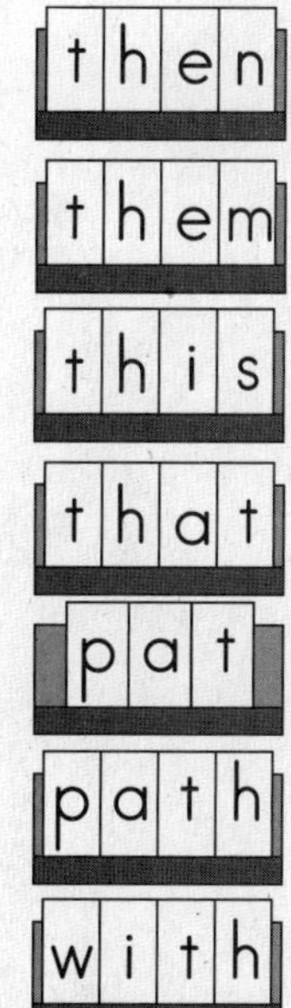

PRETEACH Place the letters *t*, *h*, *e*, and *n* in a Word Builder Slide your hand under the letters as you slowly elongate the sounds /tthheenn/. Have children do the same. Then read the word naturally—*then*. Have children do the same.

Have children blend and read new words by telling them:

Change *n* to *m*. What word did you make? *(them)*

Change *em* to *is*. What word did you make? *(this)*

Change *is* to *at*. What word did you make? *(that)*

Change *th* to *p*. What word did you make? *(pat)*

Add *h* to the end of *pat*. What word did you make? *(path)*

Change the *pa* to *wi*. What word did you make? *(with)*

Distribute *Intervention Practice Book* page 22 to children.

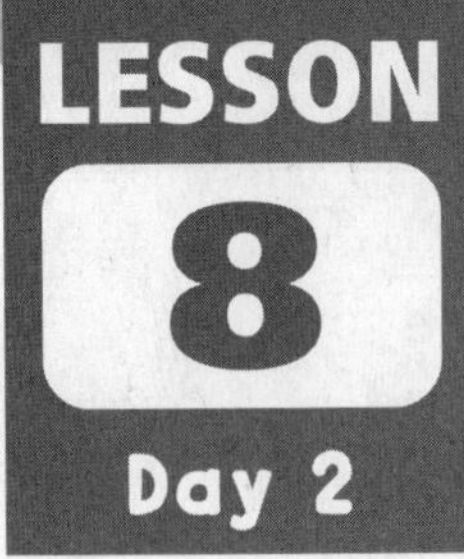

Warm-Up: Phonemic Awareness

Phoneme Isolation Say the word *thumb* aloud, and have children repeat it. Tell children to listen to the /th/ sound at the beginning of *thumb*. Then say the words *third* and *ten*, and have children repeat both words. Ask: **Which of these words has the /th/ sound you hear in *thumb*?** (*third*)

Continue with the words *thorn*, *think*, *too*; *path*, *bed*, *bath*; *with*, *moth*, *pat*

MATERIALS

Word Builder

Word Builder Cards a, b, e, h, m, n, p, t

Boots for Red

Phonics: Word Building with /th/th

RETEACH Place the letters *t*, *h*, *e*, and *n* in a Word Builder and have children do the same. Model how to blend the word *then*. Slide your hand under the letters as you slowly elongate the sounds /tthheenn/. Have children do the same. Then read the word naturally—*then*. Have children do the same.

Have children blend and read new words by telling them:

Change *th* to *p*. What word did you make? *(pen)*

Change *e* to *a*. What word did you make? *(pan)*

Change *n* to *th*. What word did you make? *(path)*

Change *p* to *b*. What word did you make? *(bath)*

Change *b* to *m*. What word did you make? *(math)*

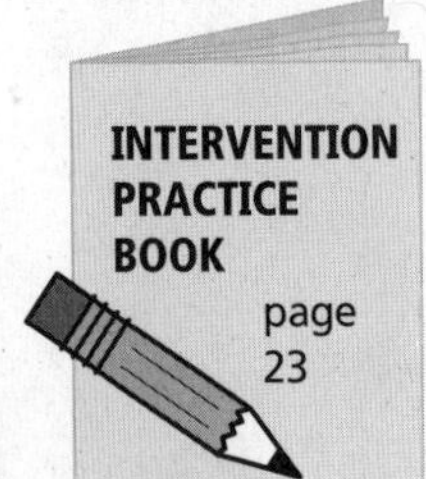

High-Frequency Words

RETEACH ***put, friends, new, she, use, could*** Write the word *pit*, and have children read it. Then write the word *put* next to *pit*, and have children read the word. **How are these words the same? How are they different? Let's read them again.**

pit put

Repeat the procedure with *ends/friends*, *see/she*, *is/use*, and *could/cot*.

Read: *Boots for Red*

Boots for Red

Distribute copies of the book to children and read the title aloud. Ask children to frame the word *Red*. Tell them *Red* is the name of the pig, so it begins with a capital letter in the story. Ask children to point to the names of the people who wrote and illustrated the book. Read their names aloud. Ask children what the author does (*writes the story*) and what the illustrator does (*draws the pictures*). Then choral read the book with children. Let your voice fade if children start to gain control of the text.

Phonics: Reading Sentences with /th/th

PRETEACH Distribute *Intervention Practice Book* page 23 to children. Point to the first sentence, and have children read it aloud. Ask them to find the word *this*, frame it with their fingers, and circle the word. Then work with children to complete the page.

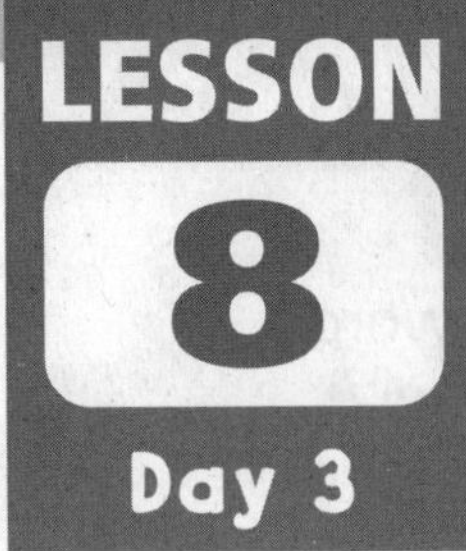

LESSON 8

Day 3

MATERIALS

Word Builder

Word Builder Cards a, e, h, m, n, p, t, t

Picture Cards drum, hat, jet, kite, map, nine, pen, red, sled, thumb, wagon

Boots for Red

Warm-Up: Phonemic Awareness

Phoneme Blending Tell children that they are going to play a guessing game. Then say: **I'm thinking of a word that is an insect. It has wings. It is a /m/-/o/-/th/. What's my word?** (*moth*) Continue with the following words: /th/-/i/-/n/ (*thin*), /th/-/e/-/m/ (*them*), /b/-/a/-/th/ (*bath*), /m/-/a/-/th/ (*math*).

Phonics: Reading Sentences with /th/th

RETEACH Help children blend and read new words and sentences shown. Have them read the sentence, blending each word in sequence. The high-frequency words are underlined; children should read these as a unit, not blending the sounds.

that this moth thin

Then <u>I</u> had *a* bath.

<u>Walk</u> with them.

Can <u>you</u> <u>do</u> math?

<u>Go</u> back <u>down</u> <u>the</u> path.

High-Frequency Words

RETEACH ***put, friends, new, she, use, could*** Write the following sentence on tag board and display it in a pocket chart along with the Picture Cards *hat*, *jet*, *kite*, *map*, *pen*, *thumb*. Call on children to choose a Picture Card to complete the sentence and to read it aloud. Then ask: **Could she really put a ______ in a sack?**

PICTURE CARDS

Could she put her ______ in a sack?

Do the same for the following sentence and Picture Cards *drum*, *nine*, *red*, *sled*, *wagon*.

I can use my new ______ with friends.

Read: *Boots for Red*

Boots for Red

Distribute copies of the book and have children put their fingers on the title. Ask what this book is about. Then guide children through the book as they read.

Pages 2–3: Have children read the pages to find out what Red has.

What does Red have? (*new boots*) **Find and read the sentence that tells how Red feels about her boots.** (*She likes new boots.*) **What word means the same as Red?** (*she*) **Find and frame that word.**

Pages 4–5: Have children read the pages to find out what Red does.

What does Red do? (*has a bath*) **What happens to Red? Find and read the sentence that tells.** (*She is all wet!*)

Pages 6–7: Have children read to find out what happens when Red gets out of the bath.

What happened to Red's new boots? Find and read the sentence that tells. (*Her boots are little!*) **What do you think made them shrink?** (*the water*)

Page 8: Have children read to find out how Red solves her problem.

How does Red solve her problem? (*Red gets new boots.*) **Do you think Red will take a bath in her new boots?**

Ask children to use the pictures to help summarize the book.

Phonics: Building Words

PRETEACH Place the letters *t*, *h*, *e*, and *m* in a Word Builder and have children do the same. Slide your hand under the letters as you blend the sounds—/tthheemm/. Then read the word naturally—*them*. Have children repeat after you. Then have children build and read new words.

Change *m* to *n*. What word did you make? (*then*)

Change *e* to *a*. What word did you make? (*than*)

Change *n* to *t*. What word did you make? (*that*)

Take *th* away. What word did you make? (*at*)

Add *p* in front of *a* and *t*. What word did you make? (*pat*)

Add *h* after *t*. What word did you make? (*path*)

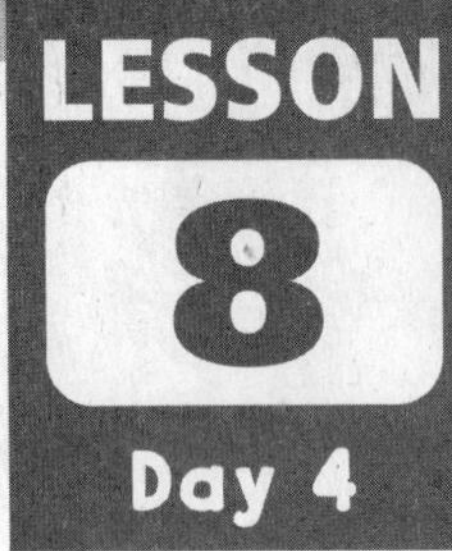

MATERIALS

Picture Cards fish, nut, rose, six, sun, thumb

Write-on/Wipe-off Boards with disks

Word Cards could, friends, new, put, said, she, use, was

Word Builder

Word Builder Cards a, e, h, i, m, n, p, s, t, t, w

Boots for Red

Warm-Up: Phonemic Awareness

PICTURE CARDS

Phoneme Segmentation Have children use the three boxes on the Write-on/Wipe-off Boards. Remind children that the boxes stand for the sounds in words. Show the Picture Card *thumb* and ask: **What is the first sound you hear in *thumb*?** (/th/) Have children place a disk in the first box. Then have children name the second sound in *thumb* (/u/) and place a disk in the second box. Then have them identify the last sound in *thumb* (/m/) and place a disk in the third box. Point to each box in sequence as children say the word. **How many sounds do you hear in *thumb*?** (*three*) Repeat this procedure with the following Picture Cards: *fish*, *nut*, *rose*, *six*, *sun*.

Phonics: Building Words

RETEACH Put the letters *t*, *h*, *i*, and *s* in a Word Builder and have children do the same. Slide your hand under the letters as you blend the sounds—/tthhiiss/. Then read the word naturally—*this*. Have children repeat after you. Then have children build and read new words.

Change *is* to *en*. What word did you make? *(then)*

Change *n* to *m*. What word did you make? *(them)*

Change *em* to *at*. What word did you make? *(that)*

Change *th* to *p*. What word did you make? *(pat)*

Add *h* after *t*. What word did you make? *(path)*

Change *pa* to *wi*. What word did you make? *(with)*

Distribute *Intervention Practice Book* page 24 to children.

put

friends

new

she

use

could

was

said

High-Frequency Words

RETEACH ***put, friends, new, she, use, could, was, said*** Distribute word cards with the words listed above. Have partners take turns displaying the words for each other and reading them. After they read each word, have children spell the word and then repeat it. Then have them spell the word again and write it on a sheet of paper.

Read: *Boots for Red*

Boots for Red

Focus Skill **Following Directions** Explain to children that it is important to listen carefully when someone gives directions. Point out that it could cause problems if they miss a step. Have children reread *Boots for Red* and then discuss what step Red missed when getting ready for her bath. (*She didn't take off her boots.*) Have children give directions for Red to follow to prepare for a bath.

Phonics: Phonograms -est, -ent

PRETEACH Write the letters *-est* and *-ent* at the top of a sheet of chart paper. Have children suggest words that end with *-est* and say what letters they would need to write the words. Then write the words underneath the heading *est*. Use the same procedure for *-ent*. Then have children read each column of words. End the activity by pointing to words at random and having children read the words.

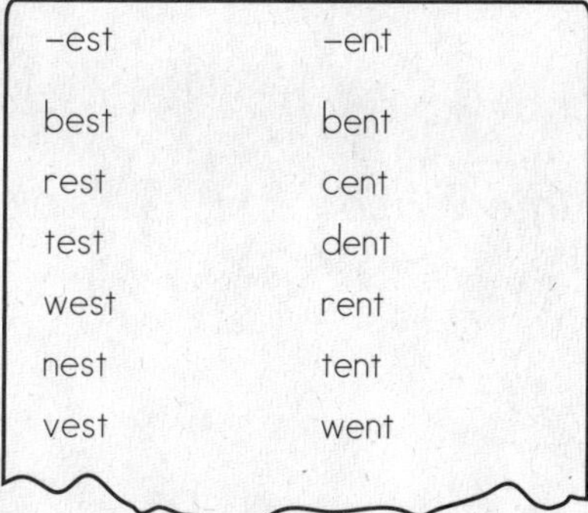

–est	–ent
best	bent
rest	cent
test	dent
west	rent
nest	tent
vest	went

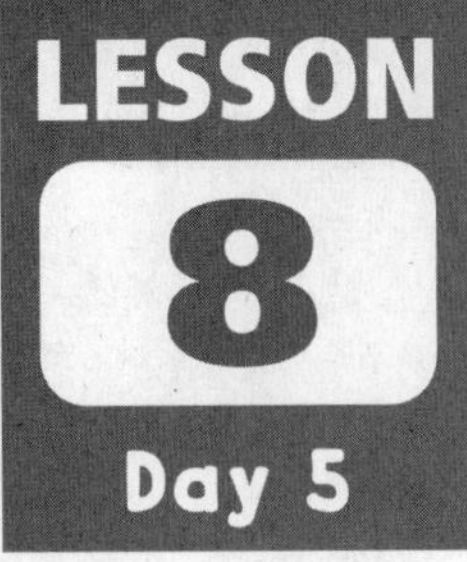

Warm-Up: Phonemic Awareness

Phoneme Blending Tell children that together you are going to play a puzzle game. Tell them that you are going to say some words sound by sound, and that they should put the sounds together like pieces of a puzzle to figure out the word. **Listen: /th/-/i/-/k/. What word does /th/-/i/-/k/ say?** (*thick*) Continue with the following words:

/th/-/ē/-/f/ (*thief*)	**/th/-/ī/** (*thigh*)	**/th/-/ôr/-/n/** (*thorn*)
/m/-/u/-/g/ (*mug*)	**/b/-/u/-/s/** (*bus*)	**/s/-/u/-/n/** (*sun*)

MATERIALS

Write-on/Wipe-off Boards

Word Cards could, friends, her, new, put, she, use, with

Word Builder

Word Builder Cards b, g, m, r, s, t, u

Phonics: Phonograms -est, -ent

RETEACH Write the word *best* on a Write-on/ Wipe-off Board and have children do the same. Then have them read the word. Ask: **What letter should we write if we want to change *best* to *pest*?** (*p*) **Let's do that.** Continue the activity with the following words: *nest*, *rest*, *jest*, and *test*. Repeat the activity, using the words *bent*, *dent*, *rent*, *sent*, *went*, and *tent*.

High-Frequency Words

Cumulative Review *put, friends, new, she, use, could, her, with* Place the words in a pocket chart. Say aloud one of the words and use it in a sentence. Have a volunteer find and point to the word. Have children clap and say the spelling of the word. Then have them write it. Have children read aloud their list of words.

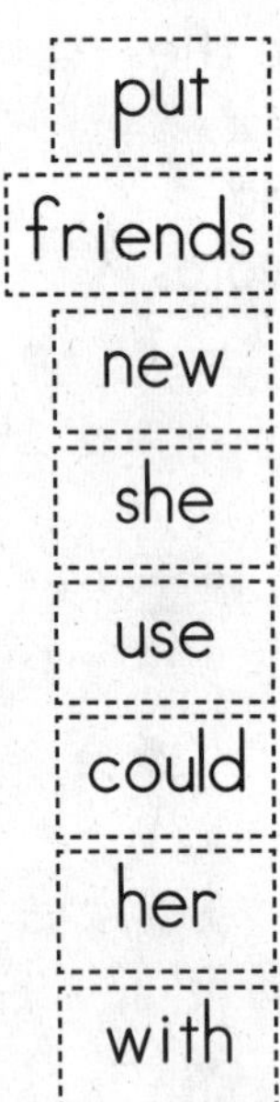

Read: Self-Selected Reading

Have children select a book to read from their browsing boxes. After they have completed their reading, have them tell you what they were most successful in during the reading of the book.

Phonics: Short Vowel /u/u

RETEACH Write the letter *u* on the board or on chart paper. The letter *u* can stand for the /u/ sound, the sound in words such as *bus*, *mud*, and *rug*. Point to the letter *u* and say /u/. Have children repeat the sound as you touch the letter *u* several times.

Use the Word Builder and Word Builder Cards to model blending words.

Place the Word Builder Cards *b*, *u*, and *s* in the Word Builder. Point to the *b* and say /b/. Point to *u* and say /u/.

Slide the *u* next the *b*. Move your hand under the letters and blend the sounds, elongating them /bbuu/. Have children repeat after you.

Point to the *s*. Say /s/. Slide the *s* next to *bu*. Slide your hand under *bus* and blend by elongating the sounds /bbuuss/. Have children repeat.

Then have children read the word *bus* along with you.

Follow the same procedure for the words *bug*, *rug*, *mug*, and *must*.

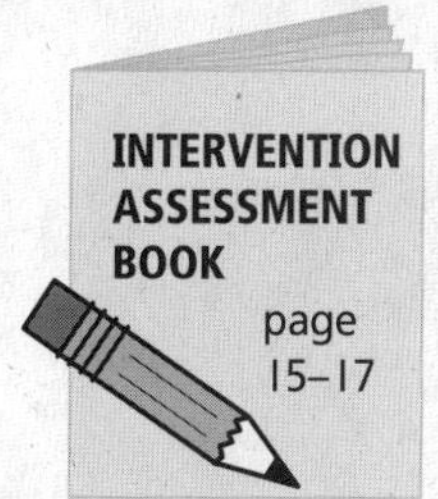

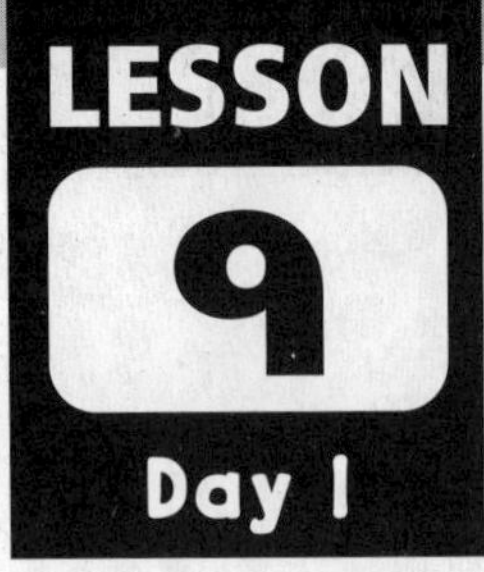

Warm-Up: Phonemic Awareness

Onset and Rime Tell children that you are going to say some words, but you are going to say them in parts. Have children listen to see if they can figure out the word. Demonstrate by saying: **/b/-ug—What word did I say?** (*bug*)

/p/-up	**/n/-ut**	**/c/-up**	**/b/-us**
/th/-umb	**/r/-ush**	**/s/-uch**	**/f/-uzz**

MATERIALS

Word Cards gives, he, night, out, people, says, when, your

Word Builder

Word Builder Cards b, g, m, r, s, t, u

Alphabet Masters Uu

A Bug and a Pup

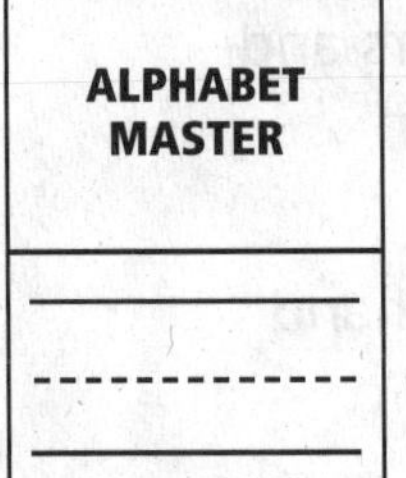

Phonics: Short Vowel /u/u

RETEACH blending Display Alphabet Master *Uu*. This letter is *u*. The letter *u* can stand for the /u/ sound, the short sound of the letter *u*, in words such as *us*, *up*, and *umbrella*. Point to the Alphabet Master and say /u/. Tell children that the /u/ sound appears in the middle of words such as *fun*, *hug*, and *tub*. Have children repeat the sound as you touch the letter several times.

Use the Word Builder Cards and a pocket chart to model blending words.

Place the Word Builder Cards *u* and *s* in the Word Builder. Point to the *u* and say /u/. Point to the *s* and say /s/.

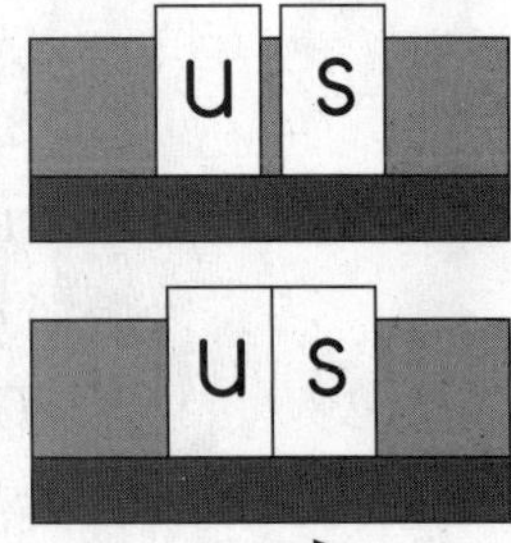

Slide the s next to the *u*. Move your hand under the letters and blend the sounds, elongating them /uuss/. Have children repeat after you. Then say the word naturally—*us*. Have children do the same.

Place the Word Builder Cards *b*, *u*, and *g* in the Word Builder. Follow a similar procedure to blend and read the word *bug*.

High-Frequency Words

PRETEACH *people, he, says, your, gives, when, night, out*

Display the word card *people*. **This word is *people*. (Child's name) and (child's name) are two people in our class. Read the word with me—*people*. Spell the word with me—*p-e-o-p-l-e*. Read the word with me. What is this word?** (*people*)

Follow the same procedure for the words *he*, *says*, *your*, *gives*, *when*, *night*, and *out*.

people
he
says
your
gives
when
night
out

he—**He is a boy I used to know.**

says—**She says to please sit down.**

your—**Your sack is very heavy.**

gives—**That TV station gives the news.**

when—**When do we go?**

night—**I cannot see well at night.**

out—**We will go out to eat.**

Then place the eight words in a pocket chart and have volunteers read the words, as you randomly point to them.

Read: *A Bug and a Pup*

A Bug and a Pup

Story Word Write the word *surprise* on the board. Point to the word, read it aloud, and have children repeat the word. Ask volunteers to talk about surprises they have had or have heard about. As children read the story, provide help for anyone who needs help with the word *surprise.*

Distribute copies of the book and ask children what they think the story will be about. Have children put their finger on the title. Have them follow along as you read the title aloud. Echo read the book with children. Read page 2 aloud and then have children read it to you. Follow this procedure throughout the book.

Phonics: Word Building with /u/u

PRETEACH Place the letters *u* and *s* in a Word Builder and have children do the same. Model how to blend the word *us*. Slide your hand under the letters as you slowly elongate the sounds /uuss/. Have children do the same. Then read the word naturally—*us*. Have children do the same.

Have children blend and read new words by telling them:

Add *b* to the front of *u* and *s*. What word did you make? *(bus)*

Change *s* to *g*. What word did you make? *(bug)*

Change *b* to *r*. What word did you make? *(rug)*

Change *r* to *m*. What word did you make? *(mug)*

Change the *g* to *st*. What word did you make? *(must)*

Distribute *Intervention Practice Book* page 25 to children.

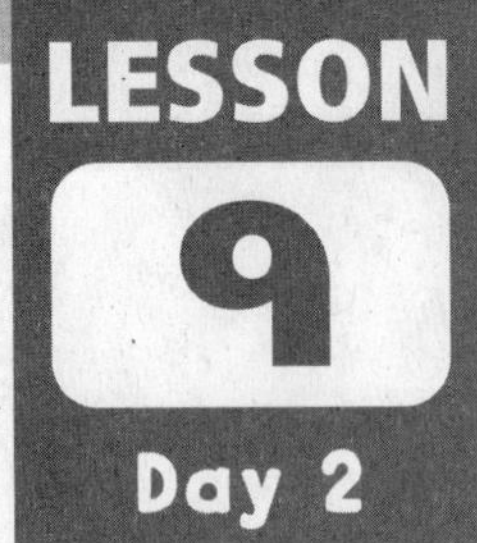

Warm-Up: Phonemic Awareness

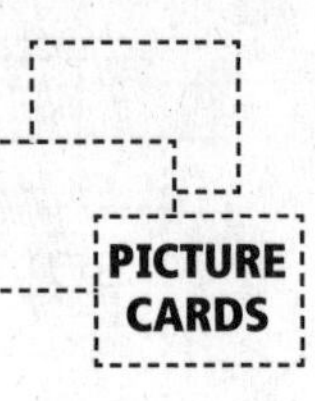

Phoneme Isolation Display the Picture Cards *sun*, *nut*, and *net*. Point to the sun, and have children say the word *sun* aloud. Tell children to listen to the /u/ sound in the middle of the word *sun*. Have them say the names of the other two pictures aloud. Ask: **What other picture name has the same /u/ sound you hear in *sun*?** (*nut*)

Continue with the words *bug*, *bed*, *thumb*; *cup*, *nut*, *clock*; *thumb*, *sun*, *clam*.

MATERIALS

Word Builder

Word Builder Cards b, g, m, r, s, t, u

Picture Cards bed, bug, clam, clock, cup, net, nut, sun, thumb

A Bug and a Pup

Phonics: Word Building with /u/u

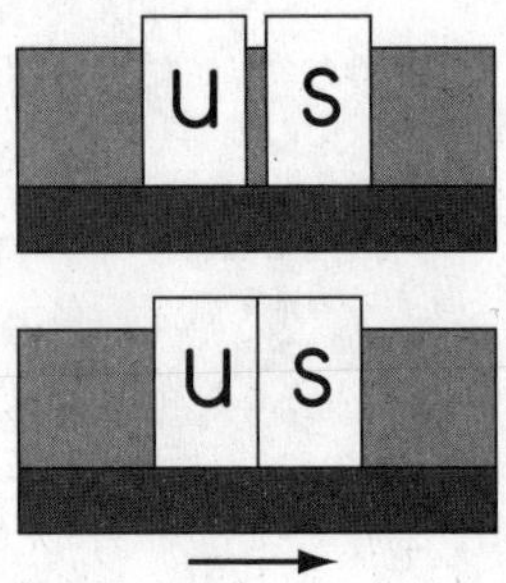

RETEACH Place the letters *u* and *s* in a Word Builder and have children do the same. Model how to blend the word *us*. Slide your hand under the letters as you slowly elongate the sounds /uuss/. Have children do the same. Then read the word naturally—*us*. Have children do the same.

Have children blend and read new words by telling them:

Add a *b* to the front of *u* and *s*. What word did you make? (*bus*)

Change the *s* to *g*. What word did you make? (*bug*)

Change the *b* to *m*. What word did you make? (*mug*)

Change the *g* to *st*. What word did you make? (*must*)

Change the *m* to *r*. What word did you make? (*rust*)

Change the *st* to *g*. What word did you make? (*rug*)

High-Frequency Words

RETEACH ***people, he, says, your, gives, when, night, out***
Write the word *she*, and have children read it. Then write the word *he* next to *she*, and have children read the word. **How are these words the same? How are they different? Let's read them again.**

she he

Repeat the procedure with *little/people*, *said/says*, *you/your*, *got/gives*, *hen/when*, *not/night*, and *too/out*.

Read: *A Bug and a Pup*

A Bug and a Pup

Distribute copies of the book to children and read the title aloud, tracking the print left to right. Ask children to point to the words that have the /u/ sound in them. (*Bug, Pup*) Ask children to point to the names of the people who wrote and illustrated the book. Read their names aloud. Then choral read the book with children, letting your voice fade if children start to gain control of the text.

Phonics: Reading Sentences with /u/u

PRETEACH Distribute *Intervention Practice Book* page 26 to children. Point to the first sentence and have children read it aloud. Ask them to find the word *run*, frame it with their fingers, and circle the word. Then work with children to complete the page.

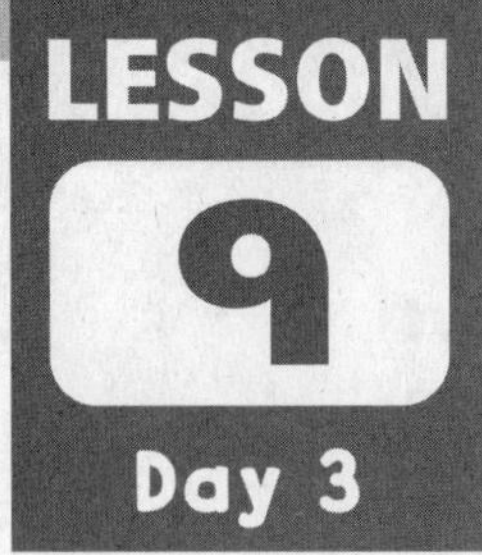

LESSON 9

Day 3

MATERIALS

Word Builder

Word Builder Cards c, h, n, o, p, p, t, u

Picture Cards bat, box, can, cat, drum, lamp, mule, pig, quilt, rose, smile, sock

A Bug and a Pup

Warm-Up: Phonemic Awareness

Phoneme Blending Tell children that they are going to play a guessing game. Then say: **I'm thinking of a word that is an animal. It is a kind of bird. It is a /d/-/u/-/k/. What's my word?** (*duck*) Continue with the following words: /k/-/u/-/t/ (*cut*), /b/-/u/-/n/ (*bun*), /d/-/u/-/g/ (*dug*), /b/-/u/-/d/ (*bud*).

Phonics: Reading Sentences with /u/u

RETEACH Help children blend and read new words and sentences shown. Have them read the sentence, blending each word in sequence. The high-frequency words are underlined; children should read these as a unit, not blending the sounds.

tug **luck** **sub** **gum**

<u>I</u> fell in <u>the</u> mud.

<u>She</u> cut <u>her</u> leg.

Sit in <u>the</u> tub.

Can <u>I</u> <u>have</u> a hug?

High-Frequency Words

RETEACH ***people, he, says, your, gives, when, night, out***

Write the following sentence on tag board and display it in a pocket chart along with the Picture Cards *bat*, *cat*, *drum*, *lamp*, *quilt*. Call on children to choose a Picture Card to complete the sentence and to read it aloud. Then ask: **Do people really play with a ______ at night?**

PICTURE CARDS

People like to play with a ______ at night.

Do the same for the following sentence and Picture Cards *box*, *can*, *quilt*, *rose*, *smile*.

He gives a ______ when he sees your pet.

Do the same for the following sentence and Picture Cards *cat*, *mule*, *pig*, *sock*, *rose*.

She says that the ______ likes to go out in the sun.

Read: *A Bug and a Pup*

A Bug and a Pup

Distribute copies of the book and have children put their finger on the title. Ask what this book is about. Then guide children through the book as they read.

Pages 2–3: Have children read the pages to find out what the bug can do.

What does the girl want to know? (*Can the bug come out?*) **Can the bug come out of the jar?** (*yes*) **Find and read the sentence that tells.** (*He can come out.*) **Why could the bug get out?** (*He was little.*)

Pages 4–5: Have children read the pages to find out what the pup can do.

Can the pup come out of the car? (*yes*) **Find and read the sentence that tells. What word means the same as pup?** (*He*) **Find and frame that word.**

Pages 6–8: Have children read to find out what happens when the bug meets the pup.

What does the bug say to the pup? (*I'll get you.*) **Why do you think the bug wants to get the pup?** (*Possible response: to tease the pup.*) **What is the surprise at the end?** (*The bug lands on the pup's nose.*)

Ask children to use the pictures to help summarize the book.

Phonics: Building Words

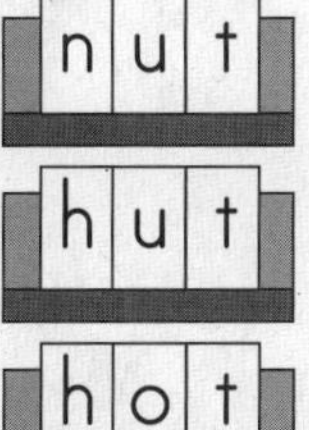

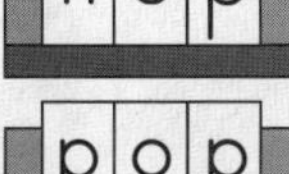

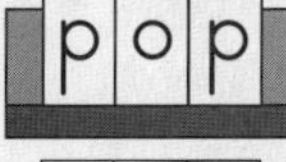

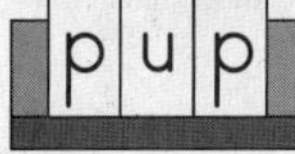

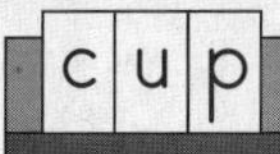

PRETEACH Put the letters *n*, *u*, *t* in a Word Builder and have children do the same. Slide your hand under the letters as you blend the sounds—/nnuutt/. Then read the word naturally—*nut*. Have children repeat after you. Then have children build and read new words.

Change the *n* to *h*. What word did you make? *(hut)*

Change the *u* to *o*. What word did you make? *(hot)*

Change the *t* to *p*. What word did you make? *(hop)*

Change the *h* to *p*. What word did you make? *(pop)*

Change the *o* to *u*. What word did you make? *(pup)*

Change the first *p* to *c*. What word did you make? *(cup)*

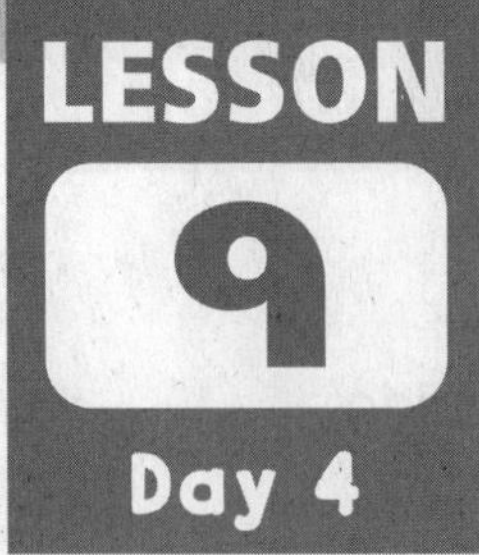

MATERIALS

Picture Cards bug, cup, kite, rose, sun, ten

Write-on/Wipe-off Boards with disks

Word Cards gives, her, night, out, people, says, she, use, when, your

Word Builder

Word Builder Cards b, d, g, m, r, s, t, u

A Bug and a Pup

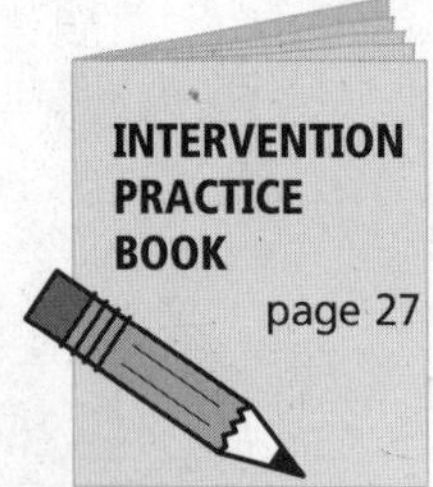

Warm-Up: Phonemic Awareness

Phoneme Segmentation. Have children use the three boxes on the Write-on/Wipe-off Boards. Remind children that the boxes stand for the sounds in words. Show the Picture Card *bug* and ask: **What is the first sound you hear in *bug*?** (/b/) Have children place a disk in the first box. Then have children name the second sound in *bug* (/u/) and place a disk in the second box. Then have them identify the last sound in *bug* (/g/) and place a disk in the third box. Point to each box in sequence as children say the word. **How many sounds do you hear in *bug*?** (*three*) Repeat this procedure with the following Picture Cards: *cup*, *kite*, *rose*, *sun*, *ten*.

PICTURE CARDS

Phonics: Building Words

RETEACH Put the letters *u* and *s* in a Word Builder and have children do the same. Slide your hand under the letters as you blend the sounds—/uuss/. Then read the word naturally—*us*. Have children repeat after you. Then have children build and read new words.

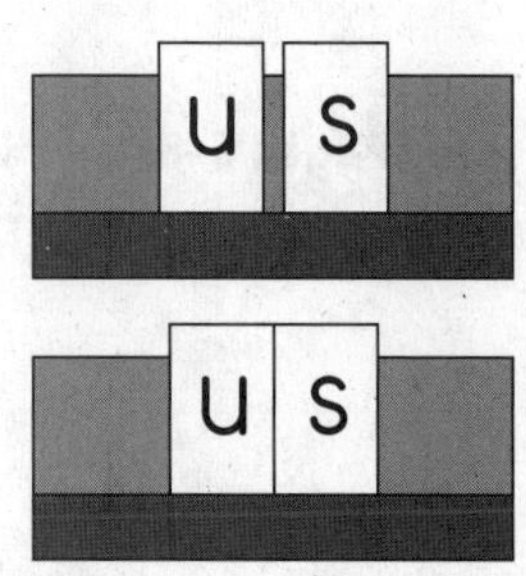

Add *b* to the front of *u* and *s*. What word did you make? (*bus*)
Change *s* to *g*. What word did you make? (*bug*)
Change *b* to *r*. What word did you make? (*rug*)
Change *r* to *m*. What word did you make? (*mug*)
Change *g* to *st*. What word did you make? (*must*)
Change *m* to *d*. What word did you make? (*dust*)

Distribute *Intervention Practice Book* page 27 to children.

people
he
says
your
gives
when
night
out
she
use

High-Frequency Words

RETEACH ***people, he, says, your, gives, when, night, out, she, use*** Distribute word cards with the words listed above. Have partners take turns displaying the words for each other and reading them. After they read each word, have children spell the word and then repeat it. Then have them spell the word again and write it on a sheet of paper.

Read: *A Bug and a Pup*

Focus Skill **Cause/Effect** Explain to children that figuring out why things happen in stories can help them understand what they read. Have children reread *A Bug and a Pup* and then discuss why they think the pup was surprised. Have children work together to write a sentence to explain why the pup was surprised.

A Bug and a Pup

Phonics: Blends with r

PRETEACH Write the letters *br*, *cr*, *dr*, *fr*, *gr*, *pr*, and *tr* at the top of a sheet of chart paper. Have children suggest words that begin with *br*. Add word suggestions of your own, as necessary. Then write the words underneath the heading *br*. Use the same procedure for *cr*, *dr*, *fr*, *gr*, *pr*, and *tr*. Then have children read each column of words. End the activity by pointing to words at random and having children read the words.

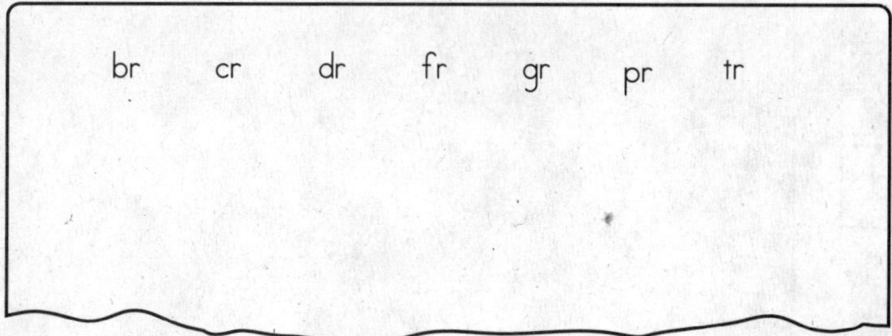

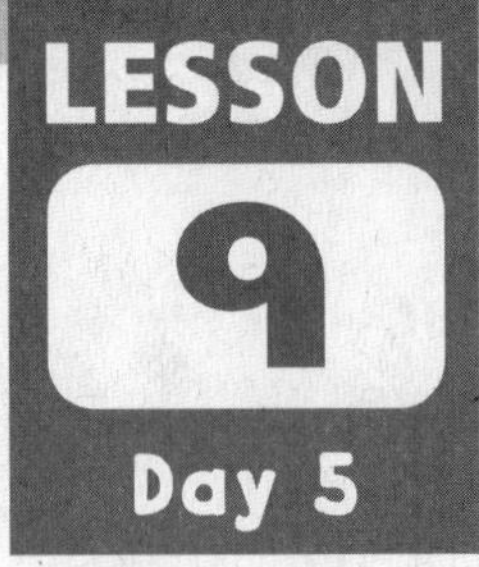

Warm-Up: Phonemic Awareness

Phoneme Blending Tell children that they are going to be builders and that they will put some sounds together to figure out a word. **Listen: /h/-/u/-/g/. What word does /h/-/u/-/g/ say?** (*hug*) Continue with the following words:

/d/-/u/-/k/ (*duck*)	**/r/-/u/-/b/** (*rub*)	**/h/-/u/-/m/** (*hum*)
/h/-/a/-/ng/ (*hang*)	**/s/-/i/-/ng/** (*sing*)	**/r/-/i/-/ng/** (*ring*)

MATERIALS

Write-on/Wipe-off Boards

Word Cards people, he, says, your, gives, put, new, could

Word Builder

Word Builder Cards a, h, i, g, n, r, s

Phonics: Blends with r

RETEACH Write the word *crab* on a Write-on/Wipe-off Board and have children do the same. Then have them read the word. Ask: **What letter should we write if we want to change *crab* to *grab*?** (*g*) **Let's do that.** Continue the activity with the word: *drab*. Repeat the activity, using the words *drill*, *grill*, *frill*, *prop, crop, brick*, and *trick*.

High-Frequency Words

people

he

says

your

gives

put

new

could

Cumulative Review *people, he, says, your, gives, put, new, could* Place the words in a pocket chart. Say aloud one of the words and use it in a sentence. Have a volunteer find and point to the word. Have children clap and say the spelling of the word. Then have them write it. Have children read aloud their list of words.

Read: Self-Selected Reading

Have children select a book to read from their browsing boxes. After they have completed their reading, have them tell you what they were most successful in during the reading of the book.

Phonics: Diphthong /ng/ng

PRETEACH Write the letters *ng* on the board or on chart paper. **The letters *ng* can stand for the /ng/ sound, the sound in words such as *sing*, *sang*, and *ring*.** Point to the letters *ng* and say /ng/. Have children repeat the sound as you touch the letters *ng* several times.

Use the Word Builder and Word Builder Cards to model blending words.

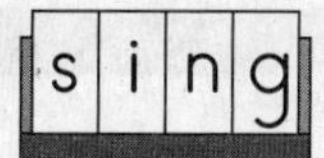

Place the Word Builder Cards *s*, *i*, *n*, and *g* in the Word Builder. Point to the *s* and say /s/. Point to *i* and say /i/.

Slide the *i* next to the *s*. Move your hand under the letters and blend the sounds, elongating them /ssii/. Have children repeat after you.

Point to the *ng*. Say /ng/. Slide the *ng* next to *si*. Slide your hand under *sing* and blend by elongating the sounds /ssiinngg/. Have children repeat.

Then have children read the word *sing* along with you.

Follow the same procedure for the words *sang*, *hang*, *rang*, and *ring*.

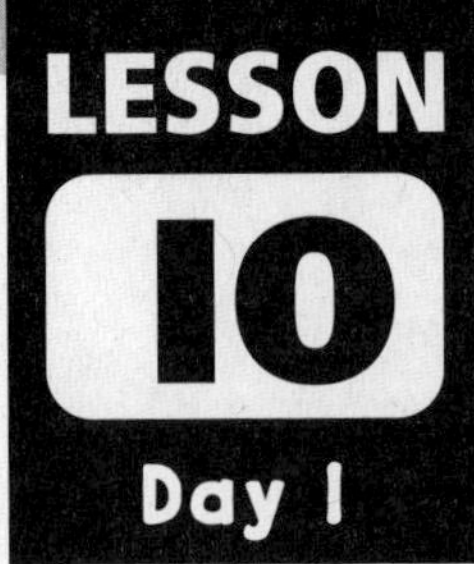

Warm-Up: Phonemic Awareness

Onset and Rime Tell children that you are going to say some words, but you are going to say them in parts. Have children listen to see if they can figure out the word. Demonstrate by saying: **/s/ -ing—What word did I say?** *(sing)*

/r/-ing	**/th/-ing**	**/k/-ing**	**/w/-ing**
/b/-ang	**/r/-ang**	**/s/-ong**	**/l/-ung**

MATERIALS

Word Cards for eat, from, gone, grows, or, two

Word Builder

Word Builder Cards a, b, g, h, i, r, n, s

Frogs

Phonics: Diphthong /ng/ng

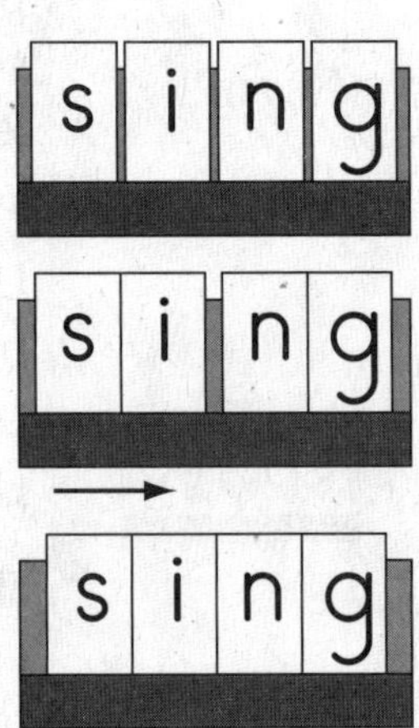

RETEACH Blending. Write the letters *n* and *g* on chart paper, and display them for children. **These letters are *n* and *g*, and when the letters *n* and *g* are together, they can stand for the /ng/ sound in words such as *sing, sang,* and *song.*** Point to the letters *ng* and say /ng/. Tell children that the /ng/ sound does not appear at the beginning of words, only after a vowel. Have children repeat the sound as you touch the letters several times.

Use the Word Builder Cards and a pocket chart to model blending words.

Place the Word Builder Cards *s, i, n,* and *g* in the Word Builder. Point to the *s and* say /s/. Point to the *i* and say /i/.

Slide the *i* next to the *s*. Move your hand under the letters and blend the sounds, elongating them /ssii/. Have children repeat after you. Point to the letters *ng* and say /ng/. Slide the *ng* next to *si.* Slide your hand under *sing* and blend by elongating the sounds—/ssiinngg/. Have children do the same. Then say the word naturally—*sing.* Have children do the same.

High-Frequency Words

PRETEACH ***eat, from, or, grows, two, gone*** Display the word card *eat*. **This word is *eat*. We *eat* lunch at (time). Read the word with me—*eat*. Spell the word with me —*e-a-t*. Read the word with me. What is this word?** *(eat)*

eat

from

or

Follow the same procedure for the words *from, or, grows, two,* and *gone.*

from—**Where are you from?**

or—**Do you prefer dogs or cats?**

grows
two
gone

grows—**Lettuce grows in my garden.**

two—**I have two dollars to spend.**

gone—**I will be gone during the summer break.**

Then place the six words in a pocket chart and have volunteers read the words, as you randomly point to them.

Read: *Frogs*

Frogs

Story Word Write the word *tadpole* on the board. Point to the word, read it aloud, and have children repeat the word. Ask volunteers to talk about *tadpoles*, discussing what *tadpoles* look like, where and how they live, and how they grow into frogs. As children read the story, provide help with the word *tadpole* for anyone who needs it.

Distribute copies of the book and ask children what they think the story will be about. Have children put their finger on the title. Have them follow along as you read the title aloud. Echo read the book with children. Read page 2 aloud and then have children read it to you. Follow this procedure throughout the book.

Phonics: Word Building with /ng/ng

sing
sang
hang
rang
ring
bring

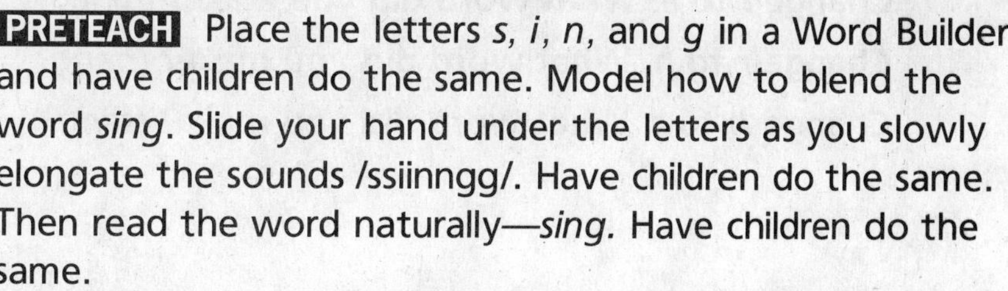

PRETEACH Place the letters *s*, *i*, *n*, and *g* in a Word Builder and have children do the same. Model how to blend the word *sing*. Slide your hand under the letters as you slowly elongate the sounds /ssiinngg/. Have children do the same. Then read the word naturally—*sing*. Have children do the same.

Have children blend and read new words by telling them:

Change *i* to *a*. What word did you make? *(sang)*

Change *s* to *h*. What word did you make? *(hang)*

Change *h* to *r*. What word did you make? *(rang)*

Change *a* to *i*. What word did you make? *(ring)*

Add *b* to the beginning of *ring*. What word did you make? *(bring)*

Distribute *Intervention Practice Book* page 28 to children.

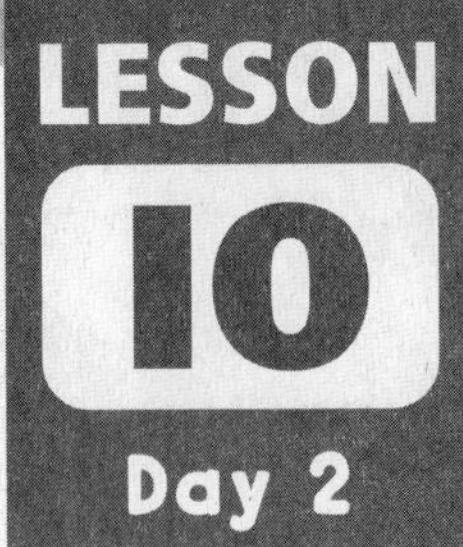

Warm-Up: Phonemic Awareness

Phoneme Isolation Say the word *rung* aloud and have children repeat it. Tell children to listen to the /ng/ sound at the end of *rung*. Then say the words *run* and *rang*. Ask: **Which of these words has the /ng/ sound you hear in *rung*?** *(rang)* Continue with the words *thing, thin, ring; gong, song, sun; bring, drag, hang.*

MATERIALS

Word Builder

Word Builder Cards
a, b, g, h, i, n, r, s

Frogs

Phonics: Word Building with /ng/ng

RETEACH Place the letters *s, i, n,* and *g* in a Word Builder and have children do the same. Model how to blend the word *sing*. Slide your hand under the letters as you slowly elongate the sounds /ssiinngg/. Have children do the same. Then read the word naturally—*sing*. Have children do the same.

Have children blend and read new words by telling them:

Change *s* to *br*. What word did you make? *(bring)*

Take away *b*. What word did you make? *(ring)*

Change *i* to *a*. What word did you make? *(rang)*

Change *r* to *h*. What word did you make? *(hang)*

Change *h* to *s*. What word did you make? *(sang)*

High-Frequency Words

RETEACH ***from, eat, or, grows, two, gone*** Write the word *for*, and have children read it. Then write the word *or* next to *for*, and have children read the word. How are these words the same? How are they different? Let's read them again.

for   or

Repeat the procedure with *mom/from*, *at/eat*, *go/grows*, and *one/gone*.

Read: *Frogs*

Frogs

Distribute copies of the book and read the title aloud. Ask children to point to the title. Ask children to tell what they know about frogs. Then choral read the book with children. Let your voice fade if children start to gain control of the text.

Phonics: Reading Sentences with /ng/ng

PRETEACH Distribute *Intervention Practice Book* page 29 to children. Point to the first sentence and have children read it aloud. Ask them to find the word *rang*, frame it with their fingers, and circle the word. Then work with children to complete the page.

LESSON 10 Day 3

MATERIALS

Word Builder

Word Builder Cards a, b, g, h, i, n, r, t

Picture Cards: bug, cat, clam, egg, fish, goat, jet, leaf, plum, rose, sock

Frogs

Warm-Up: Phonemic Awareness

Phoneme Blending Tell children that they are going to play a guessing game. Then say: **I'm thinking of a word that helps birds fly. It is also on an airplane. It is a /w/-/i/-/ng/. What's my word?** *(wing)* Continue with the following words: /th/-/i/-/ng/ *(thing)*, /s/-/o/-/ng/ *(song)*, /r/-/o/-/ng/ *(wrong)*, /h/-/u/-/ng/ *(hung)*.

Phonics: Reading Sentences with /ng/ng

RETEACH Help children blend and read new words and sentences shown. Have them read the sentence, blending each word in sequence. The high-frequency words are underlined; they should read these as a unit, not blending the sounds.

sung **thing** **ping** **hang**

<u>She</u> sang a song.

I <u>like</u> a long <u>walk</u>.

Bring <u>the</u> king <u>that</u> ring.

Can I <u>make</u> *a* bang on that gong?

High-Frequency Words

RETEACH ***eat, from, grows, or, two, gone*** Write the following sentence on tag board and display it in a pocket chart along with the Picture Cards *rose, leaf, jet, fish*. Call on children to choose a Picture Card to complete the sentence and to read it aloud. Then ask: **Does a __ really grow out back?**

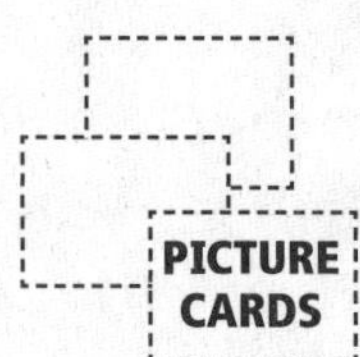

A ________________ grows out back.

Do the same for the following sentence and Picture Cards *goat, bug, cat, jet, leaf, egg*.

Two are gone, but one _____ is still here.

Do the same for the following sentence and Picture Cards *clam, egg, sock, plum, jet*.

Eat one _____ from the pot or the dish.

Read: *Frogs*

Distribute copies of the book and have children read aloud the title. Ask what information they learned from the book. Then guide children through the book as they read.

Pages 2–3: Have children read the pages to find out where tadpoles come from and what they do.

> **Where do tadpoles come from?** (*frog eggs*) **Find and read the sentence that tells. What do tadpoles do?** (*They swim.*) **Find and read the sentence that tells.**

Pages 4–5: Have children read the pages to find out what else tadpoles do and where frog eggs come from.

> **Name something else tadpoles do.** (*eat*) **Find and frame the sentence that tells. Where do frog eggs come from?** (*frogs*) **Find and read the sentence that tells.**

Pages 6–8: Have children read to find out more about frogs.

> **What don't frogs do?** (*sing*) **What do frogs do?** (*eat bugs*) **Find and frame the sentence that tells. What do frogs do fast?** (*They eat fast.*)

Ask children to use the pictures to help summarize the book.

Phonics: Building Words

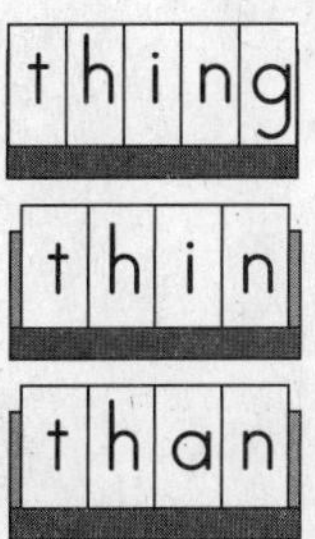

PRETEACH Put the letters *t, h, i, n, g* in a Word Builder and have children do the same. Slide your hand under the letters as you blend the sounds—/tthhiinngg/. Have children do the same. Then read the word naturally—*thing*. Have children do the same. Then have children build and read new words.

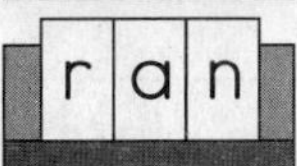

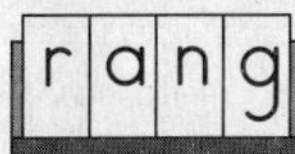

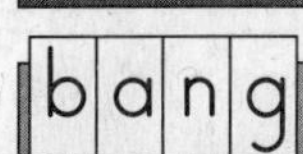

Take away the *g*. What word did you make? (*thin*)
Change *i* to *a*. What word did you make? (*than*)
Change *th* to *r*. What word did you make? (*ran*)
Add *g* to *ran*. What word did you make? (*rang*)
Change *r* to *b*. What word did you make? (*bang*)

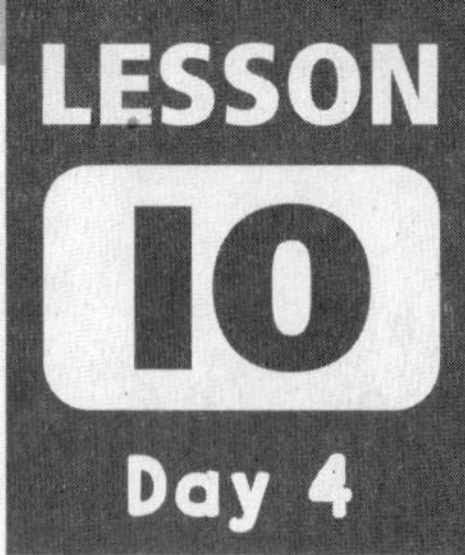

MATERIALS

Picture Cards none

Write-on/Wipe-off Boards with disks

Word Cards for eat, from, gone, grows, or, two, when, your

Word Builder

Word Builder Cards a, b, g, h, i, n, r, s

Frogs

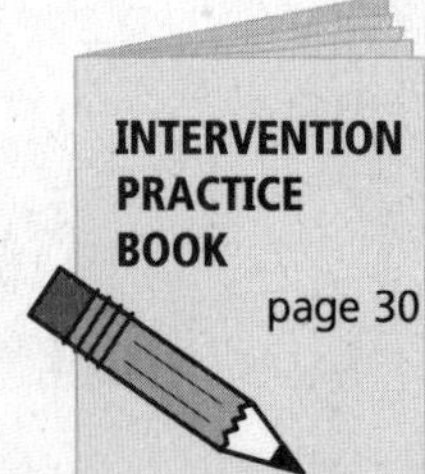

Warm-Up: Phonemic Awareness

Phoneme Segmentation. Have children use the three boxes on the Write-on/Wipe-off Boards. Remind children that the boxes stand for the sounds in words. Say the word *wing* and ask: **What is the first sound you hear in *wing?*** (/w/) Have children place a disk in the first box. Then have children name the second sound in *wing* (/i/) and place a disk in the second box. Then have them identify the last sound in *wing* (/ng/) and place a disk in the third box. Point to each box in sequence as children say the word. **How many sounds do you hear in *wing*?** (three) Repeat this procedure with the following words: *fang, song, lung, rang.*

Phonics: Building Words

RETEACH Put the letters *s, i, n,* and *g* in a Word Builder and have children do the same. Slide your hand under the letters as you blend the sounds—/ssiinngg/. Then read the word naturally—*sing*. Have children repeat after you. Then have children build and read new words.

Change i to a. What word did you make? *(sang)*

Change s to h. What word did you make? *(hang)*

Change h to r. What word did you make? *(rang)*

Change a to i. What word did you make? *(ring)*

Add b to the beginning of ring. What word did you make? *(bring)*

Distribute *Intervention Practice Book* page 30 to children.

High-Frequency Words

RETEACH ***from, eat, or, grows, two, gone, your, when*** Distribute word cards with the words listed above. Have partners take turns displaying the words for each other and reading them. After they read each word, have children spell the word and then repeat it. Then have them spell the word again and write it on a sheet of paper.

from	when
eat	of
or	so
grows	don't
two	now
gone	want
your	

Read: *Frogs*

Details Remind children that details can help them understand information that they read. Tell them that details can also help them picture what happens in a story. Have children reread *Frogs* and then together make a list of story details.

Frogs
eat bugs
eat fast
have eggs
don't sing

Phonics: Phonograms -ang, -ing

PRETEACH Write the letters *ang* and *ing* at the top of a sheet of chart paper. Have children suggest words that end with *-ang* and say what letters they would need to write the words. Then write the words underneath the heading *ang.* Use the same procedure for words that end with *-ing*. Then have children read each column of words. End the activity by pointing to words at random and having children read the words.

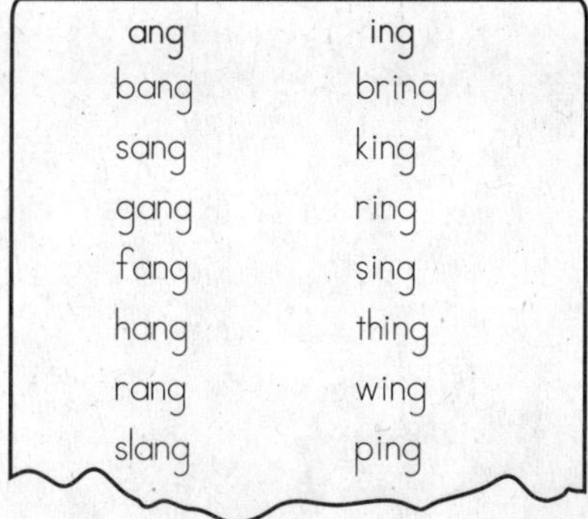

ang
bang
sang
gang
fang
hang
rang
slang
ing
bring
king
ring
sing
thing
wing
ping

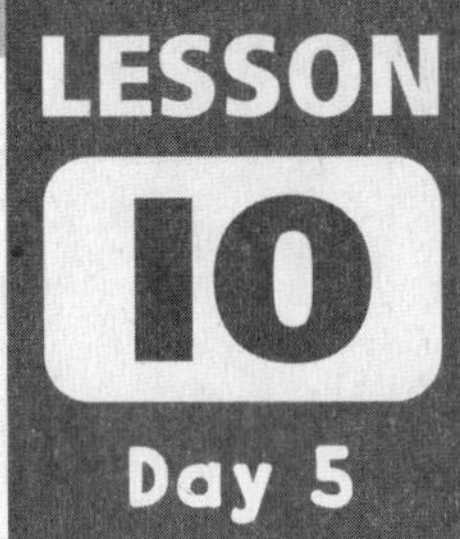

MATERIALS

Write-on/Wipe off Boards

Word Cards for eat, from, gone, grows, he, or, two, your

Word Builder

Word Builder Cards c, f, k, m, n, o, r

from

eat

or

grows

two

gone

your

he

Warm-Up: Phonemic Awareness

Phoneme Blending Tell children that together you are going to play a game of "Fix It." Tell them that you are going to say some words that are all broken and they should listen to see if they can put them together to figure out the word. **Listen: /b/-/r/-/i/-/ng/. What word does /b/-/r/-/i/-/ng/ say?** *(bring)* Continue with the following words:

/k/-/i/-/ng/ *(king)*	**/s/-/l/-/i/-/ng/** *(sling)*	**/b/-/a/-/ng/** *(bang)*
/f/-/ôr/-/k/ *(fork)*	**/k/-/ôr/-/n/** *(corn)*	**/m/-/ôr/** *(more)*

Phonics: Phonograms -ang, -ing

RETEACH Write the word *bang* on a Write-on/Wipe-off Board and have children do the same. Then have them read the word. Ask: **What letter should we write if we want to change *bang* to *fang*?** (f) **Let's do that.** Continue the activity with the following words: *hang, rang, sang.* Repeat the activity, using the words *bring, king, ring, sing, swing, thing.*

High-Frequency Words

Cumulative Review *from, eat, or, grows, two, gone, your, he* Place the words in a pocket chart. Say aloud one of the words and use it in a sentence. Have a volunteer find and point to the word. Have children clap and say the spelling of the word. Then have them write it. Have children read aloud their list of words.

Read: Self-Selected Reading

Have children select a book to read from their browsing boxes. After they have completed their reading, have them tell you about words they figured out during the reading of the book.

Phonics: R-controlled /ôr/or, ore

PRETEACH Write the letters *or* and *ore* on the board or on chart paper. The letters *or* and *ore* can stand for the /ôr/ sound, the sound in words such as *fork*, *born*, and *more*. Point to the letters *or* and *ore* and say /ôr/. Have children repeat the sound as you touch the letters *or* and *ore* several times.

Use the Word Builder and Word Builder Cards to model blending words.

Place the Word Builder Cards *f*, *o*, *r*, and *k* in the Word Builder. Point to the *f* and say /f/. Point to *or* and say /ôr/.

Slide the *or* next the *f*. Move your hand under the letters and blend the sounds, elongating them /ffôôrr/. Have children repeat after you.

Point to the *k*. Say /k/. Slide the *k* next to *for*. Slide your hand under *fork* and blend by elongating the sounds /ffôôrrkk/. Have children repeat after you.

Then have children read the word *fork* along with you.

Follow the same procedure for the words *corn*, *cork*, *for*, and *more*.

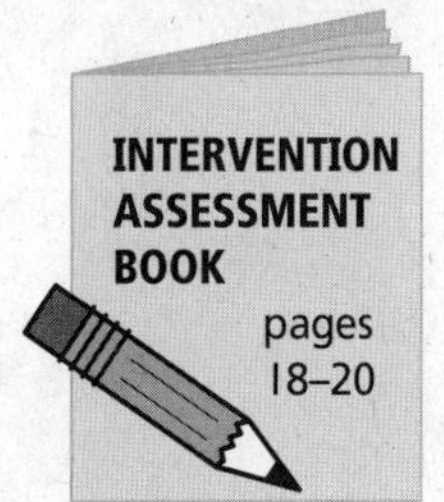

MATERIALS

Word cards for be, good, Mr., need, right, saw, time, today, try

Word Builder

Word Builder Cards c, e, f, k, m, n, o, r

Sport Will Try

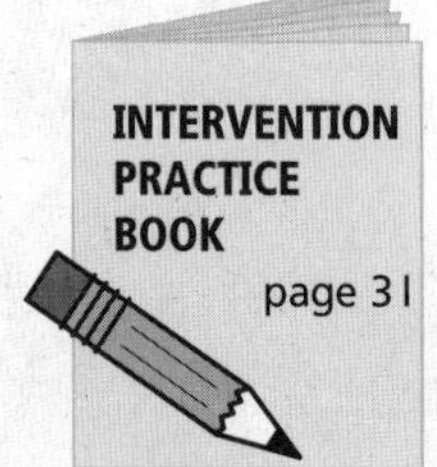

Warm-Up: Phonemic Awareness

Onset and Rime Tell children that you are going to say some words, but you are going to say them in parts. Have children listen to see if they can figure out the word. Demonstrate by saying: **/f/-ort—What word did I say? fort**

/c/-orn	**/th/-orn**	**/f/-ork**	**/b/-orn**
/f/-orth	**/p/-orch**	**/sh/-ort**	**/s/-ort**

Phonics: R-controlled /ôr/or, ore

RETEACH Blending Write the letters *or* on the board. **These letters are *or*. The letters *or* can stand for the /ôr/ sound, the sound in words such as *port* and *torn*.** Point to the letters on the board and say /ôr/. Then write *ore* on the board. Identify them, say /ôr/ and explain that the letters *ore* can stand for the /ôr/ sound in words such as *store, more,* and *score.* Point out that when /ôr/ appears at the end of a word, it is sometimes spelled with *a* silent *e* at the end. Have children repeat the sound as you touch the letters *or* and *ore* several times.

Use the Word Builder Cards and a pocket chart to model blending words.

Place the Word Builder Cards *f, o,* and *r* in the Word Builder. Point to the *f* and say /f/. Point to the *or* and say /ôr/.

Slide the *or* next to the *f*. Move your hand under the letters and blend the sounds, elongating them /ffoorr/. Have children do the same. Then say the word naturally—*for*. Have children do the same.

Place the Word Builder Cards *c, o, r,* and *e* in the Word Builder. Point to the *c* and say /c/. Point to the *ore* and say /ôr/.

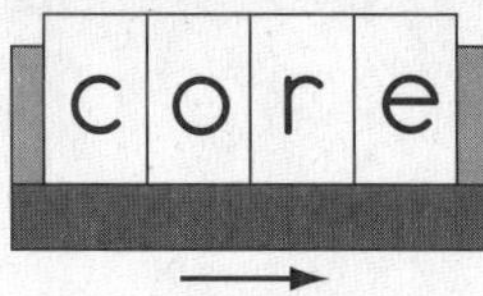

Slide the *ore* next to the *c*. Move your hands under the letters and blend the sounds, elongating them /ccoorr/.

Have children repeat. Then have children read the word *core* along with you.

time
try
need
saw
be
our
right
good
Mr.
today

High-Frequency Words

PRETEACH ***time, try, need, saw, be, our, right, good, Mr., today*** Display the word card *time*. **This word is *time*. It is time for lunch. Read the word with me—*time*. Spell the word with me—*t-i-m-e*. Read the word with me. What is this word?** *(time)* Follow the same procedure for the words *try, need, saw, be, our, right, good, today* and *Mr.*

try—**I try my best.**

need—**Do you need a hug?**

saw—**He saw me at the market yesterday.**

be—**I will be there soon.**

our, right—**Our answer is right.**

good, today—**Make good choices today.**

Mr.—**Mr. (teacher's name) teaches (grade level) grade.**

Then place the ten words in a pocket chart and have volunteers read the words, as you randomly point to them.

Read: *Sport Will Try*

Distribute copies of the book. Have children put their finger on the title as you read it aloud. Then have them frame and read each word. Echo read the book with children. Read page 2 aloud and then have children read it to you. Follow this procedure throughout the book.

Phonics: Word Building with R-controlled /ôr/or, ore

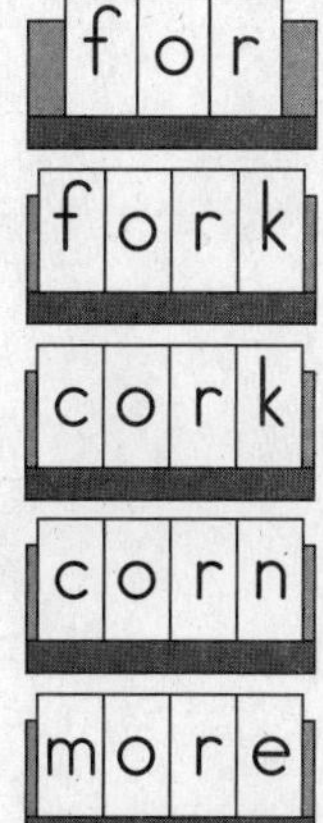

PRETEACH Place the letters *f,o,* and *r* in a Word Builder and have children do the same. Model how to blend the word *for*. Slide your hand under the letters as you slowly elongate the sounds /ffôorr/. Have children do the same. Then read the word naturally—*for.* Have children do the same. Have children blend and read new words by telling them:

Add *k* to the end of *for*. What word did you make? *(fork)*

Change *f* to *c*. What word did you make? *(cork)*

Change *k* to *n*. What word did you make? *(corn)*

Change *c* to *m*. Change *n* to *e*. What word did you make? *(more)*

Distribute *Intervention Practice Book* page 31 to children.

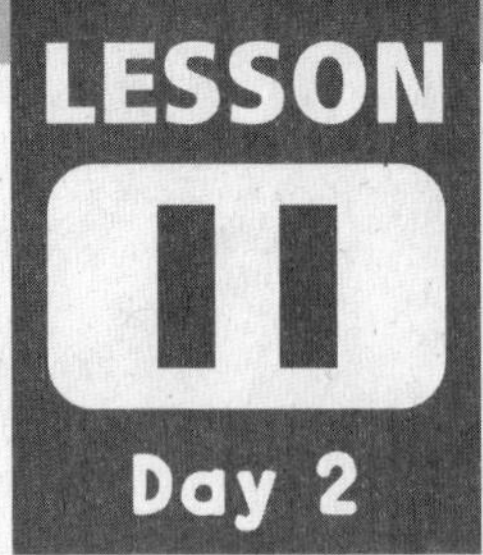

MATERIALS

Word Builder

Word Builder Cards c, e, f, k, m, n, o, r

Sport Will Try

Warm-Up: Phonemic Awareness

Phoneme Isolation Say the word *born* aloud and have children repeat it. Tell children to listen to the /ôr/ in the middle of *born*. Then say the words *short* and *bring* and have children repeat both words. Ask: **Which of these words has the /ôr/ sound you hear in *born*?** *(short)*

Continue with the words *stork, sob, sport; more, men, tore; core, port, pot.*

Phonics: Word Building with /ôr/or, ore

RETEACH Place the letters *f, o,* and *r* in a Word Builder and have children do the same. Model how to blend the word *for*. Slide your hand under the letters as you slowly elongate the sounds /ffoorr/. Have children do the same. Then read the word naturally—*for*. Have children do the same.

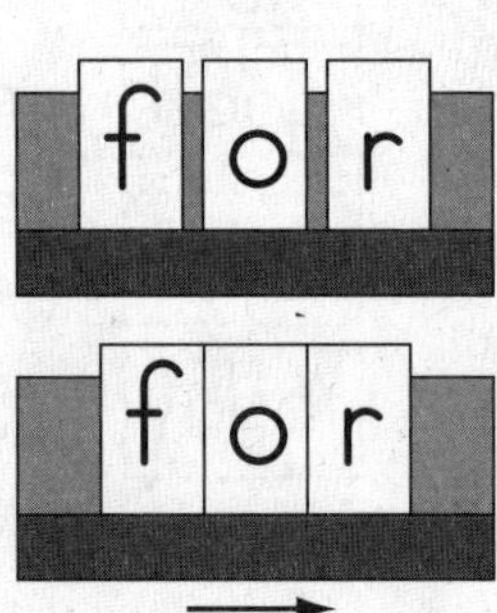

Have children blend and read new words by telling them:

Take away *f*. What word did you make? *(or)*

Add *e* after *r*. What word did you make? *(ore)*

Add m in front of *o*. What word did you make? *(more)*

Change *m* to *c*. What word did you make? *(core)*

Change e to *n*. What word did you make? *(corn)*

Change *n* to *k*. What word did you make? *(cork)*

Change c to *f*. What word did you make? *(fork)*

High-Frequency Words

RETEACH ***try, time, need, saw, be, our, right, good, Mr., today*** Write the word *sat*, and have children read it. Then write the word *saw* next to *sat*, and have children read the word. **How are these words the same? How are they different? Let's read them again.**

sat saw

Repeat the procedure with *my/try, like/time, see/need, we/be, your/our, go/good, me/Mr.*, and *they/today.*

Sport Will Try

Read: *Sport Will Try*

Distribute copies of the book. Ask children to point to the title and read it aloud. Then have children point to the names of the people who wrote and illustrated the book. Ask children who the story is about, and have them frame the name in the title. *(Sport)* Then choral read the book with children. Let your voice fade if children start to gain control of the text.

Phonics: Reading Sentences with /ôr/or, ore

PRETEACH Distribute *Intervention Practice Book* page 32 to children. Point to the first sentence and have children read it aloud. Ask them to find the word *fort*, frame it with their fingers, and circle the word. Then work with children to complete the page.

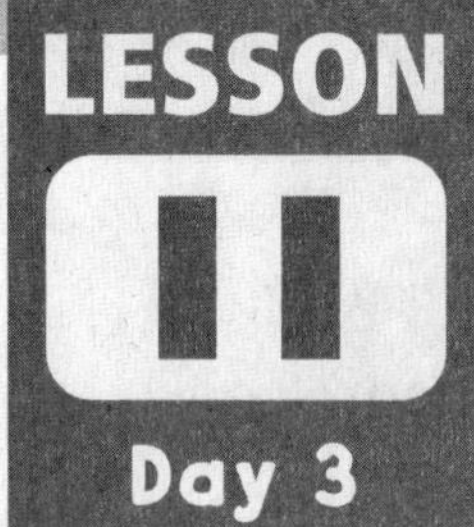

Warm-Up: Phonemic Awareness

Phoneme Blending Tell children that they are going to play a guessing game. Then say: **I'm thinking of a word that is a vegetable. It is yellow. It is /k/-/ôr/-/n/. What's my word?** *(corn)* Continue with the following words: /p/-/ôr/-/k/ *(pork)*, /t/-/ôr/-/n/ *(torn)*, /h/-/ôr/-/s/ *(horse)*, /f/-/ôr/-/t/ *(fort)*.

MATERIALS

Word Builder

Word Builder Cards e, f, o, r, s, t

Picture Cards: boat, bug, cat, clam, clock, jet, mule, plum, red, ship

Sport Will Try

Phonics: Reading Sentences with R-controlled /ôr/or, ore

RETEACH Help children blend and read new words and sentences shown. Have them read the sentence, blending each word in sequence. The high-frequency words are underlined; they should read these as a unit, not blending the sounds.

form **port** **forth** **worn**

Will <u>you</u> <u>eat</u> more pork?

<u>Go</u> <u>to</u> <u>the</u> store with <u>me.</u>

<u>Play</u> <u>your</u> horn.

<u>His</u> pet <u>was</u> born in a fort.

High-Frequency Words

RETEACH ***try, time, need, saw, be, our, right, good, Mr., today*** Write the following sentence on tag board and display it in a pocket chart along with the Picture Cards *boat, clam, clock, jet, mule, ship.* Call on children to choose a Picture Card to complete the sentence and to read it aloud. Then ask: **Can a ______ really be right on time?**

PICTURE CARDS

Our ______ is right on time today.

Do the same for the following sentence and Picture Cards *bug, cat, mule, plum.*

Mr. Ed saw the ______ try to hop.

Do the same for the following sentence and Picture Cards *cat, plum, clock, jet, red.*

I need the ______ to be good.

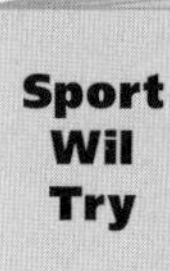

Read: *Sport Will Try*

Distribute copies of the book and have children read aloud the title. Ask children to retell the story. Then guide children through the book as they read.

Pages 2–3: Have children read the pages to find out what Sport tried to do.

Who did Sport see? *(He saw the big dogs.)* **What did Sport try to do?** *(jump up onto the rock)* **Could he do it?** *(no)* **Why couldn't he do it?** *(He was too little.)* **Find and read the sentence that tells.**

Pages 4–5: Have children read the pages to find out what Sport will try next.

What did Sport try to do next? *(tug the rope)* **Could Sport tug the rope?** *(no)* **Find and frame the sentences that tell. Why do you think Sport tried to tug?** *(Because he saw the big dogs do it.)*

Pages 6–8: Have children read to find out what else Sport tried to do.

What else did Sport try to do? *(run)* **Find and frame the sentence that tells. Why can Sport jump and run at the end of the story?** (*Because now he is big*)

Ask children to use the pictures to help summarize the book.

Phonics: Building Words

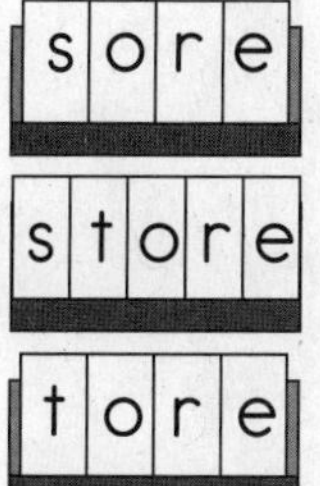

PRETEACH Put the letters *s, o, r, e* in a Word Builder and have children do the same. Slide your hand under the letters as you blend the sounds—/ssôôrr/. Then read the word naturally—*sore.* Have children repeat after you. Then have children build and read new words.

Add *t* after the *s*. What word did you make? *(store)*

Take away *s*. What word did you make? *(tore)*

Take away *t*. What word did you make? *(ore)*

Take away *e*. What word did you make? *(or)*

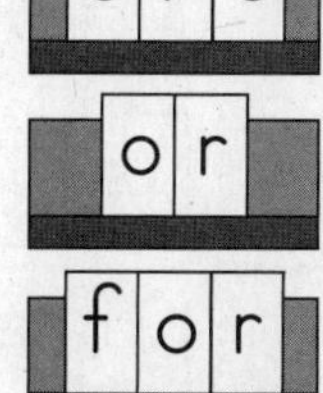

Add *f* to the beginning of *or*. What word did you make? *(for)*

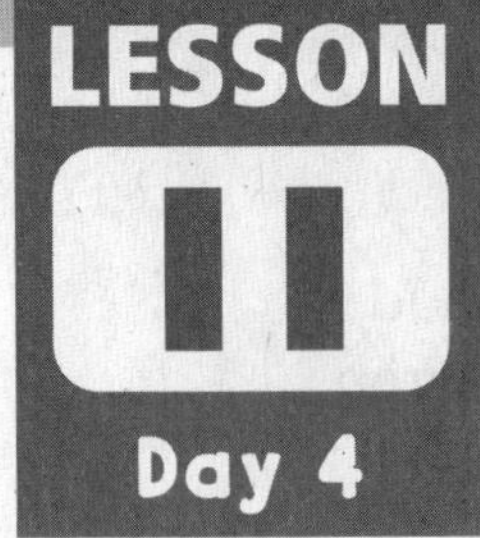

MATERIALS

Picture Cards: none

Write-on/Wipe-off Boards with disks

Word Cards for be, from, good, need, our, saw, time, try, two

Word Builder

Word Builder Cards c, e, f, k, n, o, r, s, t

Sport Will Try

Warm-Up: Phonemic Awareness

Phoneme Segmentation Have children use the three boxes on the Write-on/Wipe-off Boards. Remind children that the boxes stand for the sounds in words. Say the word *thorn* and ask: **What is the first sound you hear in *thorn*?** (/th/) Have children place a disk in the first box. Then have children name the second sound in *thorn* (/ôr/) and place a disk in the second box. Then have them identify the last sound in *thorn* (/n/) and place a disk in the third box. Point to each box in sequence as children say the word. **How many sounds do you hear in *thorn*?** (three) Repeat this procedure with the following words: *form, rang, corn, port.*

Phonics: Building Words

RETEACH Put the letters *f, o,* and *r* in a Word Builder and have children do the same. Slide your hand under the letters as you blend the sounds—/ffôôrr/. Then read the word naturally—*for*. Have children repeat after you. Then have children build and read new words.

Add *k* to the end of *for*. What word did you make? *(fork)*

Change *f* to *c*. What word did you make? *(cork)*

Change *k* to *n*. What word did you make? *(corn)*

Take away *c* and *n*. What word did you make? *(or)*

Add *e* to the end. What word did you make? *(ore)*

Add *t* to the beginning. What word did you make? *(tore)*

Add *s* to the beginning of *tore*. What word did you make? *(store)*

Distribute *Intervention Practice Book* page 33 to children.

High-Frequency Words

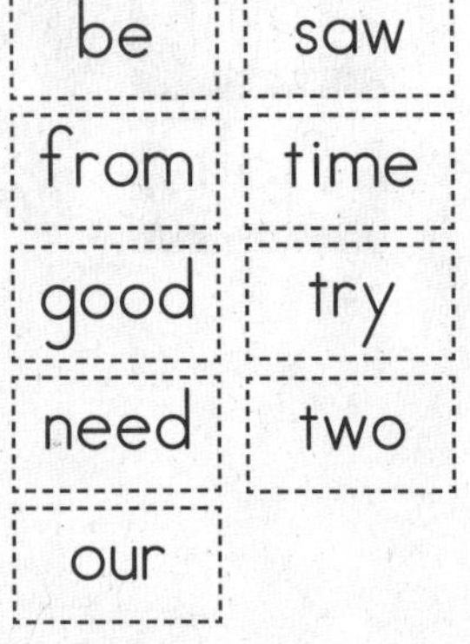

RETEACH ***be, from, good, need, our, saw, time, try, two*** Distribute word cards with the words listed above. Have partners take turns displaying the words for each other and reading them. After they read each word, have children spell the word and then repeat it. Then have them spell the word again and write it on a sheet of paper.

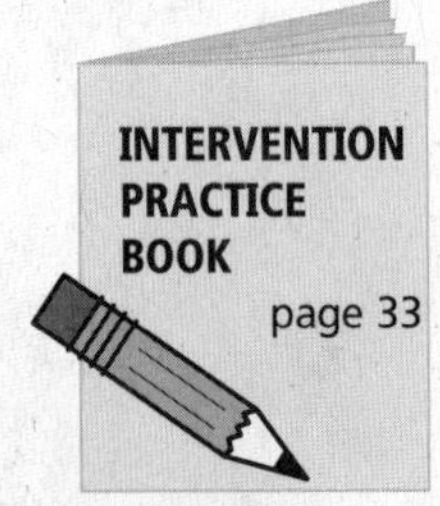

Sport Will Try

Read: *Sport Will Try*

Character Remind children when they read a story they should think about who the characters are and what they say, do, and feel. Understanding the characters helps readers to know what happens in a story. Ask children how they think Sport felt during different parts of the story. Have children reread *Sport Will Try* and then together make a list of what they know about Sport.

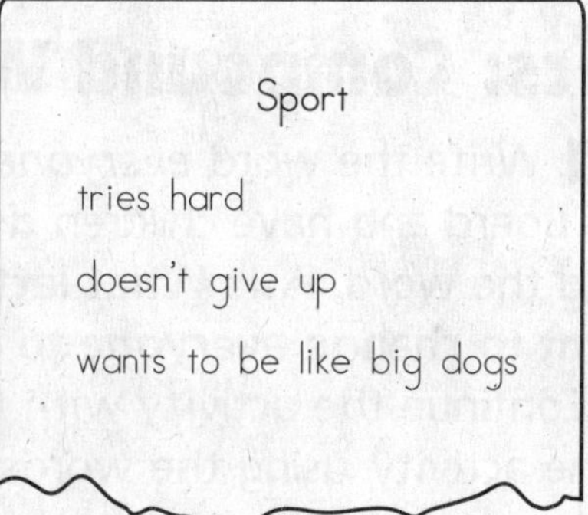

Sport
tries hard
doesn't give up
wants to be like big dogs

Phonics: Compound Words

PRETEACH Explain to children that compound words are made up of two or more shorter words. Write the words *popcorn*, *downhill*, *everyone*, *bathtub*, *lipstick*, *bedtime*, and *nighttime* on a sheet of chart paper. Ask children what two words make up each of the compound words listed. Help children detect the definition by using the two parts of the compound word to state the meaning. For example, *popcorn* is corn that has been popped; *downhill* means "down the hill," and so on. End the activity by inviting children to brainstorm other compound words.

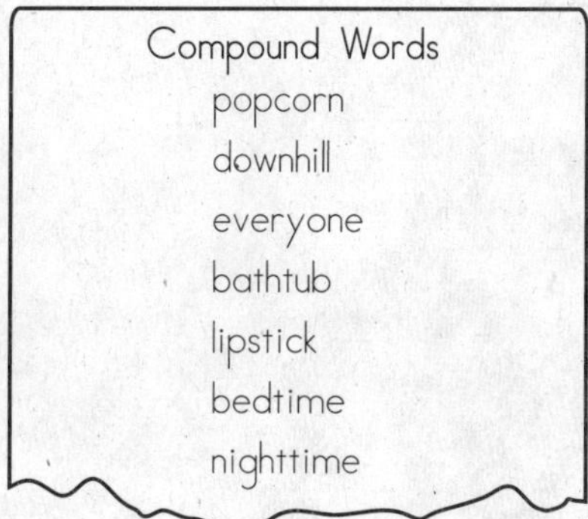

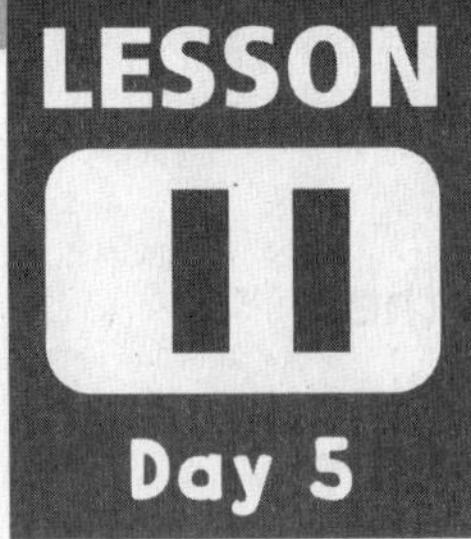

Warm-Up: Phonemic Awareness

Phoneme Blending Tell children that together you are going to play a game. Tell them that you are going to say some sounds that they should put together to figure out a whole word. Listen: **/f/-/ôr/-/m/. What word does /f/-/ôr/-/m/ say?** *(form)* Continue with the following words:

/s/-/ôr/-/t/ *(sort)* **/w/-/ôr/-/n/** *(worn)* **/sh/-/ôr/** *(shore)*
/sh/-/i/-/p/ *(ship)* **/sh/-/o/-/k/** *(shock)* **/w/-/i/-/sh/** *(wish)*

MATERIALS

Write-on/Wipe off Boards

Word Cards for from, good, need, or, saw, time, try, two

Word Builder

Word Builder Cards a, d, i, h, o, p, s, t, w

Phonics: Compound Words

RETEACH Write the word *everyone* on a Write-on/Wipe-off Board and have children do the same. Then have them read the word. Ask: **What letters should we write if we want to change *everyone* to *everyday*?** *(day)* **Let's do that.** Continue the activity with the word *everything.* Repeat the activity, using the words *bedtime, nighttime,* and *daytime; popcorn* and *corncob; uphill* and *downhill.*

High-Frequency Words

from
good
or
need
two
saw
time
try

Cumulative Review *from, good, need, or, saw, time, try, two* Place the words in a pocket chart. Say aloud one of the words and use it in a sentence. Have a volunteer find and point to the word. Have children clap and say the spelling of the word. Then have them write it. Have children read aloud their list of words.

Read: Self-Selected Reading

Have children select a book to read from their browsing boxes. After they have completed their reading, have them tell you what they were most successful in during the reading of the book.

Phonics: Digraph /sh/sh

PRETEACH Write the letters *sh* on the board or on chart paper. **The letters *sh* can stand for the /sh/ sound, the sound in words such as *ship*, *shop*, and *wish*.** Point to the letters *sh* and say /sh/. Have children repeat the sound as you touch the letters *sh* several times.

Use the Word Builder and Word Builder Cards to model blending words.

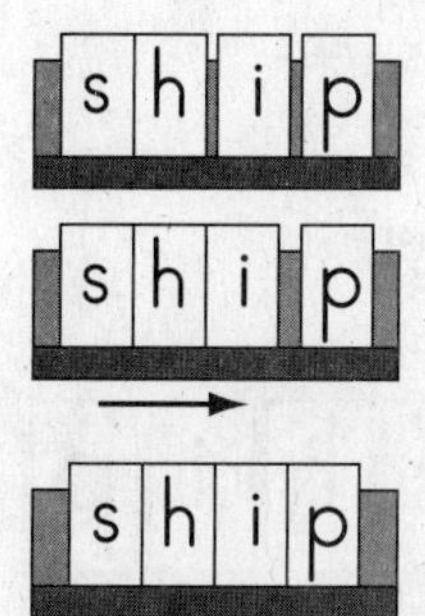

Place the Word Builder Cards *s,h, i,* and *p* in the Word Builder. Point to the *sh* and say /sh/. Point to *i* and say /i/.

Slide the *i* next to the *sh*. Move your hand under the letters and blend the sounds, elongating them /sshhii/. Have children repeat after you.

Point to the *p.* Say /p/. Slide the *p* next to *shi*. Slide your hand under *ship* and blend by elongating the sounds /sshhiipp/. Have children repeat.

Then have children read the word *ship* along with you.

Follow the same procedure for the words *shop, shot, wish, dish*, and *dash.*

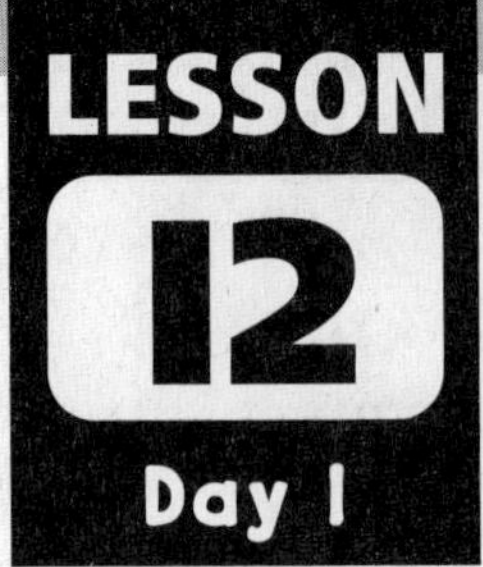

Warm-Up: Phonemic Awareness

Onset and Rime Tell children that you are going to say some words, but you are going to say them in parts. Have children listen to see if they can figure out the word. Demonstrate by saying: **/sh/+-ore—What word did I say?** *(shore)*

/sh/-out	**/sh/-irt**	**/sh/-ut**
/w/-ash	**/h/-ush**	**/c/-ash**

MATERIALS

Word Cards for some, their, many, how, away, funny, hide, food

Word Builder

Word Builder Cards a, d, h, i, o, p, s, t, w

Flip, the Funny Fish

Phonics: Blending Digraph /sh/ sh

RETEACH Blending Write the letters sh on the board. **These letters are *s* and *h*. The letters *sh* can stand for the /sh/ sound in words such as *ship*, *shop*, and *shot*.**

Point to the letters and say /sh/. Tell children that the /sh/ sound appears at the end of words like *wish*, *dish*, and *dash*. Have children repeat the sound as you touch the letters several times.

Use the Word Builder Cards and a pocket chart to model blending words.

Place the Word Builder Cards *s, h, i,* and *p* in the Word Builder with the *s* and *h* next to each other. Point to the *sh* and say /sh/. Point to the *i* and say /i/. Slide the *i* next to the *sh*. Move your hand under the letters and blend the sounds, elongating them /sshhii /. Have children repeat after you. Point to the letter *p* and say /p/. Have children say /p/ as you point to *p*. Slide *p* next to *shi*. Slide your hand under *ship* and blend by elongating the sounds—/sshhiipp /. Have children repeat. Then have children read the word *ship* along with you.

s h i p

s h i p

s h i p

s h i p

Place the Word Builder Cards *w, i, s,* and *h* in the Word Builder with the *s* and *h* next to each other. Point to the *w* and say /w/. Point to the *i* and say /i/. Point to the *sh* and say /sh/. Slide the *w* next to the *i*. Move your hand under the letters and blend the sounds, elongating them /wwii /. Slide the *sh* next to the *wi*. Move your hand under the letters and blend the sounds, elongating them /wwiisshh/. Have children repeat after you. Then say the word naturally—*wish*. Have children do the same.

High-Frequency Words

some
their
many
how
away
funny
hide
food

PRETEACH ***some, their, many, how, away, funny, hide, food***
Display the word card *some*. **This word is *some*. (Child's name) wants some ham. Read the word with me—*some*. Spell the word with me—*s-o-m-e*. Read the word with me. What is this word?** *(some)*

Follow the same procedure for the rest of the words.

their— **Their cat plays with a ball.**

many—**They got many calls.**

how—**How do you play that game?**

away—**They walk away quickly.**

funny—**The joke was funny.**

hide—**The pigs hide in the pen.**

food—**The food tasted good.**

Then place the eight words in a pocket chart and have volunteers read the words, as you randomly point to them.

Read: *Flip, the Funny Fish*

Flip, the Funny Fish

Distribute copies of the book and have children put their finger on the title. Have children follow along as you read the title aloud. Then have them frame the word *funny* and the word *fish*. Echo read the book with children. Read page 2 aloud and then have children read it to you. Follow this procedure throughout the book.

Phonics: Word Building with /sh/sh

PRETEACH Place the letters *s,h, o* and *p* in a Word Builder and have children do the same. Model how to blend the word *shop*. Slide your hand under the letters as you slowly elongate the sounds /sshhoopp/. Have children do the same. Then read the word naturally—*shop*. Have children do the same. Then say:

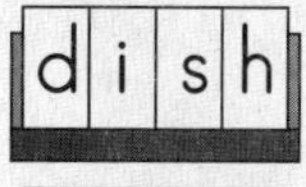

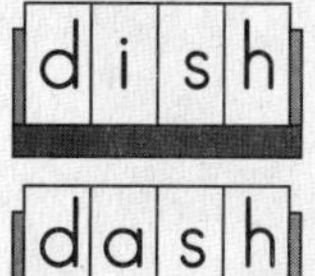

Change *p* to *t*. What word did you make? *(shot)*

Place the letters *d, i, s,* and *h* in a Word Builder and have children do the same. Model how to build the word *dish*. Then have children change *i* to *a* to build and read the word *dash*.

Distribute *Intervention Practice Book* page 34 to children.

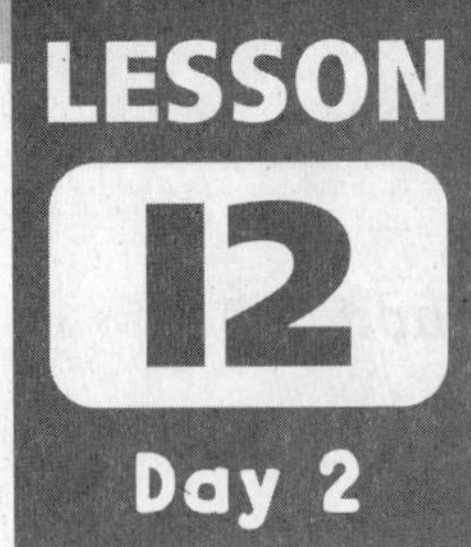

Warm-Up: Phonemic Awareness

Phoneme Isolation. Say the word *shut* aloud and have children repeat it. Tell children to listen to the /sh/ sound at the beginning of *shut*. Then say the words *shine* and *time*. Ask: **Which of these words has the /sh/ sound you hear in *shut*?** (*shine*) Continue with the words *fish, wash, sat; lash, wish, make; ship, shape, said; shut, shoe, has.*

MATERIALS

Word Builder

Word Builder Cards a, c, d, h, i, o, p, s, t, u, w

Flip, the Funny Fish

Phonics: Word Building with /sh/sh

RETEACH Place the letters *s, h, i,* and *p* in a Word Builder and have children do the same. Model how to blend the word *ship*. Slide your hand under the letters as you slowly elongate the sounds /sshhiipp/. Have children do the same. Then read the word naturally—*ship*. Have children do the same.

Have children blend and read new words by telling them:

Change *i* to *o*. What word did you make? *(shop)*

Change p to t. What word did you make? *(shot)*

Change o to u. What word did you make? *(shut)*

Place the letters *w, i, s,* and *h* in a Word Builder and have children do the same. Model how to blend the word *wish.* Slide your hand under the letters as you slowly elongate the sounds /wwiisshh/. Have children do the same. Then read the word naturally—*wish*. Have children do the same.

Have children blend and read new words by telling them:

Change *w* to *d*. What word did you make? *(dish)*

Change *i* to *a*. What word did you make? *(dash)*

Change *d* to *c*. What word did you make? *(cash)*

High-Frequency Words

RETEACH ***some, their, many, how, away, funny, hide, food***
Write the word *the* and have children read it. Then write the word *their* next to *the* and have children read the word. **How are these words the same? How are they different? Let's read them again.**

the **their**

Call attention to the *ir* added to *the* to make *their* by underlining *ir* in color.

Repeat the procedure with *so/some, man/many, fun/funny,* and *hid/hide.* To call attention to the differences between *now/how, play/away,* and *too/food*, circle in color the letters that change.

Read: *Flip, the Funny Fish*

Flip, the Funny Fish

Distribute copies of the book to children and have a volunteer read the title aloud. Ask children to frame the word that has the /sh/ sound at the end (*fish*). Ask children to frame the word that has the word *fun* within it (*funny*). Point to the comma and tell the children that this is a comma. Explain that commas can be used to separate different parts of a sentence or title. Point out that the words that come after the comma in this title—*the Funny Fish*—tell about Flip. Ask children to point to the names of the people who wrote and illustrated the book. Read their names aloud. Then choral read the book with children. Let your voice fade if children start to gain control of the text.

Phonics: Reading Sentences with /sh/sh

PRETEACH Distribute *Intervention Practice Book* page 35 to children. Point to the first sentence and have children read it aloud. Ask them to find the word *shut*, frame it with their fingers, and circle the word. Then work with children to complete the page.

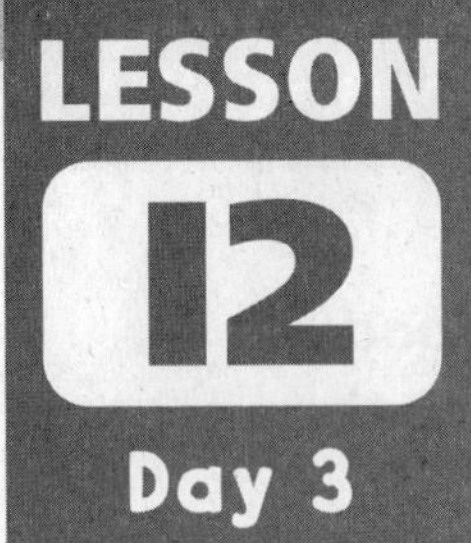

MATERIALS

Picture Cards: bat, bed, boat, bug, cat, clock, drum, egg, fox, goat, jeep, kite, lock, nut, plum, sled, train

Word Builder

Word Builder Cards s, h, i, p, o, t

Flip, the Funny Fish

Warm-Up: Phonemic Awareness

Phoneme Blending Tell children they are going to play a guessing game. Then say: **I'm thinking of a word that is something you put on your foot. It is a /sh//ū/. What's my word?** *(shoe).* Continue with the following words: /sh/-/ă/-/k/ *(shack)*, /sh/-/ā/-/d/ *(shade)*, /sh/-/ā/-/k/ *(shake)*, /sh/-/ē/-/t/ *(sheet)*, /sh/-/ī/-/n/ *(shine)*, and /sh/-/ō/ *(show)*.

Phonics: Reading Sentences with /sh/sh

RETEACH Help children blend and read new words and sentences shown. Have them read the sentence, blending each word in sequence. The high-frequency words are underlined; they should read these as a unit, not blending the sounds.

shut **cash** **hush** **shot**

That shop had pets.

I wish for a <u>friend</u> <u>to</u> <u>play</u> with.

That <u>night</u>, <u>the</u> ship <u>was</u> <u>gone</u>.

<u>Put</u> <u>the</u> <u>new</u> dish <u>where</u> <u>she</u> can <u>use</u> it.

High-Frequency Words

RETEACH ***some, their, many, how, away, funny, hide, food*** Write the following sentence on tag board and display it in a pocket chart along with the Picture Cards *bed, clock, egg, kite, nut,* and *plum*. Call on children to choose a Picture Card to complete the sentence and to read it aloud. Then ask: **Do some people really eat ______?**

PICTURE CARDS

For food some people eat one ______.

Do the same for the following sentence and Picture Cards *bug, cat, fox, nut,* and *sled*.

How can a ______ hide?

Do the same for the following sentence and Picture Cards *bat, bug, drum, goat,* and *plum.*

That ______ is their funny pet.

Do the same for the following sentence and Picture Cards *boat, drum, jeep, lock, clock,* and *train.*

Many people go away in a ______.

Read: *Flip, the Funny Fish*

Distribute copies of the book and have children read aloud the title. Ask what they think this book will be about. Then guide children through the book as they read.

Pages 2–3: Have children read the page to find out what Flip liked to do.

What did Flip like to do? *(hide)* **Find and read the sentence that tells. What word means the same as *Flip*. Find and frame that word.** *(He)*

Who wanted Flip? *(Tom)* **Find and read the sentence that tells.**

Pages 4–5: Have children read the pages to find out more about Flip.

What did Flip do? *(Flip swam away from Tom.)* **Who else saw and wanted Flip?** *(Trish)* **What do you think Flip will do?**

Pages 6–8: Have children read the pages to find out what Flip does now.

Does Flip want Trish? *(No)* **What did Flip do?** *(Flip swam away.)* **Find and frame the sentence.**

Who saw Flip last? *(Ken saw Flip.)* **Find and read the sentence that tells.**

Did Flip hide from Ken? *(No)* **Find and read the sentence that tells what Flip thinks about Ken.** *(Flip likes Ken.)*

Ask children to use the pictures to help summarize the book.

Phonics: Building Words

PRETEACH Put the letters *s*, *h*, *i*, and *p* in a Word Builder and have children do the same. Slide your hand under the letters as you blend the sounds—/sshhiipp/. Then read the word naturally—*ship*. Have children repeat after you. Then have children build and read new words.

Change *i* to *o*. What word did you make? *(shop)*

Change *p* to *t*. What word did you make? *(shot)*

Take the *s* away. What word did you make? *(hot)*

Change *o* to *i*. What word did you make? *(hit)*

Change *t* to *s*. What word did you make? *(his)*

Take the *h* away. What word did you make? *(is)*

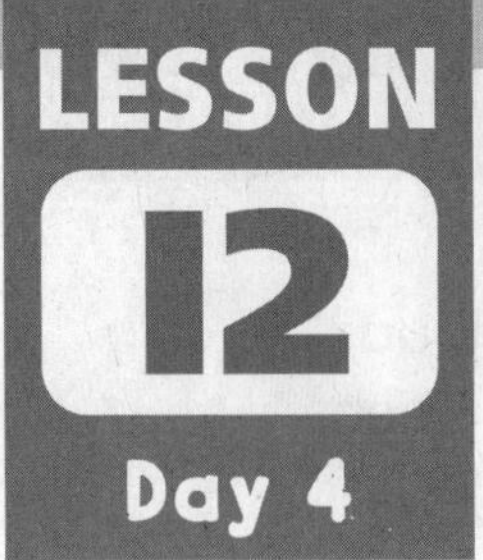

MATERIALS

Picture Cards fish, nut, ship, yarn

Write-on/Wipe-off Boards with disks

Word Cards for some, their, many, how, away, hide, be, try

Word Builder

Word Builder Cards a, d, h, i, s, w, o, p

Flip, the Funny Fish

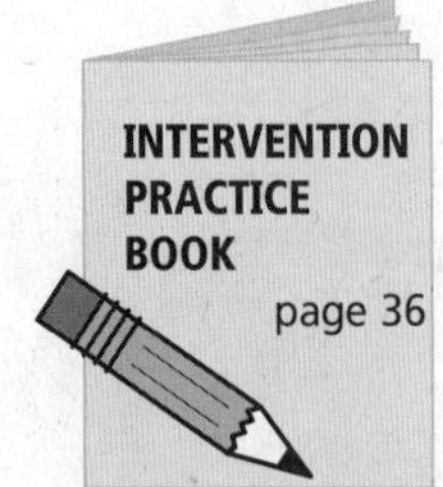

Warm-Up: Phonemic Awareness

Phoneme Segmentation Have children use the three boxes on the Write-on/Wipe-off Boards. Remind children that the boxes stand for the sounds in words. Show the Picture Card *fish* and ask: What is the first sound you hear in *fish*? (/f/) Have children place a disk in the first box. Then have children name the second sound in *fish* (/i/) and place a disk in the second box. Then have them identify the last sound in *fish* (/sh/) and place a disk in the third box. Point to each box in sequence as children say the word. **How many sounds do you hear in *fish*?** (three) Repeat this procedure with the following Picture Cards: *nut, ship, yarn.*

Phonics: Building Words

RETEACH Put the letters *w, i, s,* and *h* in a Word Builder and have children do the same. Slide your hand under the letters as you blend the sounds—/wwiisshh/. Then read the word naturally—*wish.* Have children repeat after you. Then have children build and read new words.

Change the *w* to *d*. What word did you make? *(dish)*

Change the *i* to *a*. What word did you make? *(dash)*

Take away the *d* and the *a*. Then add *op* after *sh*. What word did you make? *(shop)*

Change the *o* to *i*. What word did you make? *(ship)*

Distribute *Intervention Practice Book* page 36 to students.

High-Frequency Words

RETEACH ***some, their, many, how, away, hide, be, try*** Distribute word cards with the words listed above. Have partners take turns displaying the words for each other and reading them. After they read each word, have children spell the word and then repeat the word. Then have them spell the word again and write it on a sheet of paper.

Flip, the Funny Fish

Read: *Flip, the Funny Fish*

Focus Skill **Details.** Remind children that details can help them understand information that they read. Tell them that details can also help them picture what happens in a story. Have children reread *Flip, the Funny Fish* and then together make a list of story details.

Phonics: Blends with s and Blends with r

PRETEACH Write the following blends at the top of a sheet of chart paper: *br, cr, dr, fr, gr, tr* and *sc, sk, sm, sn, sp, st*. Have children suggest words that begin with these blends and say what letters they would need to write the words. Write the words underneath the appropriate headings. Then have the children read each column of words. End the activity by pointing to words at random and having children read the words.

br	cr	dr	fr	gr	tr	sc	sk	sm	sn	sp	st
brick	crash	drip	frog	grill	trip	scab	skim	smog	snack	spin	still
brag	crib	drop	frill	grit	trap	scat	skip	smack	snip	spill	stick

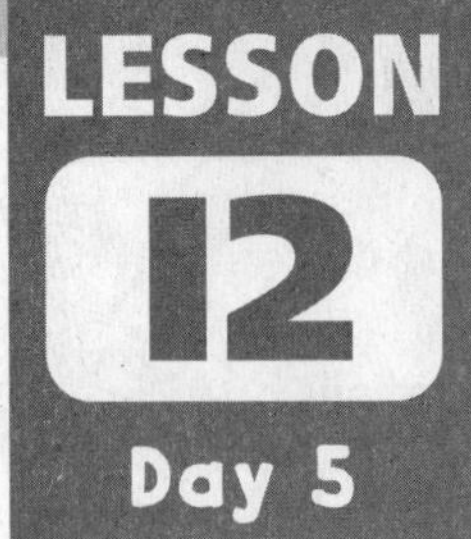

LESSON 12

Day 5

MATERIALS

Write-on/Wipe off Boards

Word Cards for some, their, many, how, away, saw, our, be

Word Builder

Word Builder Cards a, c, h, i, m, n, p, t

Warm-Up: Phonemic Awareness

Phoneme Blending Tell children that together you are going to play a puzzle game. Tell them that you are going to say some words in pieces, like a puzzle, and they should listen to see if they can put the puzzle pieces together to figure out the word. **Listen: /sh/-/i/-/p/. What word does /sh/-/i/-/p/ say?** *(ship)* Continue with the following words.

/ch/-/i/-/p/ *(chip)*	**/k/-/a/-/sh/** *(cash)*	**/hw/-/i/-/ch/** *(which)*
/s/-/t/-/ôr/ *(store)*	**/b/-/a/-/sh/** *(bash)*	**/ch/-/o/-/p/** *(chop)*

Phonics: Blends with s and Blends with r

RETEACH Write the word *trip* on a Write-on/ Wipe-off Board and have children do the same. Then have them read the word. Ask: **What letter should we write if we want to change *trip* to *trap*?** *(a)* **Let's do that.** Continue the activity with the following words: *brick* and *bring*. Repeat the activity, using the words *swish* and *swing*, *snip* and *snap*.

High-Frequency Words

Cumulative Review *some, their, many, how, away, saw, our, be* Place the words in a pocket chart. Say aloud one of the words and use it in a sentence. Have a volunteer find and point to the word. Have children clap and say the spelling of the word. Then have them write it. Have children read aloud their list of words.

some

their

many

how

away

saw

our

be

Read: Self-Selected Reading

Have children select a book to read from their browsing boxes. After they have completed their reading, suggest that they show you a word they figured out as they read the book.

Phonics: Digraph /ch/ ch, tch

PRETEACH Write the letters *ch* and *tch* on the board or on chart paper. **The letters *ch* and *tch* can stand for the /ch/ sound, the sound in words such as *chip*, *match*, and *chat*.** Point to the letters *ch* and *tch* and say /ch/. Have children repeat the sound as you touch the letters *ch* and *tch* several times.

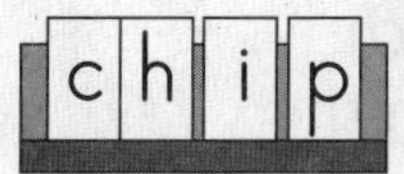

Use the Word Builder and Word Builder Cards to model blending words. Place the Word Builder Cards *c*, *h*, *i*, and *p* in the Word Builder. Point to the ch and say /ch/. Point to the *i* and say /i/.

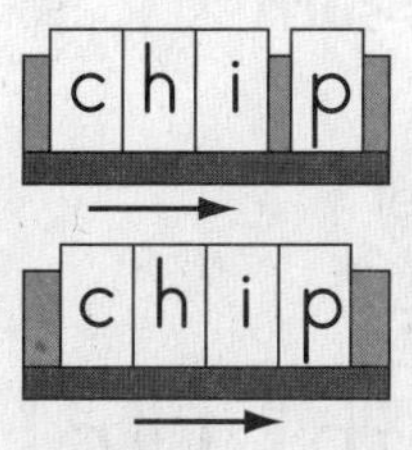

Slide the *i* next to the *ch*. Move your hand under the letters and blend the sounds, elongating them /cchhii/. Have children repeat after you. Point to the letter *p* and say /p/. Slide the *p* next to the *chi*. Slide your hand under *chip* and blend by elongating the sounds /cchhiipp/. Have children repeat. Then have children read the word *chip* along with you.

Follow the same procedure for the words *chin*, *match*, *catch*, *inch*, and *chat*.

INTERVENTION ASSESSMENT BOOK
pages 21–22

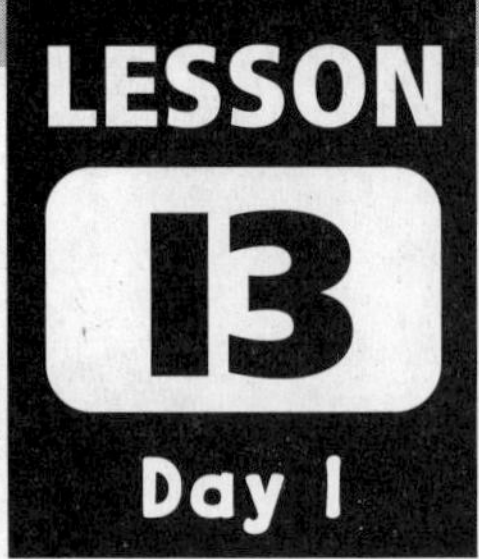

Warm-Up: Phonemic Awareness

Onset and Rime Tell children that you are going to say some words, but you are going to say them in parts. Have children listen to see if they can figure out the word. Demonstrate by saying **/ch/-at—What word did I say?** (*chat*)

/m/-uch	**/h/-atch**	**/ch/-um**
/b/-atch	**/ch/-ill**	**/ch/-ild**

MATERIALS

Word Cards for air, animals, around, fly, live, soon, turns

Word Builder

Word Builder Cards a, c, h, i, m, n, o, p, t

Soon I Will

Phonics: Digraph /ch/ ch, tch

RETEACH **Blending** Write *ch* on the board or chart paper. **These letters are *c* and *h*. The letters *ch* can stand for the /ch / sound.** Point to the letters and say /ch/. Tell children that the /ch / sound appears at the beginning of words such as *chin*, *chip*, and *chat* and at the end of words such as *inch* and *much*. Have children repeat the sound as you touch the letters several times. Then write the letters *tch*. **These letters are *t*, *c*, and *h*. When they come together, the letters *tch* also can stand for the /ch/ sound at the end of words such as *catch* and *match*.**

Use the Word Builder Cards and a pocket chart to model blending words.

Place the Word Builder cards *c*, *h*, *i*, and *p* in the Word Builder with the *c* and *h* next to each other. Point to the *ch* and say /ch/. Point to the *i* and say /i/. Slide the *i* next to the *ch*. Move your hand under the letters and blend the sounds, elongating them /cchhii/. Point to the letter *p* and say /p/. Have children say /p/ as you point to *p*. Slide *p* next to *chi*. Slide your hand under *chip* and blend by elongating the sounds—/cchhiipp/. Have children repeat after you. Then say the word naturally—*chip*. Have children do the same.

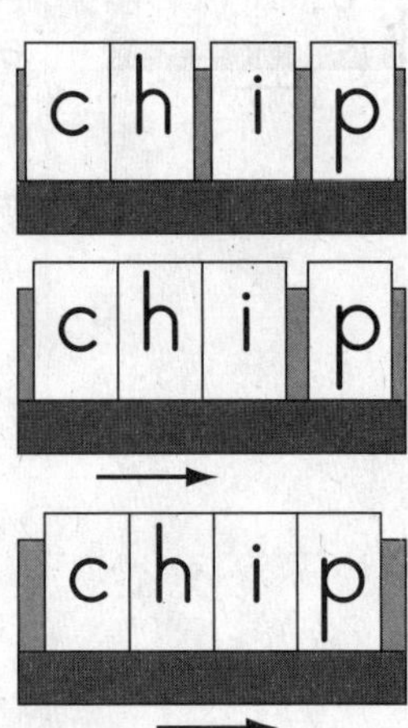

Place the Word Builder Cards *m*, *a*, *t*, *c* and *h* in the Word Builder with the *t*, *c*, and *h* next to each other. Point to the *m* and say /m/. Point to the *a* and say /a/. Slide the *a* next to the *m*. Move your hand under the letters and blend the sounds, elongating them /mmaa/. Have children repeat after you. Point to the letters *tch* and say /ch/. Have children say /ch/ as you point to *tch*. Slide tch next to *ma*. Slide your hand under *match* and blend by elongating the sounds—/mmaattcchh/. Have children repeat. Then have children read the word *match* along with you.

High-Frequency Words

air
around
live
animals
soon
fly
turns

PRETEACH ***air, around, live, animals, soon, fly, turns.*** Display the word card *air*. **This word is *air*. The bird flies through the air. Read the word with me—*air*. Spell the word with me—*a-i-r*. Read the word with me. What is this word?** (*air*) Follow the same procedure for the words *around*, *live*, *animals*, *soon*, *fly*, and *turns*.

around—**There were many animal tracks around the pond.**

live—**Polar bears live where it is cold.**

animals—**We saw many kinds of animals at the zoo.**

soon, *fly*—**Soon the bird will be able to fly.**

turns—**We take turns playing with the toy.**

Then place the seven words in a pocket chart and have volunteers read the words, as you randomly point to them.

Read: *Soon I Will*

Distribute copies of the book and have children put their finger on the title. Have children follow along as you read the title aloud. Then have them frame the word *soon*. Echo read the book with children. Read page 2 aloud and then have children read it to you. Follow this procedure throughout the book.

Phonics: Word Building with /ch/ch, tch

PRETEACH Place the letters *c*, *h*, *i*, and *n* in a Word Builder and have children do the same. Model how to blend the word *chin*. Slide your hand under the letters as you slowly elongate the sounds /cchhiinn/. Have children repeat. Then read the word naturally—*chin*. Have children repeat.

Have children blend and read new words by telling them:

Change *n* to *p*. What word did you make? *(chip)*

Change *i* to *o*. What word did you make? *(chop)*

Change *o* to *a*. What word did you make? *(chap)*

Take away the *a* and *p*. Put *it* in front of *ch*. What word did you make? *(itch)*

Distribute *Intervention Practice Book* page 37 to children.

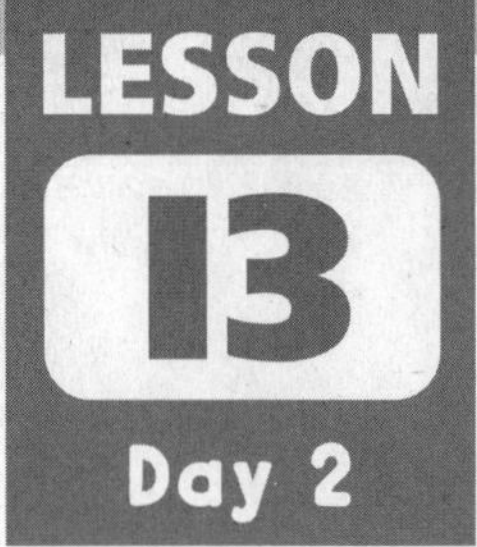

MATERIALS

Word Builder

Word Builder Cards a, c, d, h, i, n, p, t

Soon I Will

Warm-Up: Phonemic Awareness

Phoneme Isolation Say the word *chip* aloud and have children repeat it. Tell children to listen to the /ch/ sound at the beginning of *chip*. Then say the words *chin* and *corn*. Ask: **Which of these has the /ch/ sound that you hear in *chip*?** (*chin*) Continue with the words *clock*, *patch*, *beach*; *much*, *peach*, *pack*; *save*, *champ*, *choose*.

Phonics: Word Building with /ch/ch, tch

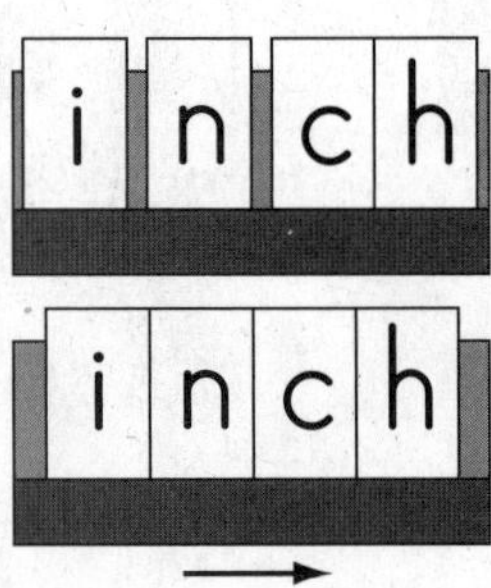

RETEACH Place the letters *i*, *n*, *c*, and *h* in a Word Builder with the *ch* together and have children do the same. Model how to blend the word *inch*. Slide your hand under the letters as you slowly elongate the sounds /iinncchh/. Have children do the same. Then read the word naturally—*inch*. Have children do the same.

Have children blend and read new words by telling them:

Change *n* to *t*. What word did you make? *(itch)*

Add *d* in front of *i*. What word did you make? *(ditch)*

Change *d* to *p*. What word did you make? *(pitch)*

Change *i* to *a*. What word did you make? *(patch)*

High-Frequency Words

RETEACH ***fly, air, around, live, animals, soon, loose, turns***
Write the word *try* and have children read it. Then write the word *fly* next to *try* and have children read the word. **How are these words the same? How are they different? Let's read them again.**

Repeat the procedure with *their/air*, *out/around*, *all/animals*, *too/soon*, *taps/turns*.

Soon I Will

Read: *Soon I Will*

Distribute copies of the book and read the title aloud. Have children frame the word *Soon*. Point to the word *I*. Tell children that the word *I* takes the place of a person's own name. Ask children to point to the names of the people who wrote and illustrated the book. Read their names aloud. Then choral read the book with children. Let your voice fade if children start to gain control of the text.

Phonics: Reading Sentences with /ch/ch, tch

PRETEACH Distribute *Intervention Practice Book* page 38 to children. Point to the first sentence and have children read it aloud. Ask them to find the word *chick*, frame it with their fingers, and circle the word. Then work with children to complete the page.

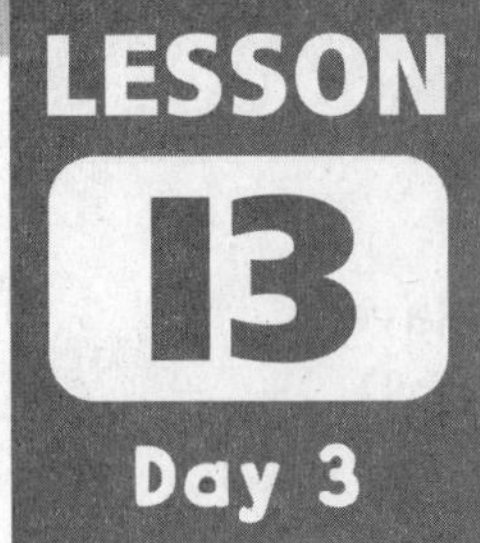

Warm-Up: Phonemic Awareness

Phoneme Blending Tell children that they are going to play a guessing game. Then say: **I'm thinking of a word that means the same as friend. It is /ch/-/u/-/m/. What's my word?** (*chum*) Continue with the following words: /ch/-/i/-/k/ (*chick*), /l/-/a/-/ch/ (*latch*), /ch/-/a/-/p/ (*chap*), and /p/-/a/-/ch/ (*patch*).

MATERIALS

Picture Cards: bat, boat, bug, cat, drum, fan, goat, jeep, jet, kite, lamp, map, pig, seal, six, train, zebra

Word Builder

Word Builder Cards a, c, d, h, i, m, p, t, h

Soon I Will

Phonics: Reading Sentences with /ch/ch, tch

Help children blend and read new words and sentences shown. Have them read the sentence, blending each word in sequence. The high-frequency words are underlined; children should read these as a unit, not blending the sounds.

much **hatch** **chill** **itch**

Trish had some food on her chin.

Ben is such a good friend to them.

She could call them and chat when they all go away.

Can we watch the chick hatch?

High-Frequency Words

RETEACH ***air, around, live, animals, soon, fly, turns*** Write the following sentence on tag board and display it in a pocket chart along with the Picture Cards *bat*, *goat*, *kite*, *jet*, *train*. Call on children to choose a Picture Card to complete the sentence and read it aloud. Then ask: **Can a ______ really fly in the air?**

PICTURE CARDS

The ______ can fly in the air.

Do the same for the following sentence and Picture Cards *bug*, *goat*, *pig*, *seal*, *zebra*.

The cat and the ______ are animals that live here.

Do the same for the following sentence and Picture Cards *cat*, *fan*, *jeep*, *six*, *lamp*, *map*.

The ______ turns around.

Do the same for the following sentence and Picture Cards *boat*, *drum*, *jet*, *map*, *six*, *train*.

The ______ will come soon.

Soon I Will

Read: *Soon I Will*

Distribute copies of the book and have children read aloud the title. Ask children what they think this book will be about. Then guide children through the book as they read.

Pages 2–3: Have children read the pages to find out who is telling this story.

> **Who is telling the story?** (*an egg; a baby bird*) **Find and frame the word that tells what the egg will do soon.** (*hatch*)

Pages 4–5: Have children read to find out what the bird does after it is hatched.

> **What does the bird do after it is hatched? Find and read the sentence that tells.** (*I beg for food.*) **Who brings the food?** (*Mama*)

Pages 6–7: Have children read to find out what the bird wants to do.

> **What does the bird want to do?** (*fly*) **Find and read the sentence that tells. Where does the bird want to fly?** (*in the air*)

Page 8: Have children read to find out what the bird can do.

> **What can the bird do now?** (*fly*) **Find and read the sentence that tells.**

Ask children to use the pictures to help summarize the book.

Phonics: Building Words

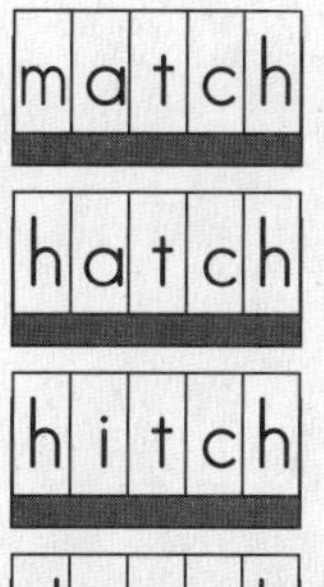

PRETEACH Put the letters *m*, *a*, *t*, *c*, and *h* in a Word Builder and have children do the same. Slide your hand under the letters as you blend the sounds—/mmaattcchh/. Then read the word naturally—*match*. Have children repeat after you. Then have children build and read new words.

Change *m* to *h*. What word did you make? *(hatch)*

Change *a* to *i*. What word did you make? *(hitch)*

Change *h* to *d*. What word did you make? *(ditch)*

Change *d* to *p*. What word did you make? *(pitch)*

Change *i* to *a*. What word did you make? *(patch)*

Change *p* to *c*. What word did you make? *(catch)*

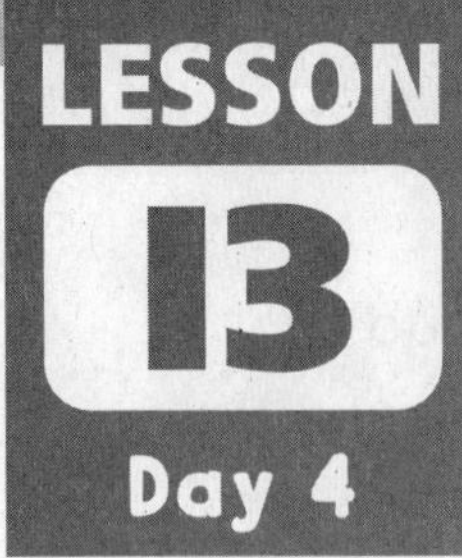

MATERIALS

Picture Cards boat, fish, lock, nine, ship, sock

Write-on/Wipe-off Boards with disks

Word Cards for animals, around, fly, how, live, many, soon

Word Builder

Word Builder Cards a, c, h, i, m, p, t

Soon I Will

Warm-Up: Phonemic Awareness

PICTURE CARDS

Phoneme Segmentation Have children use the three boxes on the Write-on/Wipe-off Boards. Remind children that the boxes stand for the sounds in words. Show the Picture Card *boat* and ask: **What is the first sound you hear in *boat*?** (/b/) Have children place a disk in the first box. Then have children name the second sound in *boat* (/ō/) and place a disk in the second box. Then have them identify the last sound in *boat* (/t/) and place a disk in the third box. Point to each box in sequence as children say the word. **How many sounds do you hear in *boat*?** (*three*) Repeat this procedure with the following Picture Cards: *fish*, *lock*, *nine*, *ship*, and *sock*.

Phonics: Building Words

RETEACH Put the letters *c*, *h*, *i*, and *p* in a Word Builder and have children do the same. Slide your hand under the letters as you blend the sounds—/cchhiipp /. Then read the word naturally—*chip*. Have children repeat after you. Then have children build and read new words.

Change *i* to *a*. What word did you make? (*chap*)

Change *ch* to *m*. What word did you make? (*map*)

Change *p* to *t*. What word did you make? (*mat*)

Add *ch* after *t*. What word did you make? (*match*)

Distribute *Intervention Practice Book* page 39 to children.

High-Frequency Words

around
live
animals
soon
fly
how
many

RETEACH ***around, live, animals, soon, fly, how, many***
Distribute word cards with the words listed above. Have partners take turns displaying the words for each other and reading them. After they read each word, have children spell the word and then repeat the word. Then have them spell the word again and write it on a sheet of paper.

Read: *Soon I Will*

Focus Skill **Predict Outcomes** Remind children that, when they read, thinking about what will happen next in a story helps readers understand what they read. Have children read *Soon I Will*, pausing after each page to predict what will happen next. Record their predictions on chart paper. Review each prediction after you read the following page.

Action	Prediction
Mama sits on the eggs.	The eggs will hatch.
Mama brings food.	The birds will grow big.
I want to fly.	The bird will fly.

Phonics: Blends with l

PRETEACH Write the letters *bl*, *cl*, *fl*, *pl*, and *sl* at the top of a sheet of chart paper. Have children suggest words that begin with these blends and say what letters they would need to write the words. Then write the words underneath the appropriate blend. Then help children read each column of words. End the activity by pointing to words at random and having children read the words.

bl	cl	fl	pl	sl
black	clap	flap	plug	slap
bled	click	flat	play	slick
block	clock	fled	plum	sled

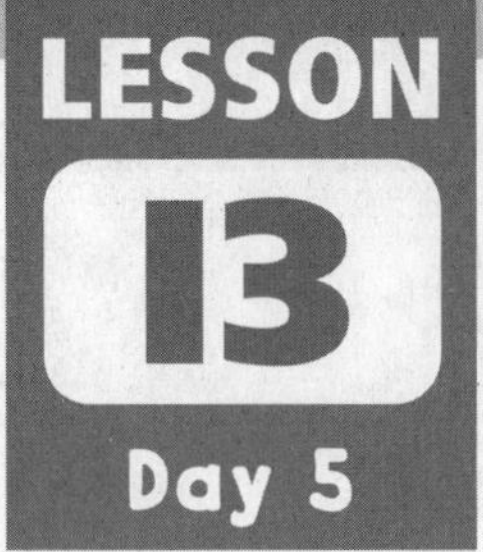
LESSON 13 Day 5

MATERIALS

Write-on/Wipe off Boards

Word Cards for air, away, fly, live, some, soon, their, turns

Word Builder

Word Builder Cards a, c, d, f, m, r, t

Warm-Up: Phonemic Awareness

Phoneme Blending Tell children that together you are going to play a game of "Fix It." Tell them that you are going to say some words that are all broken and they should listen to see if they can put the sounds together to figure out the word. **Listen: /ch/-/i/-/p/. What word does /ch/-/i/-/p/ say?** (*chip*) Continue with the following words:

/i/-/ch/ (*itch*)	**/k/-/a/-/ch/** (*catch*)	**/f/-/ar/-/m/** (*farm*)
/sh/-/är/-/k/ (*shark*)	**/kw/-/ē/-/n/** (*queen*)	**/sh/-/îr/-/t/** (*shirt*)

Phonics: Blends with l

RETEACH Write the word *black* on a Write-on/Wipe-off Board and have children do the same. Then have them read the word. Ask: **What letters should we write if we want to change *black* to *blink*?** (*ink*) **Let's do that.** Continue the activity with the words *clink* and *clap*. Repeat the activity, using the words *flap* and *flip*, *slip* and *slug*, *plug* and *plus*.

High-Frequency Words

Cumulative Review *air, live, soon, fly, turns, away, some, their* Place the words in a pocket chart. Say aloud one of the words and use it in a sentence. Have a volunteer find and point to the word. Have children clap and say the spelling of the word. Then have them write it. Have children read aloud their list of words.

air

live

soon

fly

turns

away

some

their

Read: Self-Selected Reading

Have children select a book to read from their browsing boxes. After they have completed their reading, suggest that they show you a word with *ch* or *tch* that they can read successfully.

Phonics: R-controlled vowel /är/ar

PRETEACH Write the letters *ar* on the board or on chart paper. The letters *ar* can stand for the /är/ sound, the sound in words such as *farm*, *art*, and *card*. Point to the letters *ar* and say /är/. Have children repeat the sound as you touch the letters *ar* several times.

Use the Word Builder and Word Builder Cards to model blending words. Place the Word Builder Cards *f*, *a*, and *r* in the Word Builder. Point to the *f* and say /f/. Point to the *ar* and say /är/.

Slide the *f* next to the *ar*. Move your hand under the letters and blend the sounds, elongating them /ffaarr/. Have children repeat after you. Then have children read the word *far* along with you.

Follow the same procedure for the words *farm*, *arm*, *art*, *cart*, and *card*.

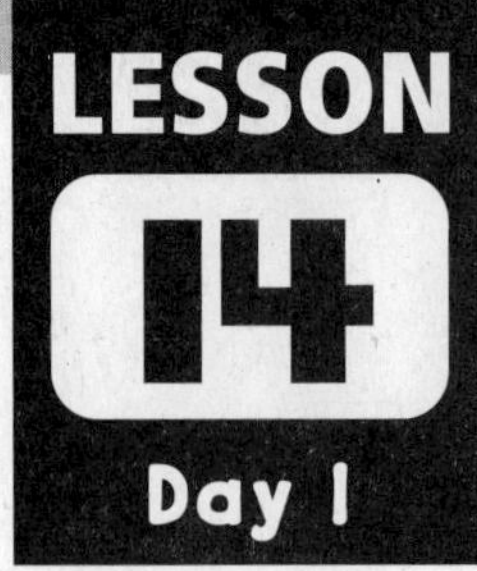

Warm-Up: Phonemic Awareness

Onset and Rime Tell children that you are going to say some words, but you are going to say them in parts. Have children listen to see if they can figure out the word. Demonstrate by saying **/d/-ark—What word did I say?** (*dark*)

MATERIALS

Word Cards for city, house, sometimes, take, there

Word Builder

Word Builder Cards a, f, m, r, t

In the City Park

/h/-arm	**/l/-ard**	**/st/-art**
/y/-ard	**/p/-art**	**/är/-cade**

Phonics: R-controlled /är/ar

RETEACH **Blending** Write the letters *a* and *r* beside each other on the board or on chart paper. **These letters are *a* and *r*. When the letters *ar* come together, they can stand for the /är/ sound you hear in the middle of words such as *start*, *tar*, and *park*.** Have children repeat the sound as you touch the letters several times.

Use the Word Builder Cards and a pocket chart to model blending words.

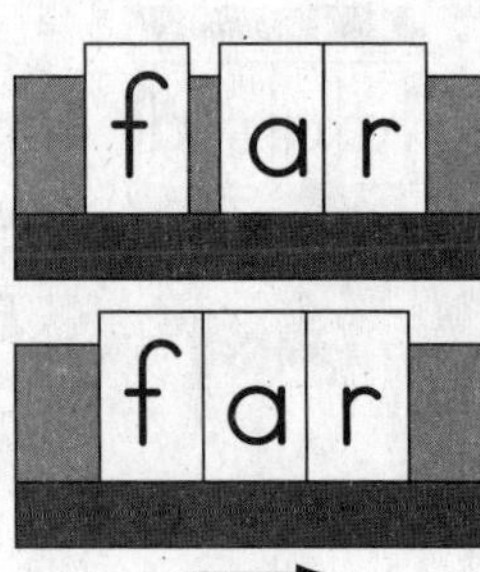

Place the Word Builder Cards *f*, *a*, and *r* in the Word Builder with the *a* and *r* next to each other. Point to the *ar* and say /är/. Point to the *f* and say /f/. Slide the *f* next to the *ar*. Move your hand under the letters and blend the sounds, elongating them /ffäärr/. Have children repeat after you. Then say the word naturally—*far*. Have children do the same.

High-Frequency Words

sometimes
take
there
city
house

PRETEACH ***sometimes, take, there, city, house*** Display the word card *sometimes*. **This word is *sometimes*. Sometimes I like to be by myself. Read the word with me—*sometimes*. Spell the word with me—*s-o-m-e-t-i-m-e-s*. Read the word with me. What is this word?** (*sometimes*)

Follow the same procedure for the words *take*, *there*, *city*, and *house*.

take—**I take the bus to school every day.**

there—**There are many ways to use math.**

city—**The city has tall buildings.**

house—**I like to visit my grandma's house.**

Then place the five words in a pocket chart and have volunteers read the words, as you randomly point to them.

Read: *In the City Park*

Distribute copies of the book and have children put their finger on the title. Have children follow along as you read the title aloud. Then have them frame the words *City* and *Park*. Echo read the book with children. Read page 2 aloud and then have children read it to you. Follow this procedure throughout the book.

Phonics: Word Building with /är/ar

PRETEACH Place the letters *f*, *a*, and *r* in a Word Builder and have children do the same. Model how to blend the word *far*. Slide your hand under the letters as you slowly elongate the sounds /ffäärr/. Have children do the same. Then read the word naturally—*far*. Have children do the same.

Have children blend and read new words by telling them:

Add *m* after the *r*. What word did you make? *(farm)*

Take *f* away. What word did you make? *(arm)*

Change *m* to *t*. What word did you make? *(art)*

Distribute *Intervention Practice Book* page 40 to children.

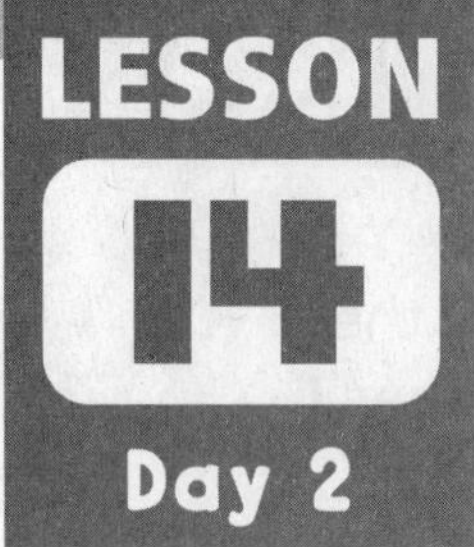

MATERIALS

Word Builder

Word Builder Cards a, c, d, h, m, r, t

In the City Park

Warm-Up: Phonemic Awareness

Phoneme Isolation Say the word *farm* aloud and have children repeat it. Tell children to listen to the /är/ sound in the middle of *farm*. Then say the words *chin* and *card*. Ask: **Which of these words has the /är/ sound that you hear in *farm*?** (*card*) Continue with the words *chart*, *card*, *cane*; *park*, *barn*, *bat*; *art*, *arm*, *ant*.

Phonics: Word Building with /är/ar

RETEACH Place the letters *a*,*r*, and *t* in a Word Builder and have children do the same. Model how to blend the word art. Slide your hand under the letters as you slowly elongate the sounds /äärrtt /. Have children do the same. Then read the word naturally—*art*. Have children do the same.

Have children blend and read new words by telling them:

Add *c* in front of *art*. What word did you make? *(cart)*

Change *t* to *d*. What word did you make? *(card)*

Change *c* to *h*. What word did you make? *(hard)*

Change *d* to *m*. What word did you make? *(harm)*

High-Frequency Words

RETEACH ***sometimes, take, there, city, house*** On the board, write the word *some* and have children read it. Then write the word *sometimes* next to *some* and have children read the word. **How are these words the same? How are they different? Let's read them again.**

some sometimes

Repeat the procedure with *make/take*, *the/there*, *cat/city*, and *how/house*.

Read: *In the City Park*

In the City Park

Distribute copies of the book to children and have a volunteer read the title aloud. Have children frame the words *City* and *Park*. Explain that, in book titles, the first word is always capitalized, as are all the other important words. Point out the capital letters at the beginning of *In*, *City*, and *Park* and have children point out the one that is the first word in the title as well as the two that are important words. Ask children to point to the names of the people who wrote and illustrated the book. Read the names aloud. Then choral read the book with children. Let your voice fade if children start to gain control of the text.

Phonics: Reading Sentences with /är/ar

PRETEACH Distribute *Intervention Practice Book* page 41 to children. Point to the first sentence and have children read it aloud. Ask them to find the word *far*, frame it with their fingers, and circle the word. Then work with children to complete the page.

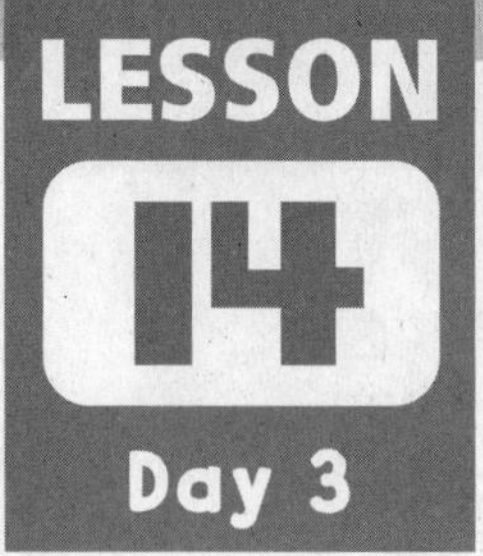

MATERIALS

Word Builder

Word Builder Cards a, b, c, d, k, m, p, r, t

Picture Cards: bed, boat, clock, egg, fan, fish, fox, jeep, nut, plum, quilt, red, six, sun, train

In the City Park

Warm-Up: Phonemic Awareness

Phoneme Blending Tell children that they are going to play a guessing game. Then say: **I'm thinking of a word that tells when something is difficult. It is /h/-/är/-/d/. What's my word?** (*hard*) Continue with the following words: /m/-/är/-/k/ (*mark*), /p/-/är/-/t/ (*part*), and /l/-/är/-/k/ (*lark*).

Phonics: Reading Sentences with /är/ar

RETEACH Help children blend and read new words and sentences shown. Have them read the sentence, blending each word in sequence. The high-frequency words are underlined; children should read these as a unit, not blending the sounds.

bark start yard part

Pitch <u>with</u> <u>that</u> arm.

<u>The</u> cart will <u>go</u> <u>down</u> <u>the</u> hill.

Will <u>the</u> car start?

<u>The</u> <u>night</u> is dark.

High-Frequency Words

RETEACH ***sometimes, take, there, city, house*** Write the following sentence on tag board and display it in a pocket chart along with the Picture Cards *egg*, *fish*, *quilt*, *nut*, *plum*, and *fan*. Call on children to choose a Picture Card to complete the sentence and to read it aloud. Then ask: **Would you really eat one _____?**

PICTURE CARDS

Sometimes I like to eat one _____.

Do the same for the following sentence and Picture Cards *clock*, *bed*, *red*, *quilt*, *six*, *fox*.

The house in the city has a _____.

Do the same for the following sentence and Picture Cards *boat*, *jeep*, *sun*, *red*, *train*.

Can you take a _____ to get there?

Read: *In the City Park*

Distribute copies of the book and have children read aloud the title. Ask children what they think this book will be about. Then guide children through the book as they read.

Pages 2–3 Have children read to find out what the people who work in the city park do.

What does the man do? (*sells hot dogs*) **Find and read the sentence that tells. What does the woman do? Find and frame those words.** (*pick up trash*)

Pages 4–5 Have children read the pages to find out what else people do.

What does the police officer do? (*stops cars*) **Find and read the sentence that tells. What does the dog walker do?** (*takes dogs out to the city park*)

Pages 6–7 Have children read the pages to find out what other jobs people have.

What does the taxi driver do? (*takes people to the park*) **What does the artist do in the park?** (*makes art*)

Page 8 Have children read to find out how the people who work in the park feel.

How do the people feel about the park? (*they like the city park*) **Find and read the sentence that tells.**

Ask children to use the pictures to help summarize the book.

Phonics: Building Words

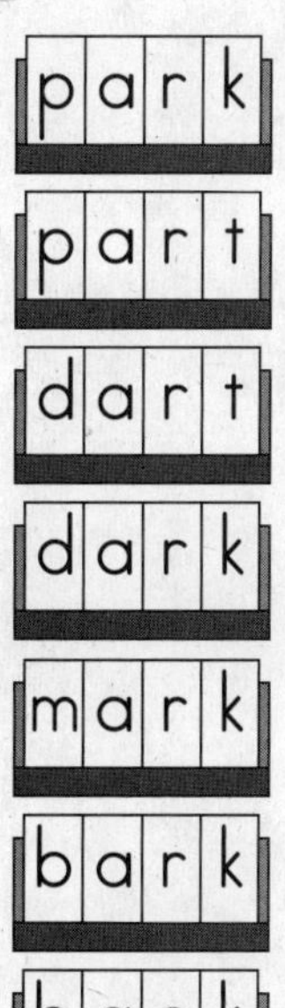

PRETEACH Put the letters *p*, *a*, *r*, and *k* in a Word Builder and have children do the same. Slide your hand under the letters as you blend the sounds—/ppäärrkk /. Then read the word naturally—*park*. Have children repeat after you. Then have children build and read new words.

Change *k* to *t*. What word did you make? *(part)*
Change *p* to *d*. What word did you make? *(dart)*
Change *t* to *k*. What word did you make? *(dark)*
Change *d* to *m*. What word did you make? *(mark)*
Change *m* to *b*. What word did you make? *(bark)*
Change *r* to *c*. What word did you make? *(back)*

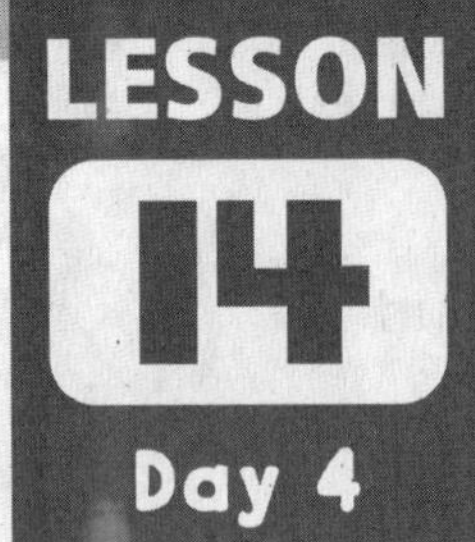

MATERIALS

Picture Cards: cup, gate, net, rake, rose

Write-on/Wipe-off Boards with disks

Word Cards for city, house, live, sometimes, soon, take, there

Word Builder

Word Builder Cards a, b, c, d, r, s, t

In the City Park

Warm-Up: Phonemic Awareness

Phoneme Segmentation Have children use the three boxes on the Write-on/Wipe-off Boards. Remind children that the boxes stand for the sounds in words. Show the Picture Card *cup* and ask: **What is the first sound you hear in *cup*?** (/k/) Have children place a disk in the first box. Then have children name the second sound in *cup* (/u/) and place a disk in the second box. Then have them identify the last sound in *cup* (/p/) and place a disk in the third box. Point to each box in sequence as children say the word. **How many sounds do you hear in *cup*?** (*three*) Repeat this procedure with the following Picture Cards: *gate*, *net*, *rake*, *rose*.

PICTURE CARDS

Phonics: Building Words

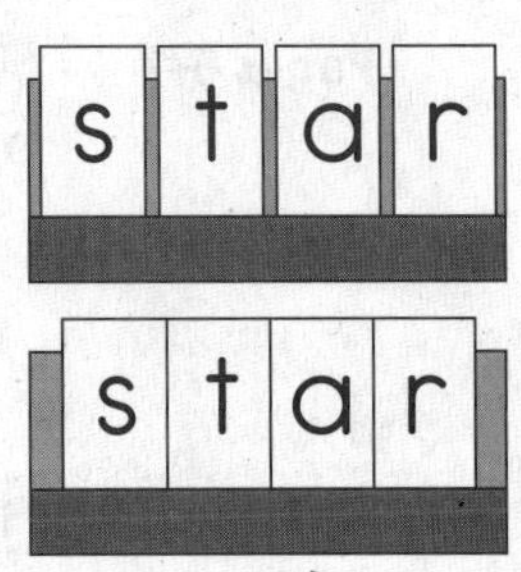

RETEACH Put the letters *s*, *t*, *a* and *r* in a Word Builder and have children do the same. Slide your hand under the letters as you blend the sounds—/ssttäärr/. Then read the word naturally—*star*. Have children repeat after you. Then have children build and read new words.

Take *s* away. What word did you make? *(tar)*

Change *t* to *b*. What word did you make? *(bar)*

Change *b* to *c*. What word did you make? *(car)*

Add *d* to the end of *car*. What word did you make? *(card)*

Change *d* to *t*. What word did you make? *(cart)*

Take *c* away. What word did you make? *(art)*

Distribute *Intervention Practice Book* page 42 to children.

High-Frequency Words

sometimes
take
there
city
house
live
soon

RETEACH ***sometimes, take, there, city, house, live, soon*** Distribute word cards with the words listed above. Have partners take turns displaying the words for each other and reading them. After they read each word, have children spell the word and then repeat the word. Then have them spell the word again and write it on a sheet of paper.

Read: *In the City Park*

In the City Park

Focus Skill **Setting.** Remind children that the setting is the place where a story takes place. Explain that understanding the setting can help readers picture what is happening in the story. Have children read *In the City Park* and then together make a list of things that make up a park.

What Makes a Park?
grass
trees
swings
slides
basketball court
fountain

Phonics: Inflections -s, -ing, -ed

PRETEACH Write the letters *-s*, *-ing*, and *-ed* at the top of a sheet of chart paper. Have children suggest words that end with *-s* and say what letters they would need to write the words. Then write the words underneath the heading *-s*. Use the same procedure for *-ing* and *-ed*. Then have children read each column of words. remind children of the three sounds *-ed* can stand for: /t/ as in *backed*; /d/ as in *lived*; /ed/ as in *ended*. End the activity by pointing to words at random and having children read the words.

–s	–ing	–ed
cats	packing	backed
bugs	falling	ended
ships	singing	dashed

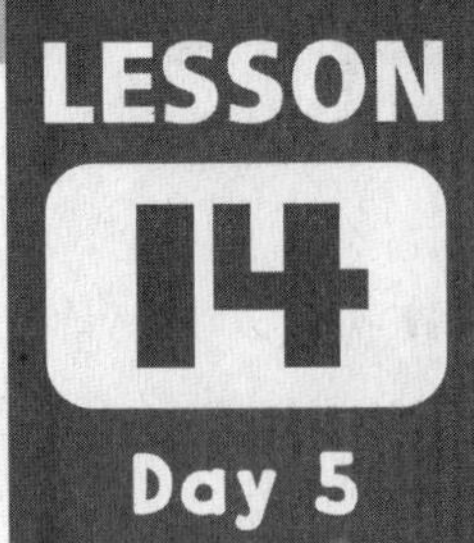

Warm-Up: Phonemic Awareness

Phoneme Blending Tell children that together you are going to play a puzzle game. Tell them that you are going to say some words in pieces like a puzzle, and they should listen to see if they can put the puzzle pieces together to figure out the word. **Listen: /k/-/är/-/d/. What word does /k/-/är/-/d/ say?** (*card*). Continue with the following words:

/f/-/är/-/m/ (*farm*)	**/s/-/t/-/är/-/k/** (*star*)	**/s/-/c/-/är/** (*scar*)
/s/-/m/-/är/-/t/ (*smart*)	**/s/-/p/-/är/-/k/** (*spark*)	**/ch/-/är/-/t/** (*chart*)

MATERIALS

Write-on/Wipe off Boards

Word Cards for around, city, house, sometimes, soon, take, there

Word Builder

Word Builder Cards c, e, h, i, k, n, q, t, u, w, z

sometimes
take
there
city
house
soon
around

Phonics: Inflections -s, -ing, -ed

RETEACH Write the word *parks* on a Write-on/ Wipe-off Board and have children do the same. Then have them read the word. Ask: **What letters should we write if we want to change *parks* to *parking*?** (*ing*) **Let's do that.** Continue the activity with the word *parked* (*ed*). Then repeat the activity with the words *starts-starting-started* and *calls-calling-called*.

High-Frequency Words

Cumulative Review *sometimes, take, there, city, house, soon, around* Place the words in a pocket chart. Say aloud one of the words and use it in a sentence. Have a volunteer find and point to the word. Have children clap and say the spelling of the word. Then have them write it. Have children read aloud their list of words.

Read: Self-Selected Reading

Have children select a book to read from their browsing boxes. After they have completed their reading, have them tell you what they were most successful in during the reading of the book.

Phonics: Digraphs /kw/ qu and /hw/ wh

PRETEACH Write the letters *qu* on the board or on chart paper. The letters *qu* can stand for the /kw/ sound, the sound you hear at the beginning of words such as *quiz*, *quit*, and *quick*. Point to the letters *qu* and say /kw/. Have children repeat the sound as you touch the letters *qu* several times.

Use the Word Builder and Word Builder Cards to model blending words.

Place the Word Builder Cards *q*, *u*, *i*, *c*, and *k* in the Word Builder. Point to the *qu* and say /kw/. Point to the *i* and say /i/.

Slide the *i* next to the *qu*. Move your hand under the letters and blend the sounds, elongating them /kkwwii/. Have children repeat after you. Point to the letters *ck*. Say /k/. Slide the *ck* next to *qui*. Slide your hand under *quick* and blend by elongating the sounds /kkwwiicckk/. Have children repeat. Then have children read the word *quick* along with you. Follow the same procedure for the words *quit* and *quiz*.

Write the letters *wh* on the board or on chart paper. **The letters *wh* can stand for the /hw/ sound, the sound you hear at the beginning of words such as *whiz*, *which*, and *when*.** Point to the letters *wh* and say /hw/. Have children repeat the sound as you touch the letters *wh* several times.

Use the Word Builder and Word Builder Cards to model blending words.

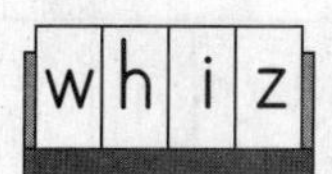

Place the Word Builder Cards *w*, *h*, *i*, and *z* in the Word Builder. Point to the *wh* and say /hw/. Point to the *i* and say /i/.

Slide the *i* next to the *wh*. Move your hand under the letters and blend the sounds, elongating them /hhwwii/. Have children repeat after you. Point to the letter *z*. Say /z/. Slide the *z* next to *whi*. Slide your hand under *whiz* and blend by elongating the sounds /hhwwiizz/. Have children repeat. Then have children read the word *whiz* along with you. Follow the same procedure for the words *which* and *when*.

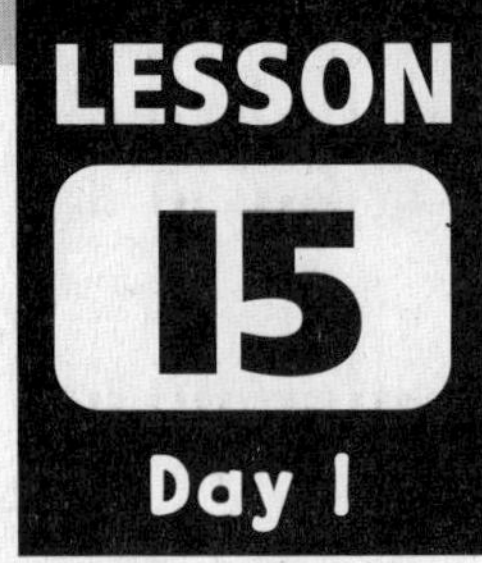

Warm-Up: Phonemic Awareness

Onset and Rime Tell children that you are going to say some words, but you are going to say them in parts. Have children listen to see if they can figure out the word. Demonstrate by saying */kw/-iet*—**What word did I say?** (*quiet*)

/hw/-ere	**/hw/-en**	**/kw/-estion**
/hw/-ite	**/kw/-ick**	**/kw/-ail**

MATERIALS

Word Builder

Word Builder Cards c, h, i, k, n, q, t, u, w, z

Word Cards for about, books, by, family, grew, read, work, writing

Alphabet Masters q

My Family Quilt

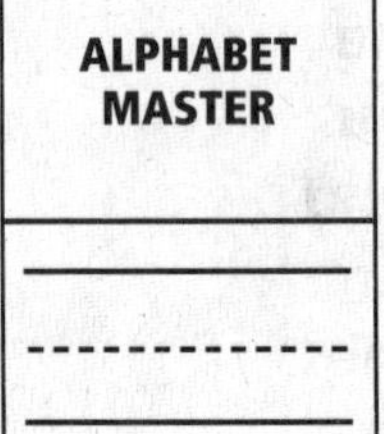

Phonics: Digraphs /kw/qu, /hw/wh

RETEACH blending Display Alphabet Master *Qq*. **This letter is *q*, and it is used with the letter *u*.** Write *qu* on the board. **The letters *qu* can stand for the /kw/ sound.** Point to the letters *qu* and say /kw/. Tell children that the /kw/ sound appears in words such as *quarter*, *quiet*, and *quilt*. Have children repeat the sound as you touch the letters *qu* several times.

Write *wh* on the board. **These letters are *w* and *h*. The letters *wh* can stand for the /hw/ sound.** Point to the letters *wh* and say /hw/. Tell children that the /hw/ sound appears in words such as *white*, *whistle*, and *whisker*. Have children repeat the sound as you touch the letters *wh* several times.

Use the Word Builder Cards and a pocket chart to model blending words.

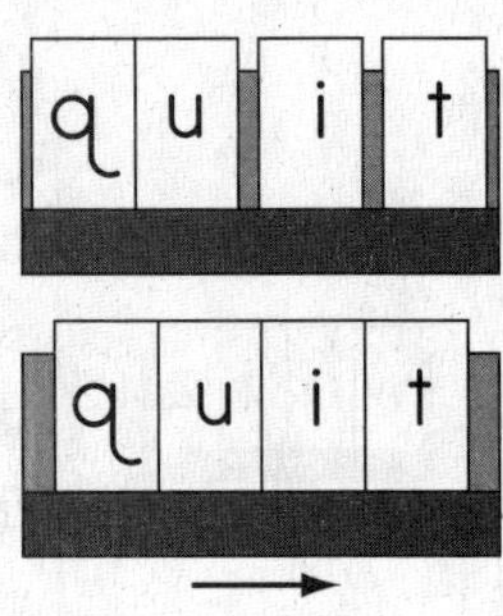

Place the Word Builder cards *q*, *u*, *i*, and *t* in the Word Builder with the *q* and *u* next to each other. Point to the *qu* and say /kw/. Point to the *i* and say /i/. Slide the *i* next to the *qu*. Move your hand under the letters and blend the sounds, elongating them /kkwwii/. Have children repeat after you. Point to the *t* and say /t/. Slide the *t* next to the *qui*. Move your hand under the letters and blend the sounds, elongating them /kkwwiitt/. Have children repeat after you. Then say the word naturally—*quit*. Have children do the same.

Use a similiar procedure for *wh* with Word Builder Cards *w*, *h*, *e*, and *n* to have children blend and read the word *when*.

High-Frequency Words

PRETEACH ***family, work, books, read, about, by, writing, grew*** Display the word card *family*. **This word is *family*. I love my family. Read the word with me—*family*. Spell the word with me—*f-a-m-i-l-y*. Read the word with me. What is this word?** (*family*) Follow the same procedure for the words *work*, *books*, *read*, *about*, *by*, *writing, grew*.

work—**I work hard at school.**

read, books—**We read lots of books.**

about—**The song is about lizards.**

by—**That picture was made by my sister.**

writing—**My mother is writing a letter.**

grew—**Mr. Sanchez grew up in Mexico.**

Then place the eight words in a pocket chart and have volunteers read the words, as you randomly point to them.

Read: *My Family Quilt*

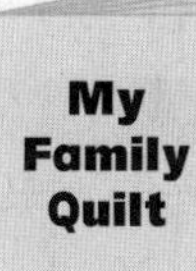

Story words Write the word *Grandpa* and read it to children. Help them read the word as needed. Distribute copies of the book and have children put their finger on the title. Read the title aloud and have them frame the words *family* and *quilt*. Echo read the book with children. Read page 2 aloud and then have children read it to you. Follow this procedure throughout the book.

Phonics: Word Building with /kw/qu, /hw/wh

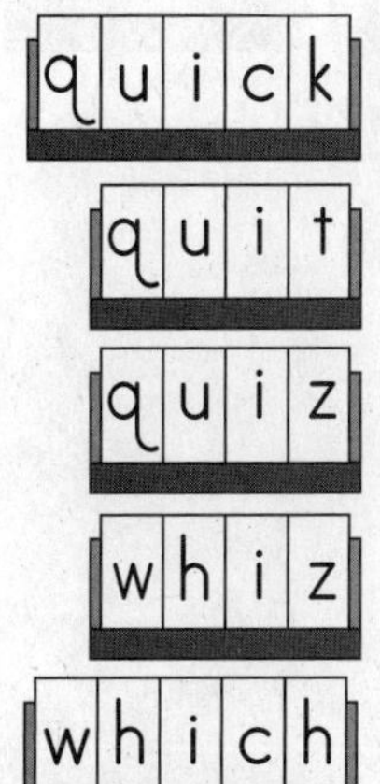

PRETEACH Place the letters *q*, *u*, *i*, *c*, and *k* in a Word Builder and have children do the same. Slide your hand under the letters as you slowly elongate the sounds /kkwwiicckk/. Have children do the same. Then read the word naturally—*quick*. Have children repeat. Have children blend and read new words by telling them:

Change *ck* to *t*. What word did you make? *(quit)*

Change *t* to *z*. What word did you make? *(quiz)*

Change *qu* to *wh*. What word did you make? *(whiz)*

Change *z* to *ch*. What word did you make? *(which)*

Distribute *Intervention Practice Book* page 142.

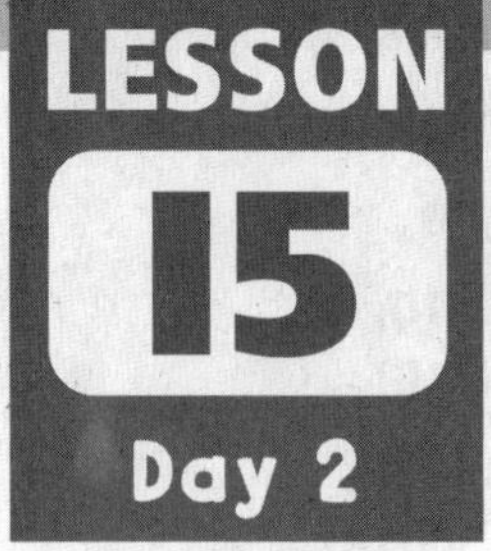

MATERIALS

Word Builder

Word Builder Cards a, c, h, i, k, p, q, u, w, z

My Family Quilt

Warm-Up: Phonemic Awareness

Phoneme Isolation Say the word *whale* aloud and have children repeat it. Tell children to listen to the /hw/ sound at the beginning of *whale*. Then say the words *whiz* and *farm*. Ask: **Which of these words has the /hw/ sound you hear in *whale*?** (*whiz*) Continue with the words *when*, *who*, *wish*; *what*, *where*, *now*.

Say the word *queen* aloud and have children repeat it. Tell children to listen to the /kw/ sound at the beginning of the word queen. Then say the words *quiz* and *itch*. Ask: **Which of these words has the /kw/ sound you hear in *queen*?** (*quiz*) Continue with the words *quick*, *quit*, *cart*; *quack*, *crack*, *quest*.

Phonics: Word Building with /kw/qu, /hw/wh

RETEACH Place the letters *w*, *h*, *i*, and *p* in a Word Builder and have children do the same. Model how to blend the word *whip*. Slide your hand under the letters as you slowly elongate the sounds /hhwwiipp/. Have children do the same. Then read the word naturally—*whip*. Have children do the same.

Have children blend and read new words by telling them:

Change *p* to *z*. What word did you make? *(whiz)*

Change *wh* to *qu*. What word did you make? *(quiz)*

Change z to *ck*. What word did you make? *(quick)*

Change *i* to *a*. What word did you make? *(quack)*

High-Frequency Words

RETEACH ***family, work, books, read, about, by, writing, grew*** Write the word *fan* and have children read it. Then write the word *family* next to fan and have children read the word. **How are these words the same? How are they different? Let's read them again:**

fan family

Repeat the procedure with *walk/work*, *look/books*, *out/about*, *try/by*, and *bring/writing*.

Read: *My Family Quilt*

My Family Quilt

Distribute copies of the book to children and read the title aloud. Again have children frame the words *family* and *quilt*. Point to the word *My*. Explain that *my* shows that something belongs to someone. Ask: **What belongs to this person?** (*the family quilt*) Tell children that other words that show belonging and ownership are *her*, *his*, *our*, *your*, and *their*.

Ask children to point to the names of the people who wrote and illustrated the book. Read the names aloud. Then choral read the book with children. Let your voice fade if children start to gain control of the text.

Phonics: Reading Sentences with /kw/qu, /hw/wh

PRETEACH Distribute *Intervention Practice Book* page 44 to children. Point to the first sentence and have children read it aloud. Ask them to find the word *when* and frame it with their fingers. Then work with children to complete the page.

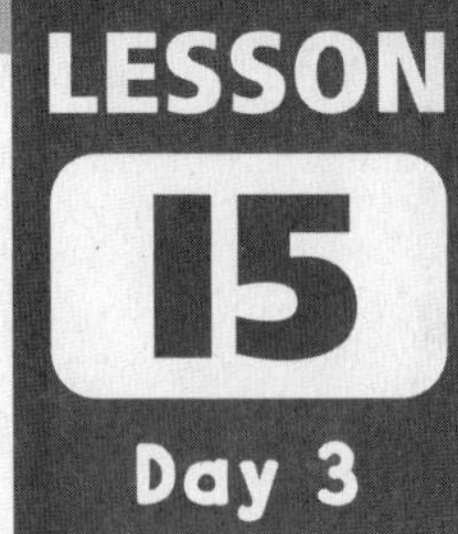

Warm-Up: Phonemic Awareness

Phoneme Blending Tell children that they are going to play a guessing game. Then say: **I'm thinking of a word that is something a duck says. It is /kw/-/a/-/k/. What's my word?** (*quack*) Continue with the following words: /hw/-/e/-/n/ (*when*), /hw/-/i/-/p/ (*whip*), and /kw/-/i/-/l/ (*quill*).

MATERIALS

Word Builder

Word Builder Cards c, d, h, h, i, m, p, r, w, z

Picture Cards: bat, bed, boat, bug, cat, clock, desk, fish, goat, jet, quilt, red, train, wagon, zebra

My Family Quilt

Phonics: Reading Sentences with /kw/qu, /hw/wh

RETEACH Help children blend and read new words and sentences shown. Have them read the sentence, blending each word in sequence. The high-frequency words are underlined; children should read these as a unit, not blending the sounds.

quest **whiz** **which** **quick**

When can <u>you</u> <u>come</u> <u>here</u>?

<u>They</u> did not quit.

We can whip <u>up</u> <u>some</u> <u>food</u>.

I <u>need</u> <u>help</u> <u>with</u> <u>the</u> quiz.

High-Frequency Words

RETEACH ***family, work, books, read, about, by, writing, grew*** Write the following sentence on tag board and display it in a pocket chart along with the Picture Cards *bed*, *clock*, *desk*, *goat*, *wagon*. Call on children to choose a Picture Card to complete the sentence and to read it aloud. Then ask: **Can you really work at a ______?**

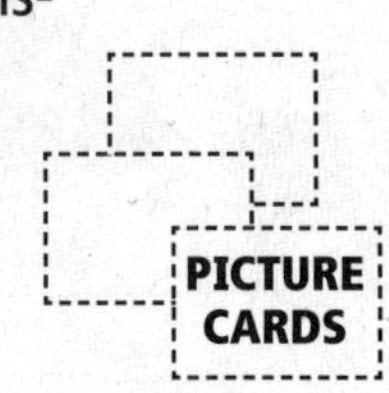

I work at my ______.

Do the same for the following sentence and Picture Cards *bat*, *bug*, *goat*, *jet*, *red*, *zebra*.

I like to read books about a ______.

Do the same for the following sentence and Picture Cards *boat*, *fish*, *jet*, *wagon*, *train*.

When Dad grew up, he went on a trip by ______.

Do the same for the following sentence and Picture Cards *cat*, *clock*, *quilt*, *desk*.

I am writing about our family ______.

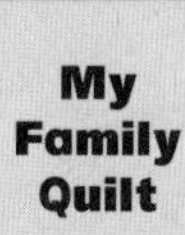

Read: *My Family Quilt*

Distribute copies of the book and have children read aloud the title. Explain that the boy is telling the story. Then guide children through the book as they read.

Pages 2–3: Have children read to find out what the quilt does.

Whose quilt is it? (*the boy's*) **What does the quilt do?** (*tells about him*) **Find and read the sentence that tells. Find and frame the word *where*. Tell them the boy lives in New Mexico.**

Pages 4–5: Have children read the pages to find out what else the quilt tells about.

What else does the quilt show? (*his house*) **Find and read the sentence that tells. Who does the quilt show?** (*the boy when he was a baby*) **Find the word that tells how the boy grew.** (*fast*)

Pages 6–7: Have children read the pages to find out more about the quilt.

What does Grandpa grow? (*corn*) **Where does he grow it?** (*on his farm*) **What is the cat's name?** (*Star*) **What does she like to do?** (*nap*)

Page 8: Have children read to find out how the quilt changed.

What was the quilt like at first? (*small*) **What happened to the quilt?** (*it grew.*)

Ask children to use the pictures to help summarize the book.

Phonics: Building Words

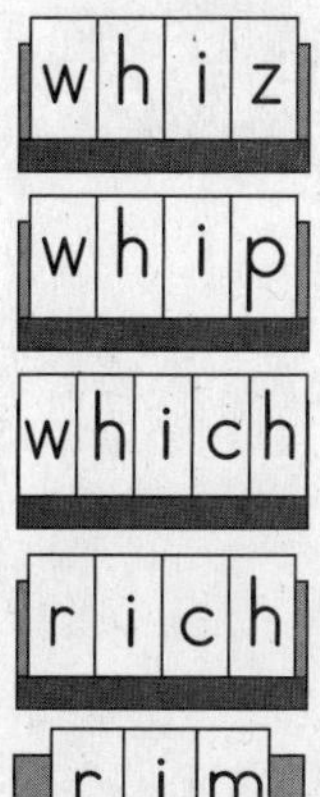

PRETEACH Put the letters *w*, *h*, *i*, and *z* in a Word Builder and have children do the same. Slide your hand under the letters as you blend the sounds—/hhwwiizz/. Then read the word naturally—*whiz*. Have children repeat after you. Then have children build and read new words.

Change *z* to *p*. What word did you make? *(whip)*

Change *p* to *ch*. What word did you make? *(which)*

Change *wh* to *r*. What word did you make? *(rich)*

Change *ch* to *m*. What word did you make? *(rim)*

Change *r* to *d*. What word did you make? *(dim)*

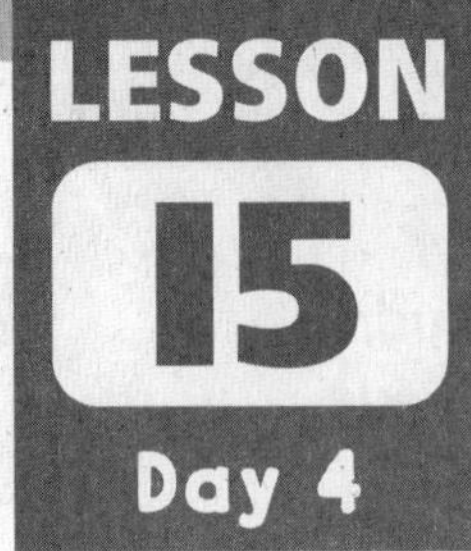

Warm-Up: Phonemic Awareness

Phoneme Segmentation Have children use the three boxes on the Write-on/Wipe-off Boards. Remind children that the boxes stand for the sounds in words. Show the Picture Card *nut* and ask: **What is the first sound you hear in *nut*?** (/n/) Have children place a disk in the first box. Then have children name the second sound in *nut* (/u/) and place a disk in the second box. Then have them identify the last sound in *nut* (/t/) and place a disk in the third box. Point to each box in sequence as children say the word. **How many sounds do you hear in *nut*?** (*three*) Repeat this procedure with the following Picture Cards: *six*, *sock*, *sun*, *ten*.

PICTURE CARDS

MATERIALS

Picture Cards: nut, six, sock, sun, ten

Write-on/Wipe-off Boards with disks

Word Cards for about, by, family, read, there, who, work

Word Builder

Word Builder Cards c, c, h, i, k, p, q, t, u, w, z

My Family Quilt

Phonics: Building Words

RETEACH Put the letters *q*, *u*, *i* and *t* in a Word Builder and have children do the same. Slide your hand under the letters as you blend the sounds—/kkwwiitt/. Then read the word naturally—*quit*. Have children repeat after you. Then have children build and read new words.

Change *t* to *z*. What word did you make? (*quiz*)

Change *z* to *ck*. What word did you make? (*quick*)

Change *qu* to *ch*. What word did you make? (*chick*)

Change *ck* to *p*. What word did you make? (*chip*)

Change *ch* to *wh*. What word did you make? (*whip*)

Distribute *Intervention Practice Book* page 45 to children.

family

work

read

about

by

who

there

High-Frequency Words

RETEACH ***family, work, read, about, by, who, there***
Distribute word cards with the words listed above. Have partners take turns displaying the words for each other and reading them. After they read each word, have children spell the word and then repeat the word. Then have them spell the word again and write it on a sheet of paper.

My Family Quilt

Read: *My Family Quilt*

Focus Skill **Characters.** Remind children that the characters are the people in a story. Knowing about a story's characters can help readers understand the story. Have children read *My Family Quilt* and then together make a list of the characters in the story.

Family
me (the narrator, the baby)
Grandpa
Star (the cat)

Phonics: Blends with l; Inflection -es

PRETEACH Write the blends *bl*, *cl*, *fl*, *gl*, *pl*, and *sl* at the top of a sheet of chart paper. Have children suggest words that contain each blend and say what letters they would need to write the words. Then write the words underneath the appropriate heading. Then have children read each column of words. End the activity by pointing to words at random and having children read the words.

Write the following words on chart paper, with the base word above its inflected form: *box-boxes, rush-rushes, porch-porches, pass-passes, buzz-buzzes*. Remind children that they have learned that the ending *-s* can be added to many words. Then explain that for words that end with certain letters, the ending is *-es* instead of just *-s*. Read each word pair to children, pointing to *-es* as you read the inflected form.

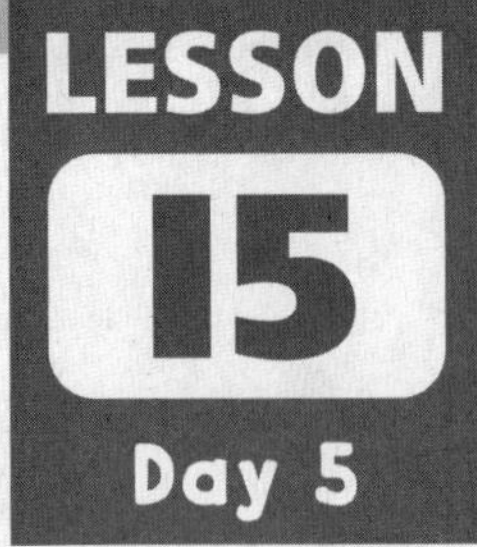

Warm-Up: Phonemic Awareness

MATERIALS

Write-on/Wipe off Boards

Word Cards for about, by, family, read, take, there

Word Builder

Word Builder Cards b, d, e, f, h, i, n, r, s, t, u

Phoneme Blending Tell children that together you are going to play a game. Tell them that you are going to say some words sound by sound and they should listen to see if they can put the sounds together to figure out the word. Listen: **/b/-/l/-/a/-/k/. What word does /b/-/l/-/a/-/k/ say?** (*black*). Continue with the following words:

/c/-/l/-/ā/-/s/ (*class*)	**/f/-/l/-/u/-/sh/** (*flush*)	**/g/-/l/-/ā/-/z/** (*glaze*)
/p/-/l/-/u/-/m/ (*plum*)	**/s/-/l/-/ā/-/t/** (*slate*)	**/b/-/l/-/ā/-/d/** (*blade*)

Phonics: Blends with l; Inflections -es

RETEACH Write the word *blink* on a Write-on/ Wipe-off Board and have children do the same. Then have them read the word. Ask: **What letters should we write if we want to change *blink* to *block*?** (*ock*) **Let's do that.** Continue the activity with the words *click* and *clock*; *flag* and *flat*; *glum* and *glob*; *plot* and *plan*; and *slam* and *slim*.

Also using the Write-on/Wipe-off boards, write *fox* and have children do the same. Have them read the word. Then ask: **What letters should we add at the end to make *foxes*?** (*es*) **Let's do that.** Continue the activity with the words *miss-misses, punch-punches, dash-dashes, fizz-fizzes.*

High-Frequency Words

family
read
about
by
take
there

Cumulative Review *family, read, about, by, take, there*
Place the words in a pocket chart. Say aloud one of the words and use it in a sentence. Have a volunteer find and point to the word. Have children clap and say the spelling of the word. Then have them write it. Have children read aloud their list of words.

Read: Self-Selected Reading

Have children select a book to read from their browsing boxes. After they have completed their reading, have them tell you what they were most successful in during the reading of the book.

Phonics: R-controlled /ûr/er, ir, ur

PRETEACH Use the Word Builder and Word Builder Cards to model blending words.

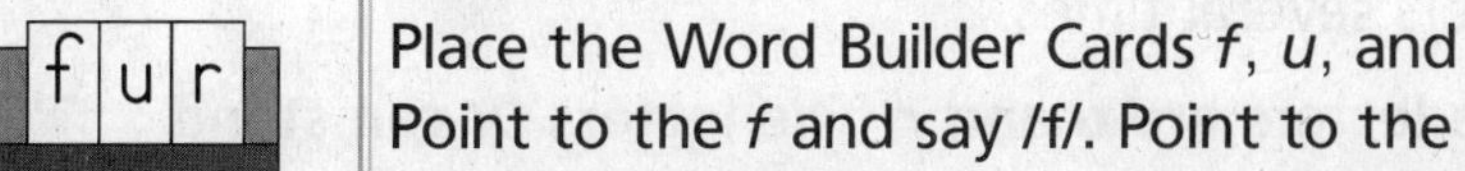

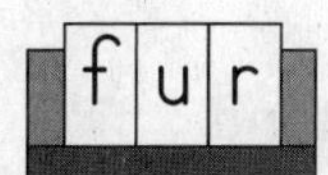

Place the Word Builder Cards *f*, *u*, and *r* in the Word Builder. Point to the *f* and say /f/. Point to the *ur* and say /ûr/.

Slide the *ur* next to the *f*. Move your hand under the letters and blend by elongating /ffûûrr/. Have children repeat. Then have children read the word *fur* along with you.

Follow the same procedure for the words *sir*, *dirt*, *bird*, *burn*, and *her*.

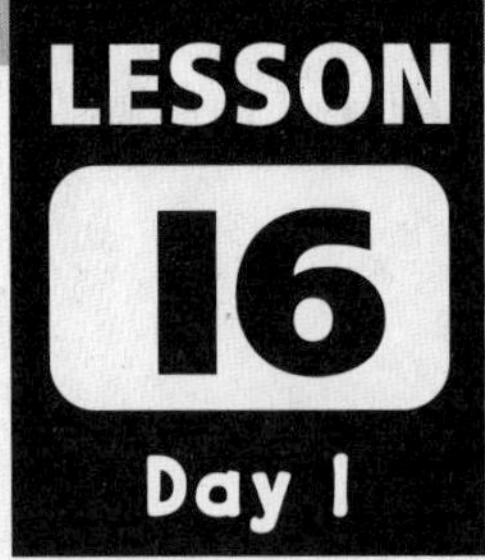

Warm-Up: Phonemic Awareness

Onset and Rime Tell children that you are going to say some words, but you are going to say them in parts. Have children listen to see if they can figure out the word. Demonstrate by saying ***/p/-urse*—What word did I say?** (*purse*)

/th/-ird	**/j/-erm**	**/st/-ern**
/p/-erch	**/b/-urst**	**/sk/-irt**

MATERIALS

Word Cards for find, follow, found, four, full, these, way, were

Word Builder

Word Builder Cards b, d, e, f, h, i, n, r, s, u

Follow Me!

Phonics: R-controlled /ûr/er, ir, ur

RETEACH **Blending** Print *er* on the board. **These letters are *e* and *r*. The letters *er* can stand for the /ûr/ sound that you hear at the end of the word *her*.** Point to the letters *er* and say /ûr/. Have children repeat the sound as you touch the letters several times.

Print *ir*. **These letters are *i* and *r*. The letters *ir* can stand for the /ûr/ sound in the middle of the word *girl*.** Point to the letters *ir* and say /ûr /. Have children repeat the sound as you touch the letters several times.

Print *ur*. **These letters are *u* and *r*. The letters *ur* can stand for the /ûr/ sound that you hear in the word *curl*.** Point to the letters *ur* and say /ûr/. Have children repeat the sound as you touch the letters several times.

Use the Word Builder Cards and a pocket chart to model blending words.

Place the Word Builder cards *s*, *i*, and *r* in the Word Builder with the *i* and *r* next to each other. Point to the *ir* and say /ûr/. Point to the *s* and say /s/. Slide the *s* next to the *ir*. Move your hand under the letters and blend the sounds, elongating them /ssûûrr/. Have children repeat after you. Then say the word naturally—*sir*. Have children do the same.

Then follow the same procedure with the word *her* for /ûr/*er* and the word *burn* for /ûr/*ur*.

High-Frequency Words

PRETEACH ***way, these, found, find, follow, full, were, four*** Display the word card *way*. **This word is *way*. I know my way home. Read the word with me—*way*. Spell the word with me—*w-a-y*. Read the word with me. What is this word?** (*way*)

way
these
found
find
follow
full
were
four

Follow the same procedure for the words *these*, *found*, *find*, *follow*, *full*, *were*, and *four*.

these—**These are my good friends.**

found—**He found his missing book.**

find—**Will you help me find my keys?**

follow—**Please, follow me this way.**

were, full—**The glasses were full of milk.**

four—**A square has four sides.**

Then place the eight words in a pocket chart and have volunteers read the words, as you randomly point to them.

Read: *Follow Me!*

Follow Me!

Distribute copies of the book and have children put their finger on the title. Read the title aloud. Then have children frame the word *follow*. Echo read the book with children. Read page 2 aloud and then have children read it to you. Follow this procedure throughout the book.

Phonics: Word Building with /ûr/er, ir, ur

PRETEACH Place the letters *f*, *u*, and *r* in a Word Builder and have children do the same. Model how to blend the word *fur*. Slide your hand under the letters as you slowly elongate the sounds /ffûûrr/. Have children do the same. Then read the word naturally—*fur*. Have children do the same.

Have children blend and read new words by telling them:

Change *f* to *b*. Add *n* after *r*. What word did you make? *(burn)*

Change *u* to *i*. Change *n* to *d*. What word did you make? *(bird)*

Change *b* to *h*. Take *d* away. Change *i* to *e*. What word did you make? *(her)*

Distribute *Intervention Practice Book* page 46 to children.

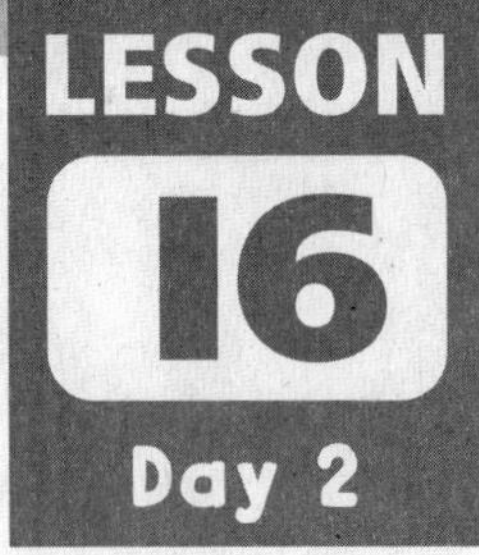

MATERIALS

Word Builder

Word Builder Cards d, e, f, h, i, n, r, s, t

Follow Me!

Warm-Up: Phonemic Awareness

Phoneme Isolation Say the word *bird* aloud and have children repeat it. Tell children to listen to the /ûr/ sound in the middle of *bird*. Then say the words *fur* and *fun*. Ask: **Which of these words has the /ûr/ sound that you hear in *bird*?** (*fur*) Continue with the words *curl*, *card*, *her*; *burst*, *pan*, *skirt*; *stir*, *surf*, *city*.

Phonics: Word Building with /ûr/er, ir, ur

RETEACH Place the letters *d*, *i*, *r*, and *t* in a Word Builder and have children do the same. Model how to blend the word *dirt*. Slide your hand under the letters as you slowly elongate the sounds /ddûûrrtt/. Have children do the same. Then read the word naturally—*dirt*. Have children do the same.

Have children blend and read new words by telling them:

Change *d* to *sh*. What word did you make? *(shirt)*

Take away *h* and *t*. What word did you make? *(sir)*

Change *s* to *f*. What word did you make? *(fir)*

Change *i* to *e*. Add *n* after the *r*. What word did you make? *(fern)*

Change *f* to *h*. Change *n* to *d*. What word did you make? *(herd)*

Take *d* away. What word did you make? *(her)*

Change *e* to *u*. Add *t* after the *r*. What word did you make? *(hurt)*

High-Frequency Words

RETEACH ***way, these, found, find, follow, full, were, four***
Write the word *play* and have children read it. Then write the word *way* next to play and have children read the word. **How are these words the same? How are they different? Let's read them again:**

play   way

Repeat the procedure with *they/these*, *out/found*, *in/find*, *now/follow*, *fly/full*, *where/were*, and *our/four*.

Read: *Follow Me!*

Follow Me!

Distribute copies of the book to children and have a volunteer read the title aloud. Have children frame the word *follow*. Ask children to point to the names of the people who wrote and illustrated the book. Read the names aloud. Then choral read the book with children. Let your voice fade if children start to gain control of the text.

Phonics: Reading Sentences with /ûr/er, ir, ur

PRETEACH Distribute *Intervention Practice Book* page 47 to children. Point to the first sentence and have children read it aloud. Ask them to find the word *shirt*, frame it with their fingers, and circle the word. Then work with children to complete the page.

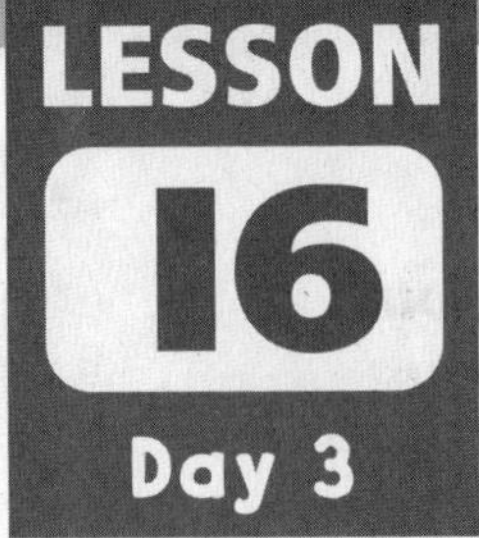

LESSON 16 Day 3

Warm-Up: Phonemic Awareness

Phoneme Blending Tell children that they are going to play a guessing game. Then say: **I'm thinking of a word that is an animal that flies. It is /b/-/ûr/-/d/. What's my word?** (*bird*) Continue with the following words: /d/-/ûr/-/t/ (*dirt*), /b/-/ûr/-/n/ (*burn*), and /s/-/û/-/r/ (*sir*).

MATERIALS

Word Builder

Word Builder Cards b, d, f, h, i, n, p, r, r, s, t, u

Picture Cards: bat, boat, box, bug, clock, cup, egg, goat, mop, mule, nest, red, rose, ship, six, thumb, wagon

Follow Me!

Phonics: Reading Sentences with /ûr/er, ir, ur

RETEACH Help children blend and read new words and sentences shown. Have them read the sentence, blending each word in sequence The high-frequency words are underlined; children should read these as a unit, not blending the sounds.

hurt **fir** **fern** **fur**

Did the car turn and go our way?

Don't let the food burn.

Try to stir the eggs.

Did she get dirt on her shirt??

High-Frequency Words

RETEACH ***way, these, found, find, follow, full, were, four***

Write the following sentence on tag board and display it in a pocket chart along with the Picture Cards *bat*, *bug*, *ship*, *wagon*, *thumb*, *mule*. Call on children to choose a Picture Card to complete the sentence and to read it aloud. Then ask: **Would you really find a _____ in a park?**

PICTURE CARDS

We found four dogs and one _____ in the park.

Do the same for the following sentence and Picture Cards *red*, *clock*, *boat*, *wagon*, *cup*, *nest*.

These new friends were on the _____.

Do the same for the following sentence and Picture Cards *rose*, *goat*, *mule*, *six*, *egg*, *wagon*.

I will follow the _____ all the way to the farm.

Do the same for the following sentence and Picture Cards *box*, *bug*, *cup*, *thumb*, *mop*, *nest*.

Did you find a full _____?

Read: *Follow Me!*

Distribute copies of the book and have children read aloud the title. Ask what this book is about. Then guide children through the book as they read.

Pages 2–3: Have children read to find out what Cat and Bird wanted to do.

What did Cat and Bird want to do? (*eat*) **What did they have?** (*a basket of food*) **What did Bird say to Cat? Find and frame those words.** (*Follow me!*)

Pages 4–5: Have children read the pages to find out where Bird leads Cat.

What did Bird find? (*a city*) **Find and read the sentence that tells. What did Cat think about the city?** (*didn't like it*) **So what did Bird say to Cat?** (*Follow me!*)

Pages 6–7: Have children read the pages to find out where Bird leads Cat now.

What did Bird find now? (*a park*) **What did Cat think?** (*Cat didn't like it*) **What did Bird do now? Find and read the sentence that tells.** (*Bird turned and followed Cat.*)

Page 8: Have children read to find out what happened when Bird followed Cat.

What happened? (*They found the perfect place to eat.*) **Where were they?** (*Back where they started.*)

Ask children to use the pictures to help summarize the book.

Phonics: Building Words

PRETEACH Put the letters *p*, *u*, *r*, and r in a Word Builder and have children do the same. Slide your hand under the letters as you blend the sounds—/ppûûrrrr/. Then read the word naturally—*purr*. Have children repeat after you. Then have children build and read new words.

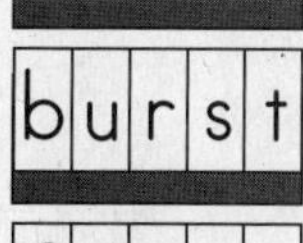

Change *p* to *b*. What word did you make? *(burr)*

Change the second *r* to *n*. What word did you make? *(burn)*

Change *n* to *st*. What word did you make? *(burst)*

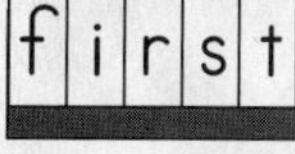

Change *bu* to *fi*. What word did you make? *(first)*

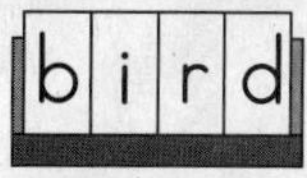

Change *f* to *b*. Change the *st* to *d*. What word did you make? *(bird)*

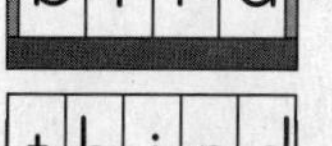

Change *b* to *th*. What word did you make? *(third)*

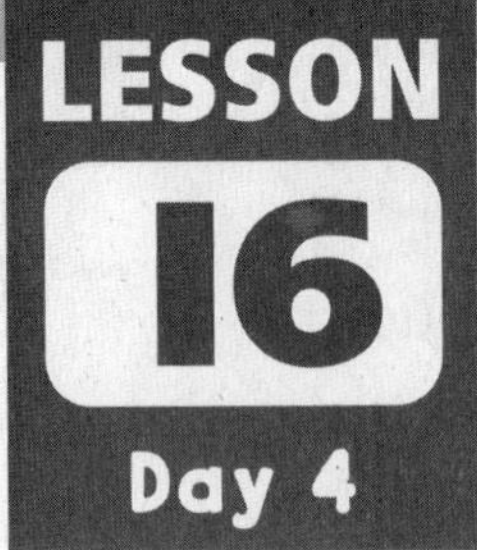

MATERIALS

Picture Cards: kite, nine, pin, red

Write-on/Wipe-off Boards with disks

Word Cards for find, found, four, full, grew, these, were, work

Word Builder

Word Builder Cards d, h, u, q, r, s, t, u, û, û

Follow Me!

Warm-Up: Phonemic Awareness

Phoneme Segmentation Have children use the three boxes on the Write-on/Wipe-off Boards. Remind children that the boxes stand for the sounds in words. Show the Picture Card *kite* and ask: **What is the first sound you hear in kite?** (/k/) Have children place a disk in the first box. Then have children name the second sound in kite (/ī/) and place a disk in the second box. Then have them identify the last sound in kite (/t/) and place a disk in the third box. Point to each box in sequence as children say the word. **How many sounds do you hear in kite?** (*three*) Repeat this procedure with the following Picture Cards: *nine*, *thumb*, *pin*, *red*.

PICTURE CARDS

Phonics: Building Words

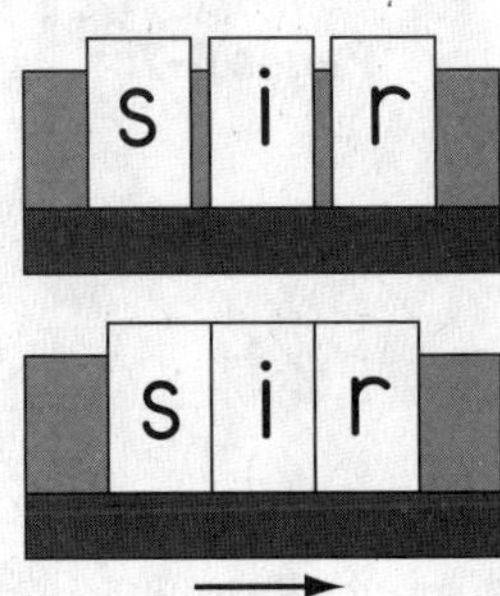

RETEACH Put the letters *s*, *i* and *r* in a Word Builder and have children do the same. Slide your hand under the letters as you blend the sounds—/ssûûrr/. Then read the word naturally—*sir*. Have children repeat after you. Then have children build and read new words.

Change *s* to *d*. Add *t* after *dir*. What word did you make? (*dirt*)

Change *d* to *sh*. What word did you make? (*shirt*)

Change *sh* to *qu*. Take *r* away. What word did you make? (*quit*)

Distribute *Intervention Practice Book* page 48 to children.

High-Frequency Words

these
found
find
full
were
four
work
grew

RETEACH ***these, found, find, full, were, four, work, grew*** Distribute word cards with the words listed above. Have partners take turns displaying the words for each other and reading them. After they read each word, have children spell the word and then repeat the word. Then have them spell the word again and write it on a sheet of paper.

Read: *Follow Me!*

Focus Skill **Setting.** Remind children that the setting is when and where a story takes place. Knowing about the setting can help readers picture and understand what happens in a story. Have children read *Follow Me!* and then together make a list of places Bird and Cat went.

Where Did They Go?
city
park

Phonics: Contractions 've, 're

PRETEACH Write the letters *'ve* and *'re* at the top of a sheet of chart paper. Explain that *'ve* and *'re* form contractions that mean *have* and *are* when they are added to other words. Write *I've, you've*, and *we've* below *'ve* and read aloud each contraction and the two words it stands for: *I've-I have*; *you've-you have*; *we've-we have*. Use a similar procedure with *'re* and *they're*, *we're* and *you're*. End the activity by pointing to words at random and having children read the words.

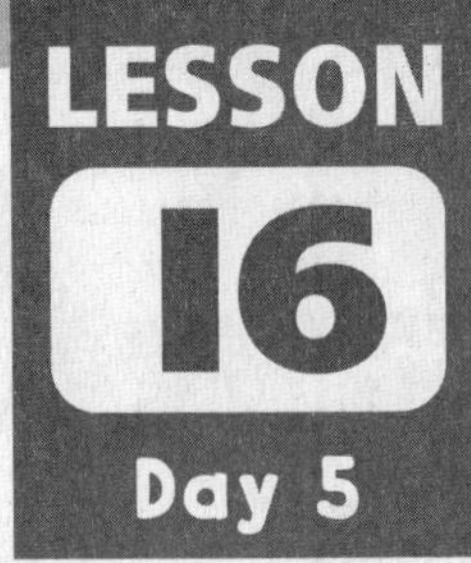

LESSON 16 Day 5

MATERIALS

Write-on/Wipe off Boards

Word Cards for about, by, four, full, read, way, were

Word Builder

Word Builder Cards c, d, d, e, f, g, g, i, l, m, p, u, w

Warm-Up: Phonemic Awareness

Phoneme Blending Tell children that together you are going to play a game of "Fix It." Tell them that you are going to say some words that are all broken and they should listen to see if they can put the sounds together to figure out the word. **Listen: /b/-/ûr/-/th/. What word does /b/-/ûr/-/th/ say?** (*birth*) Continue with the following words:

/s/-/ûr/-/f/ (*surf*)	**/s/-/t/-/ûr/** (*stir*)	**/k/-/ûr/-/b/** (*curb*)
/tw/-/ûr/-/l/ (*twirl*)	**/t//ûr/-/m/** (*term*)	**/c/-/l/-/ûr/-/ck/** (*clerk*)

Phonics: Contractions 've and 're

RETEACH Write the word *I've* on a Write-on/ Wipe-off Board and have children do the same. Then have them read the word. Ask: **What letters should we write if we want to change *I've* to *you've*?** (*you*) **Let's do that.** Continue the activity with the following words: *we've* and *they've*. Repeat the activity, using the words *you're* and *they're*, and *we're* and *you're*.

full
were
four
read
by
about
way

High-Frequency Words

Cumulative Review *full, were, four, read, by, about, way*
Place the words in a pocket chart. Say aloud one of the words and use it in a sentence. Have a volunteer find and point to the word. Have children clap and say the spelling of the word. Then have them write it. Have children read aloud their list of words.

Read: Self-Selected Reading

Have children select a book to read from their browsing boxes. After they have completed their reading, have them show you words they figured out on their own.

Phonics: Syllable /əl/-le

PRETEACH Use the Word Builder and Word Builder Cards to model blending words.

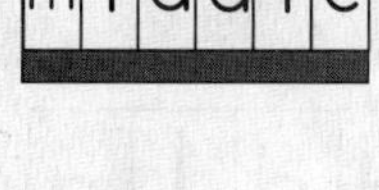

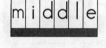

Place the Word Builder Cards *m*, *i*, *d*, *d*, *l*, and *e* in the Word Builder. Point to the *m* and say /m/. Point to the *i* and say /i/.

Slide the *i* next to the *m*. Move your hand under the letters and blend the sounds, elongating them /mmii/. Have children repeat after you. Point to the *dd* and say /d/. Have children repeat. Slide the *dd* next to the *mi*. Move your hand under the letters and blend the sounds, elongating them /mmiidddd/. Point to the letters *le*. Say /əl/. Slide the *le* next to *midd*. Slide your hand under *middle* and blend by elongating the sounds /mmiiddddəll/. Have children repeat. Then have children read the word *middle* along with you.

Follow the same procedure for the words *fiddle*, *wiggle*, *giggle*, *puddle*, and *cuddle*.

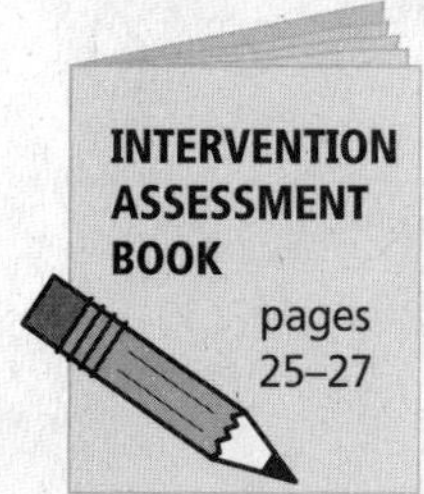

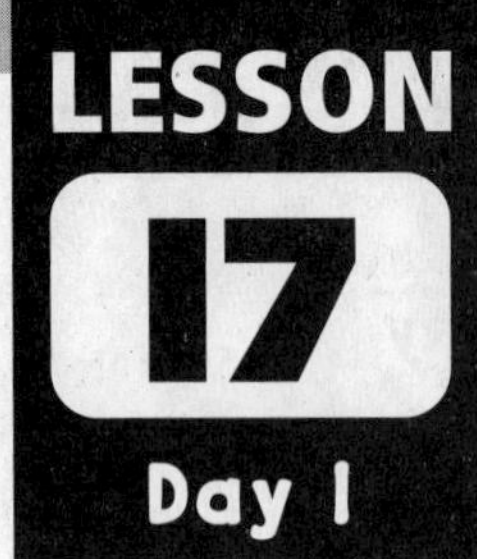

Warm-Up: Phonemic Awareness

Onset and Rime Tell children that you are going to say some words, but you are going to say them in parts. Have children listen to see if they can figure out the word. Demonstrate by saying **/n/-oodle—What word did I say?** (*noodle*)

/s/-imple	**/m/-eddle**	**/br/-ittle**	**/dr/-izzle**
/k/-obbler	**/s/-addle**	**/k/-uddle**	**/m/-iddle**

MATERIALS

Word Cards each, great, other, place, school, talk, together

Word Builder

Word Builder Cards c, d, d, e, f, i, l, m, n, p, u, z, z

Alphabet Masters Ll, Ee

My Friend

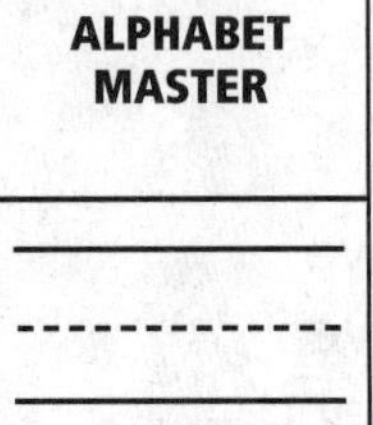

Phonics: Syllable /əl/-le

RETEACH **Blending** Display Alphabet Masters *Ll* and *Ee*. **These letters are *l* and *e*. When grouped together at the end of a two-syllable word, the letters *le* can stand for the /əl/ sound, the sound in words such as *apple*, *bubble*, and *settle*.** Have children repeat the sound as you touch the letter several times.

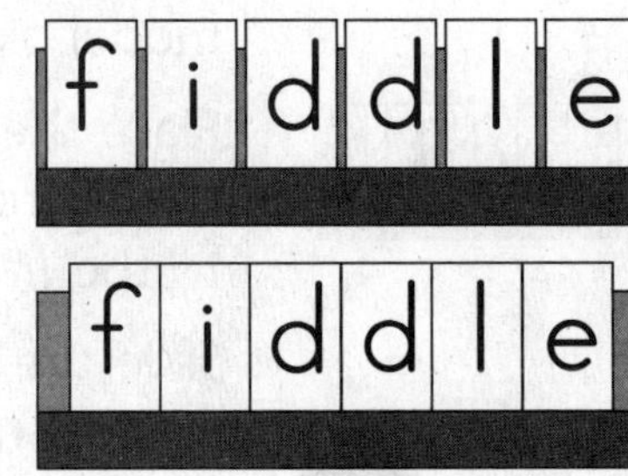

Use the Word Builder Cards and a pocket chart to model blending words.

Place the Word Builder Cards *f, i, d, d, l,* and *e* in the Word Builder. Point to the *f* and say /f/. Point to the *i* and say /i/.

Slide the *i* next to the *f*. Move your hand under the letters and blend the sounds, elongating them /ffii/. Have children repeat after you.

Point to *dd* and say /d/. Slide *dd* next to the *fi*. Move your hand under the letters and blend the sounds, elongating them /ffiidd/. Have children repeat after you.

Point to *le* and say /əl/. Slide *le* next to *fidd*. Move your hand under the letters and blend the sounds, elongating them /ffiidddələl/. Then say the word naturally—*fiddle*. Have children do the same.

High-Frequency Words

PRETEACH ***together, talk, each, other, school, place, great*** Display the word card *together*. **This word is *together*. My friend and I like to play together. Read the word with me—*together*. Spell the word with me —*t-o-g-e-t-h-e-r*. Read the word with me. What is this word?** (*together*)

together

talk
each
other
school
place
great

Follow the same procedure for the words *talk*, *each*, *other*, *school*, *place*, and *great*.

talk—**When I am scared, I *talk* to my parents.**

each—**We *each* have our own style.**

other—**One dog is brown, and the *other* is gray.**

school—**We go to [name of school] *school*.**

place—**That is your *place* in line.**

great—**They had a *great* idea for a party.**

Then place the seven words in a pocket chart and have volunteers read the words, as you randomly point to them.

Read: *My Friend*

Story words Write *uncle*, *stories*, and *whistle* on the board. Point to the words, say them aloud, and have children repeat them. Help children read these words as needed. Distribute copies of the book and have children put their fingers on the title. Have children follow along as you read the title aloud. Ask children what they think the story will be about. Echo read the book with children. Read page 2 aloud and then have children read it to you. Follow this procedure throughout the book.

Phonics: Word Building with Syllable /əl/-le

PRETEACH Place the letters *m*, *i*, *d*, *d*, *l*, and *e* in a Word Builder and have children do the same. Model how to blend the word *middle*. Slide your hand under the letters as you slowly elongate the sounds /mmiiddələl/. Have children do the same. Then read the word naturally—*middle*. Have children do the same.

Have children blend and read new words by telling them:

Change the *i* to *e*. What word did you make? *(meddle)*

Change the *e* to *u*. What word did you make? *(muddle)*

Change the *m* to *c*. What word did you make? *(cuddle)*

Change the *c* to *p*. What word did you make? *(puddle)*

Change the *dd* to *zz*. What word did you make? *(puzzle)*

Distribute *Intervention Practice Book* page 49 to children.

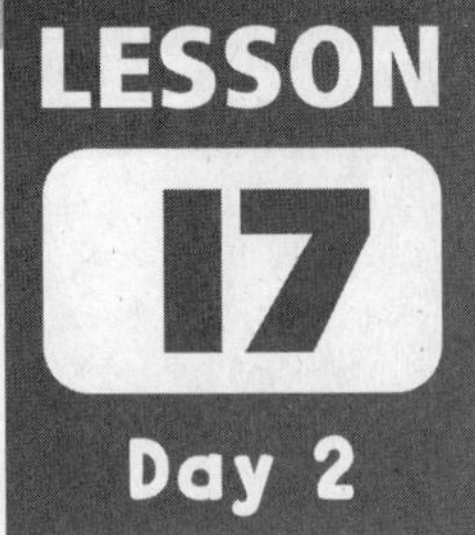

Warm-Up: Phonemic Awareness

Phoneme Isolation Say the word *struggle* aloud and have children repeat it. Tell children to listen to the /əl/ sound at the end of *struggle*. Then say the words *trouble* and *stirring*. Ask: **Which of these words has the /əl/ sound you hear at the end of *struggle*?** (*trouble*) Continue with the words *cycle*, *sick*, *gentle*; *noble*, *follow*, *people*; *able*, *beagle*, *books*.

MATERIALS

Word Builder

Word Builder Cards b, e, g, g, g, i, j, l, o, t, t, w

My Friend

Phonics: Word Building with Syllable /əl/-le

RETEACH Place the letters *w*, *i*, *g*, *g*, *l*, and *e* in a Word Builder and have children do the same. Model how to blend the word *wiggle*. Slide your hand under the letters as you slowly elongate the sounds /wwiiggələl/. Have children do the same. Then read the word naturally—*wiggle*. Have children do the same.

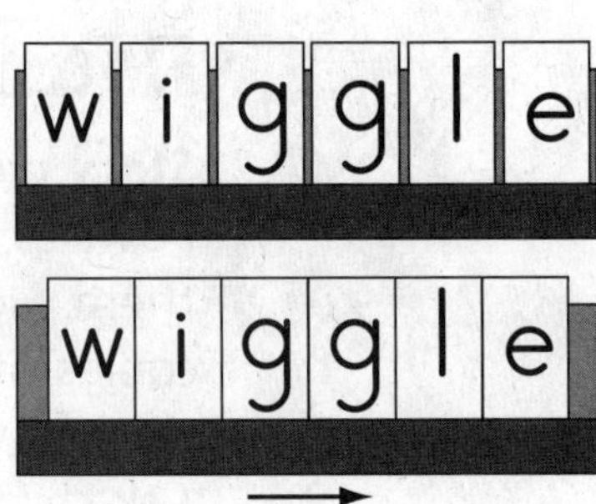

Have children blend and read new words by telling them:

Change *w* to *j*. What word did you make? *(jiggle)*

Change the *j* to *g*. What word did you make? *(giggle)*

Change *i* to *o*. What word did you make? *(goggle)*

Change the first *g* to *b*. What word did you make? *(boggle)*

Change the *gg* to *tt*. What word did you make? *(bottle)*

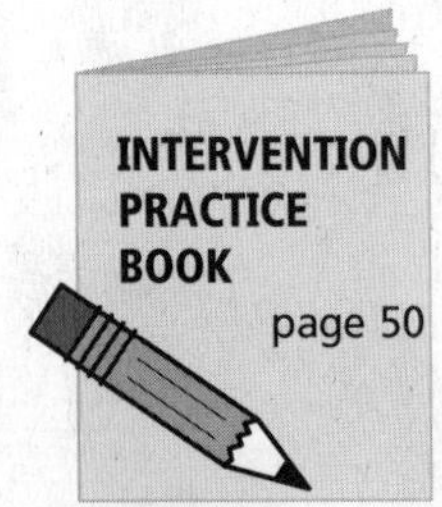

High-Frequency Words

RETEACH ***together, talk, each, other, school, place, great***
Write the words *to*, *get*, and *her* on the board and have children read them. Then write the word *together* next to *to*, *get*, and *her* and have children read the word. **How are these words the same? How are they different? Let's read them again.**

to **get** **her** **together**

Repeat the procedure with *walk/talk*, *eat/each*, *the/other*, *too/school*, *play/place*, and *eat/great*.

Read: *My Friend*

Distribute copies of the book to children and read the title aloud. Point to the word *My*. Explain to the children that this story is written in the first person, meaning that the story is told as though the author is talking about himself. **Whenever you tell a story with *I* in it, you are using the first person.** Ask children to point to the names of the people who wrote and illustrated the book. Read the names aloud. Then choral read the book with children. Let your voice fade if children start to gain control of the text.

Phonics: Reading Sentences with /əl/-le

PRETEACH Distribute *Intervention Practice Book* page 50 to children. Point to the first sentence and have children read it aloud. Ask them to find the word *fiddle*, frame it with their fingers, and circle the word. Then work with children to complete the page.

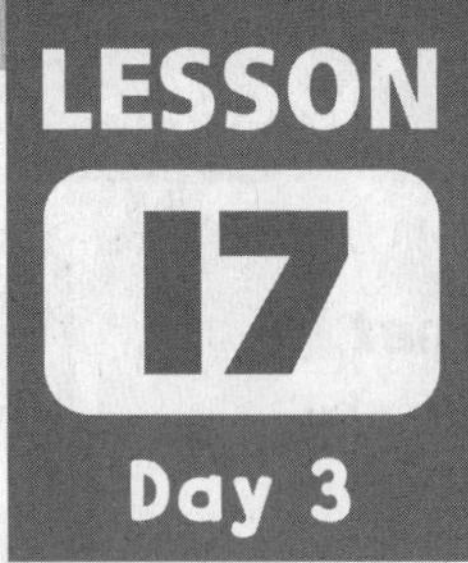

MATERIALS

Picture Cards cat, clam, desk, fan, fish, flag, goat, igloo, lamp, map, pig, thumb, train, vest, zebra

Word Builder

Word Builder Cards d, d, e, f, h, i, l, m, p, r, t, u

My Friend

Warm-Up: Phonemic Awareness

Phoneme Blending Tell children that they are going to play a guessing game. Then say: **I'm thinking of a word that is something a king lives in. It is /k/-/a/-/s/-/əl/. What's my word?** (*castle*) Continue with the following words: /p/-/ûr/-/p/-/ə l/ (*purple*), /t/-/a/-/k/-/ə l/ (*tackle*), and /hw/-/i/-/s/-/ə l/ (*whistle*).

Phonics: Reading Sentences with /əl/-le

RETEACH Help children blend and read new words and sentences shown. Have them read the sentence, blending each word in sequence. The high-frequency words are underlined; they should read these as a unit, not blending the sounds.

battle **chuckle** **bundle** **cattle**

<u>That</u> little bird can sing.

<u>The</u> kettle <u>was</u> hot.

Tickle her <u>on</u> <u>the</u> chin.

<u>You</u> <u>don't</u> paddle a ship.

High-Frequency Words

RETEACH ***together, talk, each, other, school, place, great*** Write the following sentence on tag board and display it in a pocket chart along with the Picture Cards *clam, desk, fan, fish, map, pig*. Call on children to choose a Picture Card to complete the sentence and to read it aloud. Then ask: **Can you really find a _________ at school?**

PICTURE CARDS

School is a great place for a _________.

Do the same for the following sentence and Picture Cards *vest, flag, lamp, fan, clam, thumb, train*.

They talk to each other by the _________.

Do the same for the following sentence and Picture Cards *cat, goat, igloo, pig, vest, zebra*.

We go to the farm together to see the _________.

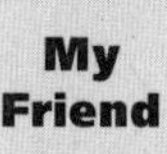

Read: *My Friend*

Distribute copies of the book and have children put their finger on the title. Ask what this book is about. Then guide children through as they read.

Pages 2–3: Have children read to find out who the friend is.

Who is the boy's friend? *(his uncle)* **Find and read the sentence that tells. When do they see each other? Find and frame the words that tell.** *(All the time.)*

Pages 4–5: Have children read the pages to find out what they do together.

What do they play? *(ball)* **Find and read the sentence that tells. Who do they like to tickle? Find and frame the words that tell.** *(each other)*

Pages 6–7: Have children read the pages to find out what else they do together.

What does the uncle do with the boy? *(puzzles)* **What does his uncle tell him?** *(stories and how to whistle)* **Find and read the sentences that tell.**

Page 8: Have children read to find out how the boy feels about his uncle.

How does the boy feel about being friends with his uncle? *(glad)*

Ask children to use the pictures to help summarize the book.

Phonics: Building Words

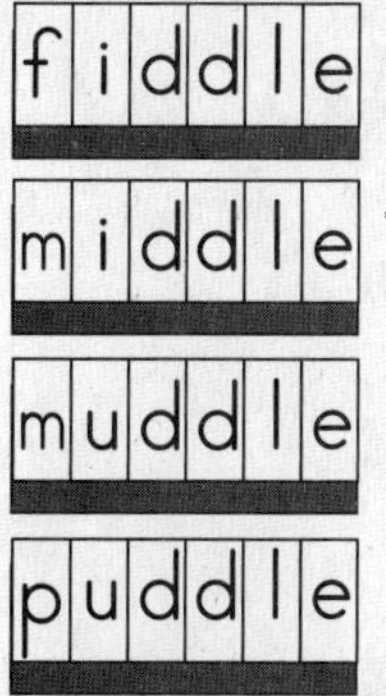

PRETEACH Place the letters *f, i, d, d, l,* and *e* in a Word Builder and have children do the same. Slide your hand under the letters as you blend the sounds—/ffiiddələl/. Then read the word naturally—*fiddle*. Have children repeat after you. Then have children build and read new words.

Change the *f* to *m*. What word did you make? *(middle)*

Change the *i* to *u*. What word did you make? *(muddle)*

Change the *m* to *p*. What word did you make? *(puddle)*

Change the *p* to *h*. What word did you make? *(huddle)*

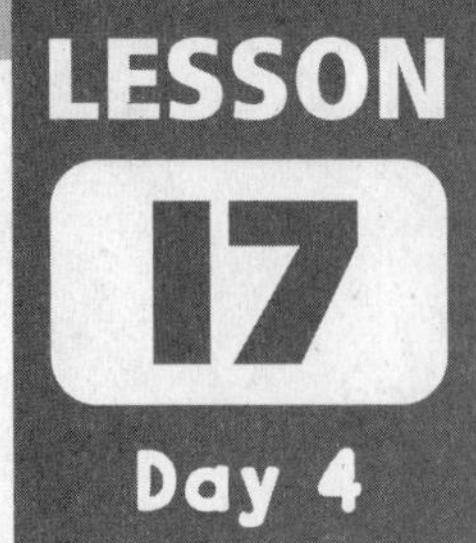

Warm-Up: Phonemic Awareness

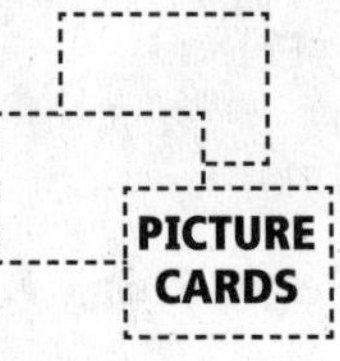

Phoneme Segmentation Distribute the four-box papers to children. Tell them that the boxes stand for sounds in words. Tell them to listen carefully as you say a word. Then say *puddle* and ask: **What is the first sound you hear in puddle?** (*/p/*) Have children place a disk in the first box to represent this sound. Next, have them name the second sound in *puddle /u/* and place a disk in the second box. Then have them identify the third sound */d/* and the last sound */l/*, and place the third and forth disks in those boxes. Point to the disks in sequence as children say the word. **How many sounds do you hear in *puddle*?** (*four*) Repeat this procedure with the words *juggle*, *giggle*, and *settle*.

MATERIALS

Papers with four boxes side by side, plus disks

Word Cards talk, each other, school, great, were, four

Word Builder

Word Builder Cards a, b, d, d, e, g, i, l, m, o, r, t, t

My Friend

Phonics: Building Words

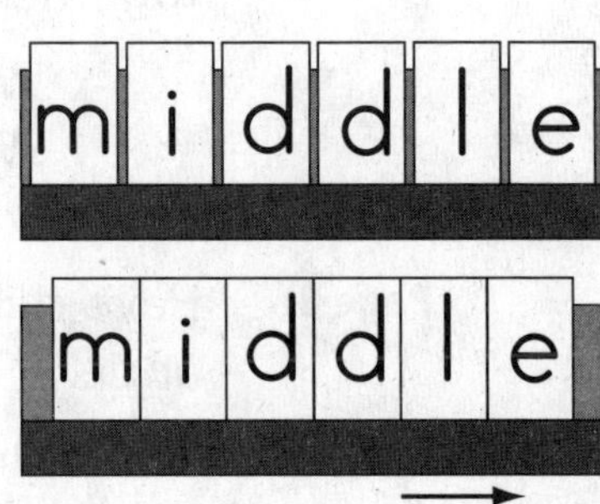

RETEACH Put the letters *m, i, d, d, l,* and *e* in a Word Builder and have children do the same. Slide your hand under the letters as you blend the sounds—/mmiidd əl/. Then read the word naturally —*middle*. Have children repeat after you. Then have children build and read new words.

Change the *m* to *gr*. What word did you make? *(griddle)*

Take away the *g*. What word did you make? *(riddle)*

Change the *idd* to *att*. What word did you make? *(rattle)*

Change the *r* to *b*. What word did you make? *(battle)*

Change the *a* to *o*. What word did you make? *(bottle)*

Distribute *Intervention Practice Book* page 51 to children.

talk

each

other

school

great

were

four

High-Frequency Words

RETEACH ***talk, each, other, school, great, were, four***

Distribute word cards with the words listed above. Have partners take turns displaying the words for each other and reading them. After they read each word, have children spell the word and then repeat the word. Then have them spell the word again and write it on a sheet of paper.

Read: *My Friend*

My Friend

Focus Skill Fact/Fiction Remind children that a fact is something true. Fiction is something that is made up. Understanding whether a story or parts of a story are fact or fiction can help readers understand what a story is about. Have children read *My Friend* and then together make a list of real and imaginary things the boy and his uncle could do together.

"Fact or Fiction?"

Play ball	fact
Walk on clouds	fiction
Tickle each other	fact
Do puzzles	fact
Fly to Mars	fiction
Make smile	fact

Phonics: Inflections er, est

PRETEACH Write the letters *er* and *est* at the top of a sheet of chart paper. Explain that the ending *-er* usually means *more than* and *-est* usually means *the most*. Have children suggest describing words (adjectives) that end with *-er*, such as *quicker*, and write the words underneath the heading *er*. Use the same procedure for *est*. Then have children read each column of words. End the activity by pointing to words at random and having children read the words.

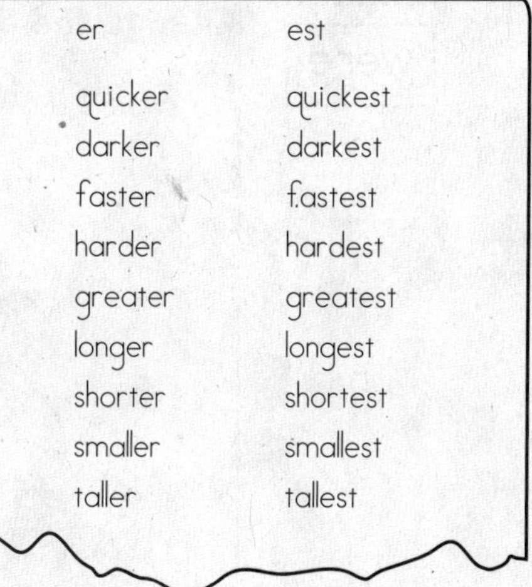

er	est
quicker	quickest
darker	darkest
faster	fastest
harder	hardest
greater	greatest
longer	longest
shorter	shortest
smaller	smallest
taller	tallest

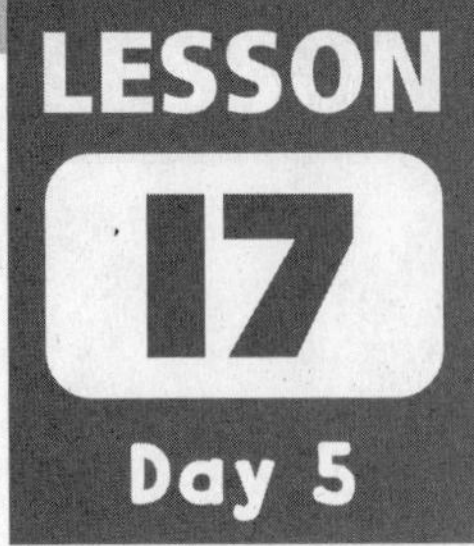

Warm-Up: Phonemic Awareness

Phoneme Blending Tell children that together you are going to play a game. Tell them that you are going to say some words sound by sound and they should listen to see if they can put the sounds together to figure out the word. **Listen: /p/-/e/-/b/-/əl/. What word does /p/-/e/-/b/-/əl/ say?** (*pebble*). Continue with the following words:

/s/-/a/-/d/-/əl/ *(saddle)*	**/s/-/ō/-/p/** *(soap)*
/r/-/i/-/d/-/əl/ *(riddle)*	**/b/-/ō/** *(bow)*
/m/-/ā/-/p/-/əl/ *(maple)*	**/r/-/ō/** *(row)*

MATERIALS

Write-on/Wipe-off Boards

Word Cards talk, each, other, school, these, were

Word Builder

Word Builder Cards a, b, d, l, o, p, r, s, t, w

Inflections: er, est

RETEACH Write the word *faster* on a Write-on/Wipe-off Board and have children do the same. Then have them read the word. Ask: **What letters should we write if we want to change *faster* to *fastest*?** (*est*) **Let's do that.** Continue the activity with the following words: *taller/tallest*, *shorter/shortest*, *longer/longest*, and *harder/hardest*.

High-Frequency Words

Cumulative Review *talk, each, other, school, these, were* Place the words in a pocket chart. Say aloud one of the words and use it in a sentence. Have a volunteer find and point to the word. Have children clap and say the spelling of the word. Then have them write it. Have children read aloud their list of words.

talk

each

other

school

these

were

Read: Self-Selected Reading

Have children select a book to read from their browsing boxes. After they have completed their reading, have them tell you what they were most successful in during the reading of the book.

Phonics: Long Vowel: /ō/ow, oa

PRETEACH Use the Word Builder and Word Builder Cards to model blending words.

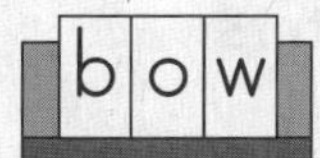

Place the Word Builder Cards *b, o,* and *w in* the Word Builder. Point to the *b* and say /b/. Point to the *ow* and say /ō/. Tell children that the letters *ow* often stand for the vowel /ō/.

Slide the *ow* next to the *b.* Move your hand under the letters and blend the sounds, elongating them /bbōō/. Have children repeat after you. Then have children read the word *bow* along with you.

Follow the same procedure for the words *low, row, road, soap,* and *boat,* pointing out that the letters *oa* as in *soap* also stand for the /ō/ sound.

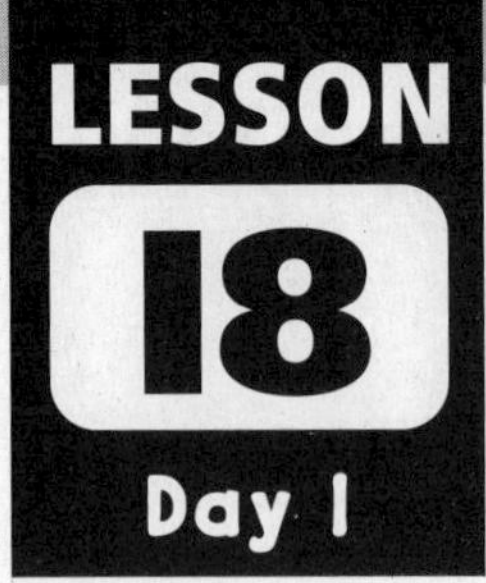

Warm-Up: Phonemic Awareness

Onset and Rime Tell children that you are going to say some words, but you are going to say them in parts. Have children listen to see if they can figure out the word. Demonstrate by saying: **/thr/-ow—What word did I say?** (*throw*)

/r/-ow	**/b/-oat**	**/l/-ow**	**/fl/-oat**
/l/-oad	**/s/-oak**	**/gr/-ow**	**/sh/-own**

MATERIALS

Word Cards door, kind, made, who, would

Word Builder

Word Builder Cards a, b, d, h, l, n, o, r, s, w

Rock Soup

Phonics: Long Vowel /ō/ow, oa

RETEACH **blending** Write *ow* on the board. **These letters are *o* and *w*. When they are together, the letters *o* and *w* can stand for the sound /ō/, the long sound of *o* at the beginning of words such as *own*, in the middle of words such as *shown*, and at the end of words such as *grow*.** Have children repeat the sound as you touch the letters *ow* several times.

Use the Word Builder Cards and a pocket chart to model blending words.

Place the Word Builder Cards *l*, *o*, and *w* in the Word Builder. Point to the *l* and say /l/. Point to the *ow* and say /ō/. Slide the *ow* next to the *l*. Move your hand under the letters and blend the sounds, elongating them /llōō/. Have children repeat after you. Then say the word naturally—*low*. Have children do the same.

Write *oa* on the board. **These letters are *o* and *a*. When they are together, the letters *o* and *a* can stand for the sound /ō/, the long sound of *o* that you hear at the beginning of words such as *oats* and in the middle of words such as *soak* and *float*.** Tell children that the spelling *oa* almost never appears at the end of words. Have children repeat the sound as you touch the letters *oa* several times.

Place the Word Builder cards *r*, *o*, *a*, and *d* in the Word Builder. Point to the *r* and say /r/. Point to the *oa* and say /ō/. Slide the *oa* next to the *r*. Move your hand under the letters and blend the sounds, elongating them /rrōō/. Have children repeat after you.

Point to the letter *d* and say /d/. Have children say /d/ as you point to *d*.

Slide *d* next to *roa*. Slide your hand under road and blend by elongating the sounds—/rrōōdd/. Have children repeat. Then have children read the word road along with you.

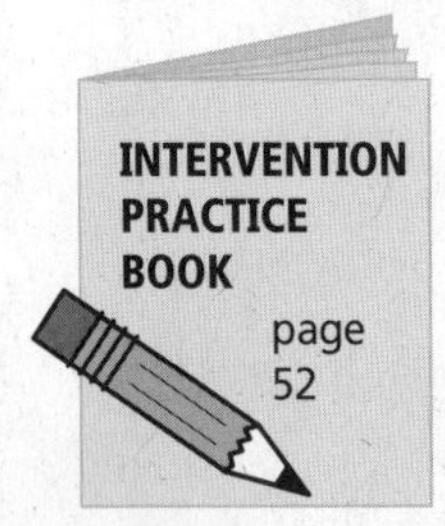

High-Frequency Words

who

would

kind

door

made

PRETEACH ***who, would, kind, door, made*** Display the word card *who*. **This word is *who*. Who is your best friend? Read the word with me—*who*. Spell the word with me—*w-h-o*. Read the word with me. What is this word?** (*who*)

Follow the same procedure for the words *would*, *kind*, *door*, and *made*. Then place the five words in a pocket chart and have volunteers read the words, as you randomly point to them.

Read: *Rock Soup*

Story Words Write the words *soup* and *greens* on the board. Read each word to children and have them repeat it. Give help if needed as children read the story.

Distribute copies of the book and have children put their fingers on the title. Have children follow along as you read the title aloud. Then have them frame the word *soup*. Ask children what they think this story will be about. Ask them what kind of soup they like to eat and if they have ever had rock soup. Echo read the book with children. Read page 2 aloud and then have children read it to you. Follow this procedure throughout the book.

Phonics: Long Vowel /ō/ow, oa

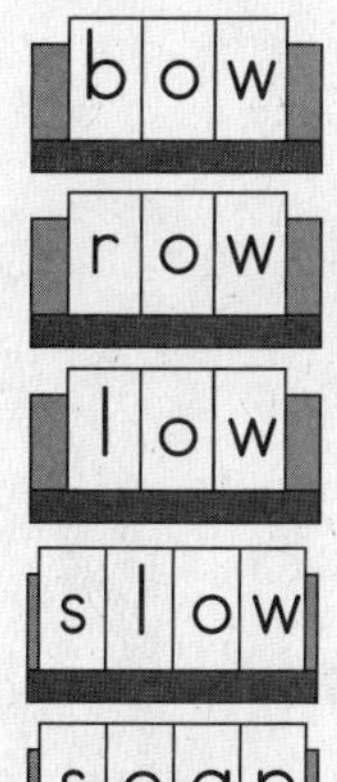

PRETEACH Place the letters *b*, *o*, and *w* in a Word Builder and have children do the same. Model how to blend the word *bow*. Slide your hand under the letters as you slowly elongate the sounds /bbōō/. Have children do the same. Then read the word naturally—*bow*. Have children do the same.

Have children blend and read new words by telling them:

Change *b* to *r*. What word did you make? *(row)*

Change *r* to *l*. What word did you make? *(low)*

Add *s* in front of *low*. What word did you make? *(slow)*

Take away the *l*. Change *w* to *a*. Add *p* after *a*. What word did you make? *(soap)*

Distribute *Intervention Practice Book* page 52 to children.

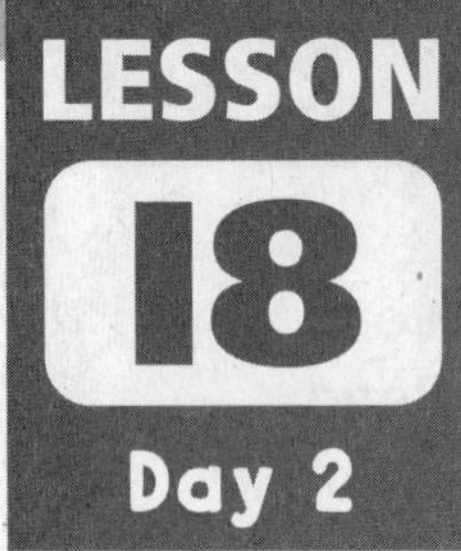

Warm-Up: Phonemic Awareness

Phoneme Isolation Display the Picture Cards *boat*, *goat*, and *mop*. Hold up the *boat*. Have children say the word boat aloud. Tell children to listen to the /ō/ sound in the middle of the word boat. Have them say the name of the other two pictures aloud. Ask: **What other picture name has the /ō/ sound you hear in *boat*?** (*goat*)

PICTURE CARDS

Continue with the Picture Cards *rose*, *lock*, *goat*; *goat*, *fox*, *rose*; *boat*, *rose*, *box*.

MATERIALS

Word Builder

Word Builder Cards a, d, l, o, r, s, t, w

Picture Cards boat, box, fox, goat, lock, mop, rose

Rock Soup

Phonics: Word Building with /ō/ow, oa

RETEACH Place the letters *r*, *o*, *a*, and *d* in a Word Builder and have children do the same. Model how to blend the word *road*. Slide your hand under the letters as you slowly elongate the sounds /rrōōdd/. Have children do the same. Then read the word naturally—*road*. Have children do the same.

Have children blend and read new words by telling them:

Change *r* to *l*. What word did you make? (*load*)

Change *l* to t. What word did you make? (*toad*)

Change *d* to *st*. What word did you make? (*toast*)

Change *t* to *r*. What word did you make? (*roast*)

Change *ast* to *w*. What word did you make? (*row*)

High-Frequency Words

RETEACH ***who, would, kind, door, made*** Write the word *what* and have children read it. Then write the word *who* next to what and have children read the word. **How are these words the same? How are they different? Let's read them again.**

what   who

Repeat the procedure with *should/would*, *for/door*, and *man/made*.

Read: *Rock Soup*

Rock Soup

Distribute copies of the book to children and read the title aloud. Have children frame the word *Soup*. Point to the word *Rock*. Ask children if they know another word that means the same thing as *rock*. *(stone)* Explain that words that mean the same thing are called synonyms, so *rock* and *stone* are synonyms. Tell children that the story *Rock Soup* is based on a folktale called *Stone Soup*. Ask children to point to the names of the people who wrote and illustrated the book. Read their names aloud. Then choral read the book with children. Let your voice fade if children start to gain control of the text.

Phonics: Reading Sentences with /ō/ow, oa

PRETEACH Distribute *Intervention Practice Book* page 53 to children. Point to the first sentence and have children read it aloud. Ask them to find the word low, frame it with their fingers, and circle the word. Then work with children to complete the page.

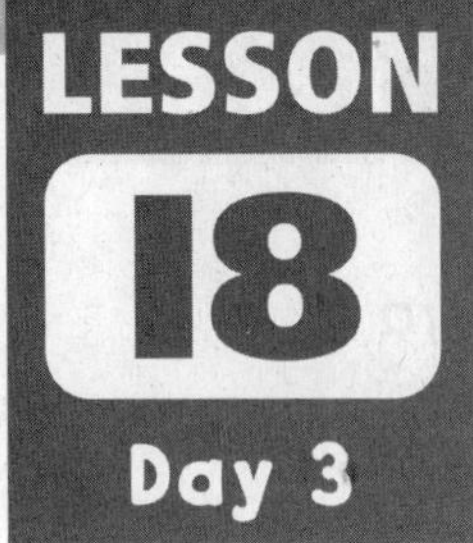

LESSON 18 Day 3

MATERIALS

Word Cards door, kind, made, who, would

Word Builder

Word Builder Cards b, g, h, i, l, n, o, r, s, t, w

Picture Cards bug, cat, clock, drum, egg, fish, hat, jeep, jet, kite, lamp, pig, quilt, seal, ship, six, ten, train

Rock Soup

Warm-Up: Phonemic Awareness

Phoneme Blending Tell children that they are going to play a guessing game. Then say: **I'm thinking of a word that is someone who leads a team. It is /k/-/ō/-/ch/. What's my word?** (*coach*) Continue with the following words: /m/-/ō/-/n/ (*moan*), /th/-/r/-/ō/ (*throw*), and /b/-/l/-/ōw/ (*blow*).

Phonics: Reading Sentences with /ō/ow, oa

RETEACH Help children blend and read new words and sentences shown. Have them read the sentence, blending each word in sequence. The high-frequency words are underlined; they should read these as a unit, not blending the sounds.

slow goat float crow

I <u>use</u> soap <u>on</u> <u>my</u> hands.

<u>We</u> can <u>eat</u> that loaf.

<u>The</u> corn can grow tall.

Load <u>the</u> dirt for <u>the</u> road.

High-Frequency Words

RETEACH ***who, would, kind, door, made*** Write the following sentence on tag board and display it in a pocket chart along with the Picture Cards *clock*, *drum*, *jeep*, *jet*, *ship*, *six*, *train*. Call on children to choose a Picture Card to complete the sentence and to read it aloud. Then ask: **Can you really go in a ______?**

PICTURE CARDS

Who would go in a ______?

Do the same for the following sentence and Picture Cards *bug*, *egg*, *hat*, *kite*, *quilt*, *ten*.

The kind man made me that ______.

Do the same for the following sentence and Picture Cards *cat*, *fish*, *lamp*, *pig*, *seal*.

There is a ______ at the door.

Read: *Rock Soup*

Rock Soup

Distribute copies of the book and have children read aloud the title. Ask what this book is about. Then guide children through as they read.

Pages 2–3: Have children read to find out what the man looked for.

What did the man look for? (*food*) **Find and read the sentence that tells.** (*A man looked for food.*) **Did people give him food?** (*no*) **What did the man do?** (*got a pot*)

Pages 4–5: Have children read the pages to find out what the man did.

What did the man fill? (*the pot*) **Find and read the words that tell. What did he put in the pot?** (*a rock*) **What did he say? Find and frame the sentences that tell.** (*I have made rock soup.*)

Pages 6–7: Have children read the pages to find out what others put in the rock soup.

What did the man put in the pot with the rock? (*greens*) **What did the girl put in the pot?** (*oats*) **Why did they add the greens and the oats?** (*The man said it would be better with greens and oats.*)

Page 8: Have children read to find out what happened.

What happened? (*the soup was made*) **Find and frame the word that describes the rock soup.** (*good*)

Ask children to use the pictures to help summarize the book.

Phonics: Building Words

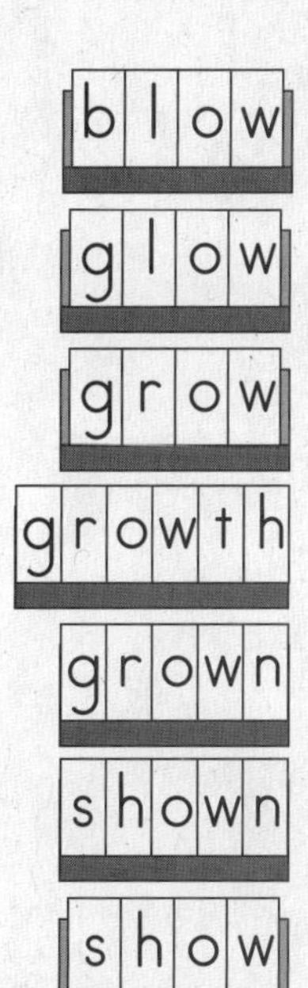

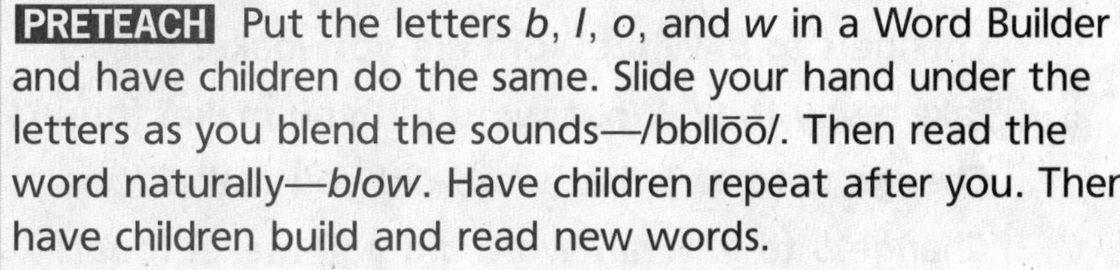

PRETEACH Put the letters *b*, *l*, *o*, and *w* in a Word Builder and have children do the same. Slide your hand under the letters as you blend the sounds—/bbllōō/. Then read the word naturally—*blow*. Have children repeat after you. Then have children build and read new words.

Change *b* to *g*. What word did you make? (*glow*)

Change *l* to *r*. What word did you make? (*grow*)

Add *th* to the end of *grow*. What word did you make? (*growth*)

Change *th* to *n*. What word did you make? (*grown*)

Change *gr* to *sh*. What word did you make? (*shown*)

Take away *n*. What word did you make? (*show*)

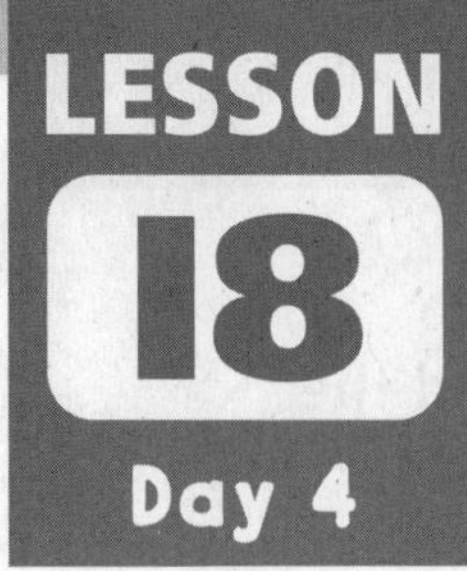

MATERIALS

Picture Cards boat, cat, cup, fan, fish, goat

Write-on/Wipe-off Boards with disks

Word Cards made, school, talk, who, would

Word Builder

Word Builder Cards a, b, g, h, l, o, r, s, t, w

Rock Soup

Warm-Up: Phonemic Awareness

Phoneme Segmentation Have children use the three boxes on the Write-on/Wipe-off Boards. Remind children that the boxes stand for the sounds in words. Show the Picture Card *goat* and ask: **What is the first sound you hear in goat?** (/*g*/) Have children place a disk in the first box. Then have children name the second sound in goat (/ō/) and place a disk in the second box. Then have them identify the last sound in goat (/*t*/) and place a disk in the third box. Point to each box in sequence as children say the word. **How many sounds do you hear in goat?** (*three*) Repeat this procedure with the following Picture Cards: *cup*, *fan*, *boat*, *fish*.

PICTURE CARDS

Phonics: Building Words

RETEACH Put the letters *t*, *h*, *r*, *o* and *w* in a Word Builder and have children do the same. Slide your hand under the letters as you blend the sounds—/ththrrōō/. Then read the word naturally—*throw*. Have children repeat after you. Then have children build and read new words.

Change *thr* to *sh*. What word did you make? (*show*)

Change *h* to *l*. What word did you make? (*slow*)

Change *s* to *b*. What word did you make? (*blow*)

Take away the *l*. What word did you make? (*bow*)

Change *w* to *at*. What word did you make? (*boat*)

Change *b* to *g*. What word did you make? (*goat*)

Distribute *Intervention Practice Book* page 54 to children.

who

would

made

talk

school

High-Frequency Words

RETEACH ***who, would, made, talk, school*** Distribute word cards with the words listed above. Have partners take turns displaying the words for each other and reading them. After they read each word, have children spell the word and then repeat the word. Then have them spell the word again and write it on a sheet of paper.

Rock Soup

Read: *Rock Soup*

Focus Skill **Character** Remind children that characters are the people or animals that a story is about. Explain that understanding the characters can help readers follow and remember what happens in the story. Have children read *Rock Soup* and then together make a list of words to describe the man who was the main character.

What Was He Like?
clever
tricky
hungry

Inflections: -ed, -s, -ing

PRETEACH Write the endings *-ed*, *-s* and *-ing* at the top of a sheet of chart paper. Explain that *-ed* means that something already happened, and that *-s* and *-ing* mean that something happens or is happening now. Have children suggest verbs that end with *-ed* and say what letters they would need to write the words. Then write the words underneath the heading *-ed*. Use the same procedure for *-s* and *-ing*. Then have children read each column of words. End the activity by pointing to words at random and having children read the words.

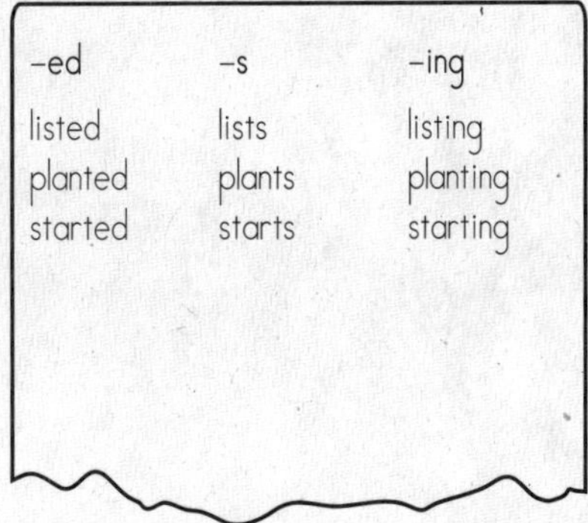

-ed
listed
planted
started
-s
lists
plants
starts
-ing
listing
planting
starting

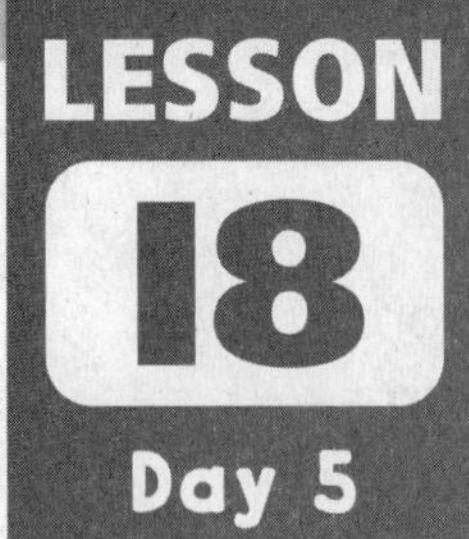

LESSON 18 Day 5

MATERIALS

Write-on/Wipe-off Boards

Word Cards each, kind, other, talk, who, would

Word Builder

Word Builder Cards a, b, e, f, m, n, t, e

Warm-Up: Phonemic Awareness

Phoneme Blending Tell children that together you are going to play a game of "Fix It." Tell them that you are going to say some words that are all broken and they should listen to see if they can put the sounds together to figure out the word. **Listen: /k/-/l/-/ō/-/k/. What word does /k/-/l/-/ō/-/k/ say?** (*cloak*). Continue with the following words:

/g/-/l/-/ō/-/t/ (*gloat*)	**/f/-/l/-/ō/** (*flow*)	**/t/-/ō/-/d/** (*toad*)
/l/-/ē/-/f/ (*leaf*)	**/b/-/ē/-/t/** (*beet*)	**/m/-/ē/** (*me*)

Inflections: -ed, -s, -ing

RETEACH Write the word talk on a Write-on/ Wipe-off Board and have children do the same. Then have them read the word. Ask: **What letter(s) should we write if we want to change talk to talks?** (*s*) **Let's do that.** Continue the activity with the word: *talked* and *talking*. Repeat the activity, using the words *packed*, *packs*, *packing*, and *walking*, *walks*, *walked*.

High-Frequency Words

Cumulative Review *who, would, kind, other, each, talk*
Place the words in a pocket chart. Say aloud one of the words and use it in a sentence. Have a volunteer find and point to the word. Have children clap and say the spelling of the word. Then have them write it. Have children read aloud their list of words.

who

would

kind

other

each

talk

Read: Self-Selected Reading

Have children select a book to read from their browsing boxes. After they have completed their reading, have them tell you what they were most successful in during the reading of the book.

Phonics: Long Vowel /ē/e, ea, ee

PRETEACH Write the letters *e, ea*, and *ee* on the board. Tell children that *e, ea*, and *ee* can all stand for the /ē/ sound. Use the Word Builder and Word Builder Cards to model blending words.

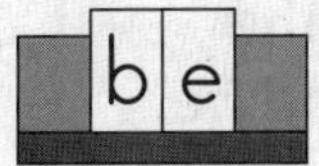

Place the Word Builder Cards *b* and *e* in the Word Builder. Point to the *b* and say /b/. Point to the *e* and say /ē/.

Slide the *e* next to the *b*. Move your hand under the letters and blend the sounds, elongating them /bbēē/. Have children repeat after you. Then have children read the word be along with you.

Follow the same procedure for the words *beet*, *bean*, *me*, *mean*, and *feet*.

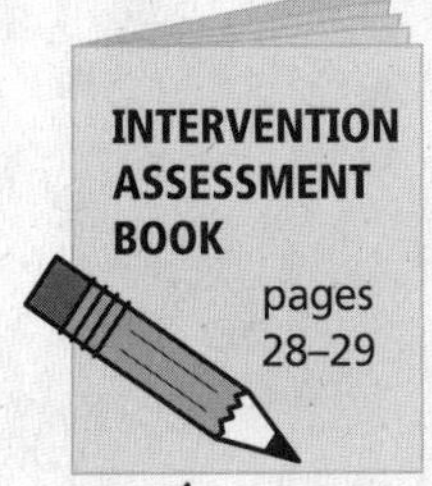

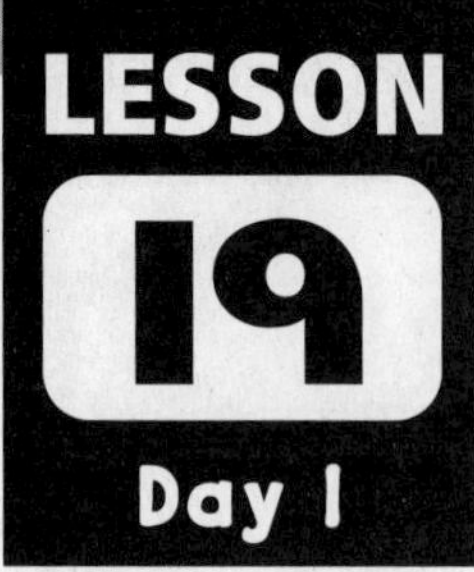

Warm-Up: Phonemic Awareness

Onset and Rime Tell children that you are going to say some words, but you are going to say them in parts. Have children listen to see if they can figure out the word. Demonstrate by saying: **/sp/-eak—What word did I say?** (*speak*)

/sh/-eet	**/kl/-ean**	**/sp/-eed**
/st/-eam	**/hw/-eel**	**/tr/-eat**

MATERIALS

word cards also, know, moved, only, room, should, those, write

Word Builder

Word Builder Cards a, b, e, e, f, l, m, n, t

Alphabet Master Ee

My Cats

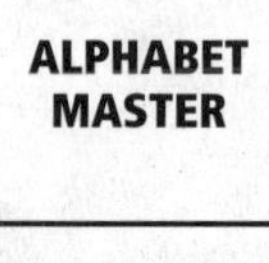

Phonics: Long Vowel /ē/e, ea, ee

RETEACH **blending** Display Alphabet Master *Ee*. **This letter is e. When the letter *e* is the only vowel at the end of a short word or syllable, it can stand for the /ē/ sound, the long sound of the letter e in words such as *me*, *be*, and *he*.** Point to the Alphabet Master and say /ē/.

Write *ea* and *ee* on the board. **When the letters *ea* or *ee* are together, they can stand for the long /ē/ sound as in words such as *eat*, *eel*, *bee*, and *beat*.** Point to the *ea* and *ee* and say /ē/. Have children repeat the sound as you touch the letters several times.

Use the Word Builder Cards and a pocket chart to model blending words.

Place the Word Builder Cards *m* and *e* in the Word Builder. Point to the *m* and say /m/. Point to the *e* and say /ē/. Slide the *e* next to the *m*. Move your hand under the letters and blend the sounds, elongating them /mmēē/. Have children repeat after you. Then say the word naturally—*me*. Have children do the same.

Use a similar procedure to blend and read the word *mean*.

High-Frequency Words

PRETEACH ***also, know, moved, only, room, should, those, write*** Display the word card *also*. **This word is *also*. I take ballet lessons and also play basketball. Read the word with me—*also*. Spell the word with me—*a-l-s-o*. Read the word with me. What is this word?** (*also*)

Follow the same procedure for the remaining words.

know—**I know how to read.**

moved—**We moved to a new apartment last year.**

also
know
moved
only
room
should
those
write

only—**Only you and I know this secret.**

room—**I share a room with my sister.**

should—**You should brush your teeth twice a day.**

those—**Those are my favorite singers.**

write—**I can write my name.**

Then place the eight words in a pocket chart and have volunteers read the words, as you randomly point to them.

Read: *My Cats*

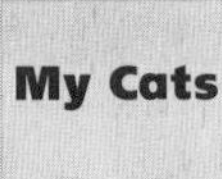

Story Words Write the words *hear* and *eyes* and read them to children. Provide help with these words as needed.

Distribute copies of the book and have children put their fingers on the title. Have them follow along as you read the title aloud. Echo read the book with children. Read page 2 aloud and then have children read it to you. Follow this procedure throughout the book.

Phonics: Word Building with /ē/e, ea, ee

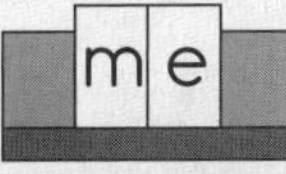

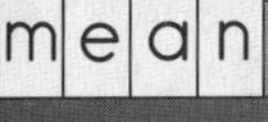

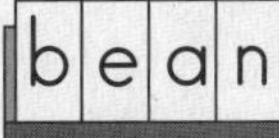

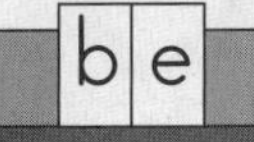

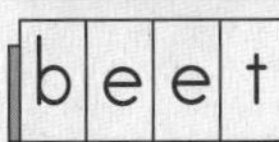

PRETEACH Place the letters *m* and *e* in a Word Builder and have children do the same. Model how to blend the word *me*. Slide your hand under the letters as you slowly elongate the sounds /mmēē/. Have children do the same. Then read the word naturally—*me*. Have children do the same.

Have children blend and read new words by telling them:

Add *an* to the end. What word did you make? (*mean*)

Change the *m* to *b*. What word did you make? (*bean*)

Take away the *an*. What word did you make? (*be*)

Add *et* to the end. What word did you make? (*beet*)

Distribute *Intervention Practice Book* page 55 to children.

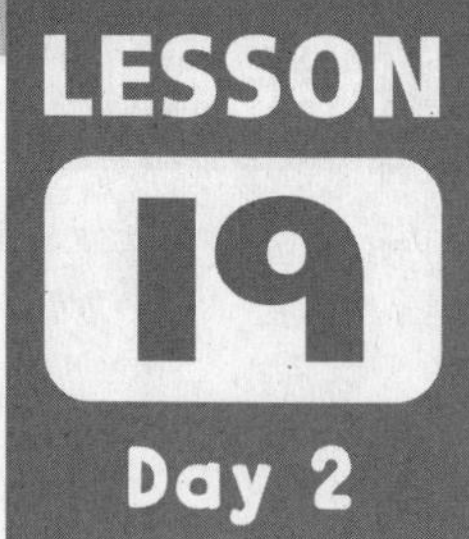

MATERIALS

Word Builder

Word Builder Cards a, e, f, h, r, t, e

Picture Cards egg, jeep, lamp, leaf, seal, ten, vest

My Cats

Warm-Up: Phonemic Awareness

PICTURE CARDS

Phoneme Isolation Display the Picture Cards *jeep*, *leaf*, and *ten*. Hold up the *jeep*. Have children say the word *jeep* aloud. Tell children to listen to the /ē/ sound in the middle of the word *jeep*. Have them say the name of the other two pictures aloud. Ask: **What other picture name has the /ē/ sound?** (*leaf*) Continue with the Picture Cards *jeep*, *seal*, *vest*; *leaf*, *lamp*, *seal*; *seal*, *egg*, *jeep*.

Phonics: Word Building with /ē/e, ea, ee

RETEACH Place the letters *h* and *e* in a Word Builder and have children do the same. Model how to blend the word *he*. Slide your hand under the letters as you slowly elongate the sounds /hhēē/. Have children do the same. Then read the word naturally—*he*. Have children do the same.

Have children blend and read new words by telling them:

Add *at* to the end. What word did you make? (*heat*)
Change *h* to *tr*. What word did you make? (*treat*)
Change *at* to *e*. What word did you make? (*tree*)
Change *t* to *f*. What word did you make? (*free*)
Take away the *r*. What word did you make? (*fee*)
Add *t* to the end. What word did you make? (*feet*)

High-Frequency Words

RETEACH ***also, know, moved, only, room, should, those, write*** Write the word *so* and have children read it. Then write the word *also* next to *so* and have children read the word. **How are these words the same? How are they different? Let's read them again:**

so | also

Repeat the procedure with *now/know*, *gives/moved*, *on/only*, *could/should*, and *writing/write*.

Read: *My Cats*

My Cats

Distribute copies of the book to children and read the title aloud. Point to the *s* at the end of the word *cats*. Explain that the *s* makes *cats* plural. **Plural means there is more than one.** Ask children to point to the names of the people who wrote and illustrated the book. Read the names aloud. Then choral read the book with children. Let your voice fade if children start to gain control of the text.

Phonics: Reading Sentences with /ē/e, ea, ee

PRETEACH Distribute *Intervention Practice Book* page 56 to children. Point to the first sentence and have children read it aloud. Ask them to find the word *feet*, frame it with their fingers, and circle the word. Then work with children to complete the page.

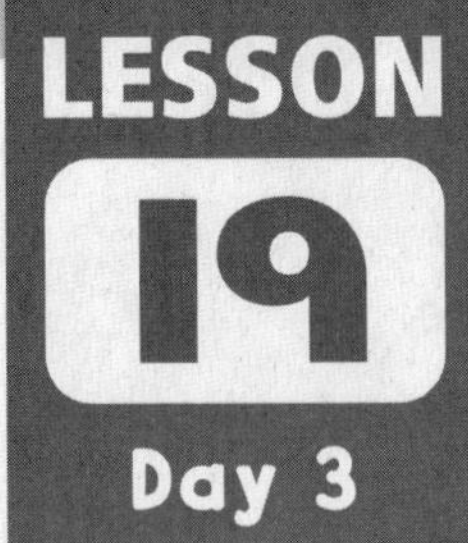

Warm-Up: Phonemic Awareness

Phoneme Blending Tell children that they are going to play a guessing game. Then say: **I'm thinking of a word that is something you put on a bed. It is a /sh/-/ē/-/t/. What's my word?** (*sheet*) Continue with the following words: /sh/-/ē/ (*she*), /m/-/ē/-/l/ (*meal*), /r/-/ē/-/ch/ (*reach*), /t/-/ē/-/th/ (*teeth*).

MATERIALS

Word Cards also, know, moved, only, room, should, those, write

Word Builder

Word Builder Cards a, d, e, l, m, o, r, t

Picture Cards cat, desk, fish, gate, hat, igloo, map, mule, pen, rake, seal, train, wagon

My Cats

Phonics: Reading Sentences with /ē/e, ea, ee

RETEACH Help children blend and read new words and sentences shown. Have them read the sentence, blending each word in sequence. The high-frequency words are underlined; they should read these as a unit, not blending the sounds.

speed **bleed** **sneak** **deal**

That team can play.

He must not peek.

The cat wants to creep.

Pig can reach the food.

High-Frequency Words

RETEACH ***also, know, moved, only, room, should, those, write*** Write the following sentence on tag board and display it in a pocket chart along with the Picture Cards *cat*, *fish*, *seal*, *gate*, *mule*. Call on children to choose a Picture Card to complete the sentence and read it aloud. Then ask: **Could a ______ really eat snacks in a room?**

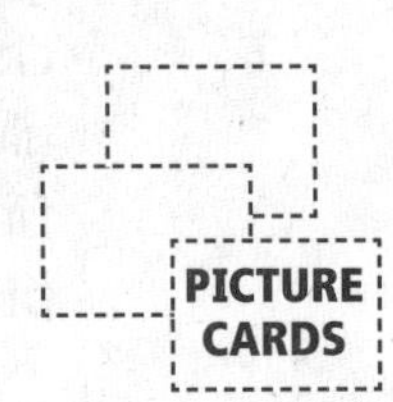

Should the ______ eat those snacks in the room?

Do the same for the following sentence and Picture Cards *desk*, *hat*, *map*, *pen*, *rake*, *train*.

I only know how to write on a ______.

Do the same for the following sentence and Picture Cards *train*, *igloo*, *wagon*, *rake*, *seal*.

We also moved to a new ______.

Read: *My Cats*

Distribute copies of the book and have children put their finger on the title. Ask what this book is about. Then guide children through as they read.

Pages 2–3: Have children read to find out who this story is about.

Who is this story about? (*a boy and his cats*)

Pages 4–5: Have children read the pages to find out what they hear.

What did the boy hear? (*his mom calling*)

What do the cats hear? (*Things the boy can not hear.*)
Find and read the sentence that tells. (*They hear things that I can not hear.*)

Pages 6–7: Have children read the pages to find out what else the boy and cats can do.

What can they do? (*smell*) **What does the boy smell?** (*dad making dinner*) **How does dinner smell? Find the sentence that tells.** (*It smells so good.*) **What do the cats smell?** (*other cats*)

Pages 8–9: Have children read to find out what else the boy and the cats do.

What do the boy and the cats know? (*when it is getting dark*) **What kinds of eyes do the cats have? Find and read the sentence that tells.** (*They have good eyes.*)

Pages 10–12: Have children read to find out what the boy and the cats do.

What time is it after they eat? (*time for bed*)

What do the boy and the cats like to do? (*sit together*) **How does the boy feel about his cats?** (*They are good pals.*)

Ask children to use the pictures to help summarize the book.

Phonics: Building Words

PRETEACH Place the letters *m*, *e*, *a*, and *l* in a Word Builder and have children do the same. Slide your hand under the letters as you blend the sounds—/mmēēll/. Then read the word naturally—*meal*. Have children repeat after you. Then have children build and read new words.

Change the *m* to *d*. What word did you make? (*deal*)
Change *d* to *r*. What word did you make? (*real*)
Change *l* to *d*. What word did you make? (*read*)
Change *e* to *o*. What word did you make? (*road*)
Change *r* to *t*. What word did you make? (*toad*)
Change the *oad* to *ea*. What word did you make? (*tea*)

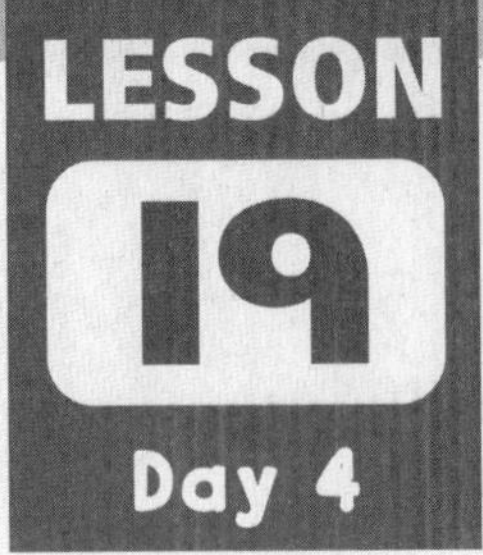

MATERIALS

Picture Cards can, jeep, leaf, net, seal

Write-on/Wipe-off Boards with disks

Word Cards also, know, only, room, should, those, who, door

Word Builder

Word Builder Cards a, b, c, e, l, n, r, s, t

My Cats

Warm-Up: Phonemic Awareness

Phoneme Segmentation Have children use the three boxes on the Write-on/Wipe-off Boards. Remind children that the boxes stand for the sounds in words. Show the Picture Card *seal* and ask: **What is the first sound you hear in seal?** (/s/) Have children place a disk in the first box. Then have children name the second sound in *seal* (/ē/) and place a disk in the second box. Then have them identify the last sound in *seal* (/l/) and place a disk in the third box. Point to each box in sequence as children say the word. **How many sounds do you hear in *seal*?** (*three*) Repeat this procedure with the following Picture Cards: *leaf*, *net*, *jeep*, *can*.

PICTURE CARDS

Phonics: Building Words

RETEACH Put the letters *b*, *e*, *a*, and *n* in a Word Builder and have children do the same. Slide your hand under the letters as you blend the sounds—/bbēēnn/. Then read the word naturally—*bean*. Have children repeat after you. Then have children build and read new words.

Change the *b* to *cl*. What word did you make? (*clean*)

Change *n* to *t*. What word did you make? (*cleat*)

Change *cl* to *tr*. What word did you make? (*treat*)

Take away *tr*. What word did you make? (*eat*)

Add an *s* in front of eat. What word did you make? (*seat*)

Distribute *Intervention Practice Book* page 57 to children.

also

know

only

room

should

those

who

door

High-Frequency Words

RETEACH ***also, know, only, room, should, those, who, door***
Distribute word cards with the words listed above. Have partners take turns displaying the words for each other and reading them. After they read each word, have children spell the word and then repeat the word. Then have them spell the word again and write it on a sheet of paper.

Read: *My Cats*

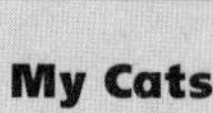

My Cats

Focus Skill **Draw Conclusions** Tell children that drawing conclusions means figuring out certain things that may not be said in the story. Explain that sometimes information from the story can help you figure out other things. Have children reread *My Cats.* Then together make a list of conclusions one can draw from the story.

What I Know
The boy likes his cats.
Dad is a good cook.
The cats are allowed on the bed.

Phonics: Contractions 's, n't, and 'll

PRETEACH Write the letters *'s*, *n't*, and *'ll* at the top of a sheet of chart paper. Explain that 's, n't, and 'll are contractions that mean *is*, *not*, and *will* when they are added to other words. Have children suggest words that end with *'s* and say what letters they would need to write the words. Then write the words underneath the heading *'s*. Use the same procedure for *n't* and *'ll*. Then have children read each column of words. End the activity by pointing to words at random and having children read the words.

's	n't	'll
she's	isn't	they'll
he's	wasn't	we'll
it's	don't	you'll
who's	can't	he'll
what's	didn't	I'll
	wasn't	she'll

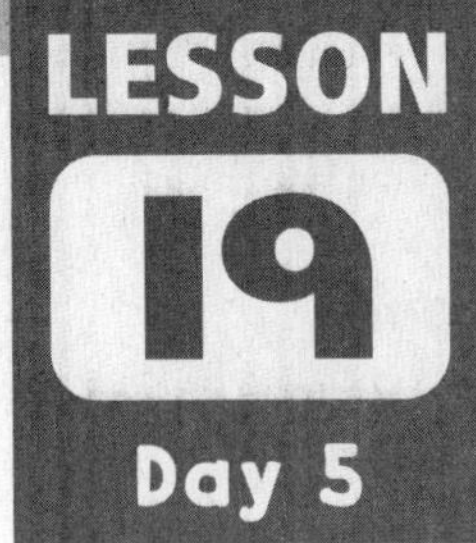

Warm-Up: Phonemic Awareness

Phoneme Blending Tell children that together you are going to play a puzzle game. Tell them that you are going to say some words in pieces like a puzzle and that they should put the pieces together to figure out the word. **Listen: /f/-/r/-/ē/. What word does /f/-/r/-/ē/ say?** (*free*). Continue with the following words:

/k/-/r/-/ē/-/k/ *(creek)*	**/p/-/l/-/ē/-/d/** *(plead)*
/s/-/w/-/ē/-/t/ *(sweet)*	**/k/-/ā/-/m/** *(came)*
/l/-/ā/-/k/ *(lake)*	**/g/-/ā/-/m/** *(game)*

MATERIALS

Write-on/Wipe-off Boards

Word Cards also, kind, made, should, those, would

Word Builder

Word Builder Cards a, c, e, g, k, l, m, t

Phonics: Contractions 's, n't, 'll

RETEACH Write the word *it* is on a Write-on/Wipe-off Board and have children do the same. Then have them read the word. Ask: **What should we do if we want to change *it* is to *it's*?** (*erase* i *in* is*; add an apostrophe*) **Let's do that.** Continue the activity with the following words: *she is/she's* and *who is/who's*. Repeat the activity, using the words *do not/don't*, *was not/wasn't*; *he will/he'll* and *you will/you'll*.

High-Frequency Words

would
kind
made
also
those
should

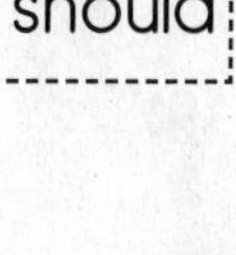

Cumulative Review *would, kind, made, also, those, should*
Place the words in a pocket chart. Say aloud one of the words and use it in a sentence. Have a volunteer find and point to the word. Have children clap and say the spelling of the word. Then have them write it. Have children read aloud their list of words.

Read: Self-Selected Reading

Have children select a book to read from their browsing boxes. After they have completed their reading, have them tell you what they were most successful in during the reading of the book.

Long Vowel: /ā/a-e

PRETEACH Use the Word Builder and Word Builder Cards to model blending words.

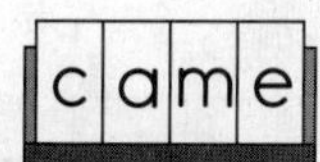

Place the Word Builder Cards *c*, *a*, *m*, and *e* in the Word Builder. Ask children to name each letter. Tell children that *e* at the end of the word is silent and helps *a* stand for /ā/, the long sound of *a* in the middle of the word lake.

Point to the *c* and say /k/. Point to the *a* and *e*. Say /ā/. Slide the *a* next to the *c*. Move your hand under the letters and blend the sounds, elongating them /kkāā/. Have children repeat after you.

Point to the *m* and say /m/. Slide *me* next to *ca*. Move your hand under the letters and blend the sounds, elongating them /kkāāmm/. Have children repeat. Then have children read the word *came* along with you.

Follow the same procedure for the words *game*, *gate*, *late*, *lake*, and *take*.

Warm-Up: Phonemic Awareness

Onset and Rime Tell children that you are going to say some words, but you are going to say them in parts. Have children listen to see if they can figure out the word. Demonstrate by saying: **/ch/-ase—What word did I say?** (*chase*)

/d/-ate	**/r/-ace**	**/s/-ame**
/g/-ave	**/l/-ate**	**/b/-ake**

MATERIALS

Word Cards over, town, world

Word Builder

Word Builder Cards a, c, e, g, k, l, m, r, t

Alphabet Masters Aa, Ee

Ann Gets a Map

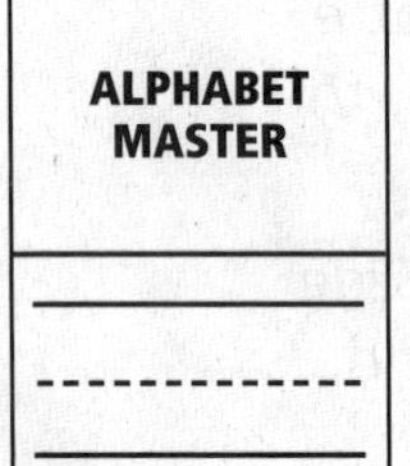

Phonics: Long Vowel /ā/a-e

RETEACH **blending** Display Alphabet Masters *Aa* and *Ee*. **These letters are *a* and *e*. When a short word has an *a*-consonant-e, the vowel *e* is silent and causes the *a* to say /ā/, the long sound of in words such as *ate*, *lake*, and *page*.** Point to the Alphabet Masters and say /ā/. Have children repeat the sound as you touch the letter *a* several times.

Use the Word Builder Cards and a pocket chart to model blending words.

Place the Word Builder Cards *c*, *a*, *m*, and *e* in the Word Builder. Point to the *c* and say /k/. Point to the *a* and say /ā/. Slide the *a* next to the *c*. Move your hand under the letters and blend the sounds, elongating them /kkāā/. Point to the *m* and say /m/. Slide the *me* next to *ca*. Move your hand under the letters and blend the sounds, elongating them /kkāāmm/. Have children repeat after you. Then say the word naturally—*came*. Have children do the same.

High-Frequency Words

over

town

world

PRETEACH ***over, town, world*** Display the word card *over*. **This word is *over*. The bird flew over the house. Read the word with me—*over*. Spell the word with me—*o-v-e-r*. Read the word with me. What is this word?** (*over*)

Follow the same procedure for the words *town* and *world*.

town—**I have lived in this town all my life.**

world—**I found the U. S. on this world map.**

Then place the three words in a pocket chart and have volunteers read the words, as you randomly point to them.

Read: *Ann Gets a Map*

Ann Gets a Map

Distribute copies of the book and have children put their finger on the title. Have children follow along as you read the title aloud. Ask children what they think this story will be about. Echo read the book with children. Read page 2 aloud and then have children read it to you. Follow this procedure throughout the book.

Phonics: Word Building with /ā/a-e

game

gate

late

PRETEACH Place the letters *g*, *a*, *m*, and *e* in a Word Builder and have children do the same. Model how to blend the word *game*. Slide your hand under the letters as you slowly elongate the sounds /ggāāmm/. Have children do the same. Then read the word naturally—*game*. Have children do the same.

Have children blend and read new words by telling them:

Change the m to t. What word did you make? *(gate)*

Change *g* to *l*. What word did you make? (*late*)

Change *t* to *k*. What word did you make? (*lake*)

Change *l* to *t*. What word did you make? (*take*)

Change *t* to *r*. What word did you make? (*rake*)

Change *r* to *c*. What word did you make? (*cake*)

Distribute *Intervention Practice Book* page 58 to children.

MATERIALS

Word Builder

Word Builder Cards a, e, g, k, l, m, s, t

Ann Gets a Map

Warm-Up: Phonemic Awareness

Phoneme Isolation Say the word *lake* aloud and have children repeat it. Tell children to listen to the /ā/ sound in *lake*. Then have them listen as you say the words *face* and *clam*. Ask: **Which of these words has the /ā/ sound you hear in *lake*?** (*face*)

Continue with the words *lace*, *lap*, *fade*; *made*, *mad*, *chase*; *plate*, *take*, *plot*.

Phonics: Word Building with /ā/a-e

RETEACH Place the letters *s*, *a*, *m*, and *e* in a Word Builder and have children do the same. Model how to blend the word *same*. Slide your hand under the letters as you slowly elongate the sounds /ssāāmm/. Have children do the same. Then read the word naturally—*same*. Have children do the same.

Have children blend and read new words by telling them:

Change the *s* to *g*. What word did you make? (*game*)
Change *m* to *t*. What word did you make? (*gate*)
Change *g* to *l*. What word did you make? (*late*)
Change *t* to *k*. What word did you make? (*lake*)
Change *l* to *t*. What word did you make? (*take*)
Change *k* to *l*. What word did you make? (*tale*)

High-Frequency Words

RETEACH ***over, town, world*** Write the word *very* and have children read it. Then write the word *over* next to *very* and have children read the word. How are these words the same? How are they different? Let's read them again:

very over

Repeat the procedure with *down/town* and *would/world*.

Read: *Ann Gets a Map*

Ann Gets a Map

Distribute copies of the book to children and read the title aloud. Point to the name *Ann*. Explain that *Ann* is a girl's name. **Names are proper nouns. Proper nouns always begin with a capital letter when they are written.** Ask children to point to the names of the people who wrote and illustrated the book. Read the names aloud. Then choral read the book with children. Let your voice fade if children start to gain control of the text.

Phonics: Reading Sentences with /ā/a-e

PRETEACH Distribute *Intervention Practice Book* page 59 to children. Point to the first sentence and have children read it aloud. Ask them to find the word *page*, frame it with their fingers, and circle the word. Then work with children to complete the page.

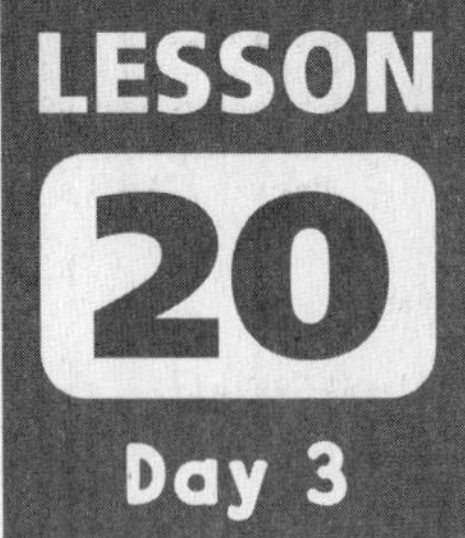

MATERIALS

Word Cards over, town, world

Word Builder

Word Builder Cards a, d, e, f, l, m, t, z

Picture Cards: bat, boat, bug, cat, flag, jet, kite, nest, octopus, ship, train, wagon

Ann Gets a Map

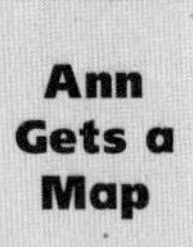

Warm-Up: Phonemic Awareness

Phoneme Blending Tell children that they are going to play a guessing game. Then say: **I'm thinking of a word that is something you do to pizza. It is /b/-/ā/-/k/. What's my word?** (*bake*) Continue with the following words: /f/-/l/-/ā/-/k/ (*flake*), /sh/-/ā/-/v/ (*shave*), /r/-/ā/-/s/ (*race*).

Phonics: Reading Sentences with /ā/a-e

RETEACH Help children blend and read new words and sentences shown. Have them read the sentence, blending each word in sequence. The high-frequency words are underlined; they should read these as a unit, not blending the sounds.

late chase tame cake

Be safe when you play.

Wave to your friends.

Run to every base.

They all sat in the shade.

High-Frequency Words

RETEACH ***over, town, world*** Write the following sentence on tag board and display it in a pocket chart along with the Picture Cards *bat*, *bug*, *octopus*, *jet*, *kite*, *wagon*. Call on children to choose a Picture Card to complete the sentence and to read it aloud. Then ask: **Can a _____ really fly over the town?**

PICTURE CARDS

The _____ can fly over the town.

Do the same for the following sentence and Picture Cards *boat*, *flag*, *nest*, *cat*, *ship*, *train*.

Take a _____ to see the world.

Read: *Ann Gets a Map*

Distribute copies of the book and have children read aloud the title. Ask them to predict what this book might be about. Then guide children through as they read.

Pages 2–5: Have children read to find out what Ann's father gave her.

> **Who is telling this story?** (*Ann*) **Why is today special?** (*She is six today; it is her birthday*) **What did Ann's dad give her?** (*a map*) **What was it a map of?** (*a park*) **Find and read the sentence that tells. Where is the park? Find and frame the words that tell.** (*in our town*)

Pages 6–7: Have children read the pages to get directions.

> **What do they follow?** (*the path*) **Where do they go?** (*by the lake*) **Where do they walk?** (*to the gate*) **Find and read the words that tell.**

Pages 8–11: Have children read to find out how to get to the gate.

> **Where do they walk past?** (*the lake*) **Where do they get to?** (*the gate*)

Page 12: Have children read to find out what happens there.

> **What does Ann see?** (*cake and friends*) **How does Ann feel?** (*surprised*) **Find and read the sentence that tells.**
>
> **Where did the map take Ann and her father?** (*to her birthday party in the park*)

Ask children to use the pictures to help summarize the book.

Phonics: Building Words

PRETEACH Put the letters *m*, *a*, *d*, and *e* in a Word Builder and have children do the same. Slide your hand under the letters as you blend the sounds—/mmāadd/. Then read the word naturally—*made*. Have children repeat after you. Then have children build and read new words.

made

maze

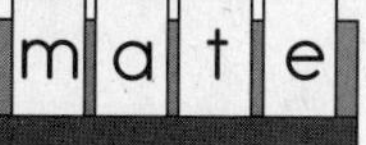

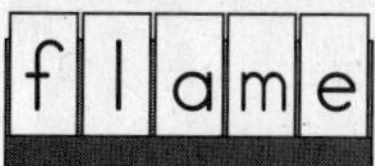

Change the *d* to *z*. What word did you make? (*maze*)

Change *z* to *t*. What word did you make? (*mate*)

Change *m* to *f*. What word did you make? (*fate*)

Change *t* to *m*. What word did you make? (*fame*)

Add *l* after *f*. What word did you make? (*flame*)

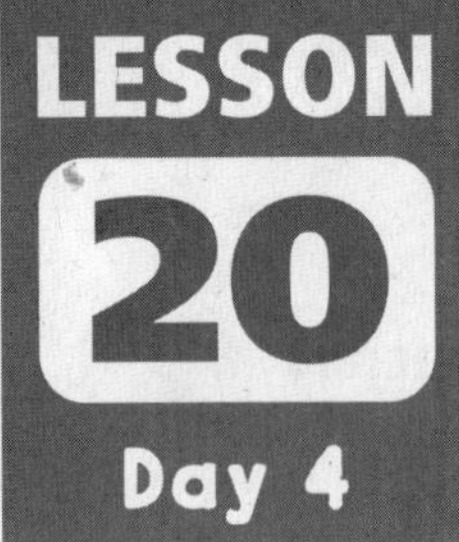

Warm-Up: Phonemic Awareness

Phoneme Segmentation Have children use the three boxes on the Write-on/Wipe-off Boards. Remind children that the boxes stand for the sounds in words. Show the Picture Card *gate* and ask: **What is the first sound you hear in gate?** (/g/) Have children place a disk in the first box. Then have children name the second sound in *gate* (/ā/) and place a disk in the second box. Then have them identify the last sound in *gate* (/t/) and place a disk in the third box. Point to each box in sequence as children say the word. **How many sounds do you hear in gate?** (*three*) Repeat this procedure with the following Picture Cards: *bed*, *map*, *nut*, *sock*, *thumb*.

PICTURE CARDS

MATERIALS

Picture Cards: bed, gate, map, nut, sock, thumb

Write-on/Wipe-off Boards with disks

Word Cards also, know, over, town, world

Word Builder

Word Builder Cards a, e, f, k, r, t, v, w

Ann Gets a Map

Phonics: Building Words

RETEACH Put the letters *r*, *a*, *k*, and *e* in a Word Builder and have children do the same. Slide your hand under the letters as you blend the sounds—/rrāākk/. Then read the word naturally—*rake*. Have children repeat after you. Then have children build and read new words.

Change the *k* to *t*. What word did you make? (*rate*)

Change *t* to *v*. What word did you make? (*rave*)

Change *r* to *w*. What word did you make? (*wave*)

Change *v* to *k*. What word did you make? (*wake*)

Change *w* to *f*. What word did you make? (*fake*)

Distribute *Intervention Practice Book* page 60 to children.

High-Frequency Words

over

town

world

know

also

RETEACH ***over, town, world, know, also*** Distribute word cards with the words listed above. Have partners take turns displaying the words for each other and reading them. After they read each word, have children spell the word and then repeat the word. Then have them spell the word again and write it on a sheet of paper.

Read: *Ann Gets a Map*

Ann Gets a Map

Focus Skill **Classify/Categorize** Remind children that being able to group together ideas that are alike in some way in a story can help them understand what they read. Have children read *Ann Gets a Map* and then together make a list of kinds of maps.

Phonics: Phonograms -ake, -ate; Inflections -ed, -ing

PRETEACH Write the letters *ake* and *ate* at the top of a sheet of paper. Have children suggest words that end with *-ake* and say what letters they would need to write the words. Write the words under *ake*. Use the same procedure for *-ate*. End the activity by pointing to words at random and having children read the words.

Write the letters *ed* and *ing* at the top of a sheet of chart paper. Explain that *-ed* and *-ing* are endings to verbs that mean something already happened or is happening. If a word ends in silent e, drop the *e* before adding *-ed* or *-ing*. Write the words *bake, fade,* and *save* and have children read them. Then write *baked, faded*, and *saved* underneath the heading *-ed*. Use the same procedure for *-ing*. Then have children read each column of words. End the activity by pointing to words at random and having children read the words.

ake	ate
make	date
take	late
cake	gate

ed	ing
baked	baking
faded	fading
saved	saving

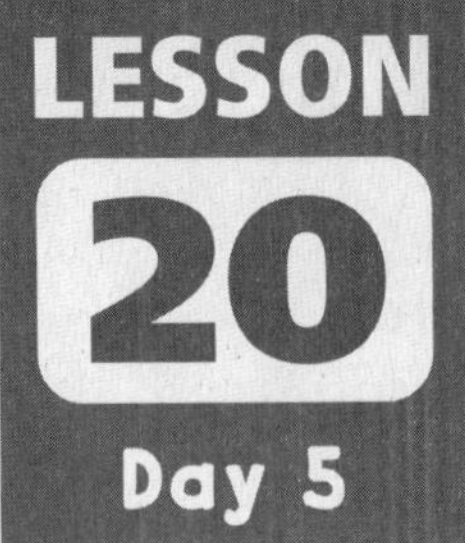

Warm-Up: Phonemic Awareness

Phoneme Blending Tell children that together you are going to play a game of "Fix It." Tell them that you are going to say some words that are all broken and they should listen to see if they can put the sounds together to figure out the word. **Listen: /s/-/l/-/ā/-/t/. What word does /s/-/l/-/ā/-/t/ say?** (*slate*). Continue with the following words:

/b/-/l/-/ā/-/m/ (*blame*)
/b/-/r/-/ā/-/v/ (*brave*)
/f/-/u/-/n/-/ē/ (*funny*)
/s/-/c/-/r/-/ā/-/p/ (*scrape*)
/j/-/e/-/l/-/ē/ (*jelly*)
/b/-/u/-/n/-/ē/ (*bunny*)

MATERIALS

Write-on/Wipe-off Boards

Word Cards moved, only, over, room, should, those, town, world, write

Word Builder

Word Builder Cards b, e, f, h, j, l, l, n, n, r, r, u, y

Phonics: Phonograms -ake, -ate; Inflections -ed, -ing

RETEACH Write the word *take* on a Write-on/Wipe-off Board and have children do the same. Then have them read the word. Ask: **What letter should we write if we want to change *take* to *lake*?** *(l)* **Let's do that.** Continue the activity with the words *late* and *date*.

Write the word *bake* on a Write-on/Wipe-off Board and have children do the same. Then have them read the word. Ask: **What letters should we write if we want to change *bake* to *baked*?** (*drop the e and add ed*) **Let's do that.** Continue the activity with the following words: *shade/shaded*, *grade/graded*. Repeat the activity, using the words *bake/baking*, *shade/shading*, *grade/grading*.

High-Frequency Words

Cumulative Review *moved, only, room, should, those, write, over, town, world* Place the words in a pocket chart. Say one of the words aloud and use it in a sentence. Have a volunteer find and point to the word. Have children clap and say the spelling of the word. Then have them write it. Have children read aloud their list of words.

Read: Self-Selected Reading

Have children select a book to read from their browsing boxes. After they have completed their reading, encourage them to show you a long *a* word they figured out.

Phonics: Long Vowel /ē/y

PRETEACH Write the letter *y* on the board or chart paper. **When the letter *y* is a vowel, it can stand for the /ē/ sound, the sound in words such as *funny*, *happy*, and *baby*.** Have children repeat the sound as you touch the letter *y* several times.

Use the Word Builder and Word Builder Cards to model blending words.

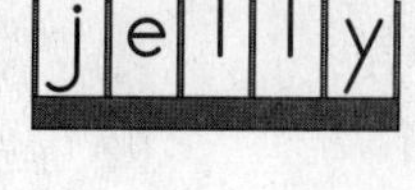

Place the Word Builder Cards *j*, *e*, *l*, *l*, and *y* in the Word Builder. Point to the *j* and say /j/. Point to the e and say /e/.

Slide the *e* next to the *j*. Move your hand under the letters and blend the sounds, elongating them /jjee/. Have children repeat after you. Point to the *ll* and say /l/. Have children repeat. Slide the *ll* next to *je*. Move your hand under the letters and blend the sounds, elongating them /jjeellll/. Point to the letter *y* and say /ē/. Slide the *y* next to *jell*. Slide your hand under *jelly* and blend by elongating the sounds /jjeellēē/. Have children repeat. Then have children read the word *jelly* along with you.

Follow the same procedure for the words *belly*, *bunny*, *funny*, *furry*, and *hurry*.

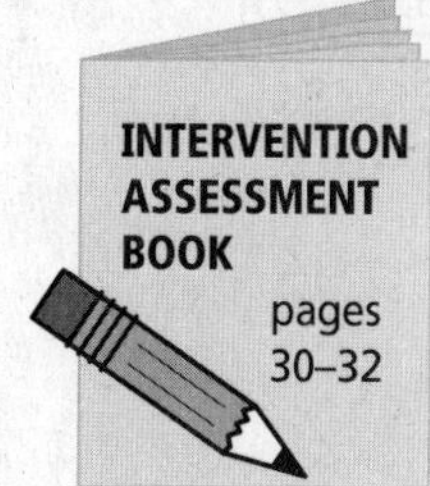

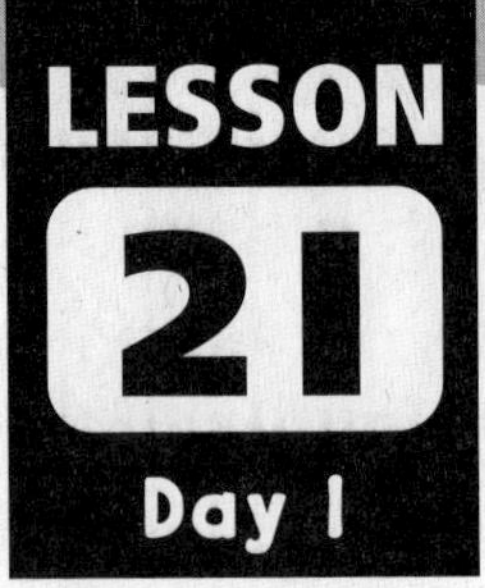

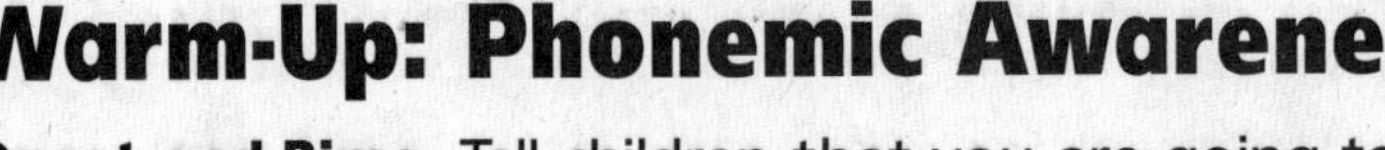

Warm-Up: Phonemic Awareness

Onset and Rime Tell children that you are going to say some words, but you are going to say them in parts. Have children listen to see if they can figure out the word. Demonstrate by saying: **/k/-ountry—What word did I say?** (*country*)

/pr/-etty	**/s/-afely**	**/n/-avy**
/d/-uty	**/l/-azy**	**/v/-ictory**

MATERIALS

Word Cards different, old, water, years

Word Builder

Word Builder Cards b, f, h, i, l, l, n, n, r, r, s, u, y

Alphabet Master Yy

A House and a Tepee

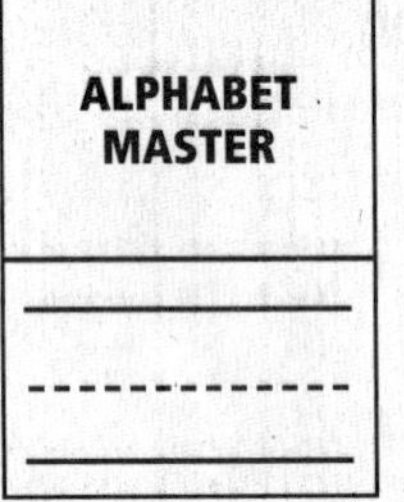

Phonics: Long Vowel /ē/y

RETEACH **blending** Display Alphabet Master *Yy*. **This letter is *y*. When the letter *y* is a vowel, it can stand for the /ē/ sound, the long sound of *e* at the end of words such as *safety*, *kitty*, and *baby*.** Point to the Alphabet Master and say /ē/. Have children repeat the sound as you touch the letter *y* several times.

Use the Word Builder Cards and a pocket chart to model blending words.

s u n n y

Place the Word Builder cards *s*, *u*, *n*, *n*, and *y* in the Word Builder. Point to the *s* and say /s/. Point to the *u* and say /u/. Slide the *u* next to the *s*. Move your hand under the letters and blend the sounds, elongating them /ssuu/. Have children repeat after you. Point to the *nn* and say /n/. Slide the *nn* next to the *su*. Move your hand under the letters and blend the sounds, elongating them /ssuunn/. Have children repeat after you. Point to the *y* and say /ē/. Slide the *y* next to the *sunn*. Move your hand under the letters and blend the sounds, elongating them /ssunnēē/. Have children repeat after you. Then say the word naturally—*sunny*. Have children do the same.

High-Frequency Words

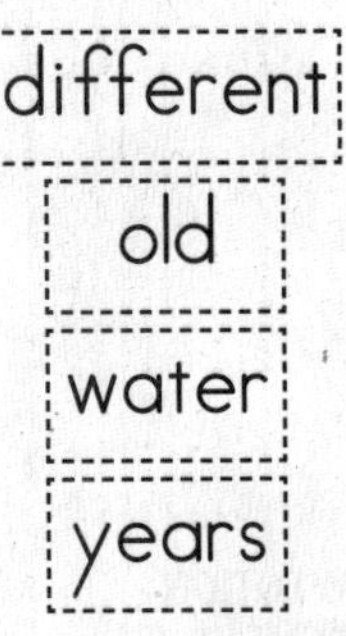

PRETEACH ***different, old, water, years*** Display the word card *different*. **This word is *different*. We each like different foods. Read the word with me—*different*. Spell the word with me—*d-i-f-f-e-r-e-n-t*. Read the word with me. What is this word?** (*different*)

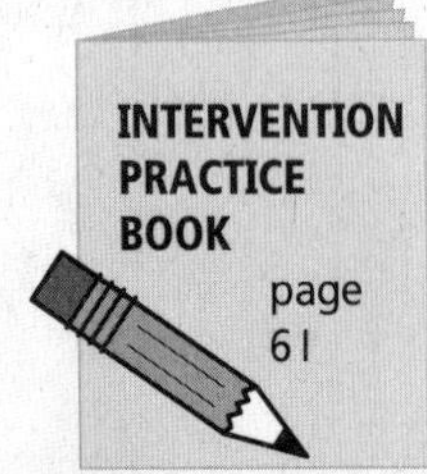

Follow the same procedure for the words old, water, and years.

old—**How old are you?**

water—**You should drink lots of water.**

years—**She is seven years old.**

Then place the four words in a pocket chart and have volunteers read the words, as you randomly point to them.

Read: *A House and a Teepee*

A House and a Teepee

Story Words Write the word *teepee*. Read the word and have children repeat it after you. Tell children that they will read about a special kind of home called a *teepee*. Help children with the word as needed.

Distribute copies of the book and have children put their finger on the title. Have children follow along as you read the title aloud. Ask children to point out the names of the people who wrote and illustrated the book. Read the names aloud. Then echo read the book with children. Read page 2 aloud and then have children read it to you. Follow this procedure throughout the book.

Phonics: Word Building with /ē/y

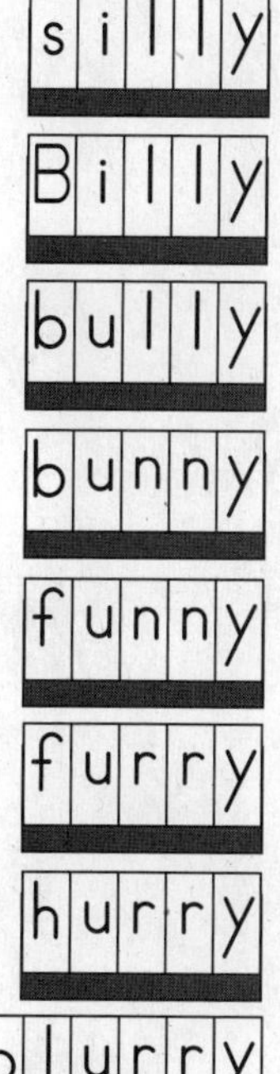

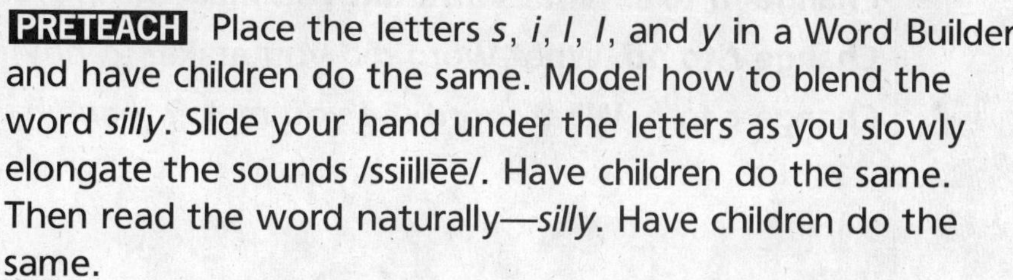

PRETEACH Place the letters *s*, *i*, *l*, *l*, and *y* in a Word Builder and have children do the same. Model how to blend the word *silly*. Slide your hand under the letters as you slowly elongate the sounds /ssiillēē/. Have children do the same. Then read the word naturally—*silly*. Have children do the same.

Have children blend and read new words by telling them:

Change *s* to *b*. What word did you make? (*Billy*)

Change *i* to *u*. What word did you make? (*bully*)

Change *ll* to *nn*. What word did you make? (*bunny*)

Change *b* to *f*. What word did you make? (*funny*)

Change *nn* to *rr*. What word did you make? (*furry*)

Change *f* to *h*. What word did you make? (*hurry*)

Change *h* to *bl*. What word did you make? (*blurry*)

Distribute *Intervention Practice Book* page 61 to children.

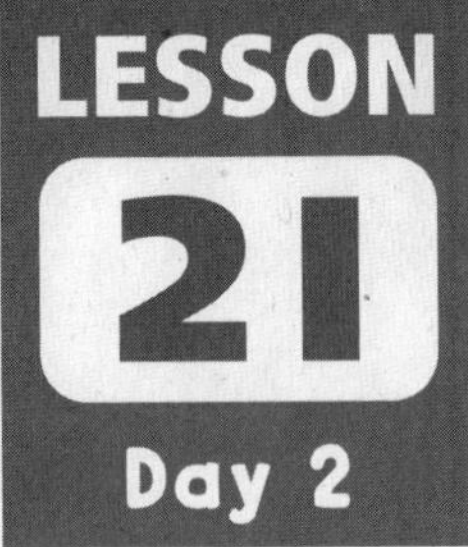

Warm-Up: Phonemic Awareness

Phoneme Isolation Say the word *tiny* aloud and have children repeat it. Tell children to listen to the /ē/ sound at the end of *tiny*. Then say the words *girl* and *quarry* and have children repeat both words. Ask: **Which of these words has the /ē/ sound you hear in *tiny*?** (*quarry*)

Continue with the words *pony*, *track*, *empty*; *army*, *swampy*, *feet*; *hurry*, *hard*, *bubbly*.

MATERIALS

Word Builder

Word Builder Cards a, b, c, e, l, l, m, o, r, r, t, y

A House and a Tepee

Phonics: Word Building with /ē/y

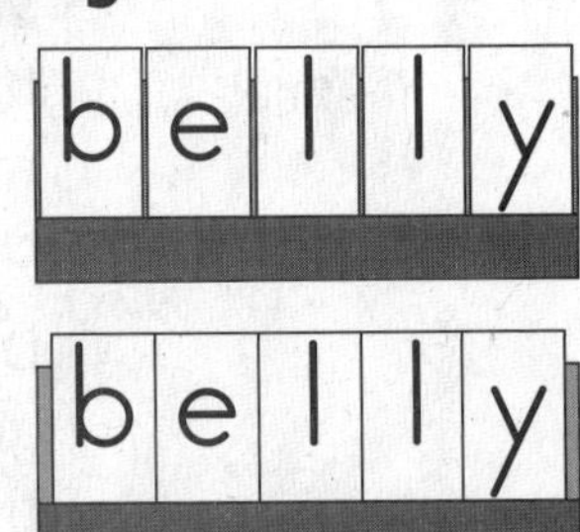

RETEACH Place the letters *b*, *e*, *l*, *l*, and *y* in a Word Builder and have children do the same. Model how to blend the word *belly*. Slide your hand under the letters as you slowly elongate the sounds /bbeellēē /. Have children do the same. Then read the word naturally—*belly*. Have children do the same.

Have children blend and read new words by telling them:

Change *ll* to *rr*. What word did you make? (*berry*)

Change *be* to *ma*. What word did you make? (*marry*)

Change *m* to *c*. What word did you make? (*carry*)

Change *r* to *nd*. What word did you make? (*candy*)

Change *c* to *h*. What word did you make? (*handy*)

High-Frequency Words

RETEACH ***different, old, water, years*** Write the word want and have children read it. Then write the word different next to want and have children read the word. How are these words the same? How are they different? Let's read them again:

want   different

Read: *A House and a Teepee*

A House and a Teepee

Distribute copies of the book to children and read the title aloud. Point to the words *A* and *a*. Have children notice that *a* is not written as a capital letter in this title except when it is at the very beginning. Explain that small words like *the*, *a*, and *and* are not written with capital letters in the title unless the words come at the beginning. Then choral read the book with children. Let your voice fade if children start to gain control of the text.

Phonics: Reading Sentences with /ē/y

PRETEACH Distribute Intervention Practice Book page 62 to children. Point to the first sentence and have children read it aloud. Ask them to find the word *jelly*, frame it with their fingers, and circle the word. Then work with children to complete the page.

LESSON 21 Day 3

Warm-Up: Phonemic Awareness

Onset and Rime Tell children that they are going to play a guessing game. Then say: **I'm thinking of a word that is something that makes you laugh. It is /f/-unny. What's my word?** (*funny*) Continue with the following words: /s/-illy (*silly*), /pr/-etty (*pretty*), and /r/-unny (*runny*).

MATERIALS

Word Builder

Word Builder Cards d, f, h, i, l, n, n, r, r, t, u, y

Picture Cards bed, box, cat, clock, desk, fish, igloo, jet, kite, nest, octopus, red, ship, six, sun

A House and a Tepee

Phonics: Reading Sentences with /ē/y

RETEACH Help children blend and read new words and sentences shown. Have them read the sentence, blending each word in sequence. The high-frequency words are underlined; they should read these as a unit, not blending the sounds.

mommy **study** **hobby** **guppy**

<u>My</u> <u>friends</u> <u>were</u> happy at the party.

I <u>have</u> a penny.

<u>My</u> daddy <u>writes</u> funny <u>books</u>.

We must hurry <u>to</u> <u>the</u> park.

High-Frequency Words

RETEACH ***different, old, water, years*** Write the following sentence on tagboard and display it in a pocket chart along with the Picture Cards *clock*, *desk*, *fish*, *kite*, *octopus*, *red*. Call on children to choose a Picture Card to complete the sentence and to read it aloud. Then ask: **Do you really want an _____?**

PICTURE CARDS

I want a different _____.

Do the same for the following sentence and Picture Cards *box*, *cat*, *jet*, *nest*, *six*, *sun*.

That _____ is two years old.

Do the same for the following sentence and Picture Cards *bed*, *clock*, *fish*, *igloo*, *octopus*, *ship*.

The _____ goes in the water.

Read: *A House and a Teepee*

Distribute copies of the book and have children put their fingers on the title. Ask what this book is about. Then guide children through as they read.

Pages 2–5: Have children read to find out what the story is about.

What does the story say about homes? Find and read the sentence that tells. (*Homes can be different*) **Where can people live?** (*in a teepee and in a house*) **When did people live in teepees?** (*many years ago*)

Pages 6–9: Have children read the pages to find out how a teepee and a house are the same and different.

What is one way a house and a teepee are different? (*the time it takes to make them*) **How many rooms in a teepee?** (*one big room*) **Find and read the sentence that tells. How many rooms in a house?** (*many different rooms*)

Pages 10–11: Have children read to find out what a house and a teepee can do.

Which home keeps a family warm in winter and fresh in summer? (*both of them*)

Page 12: Have the children read to find out what happened if people wanted to move.

Which home is easier to move? (*the teepee*)

Ask children to use the pictures to help summarize the book.

Phonics: Building Words

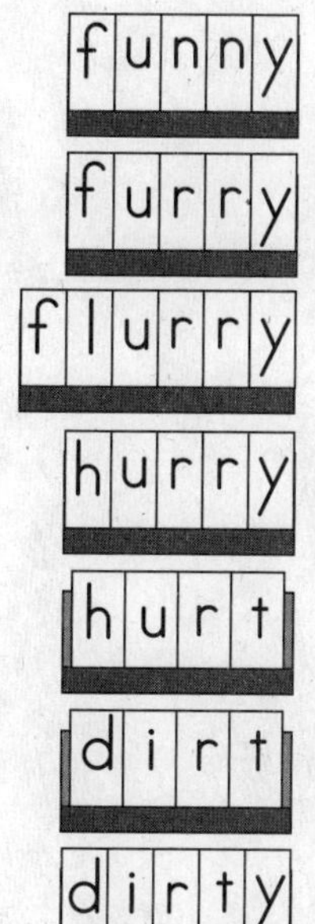

PRETEACH Put the letters *f*, *u*, *n*, *n*, and *y* in a Word Builder and have children do the same. Slide your hand under the letters as you blend the sounds—/ffuunnēē/. Then read the word naturally—*funny*. Have children repeat after you. Then have children build and read new words.

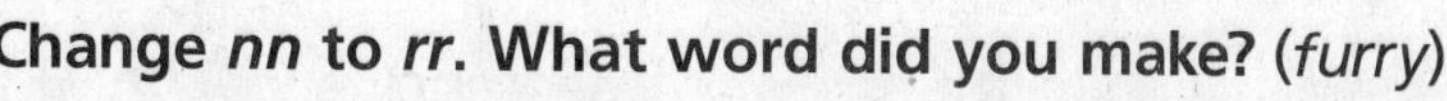

Change *nn* to *rr*. What word did you make? (*furry*)
Add *l* after the *f*. What word did you make? (*flurry*)
Change *fl* to *h*. What word did you make? (*hurry*)
Change *ry* to *t*. What word did you make? (*hurt*)
Change *hu* to *di*. What word did you make? (*dirt*)
Add *y* after the *t*. What word did you make? (*dirty*)

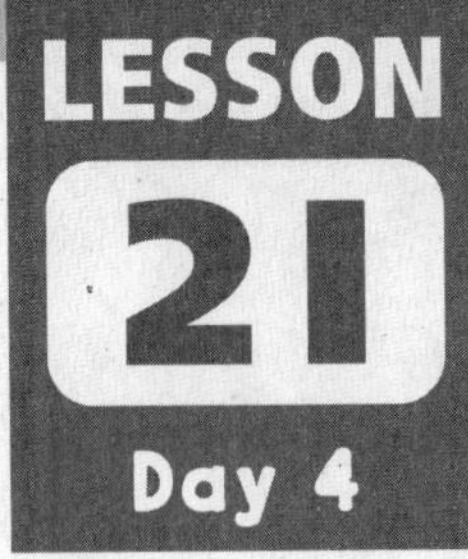

MATERIALS

Word Cards different, old, over, water, world, years

Word Builder

Word Builder Cards b, r, j, e, f, h, l, n, r, u, y, l, n

A House and a Tepee

Warm-Up: Phonemic Awareness

Phoneme Blending Tell children that they are going to be builders and put together pieces of words to make whole words. Say: **This is good on toast. It is /j/-/e/-/l/-/ē/. What word did I say?** *(jelly)* Continue with the following words: *messy*, *tiny*, *buggy*.

Phonics: Building Words

RETEACH Put the letters *j*, *e*, *l*, *l*, and *y* in a Word Builder and have children do the same. Slide your hand under the letters as you blend the sounds—/jjeellēē/. Then read the word naturally—*jelly*. Have children repeat after you. Then have children build and read new words.

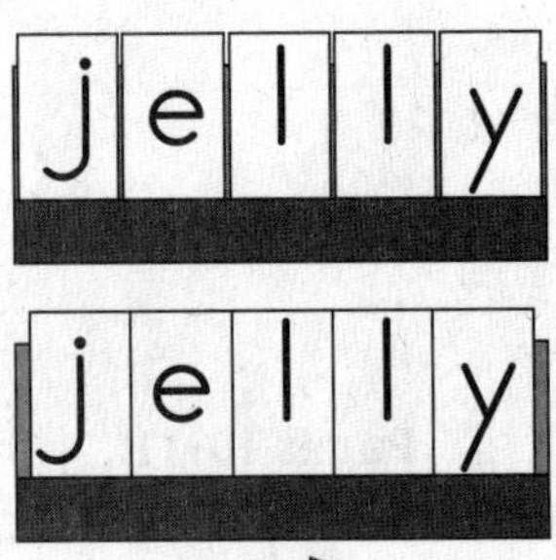

Change ***j*** **to** ***b*****. What word did you make?** *(belly)*

Change e to ***u*****. What word did you make?** *(bully)*

Change ***ll*** **to** ***nn*****. What word did you make?** *(bunny)*

Change ***b*** **to** ***f*****. What word did you make?** *(funny)*

Change ***nn*** **to** ***rr*****. What word did you make?** *(furry)*

Change the ***f*** **to** ***h*****. What word did you make?** *(hurry)*

Distribute *Intervention Practice Book* page 63 to children.

High-Frequency Words

different
old
water
years
world
over

RETEACH ***different, old, water, years, world, over***
Distribute word cards with the words listed above. Have partners take turns displaying the words for each other and reading them. After they read each word, have children spell the word and then repeat the word. Then have them spell the word again and write it on a sheet of paper.

Read: *A House and a Teepee*

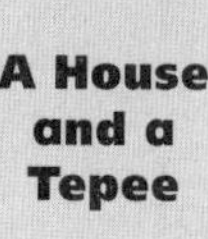

Classify/Categorize Remind children that being able to think of how certain things are alike and different can help them organize what they learn in a story. Have children reread *A House and a Teepee*. Have them make a list of what each type of home is like.

House	Teepee
takes time to make	takes little time to make
many different rooms	one big room
	can be moved

Phonics: Inflections -es, -ing, -ed

PRETEACH Write the letters *-es*, *-ing*, and *-ed* at the top of a sheet of chart paper. Explain that when words end in *y* you often have to change that *y* to the letter *i* before adding the *-es* and *-ed* endings. Help children suggest *y*-ending words that end with *-es* such as *puppies*. Then write the words underneath the heading *-es*. Use the same procedure for *-ing* and *-ed*. Then have children read each column of words. End the activity by pointing to words at random and having children read the words.

-es	-ing	-ed
puppies	hurrying	studied
parties	emptying	hurried
copies	babying	copied

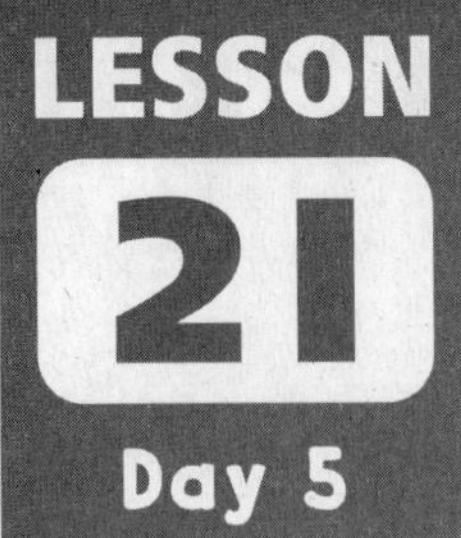

LESSON 21 Day 5

Warm-Up: Phonemic Awareness

Phoneme Blending Tell children that together you are going to play a puzzle game. Tell them that you are going to say some words in pieces like a puzzle and they should listen to see if they can put the puzzle pieces together to figure out the word. Listen: **/kw/-/är/-/ē/. What word does /kw/-/är/-/ē/ say?** (*quarry*). Continue with the following words:

/g/-/u/-/m/-/ē/ (*gummy*)
/w/-/ûr/-/ē/ (*worry*)
/d/-/ī/-/m/ (*dime*)
/s/-/ā/-/f/-/t/-/ē/ (*safety*)
/m/-/ī/-/n/ (*mine*)
/b/-/ī/-/k/ (*bike*)

MATERIALS

Write-on/Wipe-off Boards

Word Cards different, old, over, town, water, world, years

Word Builder

Word Builder Cards b, e, h, i, k, l, n, t, w

Phonics: Inflections -es, -ing, -ed

RETEACH Write the word *baby* on a Write-on/ Wipe-off Board and have children do the same. Then have them read the word. Ask: **What letter should we write if we want to change baby to babies?** (*ies*) **Let's do that.** Continue the activity with the following words: *babying* and *babied*. Repeat the activity, using the words *empty*, *empties*, *emptying*, *emptied*; *hurry*, *hurries*, *hurrying*, *hurried*.

High-Frequency Words

different
old
water
years
over
world
town

Cumulative Review *different, old, water, years, over, world, town* Place the words in a pocket chart. Say aloud one of the words and use it in a sentence. Have a volunteer find and point to the word. Have children clap and say the spelling of the word. Then have them write it. Have children read aloud their list of words.

Read: Self-Selected Reading

Have children select a book to read from their browsing boxes. After they have completed their reading, have them tell you what they were most successful in during the reading of the book.

Long Vowel /ī/i-e

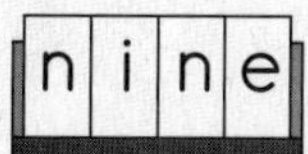

PRETEACH Use the Word Builder and Word Builder Cards to model blending words.

Place the Word Builder Cards *n*, *i*, *n*, and *e* in the Word Builder. Ask children to name each letter. Tell children that *e* at the end of the word is silent and helps *i* stand for /ī/, the long sound of *i* in the middle of the word *like*. Point to the *n* and say /n/. Point to the *i* and say /ī/.

Slide the *i* next to the *n*. Move your hand under the letters and blend the sounds, elongating them /nnīī/. Have children repeat after you. Point to the letter *n* and say /n/. Slide the *ne* next to the *ni*. Slide your hand under nine and blend by elongating the sounds /nnīīnn/. Have children repeat. Then have children read the word *nine* along with you.

Follow the same procedure for the words *line*, *like*, *bike*, *bite*, and *while*.

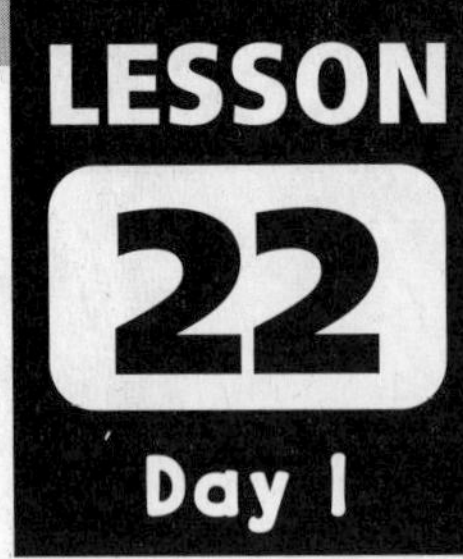

Warm-Up: Phonemic Awareness

Onset and Rime Tell children that you are going to say some words, but you are going to say them in parts. Have children listen to see if they can figure out the word. Demonstrate by saying: **/g/-ide—What word did I say?** (*guide*)

/ch/-ime	**/sp/-ine**	**/str/-ipe**
/pr/-ime	**/kw/-ite**	**/hw/-ine**

MATERIALS

Word Cards because, most, picture, why

Word Builder

Word Builder Cards b, e, h, i, k, l, n, n, t, w

Alphabet Masters Ee, Ii

Picture a Kite

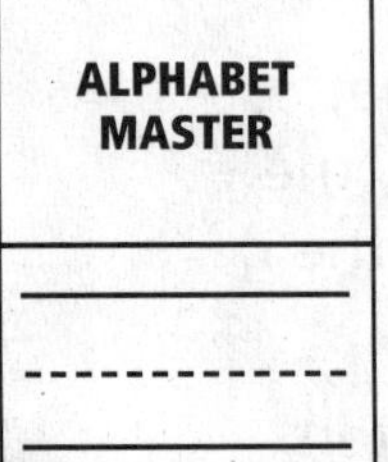

Phonics: Long Vowel /ī/i-e

RETEACH **Blending** Display Alphabet Masters *Ii* and *Ee*. **These letters are *i* and *e*. When a short word has an *i*-consonant-*e*, the vowel *e* is silent and causes the *i* to say /ī/, the long sound in words such as *nine*, *bike*, and *while*.** Point to the Alphabet Masters and say /ī/. Have children repeat the sound as you touch the letter *i* several times.

Use the Word Builder Cards and a pocket chart to model blending words.

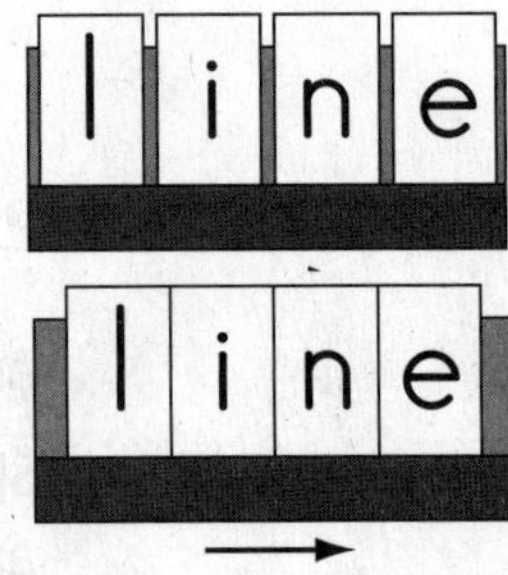

Place the Word Builder cards *l*, *i*, *n*, and *e* in the Word Builder. Point to the *l* and say /l/. Point to the *i* and say /ī/. Slide the *i* next to the *l*. Move your hand under the letters and blend the sounds, elongating them /llīī/. Have children repeat after you. Point to the *n* and say /n/. Slide the *ne* next to the *li*. Move your hand under the letters and blend the sounds, elongating them /llīīnn/. Have children repeat after you. Then say the word naturally—*line*. Have children do the same.

High-Frequency Words

because

most

picture

why

PRETEACH ***because, most, picture, why*** Display the word card *because*. **This word is *because*. Our teacher was happy because we helped each other. Read the word with me—*because*. Spell the word with me—*b-e-c-a-u-s-e*. Read the word with me. What is this word?** (*because*)

Follow the same procedure for the words *most*, *picture*, and *why*.

most—**I work hard most of the time.**

picture—**She drew that picture for her mom.**

why—**Why is the sky blue?**

Then place the four words in a pocket chart and have volunteers read the words, as you randomly point to them.

Read: *Picture a Kite*

Distribute copies of the book and have children put their finger on the title. Have children follow along as you read the title aloud. Have children find and frame the words *picture* and *kite*. Echo read the book with children. Read page 2 aloud and then have children read it to you. Follow this procedure throughout the book.

Phonics: Word Building with /ī/i-e

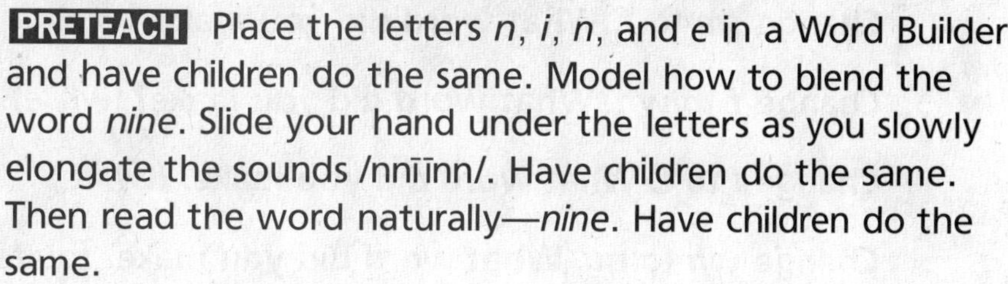

PRETEACH Place the letters *n*, *i*, *n*, and *e* in a Word Builder and have children do the same. Model how to blend the word *nine*. Slide your hand under the letters as you slowly elongate the sounds /nnīīnn/. Have children do the same. Then read the word naturally—*nine*. Have children do the same.

Have children blend and read new words by telling them:

Change the first *n* to *l*. What word did you make? (*line*)

Change *n* to *k*. What word did you make? (*like*)

Change *l* to *b*. What word did you make? (*bike*)

Change *k* to *t*. What word did you make? (*bite*)

Change *b* to *k*. What word did you make? (*kite*)

Change *k* to *wh*. What word did you make? (*white*)

Distribute *Intervention Practice Book* page 64 to children.

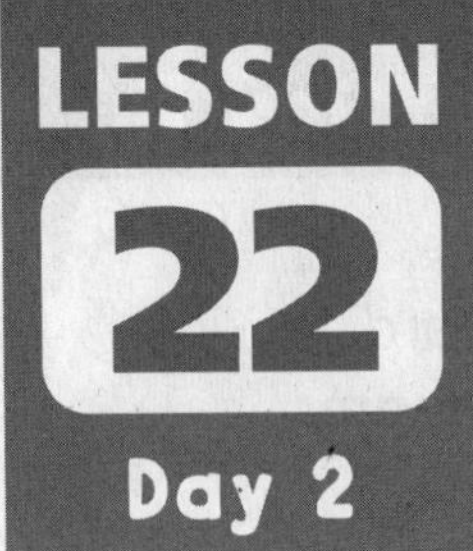

MATERIALS

Picture Cards: fish, igloo, kite, nine, pig, six, smile

Word Builder

Word Builder Cards b, e, f, h, i, l, m, q, s, t, u, w

Picture a Kite

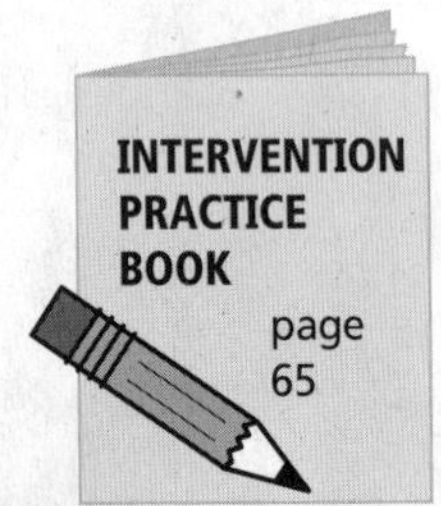

Warm-Up: Phonemic Awareness

Phoneme Isolation Display the Picture Cards *kite*, *nine*, and *pig*. Hold up the *kite*. Have children say the word *kite* aloud. Tell children to listen to the /ī/ sound in the middle of the word *kite*. Have them say the names of the other two pictures aloud. Ask: **What other picture name has the /ī/ sound you hear in** kite? (*nine*)

PICTURE CARDS

Continue with the Picture Cards *kite*, *six*, *smile*; *smile*, *igloo*, *nine*; *nine*, *kite*, *fish*.

Phonics: Word Building with /ī/i-e

RETEACH Place the letters *m*, *i*, *l*, and *e* in a Word Builder and have children do the same. Model how to blend the word *mile*. Slide your hand under the letters as you slowly elongate the sounds /mmīīll/. Have children do the same. Then read the word naturally—*mile*. Have children do the same.

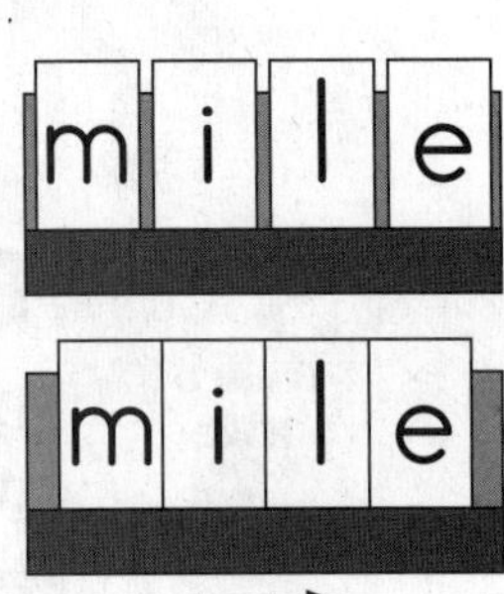

Have children blend and read new words by telling them:

Add an *s* **to the front of** *mile*. **What word did you make?** (*smile*)

Change *sm* **to** *f*. **What word did you make?** (*file*)

Change *f* **to** *wh*. **What word did you make?** (*while*)

Change *l* **to** *t*. **What word did you make?** (*white*)

Change *wh* **to** *qu*. **What word did you make?** (*quite*)

Change *qu* **to** *b*. **What word did you make?** (*bite*)

High-Frequency Words

RETEACH ***because***, ***most***, ***picture***, ***why*** Write the word *use* and have children read it. Then write the word *because* next to *use* and have children read the word. **How are these words the same? How are they different? Let's read them again:**

use　　because

Repeat the procedure with *turn/picture* and *who/why*.

Read: *Picture a Kite*

Picture a Kite

Distribute copies of the book to children and have them read the title aloud. Again have children frame the words *picture* and *kite*. Point to the word *a*. Point out that *a* is not written as a capital letter in this title. **Small words like *the*, *a*, and *and* are not important enough words to be written with capital letters in a title unless they come at the beginning.** Ask children to point to the name of the people who wrote and illustrated the book. Read the names aloud. Then choral read the book with children. Let your voice fade if children start to gain control of the text.

Phonics: Reading Sentences with /ī/i-e

PRETEACH Distribute *Intervention Practice Book* page 65 to children. Point to the first sentence and have children read it aloud. Ask them to find the word *vine*, frame it with their fingers, and circle the word. Then work with children to complete the page.

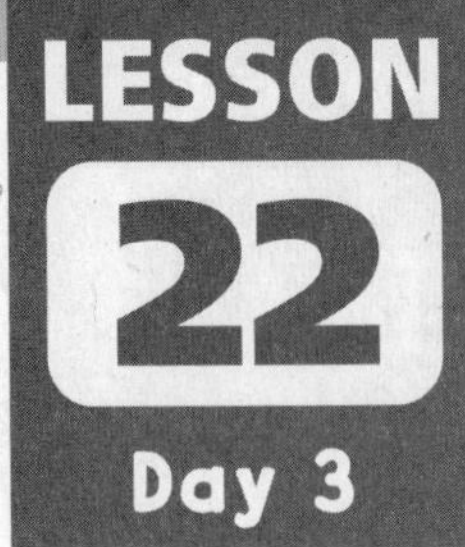

Warm-Up: Phonemic Awareness

Phoneme Blending Tell children that they are going to play a guessing game. Then say: **I'm thinking of a word that is something you can fly in the wind. It is /k/-/ī/-/t/. What's my word?** (*kite*) Continue with the following words: /d/-/ī/-/v/ (*dive*), /s/-/t/-/r/-/ī/-/p/ (*stripe*), /t/-/r/-/ī/-/b/ (*tribe*), /w/-/ī/-/f/ (*wife*).

MATERIALS

Word Cards because, most, picture, why

Word Builder

Word Builder Cards a, e, f, h, i, k, l, n, t, v

Picture Cards: bug, cat, gate, jet, lock, nut, zebra

Picture a Kite

Phonics: Reading Sentences with /ī/i-e

RETEACH Help children blend and read new words and sentences shown. Have them read the sentence, blending each word in sequence. The high-frequency words are underlined; they should read these as a unit, not blending the sounds.

spine **file** **hide** **ripe**

<u>The</u> bride wore white.

<u>She</u> <u>should</u> win <u>the</u> prize.

What <u>a</u> big smile!

Can <u>you</u> <u>play</u> <u>on</u> <u>the</u> slide?

High-Frequency Words

RETEACH ***because, most, picture, why*** Write the following sentence on tag board and display it in a pocket chart along with the Picture Cards *bug*, *cat*, *gate*, *jet*, *lock*, *nut*, *zebra*. Call on children to choose a Picture Card to complete the sentence and to read it aloud. **Then ask: Is a _____ really funny?**

PICTURE CARDS

I made a picture of the _____ because it is funny.

Do the same for the following sentences and the Picture Cards above.

Why do most people like that _____.

Read: *Picture a Kite*

Picture a Kite

Distribute copies of the book and have children put their finger on the title. Ask what this book is about. Then guide children through as they read.

Pages 2–3: Have children read to find out what is the girl's problem.

> **What is the girl's problem?** (*she can't go to sleep*) **Find and read the sentence that tells. What does Nana tell her to do?** (*get into bed and picture a kite*)

Pages 4–7: Have children read the pages to find out why she should picture a kite.

> **Why does Nana tell her to picture a kite?** (*It will help her sleep.*) **Find and read the sentence that tells. What question does the girl ask?** (*why she should picture a pink flying kite*) **Find and read her question.**

Pages 8–11: Have children read to find out what her grandmother tells her.

> **Why should the girl picture the flying kite?** (*to help her sleep*) **What does her grandmother tell her to picture the kite doing?** (*flying over the town and as the sun goes down*)

Page 12: Have children read to find out when the girl should picture the kite.

> **When should the girl picture the kite?** (*as she sleeps*) **Read the sentence that tells.**

Ask children to use the pictures to help summarize the book.

Phonics: Building Words

PRETEACH Place the letters *f*, *i*, *n*, and *e* in a Word Builder and have children do the same. Slide your hand under the letters as you blend the sounds—/ffīīnn/. Then read the word naturally—*fine*. Have children repeat after you. Then have children build and read new words.

Change the *n* to *v*. What word did you make? (*five*)

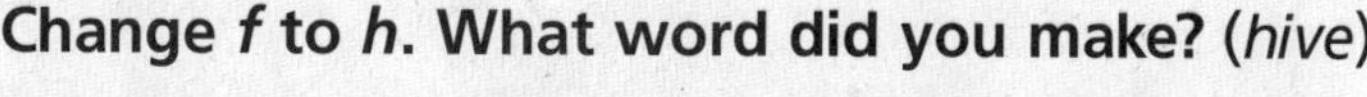

Change *f* to *h*. What word did you make? (*hive*)

Change *h* to *l*. What word did you make? (*live*)

Change *v* to *k*. What word did you make? (*like*)

Change *i* to *a*. What word did you make? (*lake*)

Change *l* to *t*. What word did you make? (*take*)

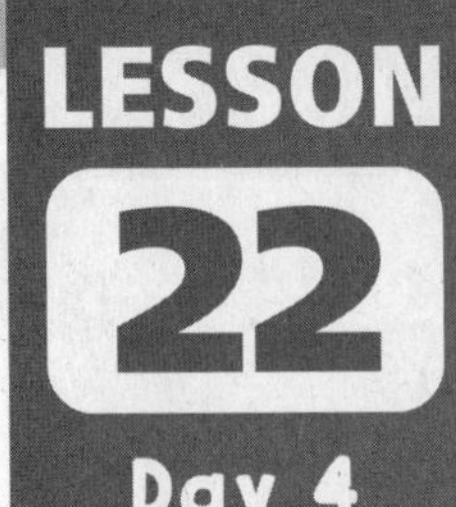

Warm-Up: Phonemic Awareness

Phoneme Segmentation Have children use the three boxes on the Write-on/Wipe-off Boards. Remind children that the boxes stand for the sounds in words. Show the Picture Card *nine* and ask: **What is the first sound you hear in nine?** (/n/) Have children place a disk in the first box. Then have children name the second sound in *nine* (/ī/) and place a disk in the second box. Then have them identify the last sound in *nine* (/n/) and place a disk in the third box. Point to each box in sequence as children say the word. **How many sounds do you hear in nine?** (*three*) Repeat this procedure with the following Picture Cards: *fan*, *hat*, *kite*, *pin*.

PICTURE CARDS

MATERIALS

Picture Cards: fan, hat, kite, pin, nine

Write-on/Wipe-off Boards with disks

Word Cards because, most, picture, water, why, years

Word Builder

Word Builder Cards e, f, h, i, l, m, r, s, v, w

Picture a Kite

Phonics: Building Words

RETEACH Put the letters *h*, *i*, *v*, and e in a Word Builder and have children do the same. Slide your hand under the letters as you blend the sounds—/hhīīvv/. Then read the word naturally—*hive*. Have children repeat after you. Then have children build and read new words.

Change the *h* to *l*. What word did you make? (*live*)

Change *v* to *m*. What word did you make? (*lime*)

Change *m* to *f*. What word did you make? (*life*)

Change *l* to *w*. What word did you make? (*wife*)

Change *f* to *s*. What word did you make? (*wise*)

Change *w* to *r*. What word did you make? (*rise*)

Distribute *Intervention Practice Book* page 66 to children.

because

most

picture

why

years

water

High-Frequency Words

RETEACH ***because, most, picture, why, years, water***
Distribute word cards with the words listed above. Have partners take turns displaying the words for each other and reading them. After they read each word, have children spell the word and then repeat the word. Then have them spell the word again and write it on a sheet of paper.

Read: *Picture a Kite*

Focus Skill **Draw Conclusions** Remind children that being able to draw conclusions or figure things the story doesn't tell directly can help them understand a story. Have children read *Picture a Kite* and then together make a list of things they figured out for themselves.

What We Know
Nana is taking care of the girl.
The girl has a good imagination.
It is bedtime.
Nana loves the girl.

Phonics: Phonograms -ine, -ite

PRETEACH Write the letters *-ine* and *-ite* at the top of a sheet of chart paper. Have children suggest words that end with *-ine* and say what letters they would need to write the words. Then write the words underneath the heading *-ine*. Use the same procedure for *-ite*. Then have children read each column of words. End the activity by pointing to words at random and having children read the words.

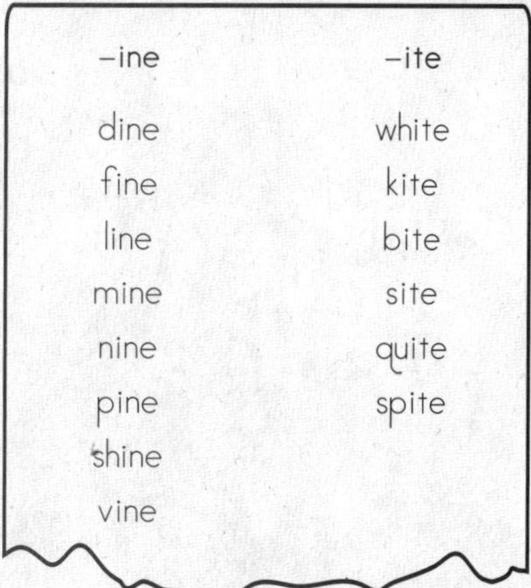

–ine	–ite
dine	white
fine	kite
line	bite
mine	site
nine	quite
pine	spite
shine	
vine	

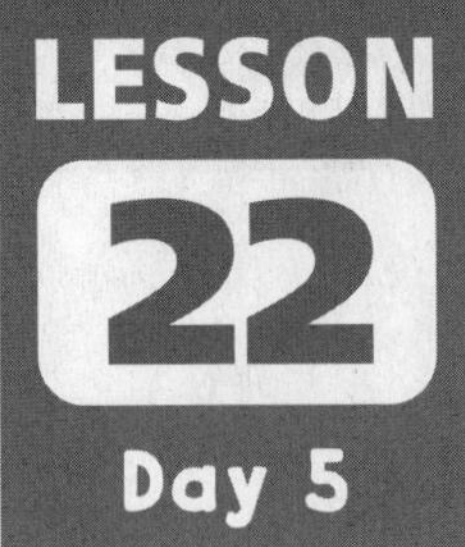

Warm-Up: Phonemic Awareness

Phoneme Blending Tell children that together you are going to play a game of "Fix It." Tell them that you are going to say some words that are all broken and they should listen to see if they can put the sounds together to figure out the word. **Listen: /h/-/ī/-/d/. What word does /h/-/ī/-/d/ say?** (*hide*) Continue with the following words:

/hw/-/ī/-/l/ (*while*)	**/p/-/r/-/ī/-/d/** (*pride*)
/p/-/r/-/ī/-/m/ (*prime*)	**/r/-/ī/-/s/** (*rice*)
/ī/-/s/ (*ice*)	**/f/-/ā/-/s/** (*face*)

MATERIALS

Write-on/Wipe-off Boards

Word Cards because, different, most, old, why, years

Word Builder

Word Builder Cards a, c, e, f, i, n, p, r, s

Phonics: Phonograms -ine, -ite

RETEACH Write the word line on a Write-on/Wipe-off Board and have children do the same. Then have them read the word. Ask: **What letter should we write if we want to change *line* to *fine*?** (*f*) **Let's do that.** Continue the activity with the following words: *nine*, *mine*, *dine*, and *spine*. Repeat the activity, using the words *bite*, *white*, *quite*, and *kite*.

High-Frequency Words

Cumulative Review *because, most, why, different, old, years* Place the words in a pocket chart. Say aloud one of the words and use it in a sentence. Have a volunteer find and point to the word. Have children clap and say the spelling of the word. Then have them write it. Have children read aloud their list of words.

because

most

why

different

old

years

Read: Self-Selected Reading

Have children select a book to read from their browsing boxes. After they have completed their reading, have them show you a word, such as a long *i* word, that they figured out on their own.

Phonics: Consonant /s/c

PRETEACH Write the letters *ce* on the board or on chart paper. **When the letter *c* is followed by *e*, it can stand for the /s/ sound in words such as *ice*, *face*, and *nice*.** Point to the letters *ce* and say /s/. Have children repeat the sound as you touch the letters *ce* several times.

Use the Word Builder and Word Builder Cards to model blending words.

Place the Word Builder Cards *i*, *c*, and *e* in the Word Builder. Point to the *i* and say /ī/. Point to the *ce* and say /s/.

Slide the *ce* next to the *i*. Move your hand under the letters and blend the sounds, elongating them /īīss/. Have children repeat after you. Then have children read the word *ice* along with you.

Follow the same procedure for the words *nice*, *rice*, *race*, *face*, and *space*.

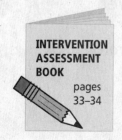

INTERVENTION ASSESSMENT BOOK
pages 33–34

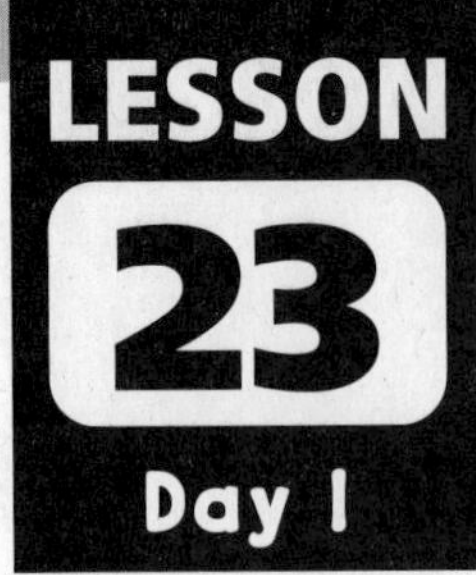

MATERIALS

Word Cards for always, does, even, pretty, say, sound

Word Builder

Word Builder Cards a, c, e, f, i, l, n, p, r, s

Alphabet Masters Cc

I Have a Robot

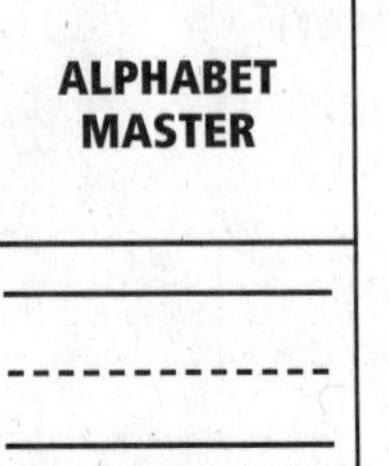

Warm-Up: Phonemic Awareness

Onset and Rime Tell children that you are going to say some words, but you are going to say them in parts. Have children listen to see if they can figure out the word. Demonstrate by saying: **/r/-ice—What word did I say?** (*rice*)

/m/-ice	**/n/-ice**	**/sp/-ice**	**/f/-ace**
/pl/-ace	**/l/-ace**	**/d/-ice**	**/pr/-ice**

Phonics: Consonant /s/c

RETEACH blending Display Alphabet Master *Cc*. **This letter is** ***c*****. When it is followed by** ***e*** **or** ***i*****, the letter** ***c*** **can stand for /s/, the sound at the end of words such as** ***face*****,** ***slice*****, and** ***nice*****.**

Have children repeat the sound as you touch the card several times.

Use the Word Builder Cards and a pocket chart to model blending words.

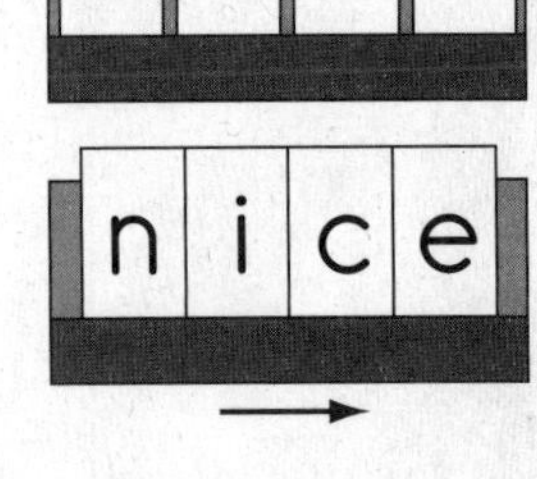

Place the Word Builder cards *n*, *i*, *c*, and *e* in the Word Builder. Point to the *n* and say /n/. Point to the *i* and *e* together and say /ī/.

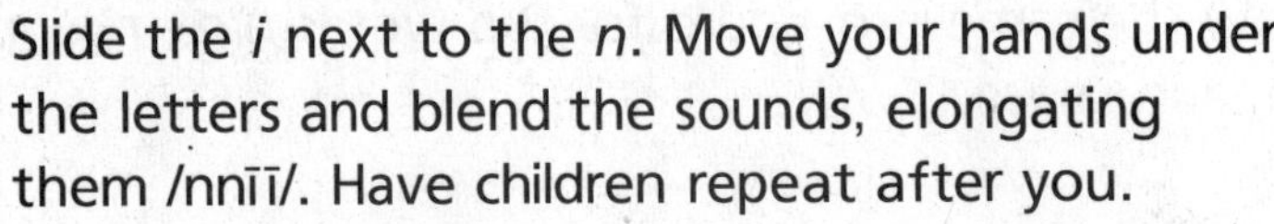

Slide the *i* next to the *n*. Move your hands under the letters and blend the sounds, elongating them /nnīī/. Have children repeat after you.

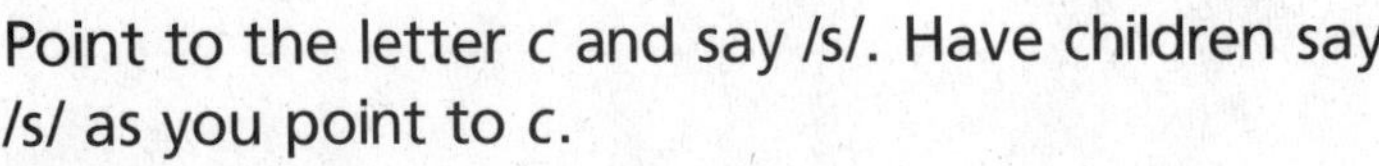

Point to the letter *c* and say /s/. Have children say /s/ as you point to *c*.

Slide *c* and *e* next to *ni*. Slide your hand under *nice* and blend by elongating the sounds—/nnīīss/. Have children repeat. Then have children read the word *nice* along with you.

High-Frequency Words

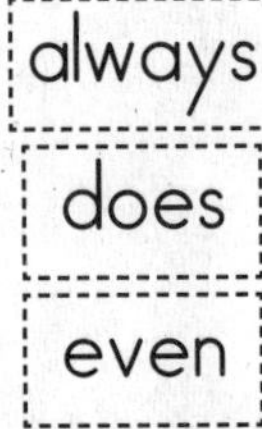

PRETEACH ***always, does, even, pretty, say, sound*** Display the word card *always*. **This word is** ***always*****. I have always wanted to visit the moon. Read the word with me—*****always*****. Spell the word with me—*****a-l-w-a-y-s*****. Read the word with me. What is this word?** (*always*)

Follow the same procedure for the words *does*, *even*, *pretty*, *say*, and *sound*.

does—**Does he have a sister?**

even—**I don't even know your name yet.**

pretty—**You painted a pretty picture.**

say—**I will say "Boo!" and scare you!**

sound—**Does the music sound nice?**

Then place the six words in a pocket chart and have volunteers read the words, as you randomly point to them.

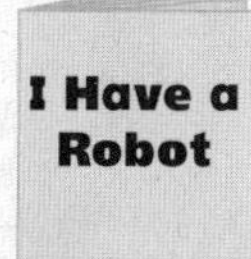

Read: *I Have a Robot*

Story words Write the words *robot* and *caterpillar* on the board. Say the words aloud and have children repeat them. Discuss with children that a robot is a machine that can do human tasks. Then point to *robot*, say it aloud, and have children repeat it. Do the same with *caterpillar*. Be sure to assist children in reading these words as they proceed with the story.

Distribute copies of the book and have children put their finger on the title. Read the title aloud while children follow along. Ask them to touch the word *I*, then the words *Have*, *a*, and *Robot*. Have volunteers choose a word in the title to read aloud. Echo read the book with children. Read page 2 aloud and then have children read it to you. Follow this procedure throughout the book.

Phonics: Word Building with /s/c

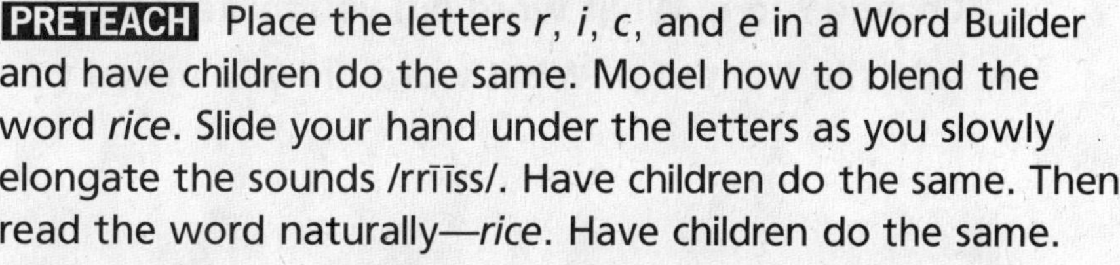

PRETEACH Place the letters *r*, *i*, *c*, and *e* in a Word Builder and have children do the same. Model how to blend the word *rice*. Slide your hand under the letters as you slowly elongate the sounds /rrīīss/. Have children do the same. Then read the word naturally—*rice*. Have children do the same.

Have children blend and read new words by telling them:

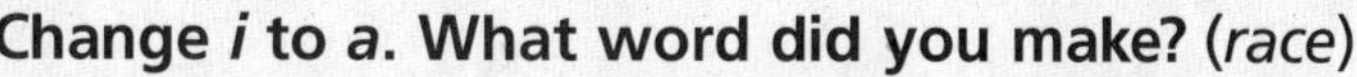

Change *i* to *a*. What word did you make? (*race*)

Change *r* to *l*. What word did you make? (*lace*)

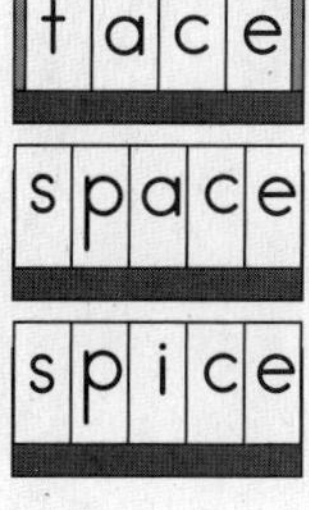

Change *l* to *f*. What word did you make? (*face*)

Change *f* to *sp*. What word did you make? (*space*)

Change *a* to *i*. What word did you make? (*spice*)

Distribute *Intervention Practice Book* page 67 to children.

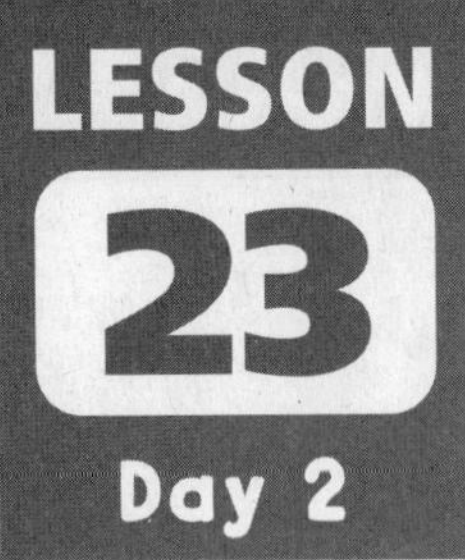

MATERIALS

Word Builder

Word Builder Cards a, c, e, f, i, n, p, r, s

I Have a Robot

Warm-Up: Phonemic Awareness

Phoneme Isolation Say the word *face* aloud and have children repeat it. Tell children to listen to the /s/ sound at the end of *face*. Then say the words *line* and *piece*. Ask: **Which of these words has the /s/ sound you hear in *face*?** (*piece*) Continue with the words *rice*, *hope*, *space*; *slice*, *race*, *lake*; *mice*, *fleece*, *gray*.

Phonics: Word Building with /s/c

RETEACH Place the letters *n*, *i*, *c*, and *e* in a Word Builder and have children do the same. Model how to blend the word *nice*. Slide your hand under the letters as you slowly elongate the sounds /nnīss/. Have children do the same. Then read the word naturally—*nice*. Have children do the same.

Have children blend and read new words by telling them:

Take away *n*. What word did you make? (*ice*)

Add *r* in front of *i*. What word did you make? (*rice*)

Change *i* to *a*. What word did you make? (*race*)

Change *r* to *f*. What word did you make? (*face*)

Change *f* to *p*. What word did you make? (*pace*)

Add *s* in front of *p*. What word did you make? (*space*)

High-Frequency Words

RETEACH ***always, does, even, pretty, say, sound*** Write the word *always* and have children read it. Then write the word *all* next to *always*. Have children read the word. **How are these words the same? How are they different? Let's read them again:**

always　　all

Repeat the procedure with *does/do*, *even/every*, *pretty/funny*, and *say/said*.

Read: *I Have a Robot*

I Have a Robot

Distribute copies of the book to children. Read page 2 with them. Have children find and point to the period at the end of the first sentence. Have children frame and read the first sentence. Then have them read the second sentence. Explain to the children that this page contains two different ideas. The ideas are separated into two sentences with a period at the end of each one. Then choral read the book with children. Let your voice fade if children start to gain control of the text.

Phonics: Reading Sentences with /s/c

PRETEACH Distribute *Intervention Practice Book* page 68 to children. Point to the first sentence and have children read it aloud. Ask them to find the word *rice*, frame it with their fingers, and circle the word. Then work with children to complete the page.

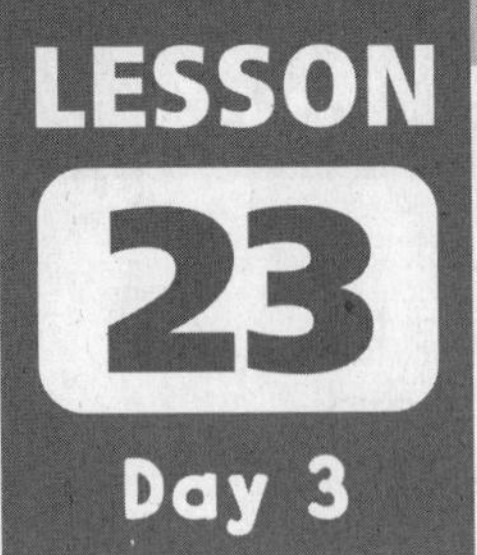

Warm-Up: Phonemic Awareness

Phoneme Blending Tell children that they are going to play a guessing game and find the word you are thinking about. Say: **I'm thinking of a word that tells how much you have to pay for something. It is a /p/-/r/-/ī/-/s/. What's my word?** (*price*) Continue with the following words: /f/-/ā/-/s/ (*face*), /m/-/ī/-/s/ (*mice*), /s/-/p/-/ā/-/s/ (*space*), /p/-/l/-/ā/-/s/ (*place*), /r/-/ī/-/s/ (*rice*).

MATERIALS

Picture Cards: clam, clock, desk, goat, jeep, mop, mule, nine, seal, ship, train

Word Builder

Word Builder Cards a, c, e, f, i, l, n, n, p, t

I Have a Robot

Phonics: Reading Sentences with /s/c

RETEACH Help children blend and read new words and sentences shown. Have them read the sentence, blending each word in sequence. The high-frequency words are underlined; children should read these as a unit, not blending the sounds.

grace **place** **brace** **twice**

I <u>put</u> ice <u>on</u> my sore face.

Mice can <u>be</u> <u>very</u> nice.

Cut <u>me</u> a slice.

I <u>like</u> space when <u>I</u> sleep.

High-Frequency Words

RETEACH ***always, does, even, pretty, say, sound*** Write the following sentence on tag board and display it in a pocket chart along with the Picture Cards *goat*, *clam*, *ship*, *jeep*, *mop*, *mule*. Call on children to choose a Picture Card to complete the sentence and read it aloud. Then ask: **Could you really be taller than a ______?**

PICTURE CARDS

I always say I am even taller than a ______.

Do the same for the following sentence and Picture Cards *nine*, *clock*, *train*, *seal*, *desk*, *goat*.

A ______ does not make a pretty sound.

I Have a Robot

Read: *I Have a Robot*

Distribute copies of the book and have children read aloud the title. Then guide children through the book as they read.

Pages 2–5: Have children read the pages to find out some of the things the robot can do.

> **Who is talking?** (*the boy*) **What does he have? Find and frame the word that tells.** (*a robot*) **What can it say? Find and read the word that tells.** (*Beep!*) **What can the boy say besides "Beep!"? Find and read the word that tells.** (*Caterpillar*) **What can the robot do?** (*roll in a circle and stop*)

Pages 6–9: Have children read to see what the robot and the boy can do.

> **Which one always looks the same, the boy or the robot?** (*the robot*) **Which one always feels the same?** (*the robot*)

Pages 10–12: Have children read to find out other things the boy and the robot can do.

> **What else can the boy do? Find and frame words that tell.** (*smile, giggle*) **What does the robot have? Find and read the word that tells.** (*eye that blinks*) **Which one can sleep?** (*the boy*)

Ask children to use the pictures to help summarize the book.

Phonics: Building Words

PRETEACH Put the letters *n*, *i*, *c*, *e* in a Word Builder and have children do the same. Slide your hand under the letters as you blend the sounds—/nīīss/. Then read the word naturally—*nice*. Have children repeat after you. Then have children build and read new words.

Change *c* to *n*. What word did you make? (*nine*)

Change the first *n* to *l*. What word did you make? (*line*)

Change *i* to *a*. What word did you make? (*lane*)

Add *p* in front of *l*. What word did you make? (*plane*)

Change *n* to *t*. What word did you make? (*plate*)

Change *t* to *c*. What word did you make? (*place*)

Take away *l*. What word did you make? (*pace*)

Change *p* to *f*. What word did you make? (*face*)

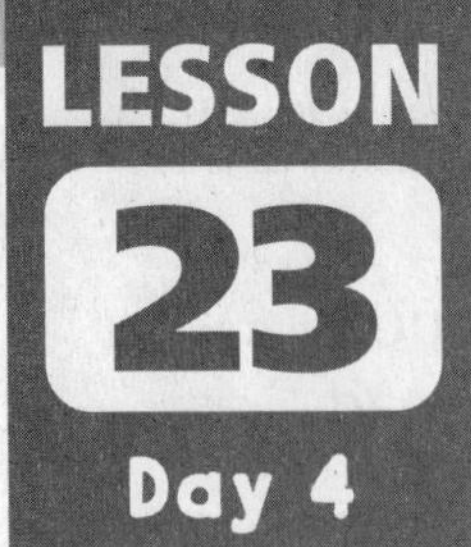

Warm-Up: Phonemic Awareness

Phoneme Segmentation Distribute four-box papers to children. Tell them that the boxes stand for the sounds in words. Show the Picture Card *lamp* and ask: **What is the first sound you hear in *lamp*?** (/l/) Have children place a disk in the first box. Next, have children name the second sound in *lamp* (/a/) and place a disk in the second box. Then have them identify the third and then the last sounds in *lamp* (/m, p/) and place disks in the third and fourth boxes. Point to each box in sequence as children say the word. **How many sounds do you hear in *lamp*?** (*four*) Repeat this procedure with the Picture Cards *vest*, *plum*, *igloo*, *train*, *clock*.

PICTURE CARDS

MATERIALS

Picture Cards: clock, igloo, lamp, plum, train, vest

Papers with four boxes side by side, plus disks

Word Cards for always, does, even, most, pretty, say, sound, why

Word Builder

Word Builder Cards a, b, c, d, e, f, i, p, r, w

I Have a Robot

Phonics: Building Words

RETEACH Put the letters *r*, *i*, *c*, *e* in a Word Builder and have children do the same. Slide your hand under the letters as you blend the sounds—/rrīīss/. Then read the word naturally—*rice*. Have children repeat after you. Then have children build and read new words.

Add *p* in front of *r*. What word did you make? (*price*)

Change *c* to *d*. What word did you make? (*pride*)

Change *p* to *b*. What word did you make? (*bride*)

Take away *b*. What word did you make? (*ride*)

Change *r* to *w*. What word did you make? (*wide*)

Change *i* to *a*. What word did you make? (*wade*)

Change *w* to *f*. What word did you make? (*fade*)

Change *f* to *c*. What word did you make? (*face*)

Distribute *Intervention Practice Book* page 69 to children.

always
does
even
pretty
say
sound
why
most

High-Frequency Words

RETEACH ***always, does, even, pretty, say, sound, why, most*** Distribute word cards with the words listed above. Have partners take turns displaying the words for each other and reading them. After they read each word, have children spell it and then repeat the word. Then have them spell the word again and write it on a sheet of paper.

I Have a Robot

Read: *I Have a Robot*

Focus Skill **Fantasy/Reality** Remind children that some stories are based on fantasy and some are based on what really could happen. Have children reread *I Have a Robot* a page at a time. As they finish each page, ask: **Could this really happen? Could a boy really do this? Could a robot really do this?** When you have finished, have children use their answers to decide whether the story is based on fantasy or on what could really happen. You may wish to have children write a sentence about one thing in the story that could happen in real life.

Phonics: Phonograms -ice, -ide

PRETEACH Write the letters *-ice* and *-ide* at the top of a sheet of chart paper. Have children suggest words that end with *-ice* and say what letters they would need to write the words. Then write the words underneath the heading *-ice*. Use the same procedure for *-ide*. Then have children read each column of words. End the activity by pointing to words at random and having children read the words.

–ice
–ide
mice
wide
rice
ride
spice
slide
slice
tide

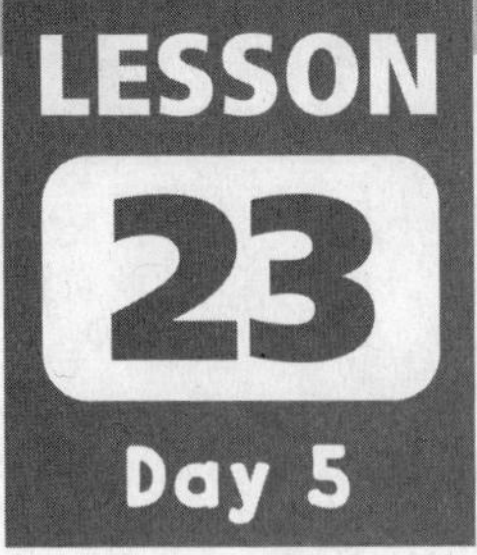

Warm-Up: Phonemic Awareness

Phoneme Blending Tell children that they are going to be builders. Tell them that you are going to say some words sound by sound and that they will put the sounds together to build the word. Listen: /s/-/l/-/ī/-/s/. **What word does /s/-/l/-/ī/-/s/ say?** (*slice*) Continue with the following words:

/r/-/ā/-/s/ *(race)*	**/w/-/ī/-/d/** *(wide)*	**/s/-/ou/-/th/** *(south)*
/r/-/a/-/sh/ *(rash)*	**/p/-/ou/-/n/-/d/** *(pound)*	**/s/-/p/-/ā/-/s/** *(space)*

MATERIALS

Write-on/Wipe off Boards

Word Cards for because, does, even, say, sound, why

Word Builder

Word Builder Cards c, d, h, l, n, o, u, w

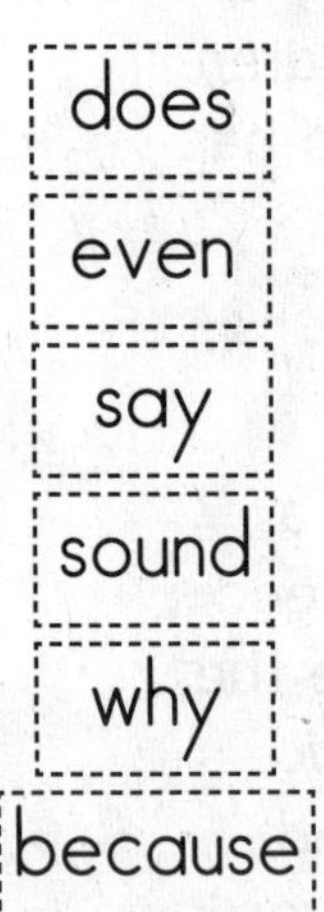

Phonics: Phonograms -ice, -ide

RETEACH Write the word *rice* on a Write-on/Wipe-off Board and have children do the same. Then have them read the word. Ask: **What letter should we change if we want to change *rice* to *ride*?** (*c to d*) **Let's do that.** Continue the activity with the following words: *slice/slide* and *price/pride*.

High-Frequency Words

Cumulative Review *does, even, say, sound, why, because*
Place the words in a pocket chart. Say aloud one of the words and use it in a sentence. Have a volunteer find and point to the word. Have children clap and say the spelling of the word. Then have them write it. Have children read aloud their list of words.

Read: Self-Selected Reading

Have children select a book to read from their browsing boxes. After they have completed their reading, suggest that they show you a word they successfully figured out on their own.

Phonics: Vowel variant /ou/ow, ou

c o w

PRETEACH Use the Word Builder and Word Builder Cards to model blending words. Place the Word Builder Cards *c*, *o*, and *w* in the Word Builder. Slide the *o* and the *w* together. Tell children that *ow* can stand for /ou/, the sound at the end of the word *how*. Point to *ow*. Say /ou/.

Point to the letter *c*. Say /k/. Slide the *ow* next to the *c*. Move your hand under the letters and blend the sounds, elongating them /kkou/. Have children repeat after you. Then have children read the word *cow* along with you.

Follow the same procedure for the words *how*, *now*, and *loud*, pointing out that the letters *ou* as in *loud* also can stand for the /ou/ sound.

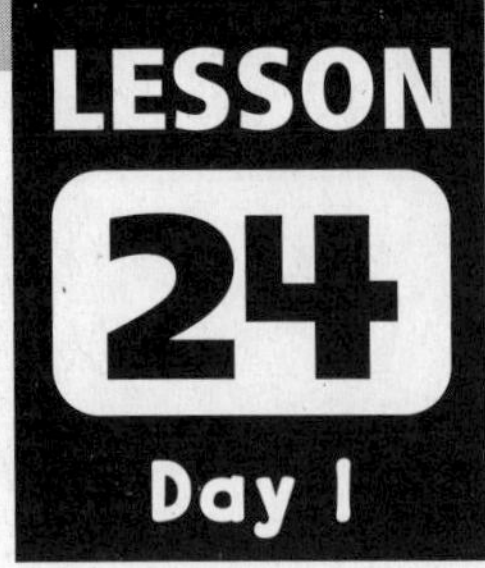

Warm-Up: Phonemic Awareness

Onset and Rime Tell children that you are going to say some words, but you are going to say them in parts. Have children listen to see if they can figure out the word. Demonstrate by saying: **/s/-outh—What word did I say?** (*south*)

/sh/-out	**/n/-ow**	**/sp/-out**	**/k/-ow**
/pl/-ow	**/f/-ound**	**/kl/-oud**	**/pr/-oud**

MATERIALS

Word Cards any, took

Word Builder

Word Builder Cards c, d, h, n, o, r, t, u, w, b

A Pet to the Vet

Phonics: Vowel Variant /ou/ow, ou

RETEACH **Blending** Write *ou* on the board. **These letters are *o* and *u*. When they are together, the letters *o* and *u* can stand for the sound /ou/, the sound in words such as *ouch*, *out*, and *shout*.** Tell children that the spelling *ou* seldom appears at the end of words. Have children repeat the sound as you touch the letters several times.

Use the Word Builder Cards and a pocket chart to model blending words. Place the Word Builder cards *o*, *u*, and *t* in the Word Builder. Point to the *ou* and say /ou/. Point to the *t* and say /t/. Slide the *t* next to the *ou*. Move your hands under the letters and blend the sounds, elongating them /oouutt/. Have children repeat after you. Then say the word naturally—*out*. Have children do the same.

Write *ow* on the board. **These letters are *o* and *w*. When they are together, the letters *o* and *w* can also stand for the sound /ou/, the sound in words such as *owl*, *plow*, and *town*.** Tell children that the spelling *ow* can come at the beginning, middle, and end of words. Have children repeat the sound as you touch the cards several times.

Place the Word Builder cards *c*, *o*, and *w* in the Word Builder. Point to the letter *c* and say /k/. Point to *ow* and say /ou/. Have children repeat the sounds. Slide *ow* next to *c*. Slide your hand under *cow* and blend by elongating the sounds—/kkoouu/. Have children repeat. Then have children read the word *cow* along with you.

High-Frequency Words

any

took

PRETEACH ***any, took*** Display the word card *any*. **This word is *any*. I do not have any pet mice. Read the word with me—*any*. Spell the word with me—*a-n-y*. Read the word with me. What is this word?** (*any*)

Follow the same procedure for the word *took*.

took—**I took my brother to the movies.**

Then place the two words in a pocket chart and have volunteers read the words, as you randomly point to them.

Read: *A Pet to the Vet*

A Pet to the Vet

Story words/Vocabulary Write the words *busy* and *care*. Say the words aloud and have children repeat them. Help children with these words as needed. Distribute copies of the book and have children put their finger on the title. Read the title aloud. Ask children to explain what a vet is. Echo read the book with children. Read page 2 aloud and then have children read it to you. Follow this procedure throughout the book.

Phonics: Word Building with /ou/ow, ou

crowd

cloud

PRETEACH Place the letters *c*, *o*, and *w* in a Word Builder and have children do the same. Slide your hand under the letters as you slowly elongate the sounds /kkoouu/. Have children do the same. Then read the word naturally—*cow*. Have children do the same.

Have children blend and read new words by telling them:

Change the *c* to *n*. What word did you make? (*now*)

Change the *n* to *br*. What word did you make? (*brow*)

Change the *b* to *c*. Add *n* after *w*. What word did you make? (*crown*)

Change the *n* to d. What word did you make? (*crowd*)

Change the *r* to *l*. Change the *w* to *u*. What word did you make? (*cloud*)

Distribute *Intervention Practice Book* page 70 to children.

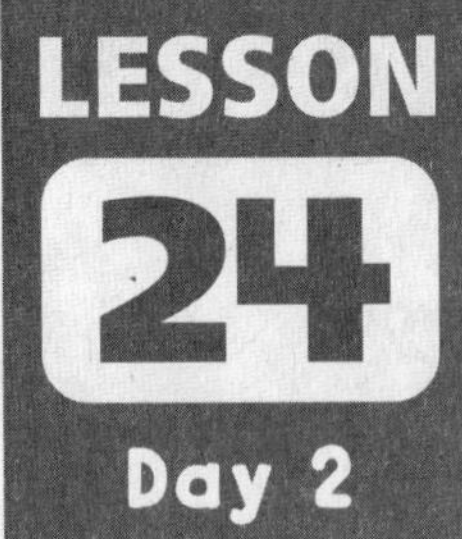

MATERIALS

Word Builder

Word Builder Cards d, e, f, g, h, l, m, n, o, r, s, t, u, w

A Pet to the Vet

Warm-Up: Phonemic Awareness

Phoneme Isolation Say the word *plow* and have children repeat it. Tell children to listen to the /ou/ sound at the end of *plow*. Then say the words *cow* and *face* and have children repeat both words. Ask: **Which of these words has the /ou/ sound you hear in *plow*?** (*cow*)

Continue with the words *crowd*, *line*, *trout*; *pound*, *spout*, *vet*; *owl*, *out*, *trap*.

Phonics: Word Building with /ou/ow, ou

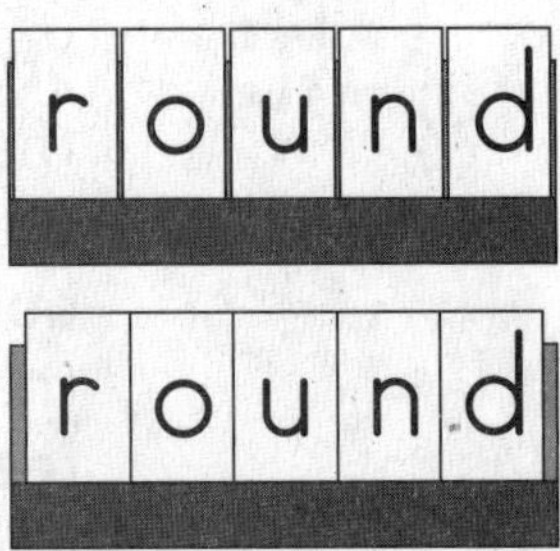

RETEACH Place the letters *r*, *o*, *u*, *n*, and *d* in a Word Builder and have children do the same. Model how to blend the word *round*. Slide your hand under the letters as you slowly elongate the sounds /rroouunndd/. Have children do the same. Then read the word naturally—*round*. Have children do the same.

Have children blend and read new words by telling them:

Add a *g* before the *r*. What word did you make? (*ground*)

Change the *u* to *w*. Change *nd* to *l*. What word did you make? (*growl*)

Change the *gr* to *h*. What word did you make? (*howl*)

Change the *w* to *u*. Change *l* to *se*. What word did you make? (*house*)

Change the *h* to *m*. Change *se* to *th*. What word did you make? (*mouth*)

High-Frequency Words

RETEACH ***any, took*** Write the word *many* and have children read it. Then write the word *any* next to *many*. Have children read the word. **How are these words the same? How are they different? Let's read them again.**

many any

Repeat the procedure with *take/took*.

A Pet to the Vet

Read: *A Pet to the Vet*

Distribute copies of the book to children. Read the title with them. Have children find and frame the two words in the title that rhyme. (*Pet, Vet*) Next, read page 2 with children. Have children frame and read the two words on this page that rhyme. (*pet, Chet*) Ask what other words rhyme with these words. Then choral read the book with children. Let your voice fade if children start to gain control of the text.

Phonics: Reading Sentences with /ou/ow, ou

PRETEACH Distribute *Intervention Practice Book* page 71 to children. Point to the first sentence and have children read it aloud. Ask them to find the word *cow*, frame it with their fingers, and circle the word. Then work with children to complete the page.

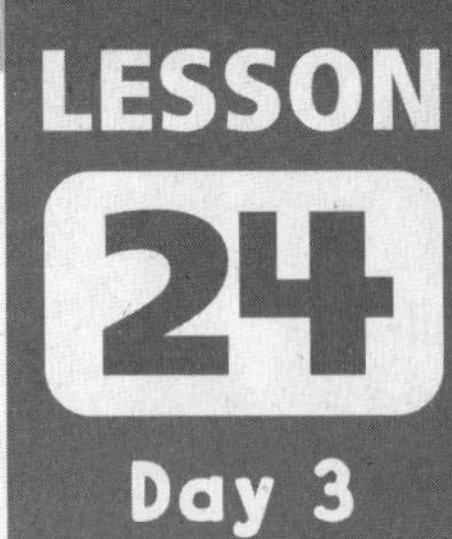

Warm-Up: Phonemic Awareness

Phoneme Blending Tell children that they are going to play a guessing game. Then say: **I'm thinking of a word that tells the shape of a circle. It is /r/-/ou/-/n/-/d/. What's my word?** (*round*) Continue with the following words: /f/-/ou/-/n/-/d/ (*found*), /m/-/ou/-/th/ (*mouth*), /p/-/l/-/ou/ (*plow*), /k/-/r/-/ou/-/d/ (*crowd*), /t/-/ou/-/n/ (*town*)

MATERIALS

Picture Cards boat, cup, egg, fish, hat, jet, nut, plum, sled, sock, train, vest

Word Builder

Word Builder Cards b, c, d, f, l, n, o, r, t, w

A Pet to the Vet

Phonics: Reading Sentences with /ou/ow, ou

RETEACH Help children blend and read new words and sentences shown. Have them read the sentence, blending each word in sequence. The high-frequency words are underlined; they should read these as a unit, not blending the sounds.

gown **ground** **trout** **plow**

<u>The</u> queen has a crown.

I found <u>a</u> brown bunny.

Now <u>I</u> see <u>a</u> cloud.

<u>I</u> am proud <u>of</u> <u>my</u> cow.

High-Frequency Words

RETEACH ***any, took*** Write the following sentence on tagboard and display it in a pocket chart along with the Picture Cards *nut*, *cup*, *plum*, *fish*, *sock*, *egg*. Call on children to choose a Picture Card to complete the sentence and read it aloud. Then ask: **Would you really eat a/n ______?**

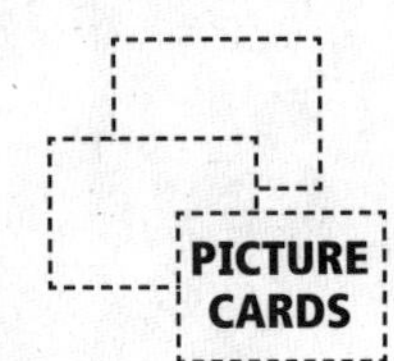

I did not have any corn for a snack, but I did have one ______.

Do the same for the following sentence and Picture Cards *boat*, *train*, *jet*, *sled*, *vest*, *hat*.

I took a ride on a ______.

A Pet to the Vet

Read: *A Pet to the Vet*

Distribute copies of the book and have children read aloud the title. Then guide children through the book as they read.

Have children read to find out about the girl's family.

Pages 2–5: **Who got a pet?** (*the girl*) **What is the pet's name?** (*Chet*) **Who else is in the family?** (*mom, baby*) **What did the girl do every day? Find and read the sentence that tells.** (*Every day I took Chet out for a walk.*)

Pages 6–9: Have children read to see where the girl and Chet are going.

What did Chet need? (*a shot*) **Find and frame the words that tell. What did the girl do?** (took Chet *downtown to the vet*) **What word describes the vet?** (*busy*) **Who was the vet taking care of when the girl got there?** (*a cat*) **Then what did the vet do?** (*Then the vet took care of a brown duck.*)

Pages 10–12: Have children read to find out if Chet gets a shot.

Did Chet like being in the office? (*no*) **Find and frame the sentence that tells.** (*Chet was not happy.*) **Does Chet need a shot?** (*no*) **Find and read the sentence that tells how Chet is.** (*Chet is just fine.*)

Ask children to use the pictures to help summarize the book.

Phonics: Building Words

t o w n

d o w n

d r o w n

f r o w n

b r o w n

c r o w n

c l o w n

PRETEACH Place the letters *t*, *o*, *w*, and *n* in a Word Builder and have children do the same. Slide your hand under the letters as you blend the sounds—/ttooouunn/. Then read the word naturally—*town*. Have children repeat after you. Then have children build and read new words.

Change the *t* to *d*. What word did you make? (*down*)

Add *r* after *d*. What word did you make? (*drown*)

Change the *d* to *f*. What word did you make? (*frown*)

Change the *f* to *b*. What word did you make? (*brown*)

Change the *b* to *c*. What word did you make? (*crown*)

Change the *r* to *l*. What word did you make? (*clown*)

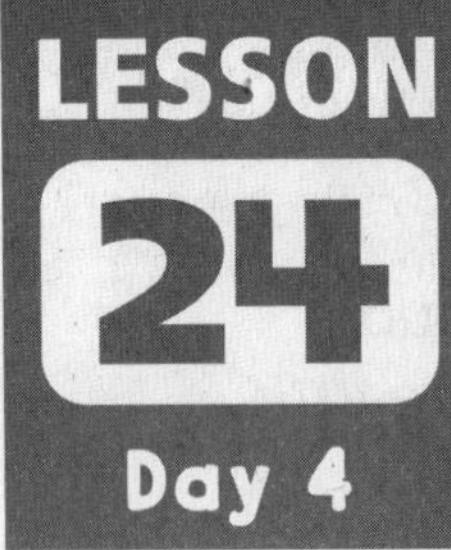

MATERIALS

Write-on/Wipe-off Boards with disks

Word Cards any, took, does, always

Word Builder

Word Builder Cards c, d, h, n, o, p, r, s, t, u

A Pet to the Vet

Warm-Up: Phonemic Awareness

Phoneme Segmentation Have children use the three boxes on the Write-on/Wipe-off Boards. Remind children that the boxes stand for the sounds in words. Say the word *plow* and ask: **What is the first sound you hear in *plow*?** (/p/) Have children place a disk in the first box. Then have children name the second sound in *plow* (/l/) and place a disk in the second box. Then have them identify the last sound in *plow* (/ou/) and place a disk in the third box. Point to each box in sequence as children say the word. **How many sounds do you hear in *plow*?** (*three*) Repeat this procedure with the following words: *down*, *shout*, *house*, *loud*, *gown*.

Phonics: Building Words

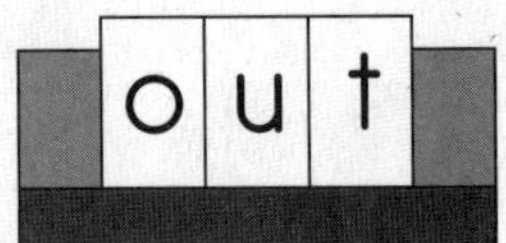

RETEACH Put the letters *o*, *u*, and *t* in a Word Builder and have children do the same. Slide your hand under the letters as you blend the sounds—/oouutt/. Then read the word naturally—*out*. Have children repeat after you. Then have children build and read new words.

Add *sh* in front of *out*. What word did you make? (*shout*)

Change the *sh* to *sc*. What word did you make? (*scout*)

Change the *c* to *p*. What word did you make? (*spout*)

Take away the *s*. What word did you make? (*pout*)

Change the *t* to *nd*. What word did you make? (*pound*)

Change the *p* to *s*. What word did you make? (*sound*)

Change the *s* to *r*. What word did you make? (*round*)

Distribute *Intervention Practice Book* page 72 to children.

any

took

does

always

High-Frequency Words

RETEACH ***any, took, does, always*** Distribute word cards with the words listed above. Have partners take turns displaying the words for each other and reading them. After they read each word, have children spell it and then repeat the word. Then have them spell the word again and write it on a sheet of paper.

Read: *A Pet to the Vet*

Focus Skill **Classify/Categorize** Remind children that stories can be easier to understand if they think of how certain things are alike. Have children reread A *Pet to the Vet*. Then ask: **How are the vet, the girl, the mother, and the baby alike?** (*All are people.*) **How are the hamster, the cat, and the duck alike?** (*All are animals; all are pets.*)

People	Pets
Vet.	Hamster
Girl	Cat
Mother	Duck
Baby	

Phonics: Phonograms -own, -ound

PRETEACH Write the letters *own* and *ound* at the top of a sheet of chart paper. Have children suggest words that end with *-own* and say what letters they would need to write the words. Then write the words underneath the heading *own*. Use the same procedure for *ound*. Then have children read each column of words. End the activity by pointing to words at random and having children read the words.

own	ound
town	hound
down	pound
brown	round
clown	sound
crown	ground
frown	wound
gown	found
drown	

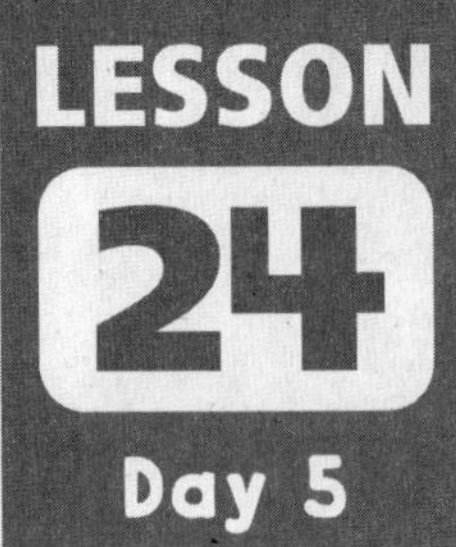

MATERIALS

Write-on/Wipe-off Boards

Word Cards any, took, always, does, say, even

Word Builder

Word Builder Cards e, f, i, l, r, s, t, y

Warm-Up: Phonemic Awareness

Phoneme Blending Tell children that together you are going to play a game of "Fix It." Tell them that you are going to say some words that are all broken and they should listen to see if they can put the sounds together to figure out the word. **Listen: /f/-/ou/-/n/-/d/. What word does /f/-/ou/-/n/-/d / say?** (*found*) Continue with the following words:

/h/-/ou/-/s/ (*house*)	**/f/-/l/-/ī/** (*fly*)	**/m/-/ou/-/th/** (*mouth*)
/r/-/ā/-/s/ (*race*)	**/s/-/ou/-/n/-/d/** (*sound*)	**/t/-/r/-/ī/** (*try*)

Phonics: Phonograms -own, -ound

RETEACH Write the word *town* on a Write-on/Wipe-off Board and have children do the same. Then have them read the word. Ask: **What letter should we change if we want to change *town* to *down*?** (*t to d*) **Let's do that.** Continue the activity with the following words: *gown*, *crown*, *brown*. Repeat with the word *sound* and the words *round*, *pound*, *found*, and *mound*.

High-Frequency Words

Cumulative Review *any, took, always, does, say, even* Place the words in a pocket chart. Say aloud one of the words and use it in a sentence. Have a volunteer find and point to the word. Have children clap and say the spelling of the word. Then have them write it. Have children read aloud their list of words.

any

took

always

does

say

even

Read: Self-Selected Reading

Have children select a book to read from their browsing boxes. After they have completed their reading, have them tell you what they were most successful in during the reading of the book.

Phonics: Long Vowel /ī/y, ie

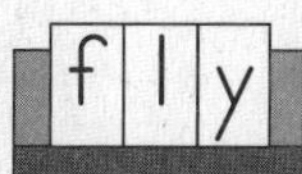

PRETEACH Use the Word Builder and Word Builder Cards to model blending words. Place the Word Builder Cards *f*, *l*, and *y* in the Word Builder. Tell children that *y* can stand for /ī/, the long *i* sound, at the end of words like *my* and *by*.

Point to the *f*. Say /f/. Point to *l* and say /l/. Slide the letters together and blend the sounds, elongating them /ffll/. Have children repeat after you.

Point to *y*. Say /ī/. Slide the *y* next to *fl*. Move your hand under the letters and blend the sounds, elongating them /ffllīī/. Have children repeat.

Then have children read the word *fly* along with you.

Follow the same procedure for the words *try* and *flies*, pointing out that the letters *ie* as in *flies* also can stand for the long *i* sound.

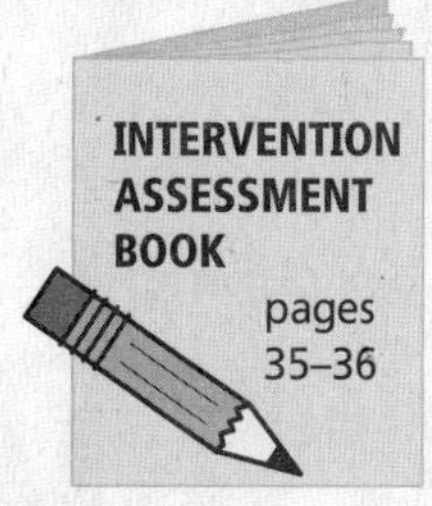

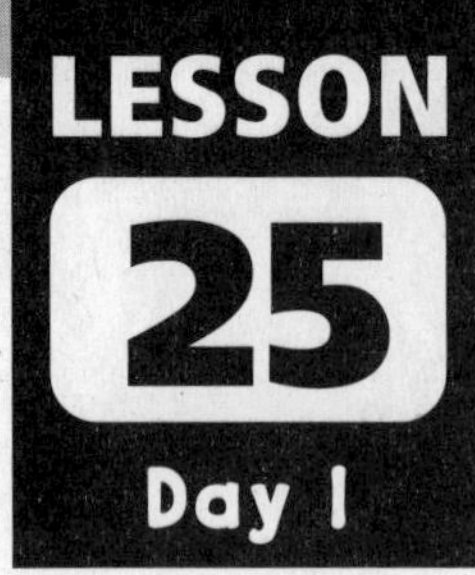

Warm-Up: Phonemic Awareness

Onset and Rime Tell children that you are going to say some words, but you are going to say them in parts. Have children listen to see if they can figure out the word. Demonstrate by saying: **/fl/-y—What word did I say?** (*fly*)

/tr/-y	**/t/-ie**	**/wh/-y**	**/fr/-y**
/sh/-y	**/m/-y**	**/p/-ie**	**/sp/-y**

MATERIALS

Word Cards again, blue, high, love, opened

Word Builder

Word Builder Cards b, c, d, e, f, i, l, m, r, y

Alphabet Masters Yy

Bears Are Big

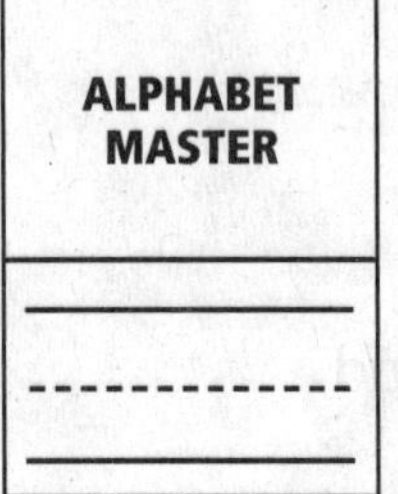

Phonics: Long Vowel /ī/y, ie

RETEACH **Blending** Display Alphabet Master *Yy*. **This letter is *y*. When it is a vowel, it can stand for the /ī/ sound, the long sound of *i* at the end of words such as *fly, by,* and *my*.** Have children repeat the sound as you touch the letter several times.

Write the letters *ie* on the board. When *i* and *e* are grouped together, they can make the sound /ī/ at the end of words such as *pie, lie,* and *tie*. Have children repeat the sound as you touch the letters several times.

Use the Word Builder Cards and a pocket chart to model blending words.

Place the Word Builder Cards *b* and *y* in the Word Builder. Point to the *b* and say /b/. Point to the *y* and say /ī/.

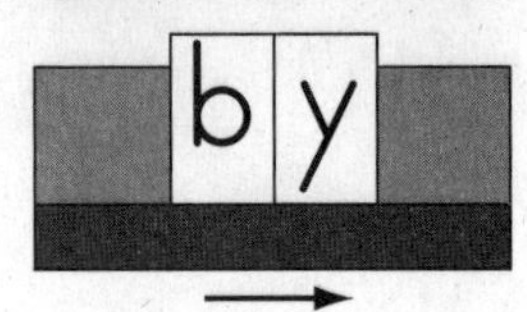

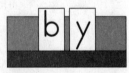

Slide the *y* next to the *b*. Move your hand under the letters and blend the sounds, elongating them /bbīī/. Have children repeat after you. Then say the word naturally—*by*. Have children do the same.

Place the Word Builder Cards *p, i,* and *e* in the Word Builder. Point to the *p* and say /p/. Point to the *ie* and say /ī/.

Slide the *ie* next to the *p*. Move your hands under the letters and blend the sounds, elongating them—/ppīī/. Have children repeat after you. Then have children read the word *pie* with you.

High-Frequency Words

again
blue
high
love
opened

PRETEACH ***again, blue, high, love, opened*** Display the word card *again*. **This word is again. I want to read that book *again*. Read the word with me—*again*. Spell the word with me—*a-g-a-i-n*. Read the word with me. What is this word?** (*again*) Follow the same procedure for the words *blue*, *high*, *love*, and *opened*.

blue—**My favorite color is blue.**

high—**I can jump high.**

love—**I love to eat peaches.**

opened—**She opened the letter and read it.**

Then place the five words in a pocket chart and have volunteers read the words, as you randomly point to them.

Read: *Bears Are Big*

Bears Are Big

Story Words Write *meadow*, *bears*, and *winter* on the board. Point to the words, say them aloud, and have children repeat them. Remember to help children with these words as they read the story.

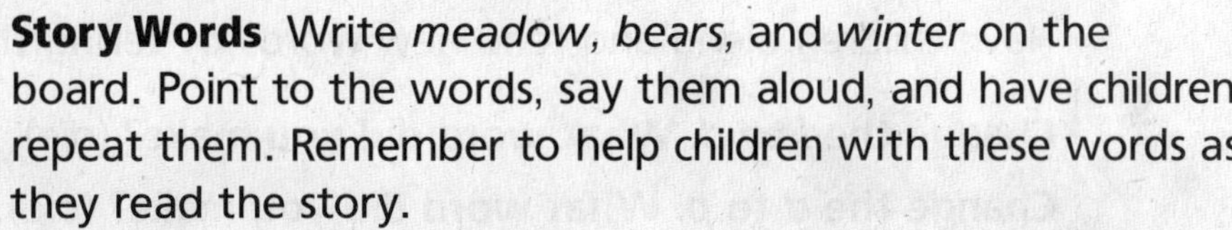

Distribute copies of the book and have children put their finger on the title. Read the title aloud while children follow along. Ask them to touch the word *Bears*, then the words *Are* and *Big*. Echo read the book with children. Read page 2 aloud and then have children read it to you. Follow this procedure throughout the book.

Phonics: Word Building with /ī/y, ie

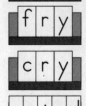

PRETEACH Place the letters *b* and *y* in a Word Builder and have children do the same. Slide your hand under the letters as you slowly elongate the sounds /bbīī/. Have children repeat. Then read the word naturally—*by.* Have children repeat. Have children blend and read new words by telling them:

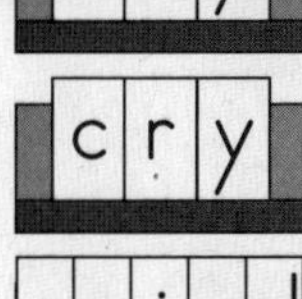

Change the *b* to *m*. What word did you make? (*my*)

Change the *m* to *fl*. What word did you make? (*fly*)

Change the *l* to an *r*. What word did you make? (*fry*)

Change the *t* to a *c*. What word did you make? (*cry*)

Change the *y* to *ied*. What word did you make? (*cried*)

Distribute *Intervention Practice Book* page 73 to children.

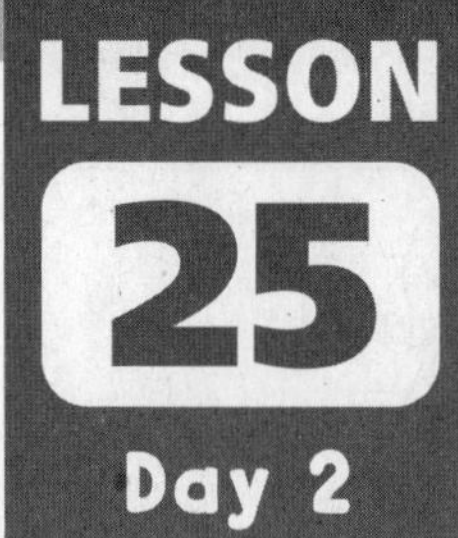

MATERIALS

Word Builder

Word Builder Cards e, i, l, p, r, s, s, t, y

Word Cards again, blue, high, love, opened

Bears Are Big

Warm-Up: Phonemic Awareness

Phoneme Isolation Say the word *why* and have children repeat it. Tell children to listen to the ī sound at the end of *why*. Then say the words *how* and *shy* and have children repeat both words. Ask: **Which of these words has the /ī/ sound?** (*shy*)

Continue with the words *sky, try, found; my, bell, fry; pie, by, green.*

Phonics: Word Building with /ī/i

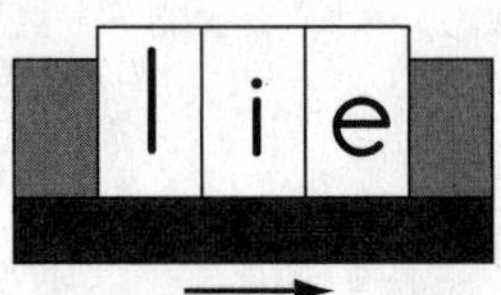

RETEACH Place the letters *l, i,* and *e* in a Word Builder and have children do the same. Model how to blend the word *lie*. Slide your hand under the letters as you slowly elongate the sounds /llīī/. Have children do the same. Then read the word naturally—*lie*. Have children do the same.

Have children blend and read new words by telling them:

Change the *l* to *d*. What word did you make? (*die*)

Change the *d* to *p*. What word did you make? (*pie*)

Add an *s* after *e*. What word did you make? (*pies*)

Add an *s* before the *p*. What word did you make? (*spies*)

Change *ies* to *y*. What word did you make? (*spy*)

Change *sp* to *tr*. What word did you make? (*try*)

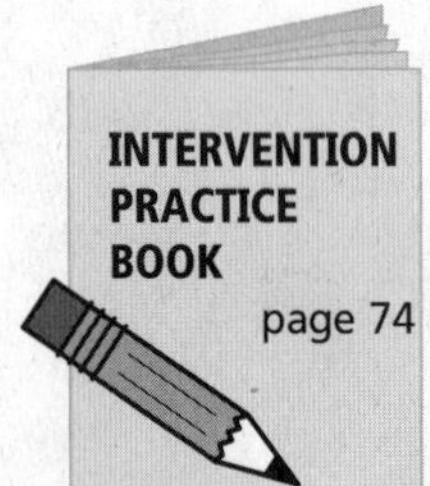

High-Frequency Words

again
blue
high
love
opened

RETEACH ***again, blue, high, love, opened*** Display the word card *again* and have children read it. Then teach children this chant to help them remember the word and its spelling: ***A-g-a-i-n, let me spell it out again***. Touch each letter in turn as you say its name. Have children repeat the chant as they use their index finger to write the letters of *again* in the air.

Repeat the procedure with the following chants:

B-l-u-e, the color blue makes me feel free.

What's high at the ends but low in the middle?

H-i-g-h will solve that riddle.

L-o-v-e, spell "love" with me.

O-p-e-n-e-d, she opened her eyes and saw a bee.

Read: *Bears Are Big*

Bears Are Big

Distribute copies of the book to children. Read pages 2 and 3 with them. Ask children if this story fits with what they know about bears in real life. Point out that some stories are fiction, meaning that they tell about things that are not real. Explain that this book is nonfiction; it tells about the real world. Have students find words and sentences that tell real things about bears. Then choral read the book with children. Let your voice fade if children start to gain control of the text.

Phonics: Reading Sentences with /ī/ y, ie

PRETEACH Distribute *Intervention Practice Book* page 74 to children. Point to the first sentence and have children read it aloud. Ask them to find the word *tie*, frame it with their fingers, and circle the word. Then work with children to complete the page.

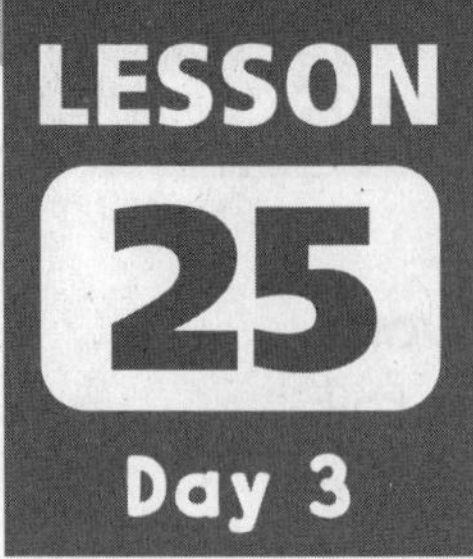

Warm-Up: Phonemic Awareness

Phoneme Blending Tell children that they are going to be detectives and find the word you are thinking about. Say: **I'm thinking of a word that means the opposite of *wet*. The word is /d/-/r/-/ī/ . What's my word?** (*dry*) Continue with the following words: /b/-/ī/ (*by*), /s/-/k/-/ī/ (*sky*), /sh/-/ī/ (*shy*), /t/-/ī/ (*tie*), /f/-/r/-/ī/ (*fry*)

MATERIALS

Picture Cards bed, bug, can, egg, fish, flag, igloo, jet, kite, map, quilt, ship, sock, sun, wagon

Word Builder

Word Builder Cards c, d, f, l, r, t, y

Bears Are Big

Phonics: Reading Sentences with /ī/ y, ie

RETEACH Help children blend and read new words and sentences shown. Have them read the sentence, blending each word in sequence. The high-frequency words are underlined; they should read these as a unit, not blending the sounds.

spy **tried** **sly** **cries**

<u>She</u> tied <u>the</u> cord.

Why did <u>they</u> cry?

Try <u>to</u> <u>walk</u> by <u>the</u> <u>house</u>.

Let's fly up <u>to</u> <u>the</u> sky.

High-Frequency Words

RETEACH ***again, blue, high, love, opened*** Write the following sentence on tag board and display it in a pocket chart along with the Picture Cards *can, igloo, bug, sun, sock, map.* Call on children to choose a Picture Card to complete the sentence and read it aloud. Then ask: **Could a ________ really be blue?**

PICTURE CARDS

I opened the box again and saw a blue ________.

Do the same for the following sentence and *Picture Cards quilt, bed, wagon, egg, fish.*

I love to lie on my ________.

Repeat for the following sentence and *Picture Cards ship, kite, bug, jet, flag.*

The bird will fly high like a ________.

Read: *Bears Are Big*

Bears Are Big

Distribute copies of the book and have children read the title. Then guide children through the book as they read.

Have children read the pages to learn about what bears eat.

Pages 2–5: **What was the bear looking for?** *(food)* **Find and frame the sentence that tells. What does the bear eat?** *(bugs, grass, nuts, sweet things)* **What will a bear do if it finds good food? Find and read the words that tell.** *(come back again and again)*

Pages 6–7: Have children read to learn about another kind of bear.

Is this bear the same size as the first? *(no)* **Where does this bear live?** *(in a meadow)* **What does this bear do?** *(eat plants and bugs and fish)*

Pages 8–9: Have children read to find out what bears do in winter.

When is there not much food for a big bear? *(in the winter)* **Find and read the words that tell. What does the bear do all winter? Why doesn't a bear need food?** *(It lies in its den and sleeps)*

Pages 10–12: Have children read to learn about polar bears.

How big is this bear? *(the biggest of all)* **How does the bear spend its time?** *(looking for food)* **How does the bear stay dry during the winter? Find and read the sentence that tells.** *(Thick fur keeps the bear warm and dry.)*

Ask children to use the pictures to help summarize the book.

Phonics: Building Words

PRETEACH Place the letters *d, r,* and *y* in a Word Builder and have children do the same. Slide your hand under the letters as you blend the sounds—/drī/. Then read the word naturally—*dry.* Have children repeat after you. Then have children build and read new words.

Change the *d* to *t*. What word did you make? (*try*)

Change the *t* to *c*. What word did you make? (*cry*)

Change the *c* to *f*. What word did you make? (*fry*)

Change the *r* to *l*. What word did you make? (*fly*)

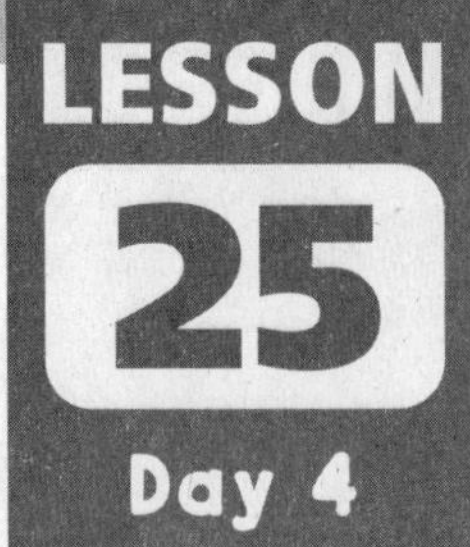

MATERIALS

Write-on/Wipe-off Boards with disks

Word Cards again, any, blue, high, love, opened, took

Word Builder

Word Builder Cards d, e, f, i, l, p, r, s, t

Bears Are Big

Warm-Up: Phonemic Awareness

Phoneme Segmentation Have children use the three boxes on the Write-on/Wipe-off Boards. Remind children that the boxes stand for the sounds in words. Say the word *cry* and ask: **What is the first sound you hear in *cry*?** (/k/) Have children place a disk in the first box. Then have children name the second sound in *cry* (/r/) and place a disk in the second box. Then have them identify the last sound in *cry* (/ī/) and place a disk in the third box. Point to each box in sequence as children say the word. **How many sounds do you hear in *cry*?** (*three*) Repeat this procedure with the following words: *fly, dry, fry, pry, sky.*

Phonics: Building Words

RETEACH Put the letters *l, i, e* in a Word Builder and have children do the same. Slide your hand under the letters as you blend the sounds—/llīī/. Then read the word naturally—*lie*. Have children repeat after you. Then have children build and read new words.

Change the *t* to *p*. What word did you make? (*pie*)

Change the *p* to *d*. What word did you make? (*die*)

Change the *p* to *t*. What word did you make? (*tie*)

Add a *d to* the end of *tie*. What word did you make? (*tied*)

Add an *r* after *t*. What word did you make? (*tried*)

Change the *t* to *f*. What word did you make? (*fried*)

Distribute *Intervention Practice Book* page 75 to children.

High-Frequency Words

RETEACH ***again, blue, high, love, opened, any, took*** Distribute word cards with the words listed above. Have partners take turns displaying the words for each other and reading them. After they read each word, have children spell it and then repeat the word. Then have them spell the word again and write it on a sheet of paper.

again

blue

high

love

opened

any

took

Bears Are Big

Read: *Bears Are Big*

Focus Skill **Cause/Effect** Remind children that knowing what happens and why it happens will help them understand the stories they read. Have children reread *Bears Are Big* one page at a time and think about why certain things happen. Ask: **Why do bears climb high in trees? What do bears do in cold weather? Why? Why would a bear go back to the same place again and again?** Have children decide on answers and compare their ideas. You may wish to have children work together to write sentences such as *Bears climb high in trees to get food.*

Phonics: Contractions 's, n't, 'll

PRETEACH Write the words *it is* on the board and have children read them. Say: **We can use an apostrophe to make the words *it is* in a shorter way.** Write *it's* next to *it is*. **The *i* in *is* becomes an apostrophe, and the words are pushed together.** Repeat with *he is/he's, that is/that's, who is/who's*, and *there is/there's*.

Write the words *was not* on the board and have children read them. Say **We can use an apostrophe to write the words *was not* in a shorter way.** Write *wasn't* next to *was not*. **The *o* in *not* becomes an apostrophe, and the words are pushed together.** Write *did not* on the board and explain that it can be written as *didn't* for short. Repeat with *is not/isn't,do not/don't, would not/wouldn't,* and *were not/weren't.*

Write the words *she will* on the board and have children read them. Say: **We can also use an apostrophe to make the words *she will* shorter.** Write *she'll* next to *she will*. Have children read the word. **The *wi* in *will* becomes an apostrophe.** Repeat with *I will/I'll, they will/they'll, we will/we'll*, and *you will/you'll.*

it is	it's	was not	wasn't	she will	she'll
he is	he's	did not	didn't	I will	I'll
that is	that's	is not	isn't	they will	they'll
who is	who's	do not	don't	we will	we'll
there is	there's	would not	wouldn't	you will	you'll
		were not	weren't		

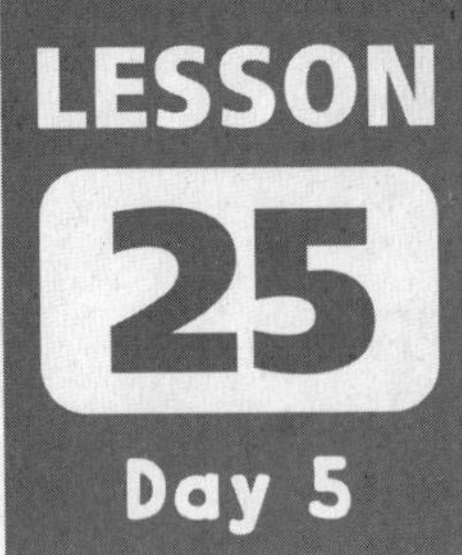

Warm-Up: Phonemic Awareness

Phoneme Blending Tell children that together you are going to play a puzzle game. Tell them that you are going to say some words in pieces like a puzzle and they should listen to see if they can put the puzzle pieces together to figure out the word. **Listen: /s/-/p/-/ī/. What word does /s/-/p/-/ī/ say?** (spy) Continue with the following words:

/p/-/l/-/ou/ *(plow)*	**/hw/-/ī/** *(why)*	**/t/-/r/ī-/d/** *(tried)*
/b/-/ō/-/n/ *(bone)*	**/r/-/ō/-/d/** *(rode)*	**/s/-/t/-/ō/-/n/** *(stone)*

MATERIALS

Write-on/Wipe-off Boards

Word Cards again, any, blue, high, love, opened, took

Word Builder

Word Builder Cards b, c, d, e, n, o, r, s

Phonics: Contractions 's, n't, 'll

RETEACH Write *he is* on a Write-on/Wipe-off Board and have children do the same. Then have them read the words. Ask: **What should we write if we want to change *he is* to *he's*?** (*'s*) **Let's do that.** Continue the activity with the following words: *she is, it is*. Write *do not* and have children do the same. Then have them read the words. Ask **What should we write to change *do not* to *don't*?** (*an apostrophe*) **Let's do that.** Repeat with the following words: *is not, does not, are not*. Then repeat with *'ll* and *he will, we will*, and *you will*.

High-Frequency Words

Cumulative Review *again, blue, high, love, opened, any, took* Place the words in a pocket chart. Say aloud one of the words and use it in a sentence. Have a volunteer find and point to the word. Have children clap and say the spelling of the word. Then have them write it. Have children read aloud their list of words.

Read: Self-Selected Reading

Have children select a book to read from their browsing boxes. After they have completed their reading, have them tell you what they were most successful in during the reading of the book.

Phonics: Long Vowel /ō/o-e

b o n e

PRETEACH Use the Word Builder and Word Builder Cards to model blending words. Place the Word Builder Cards *b, o, n,* and *e* in the Word Builder. Tell children that *e at* the end of the word helps *o* stand for /ō/, the long sound of *o* in the middle of the words *hope* and *wrote*.

Point to the letter *b*. Say /b/. Point to the *o* and *e*. Say *o*. Slide the *o* next to the *b*. Move your hand under the letters and blend the sounds, elongating them /bbōō/. Have children repeat after you.

Point to the letter *n*. Say /n/. Slide *ne* next to bo. Move your hand under the letters and blend the sounds, elongating them /bbōōnn/. Have children repeat. Then have children read the word *bone* along with you.

Follow the same procedure for the words *cone, code,* and *rose*.

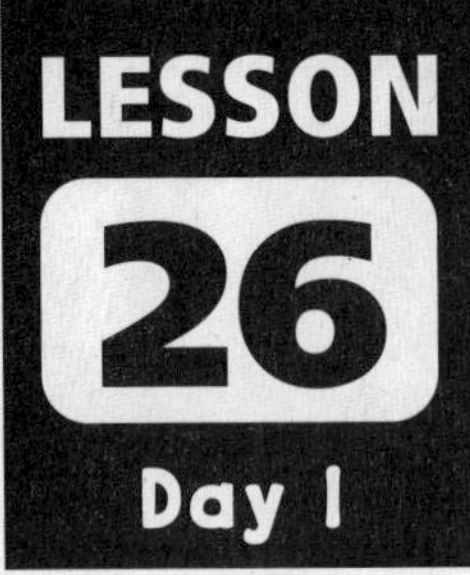

Warm-Up: Phonemic Awareness

Onset and Rime Tell children that you are going to say some words, but you are going to say them in parts. Have children listen to see if they can figure out the word. Demonstrate by saying: **/k/-one—What word did I say?** (*cone*)

/r/-obe	**/st/-one**	**/sh/-one**	**/k/-ode**
/sm/-oke	**/p/-ole**	**/r/-ope**	**/st/-ole**

MATERIALS

Word Cards another, change

Word Builder

Word Builder Cards b, c, d, e, h, l, n, o, p, r, s, t

Alphabet Masters Oo, Ee

What a Bee Can See

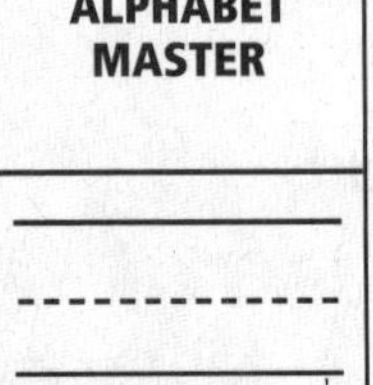

Phonics: Long Vowel /ō/o-e

RETEACH Blending Display Alphabet Masters *Oo* and *Ee*. **These letters are *o* and *e*. When a short word has an *o*-consonant-*e*, the vowel *e* is silent and causes the *o* to say /ō/, the long sound in words such as *note*, *poke*, and *hole*.** Have children repeat the sound as you touch the letters several times.

Use the Word Builder Cards and a pocket chart to model blending words.

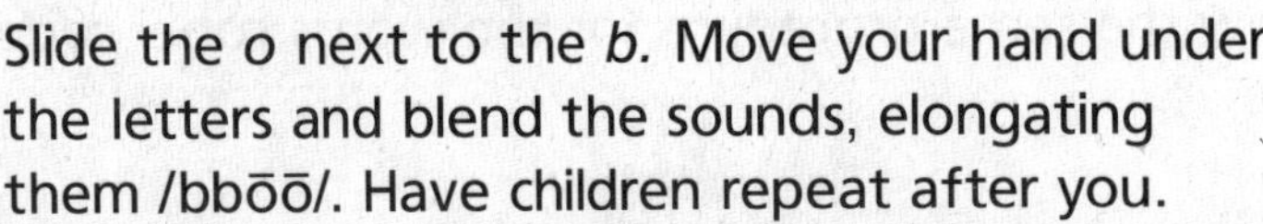

Place the Word Builder Cards *b, o, n,* and *e* in the Word Builder. Point to the *b* and say /b/. Point to the *o* and *e* and say /ō/.

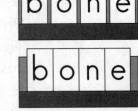

Slide the *o* next to the *b.* Move your hand under the letters and blend the sounds, elongating them /bbōō/. Have children repeat after you.

Point to the *n* and say /n/. Slide the *ne* next to *bo* and blend by elongating the sounds—/bbōōnn/. Then say the word naturally—*bone*. Have children do the same.

High-Frequency Words

PRETEACH *another, change* Display the word card *another*. **This word is *another*. I have another pencil at home. Read the word with me—*another*. Spell the word with me—*a-n-o-t-h-e-r*. Read the word with me. What is this word?** (*another*)

Follow the same procedure for the word *change*.

***change*—I will change my clothes before dinner.**

Then place the two words in a pocket chart and have volunteers read the words, as you randomly point to them.

Read: *What a Bee Can See*

What a Bee Can See

Story Words/Vocabulary Write the word *nectar* on the board. Point to the word, read it aloud, and have children repeat it after you. Discuss with children that nectar is a sweet liquid found in flowers and that bees use nectar to make honey. Next, write the words *wild* and *field*, read them aloud, and have children repeat them. Provide help with these words for any child who needs it during the reading of the story.

Distribute copies of the book and have children put their finger on the title. Read the title aloud while children follow along. Ask them to touch the words *What*, *Bee*, and *See*. Ask which of these words rhyme. (*bee*, *see*) Have volunteers choose a word in the title to read aloud. Echo read the book with children. Read page 2 aloud and then have children read it to you. Follow this procedure throughout the book.

Phonics: Word Building with /ō/o-e

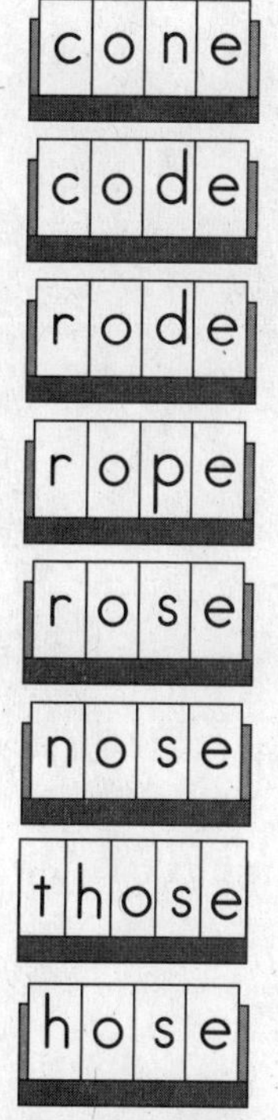

PRETEACH Place the letters *c*, *o*, *n*, and *e* in a Word Builder and have children do the same. Model how to blend the word *cone*. Slide your hand under the letters as you slowly elongate the sounds /kkōōnn/. Have children do the same. Then read the word naturally—*cone*. Have children do the same.

Have children blend and read new words by telling them:

Change the *n* to *d*. What word did you make? *(code)*

Change the *c* to *r*. What word did you make? *(rode)*

Change the *d* to *p*. What word did you make? *(rope)*

Change the *p* to *s*. What word did you make? *(rose)*

Change the *r* to *n*. What word did you make? *(nose)*

Change the *n* to *th*. What word did you make? *(those)*

Take away the *t*. What word did you make? *(hose)*

Change the *s* to *l*. What word did you make? *(hole)*

Distribute *Intervention Practice Book* page 76 to children.

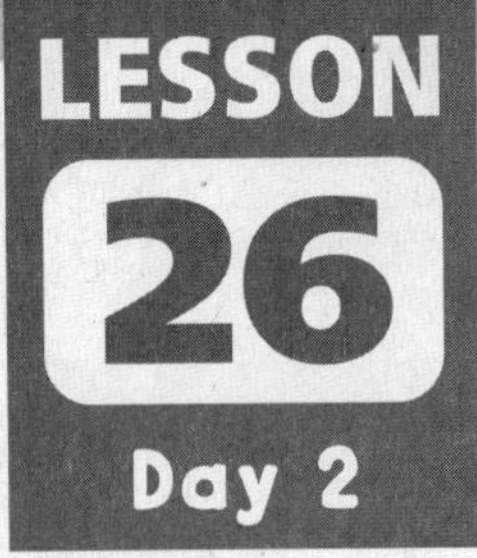

Warm-Up: Phonemic Awareness

Phoneme Isolation Say the word *rose* and have children repeat it. Tell children to listen to the /ō/ sound in the middle of *rose*. Then say the words *phone* and *try* and have children repeat both words. Ask: **Which of these words has the /ō/ sound you hear in *rose*?** (*phone*)

Continue with the words *stole, rope, smile; globe, those, steal; pole, stove, growl.*

MATERIALS

Word Builder

Word Builder Cards e, k, l, m, n, o, p, s, t, v

What a Bee Can See

Phonics: Word Building with /ō/o-e

RETEACH Place the letters *t, o, n,* and *e* in a Word Builder and have children do the same. Model how to blend the word *tone*. Slide your hand under the letters as you slowly elongate the sounds /ttōōnn/. Have children do the same. Then read the word naturally—*tone*. Have children do the same.

Have children blend and read new words by telling them:

Add *s* to the front of *tone*. What word did you make? (*stone*)

Change the *n* to *v*. What word did you make? (*stove*)

Change the *v* to *l*. What word did you make? (*stole*)

Change the *st* to *p*. What word did you make? (*pole*)

Change the *l* to *k*. What word did you make? (*poke*)

Add *s* to the front of *poke*. What word did you make? (*spoke*)

Change the *p* to *m*. What word did you make? (*smoke*)

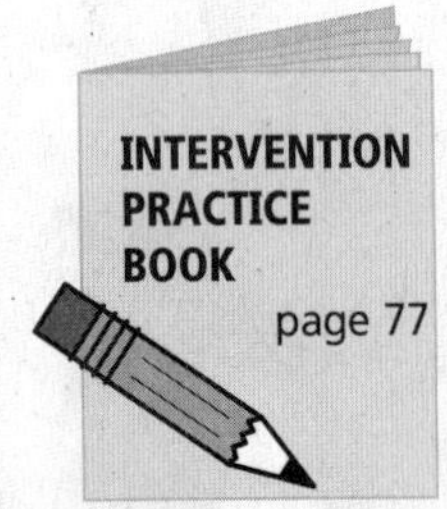

High-Frequency Words

RETEACH ***another, change*** Write the word *other* and have children read it. Then write the word *another* next to *other*. Have children read both words. **How are these words the same? How are they different? Let's read them again.**

other   another

Repeat the procedure with *clang/change*.

Read: *What a Bee Can See*

What a Bee Can See

Distribute copies of the book to children. Read page 2 with children. Have children frame and read the word *Its*. Have them find and frame *its* on page 3 as well. Point out that there are two different spellings and meanings of the word. ***Its*, with no apostrophe, means *belonging to it*, but *it's*, with an apostrophe, is a contraction, short for *it is*.** Ask which meaning is used here. Then choral read the book with children. Let your voice fade if children start to gain control of the text.

Phonics: Reading Sentences with /ō/o-e

PRETEACH Distribute *Intervention Practice Book* page 77 to children. Point to the first sentence and have children read it aloud. Ask them to find the word *hope*, frame it with their fingers, and circle the word. Then work with children to complete the page.

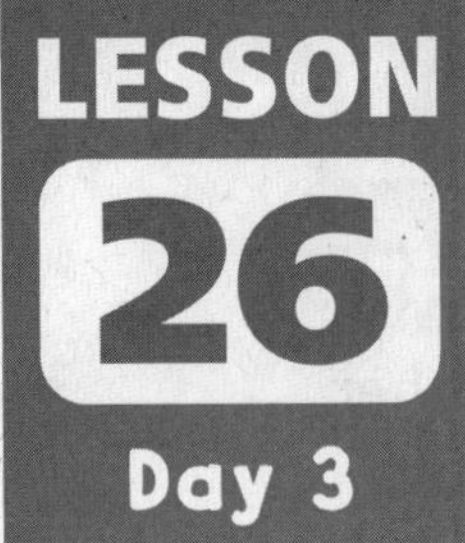

MATERIALS

Picture Cards boat, jet, mop, plum, train, wagon

Word Builder

Word Builder Cards a, d, e, h, i, o, p, r, t

What a Bee Can See

Warm-Up: Phonemic Awareness

Phoneme Blending Tell children that they are going to play a guessing game and find the word you are thinking about. Say: **I'm thinking of something used for cooking. It is a /s/-/t/-/ō/-/v/. What's my word?** (*stove*) Continue with the following words: /h/-/ō/-/p/ (*hope*), /k/-/ō/-/n/ (cone), /ch/-/ō/-/z/ (chose), /g/-/l/-/ō/-/b/ (*globe*), /s/-/m/-/ō/-/k/ (*smoke*)

Phonics: Reading Sentences with /ō/o-e

RETEACH Help children blend and read new words and sentences shown. Have them read the sentence, blending each word in sequence. The high-frequency words are underlined; they should read these as a unit, not blending the sounds.

home **robe** **drove** **slope**

I hope <u>she</u> spoke up.

<u>The</u> rose is made <u>of</u> stone.

Tell me <u>a</u> joke.

I broke my nose!

High-Frequency Words

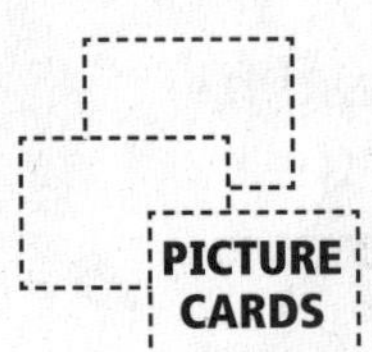

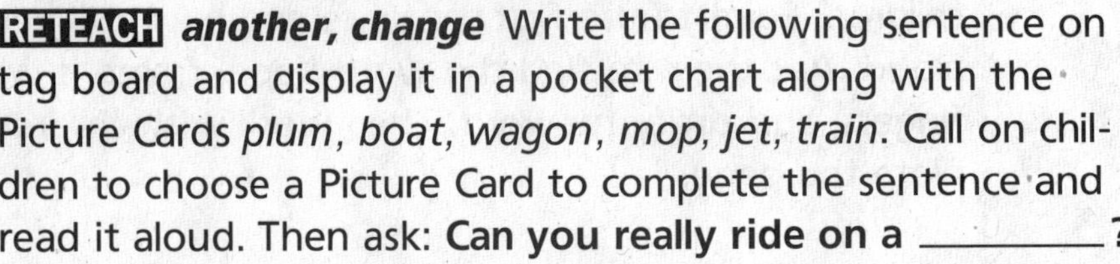

RETEACH ***another, change*** Write the following sentence on tag board and display it in a pocket chart along with the Picture Cards *plum, boat, wagon, mop, jet, train*. Call on children to choose a Picture Card to complete the sentence and read it aloud. Then ask: **Can you really ride on a ________?**

There was no room for us, so we rode on another ________.

Do the same for the following sentence and the same Picture Cards.

I need to change a wheel on my ________.

Read: *What a Bee Can See*

What a Bee Can See

Distribute copies of the book and have children read aloud the title. Then guide children through the book as they read.

Have children read the pages to find out what the bee is doing.

Pages 2–5: **What is the book about?** (*a wild bee*) **Where does the bee live?** (*in a hole in a tree*) **What is the bee looking for?** (*some food*) **Are the bee's eyes big or small?** (*big*) **How do the big eyes help the bee?** (*helps it find nectar*) **What is nectar? Read the sentence that tells. Point out and read the captions on page 5.**

Pages 6–7: Have children read to learn how bees find their food.

What color are the flowers in the first field? (*green*) **Why doesn't the bee stop?** (*it doesn't like green flowers*) **Does the bee see the red flower?** (*no*)

Pages 8–9: Have children read to find out the flowers bees can see.

Where is the bee now? (*another field*) **Why is this field different from the others?** (*The bee can see most of these flowers*) **What color flowers can the bee see best?** (*blue and yellow*) **What does the bee do?** (*drinks the nectar from the yellow and blue flowers*)

Pages 10–12: Have children read to find out how the bees work together.

Where does the bee go now? Find and frame the word that tells. (*home*) **What will the bee do at home?** (*tell the other bees about this field*) **What will the other bees do now?** (*go and collect nectar*)

Ask children to use the pictures to help summarize the book.

Phonics: Building Words

r o d e

r o p e

h o p e

h o p

h o t

h i t

h a t

PRETEACH Place the letters *r, o, d,* and *e* in a Word Builder and have children do the same. Slide your hand under the letters as you blend the sounds—/rrōōdd/. Then read the word naturally—rode. Have children repeat after you. Then have children build and read new words.

Change the *d* to *p*. What word did you make? *(rope)*

Change the *r* to *h*. What word did you make? *(hope)*

Take away the *e*. What word did you make? *(hop)*

Change the *p* to *t*. What word did you make? *(hot)*

Change the *o* to *i*. What word did you make? *(hit)*

Change the *t* to *a*. What word did you make? *(hat)*

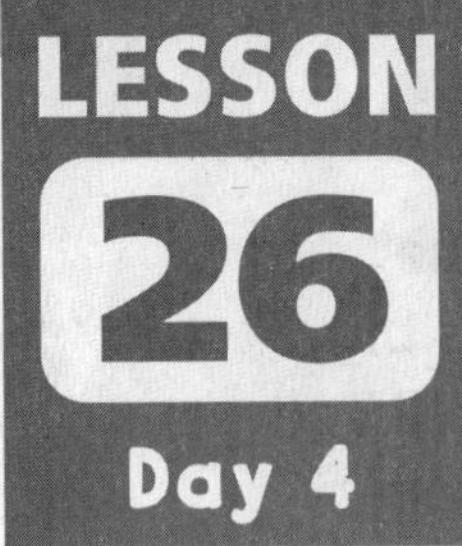

MATERIALS

Picture Cards boat, gate, goat, nine, rake, rose

Write-on/Wipe-off Boards with disks

Word Cards again, another, blue, change

Word Builder

Word Builder Cards b, c, e, g, h, l, m, o, p, r, s, t

What a Bee Can See

Warm-Up: Phonemic Awareness

Phoneme Segmentation Have children use the three boxes on the Write-on/Wipe-off Boards. Remind children that the boxes stand for the sounds in words. Show the Picture Card *rose* and ask: **What is the first sound you hear in *rose*?** (/r/) Have children place a disk in the first box. Then have children name the second sound in *rose* (/ō/) and place a disk in the second box. Then have them identify the last sound in *rose* (/z/) and place a disk in the third box. Point to each box in sequence as children say the word: **How many sounds do you hear in rose?** (*three*) Repeat this procedure with the following Picture Cards: *boat*, *goat*, *rake*, *nine*, *gate*.

Phonics: Building Words

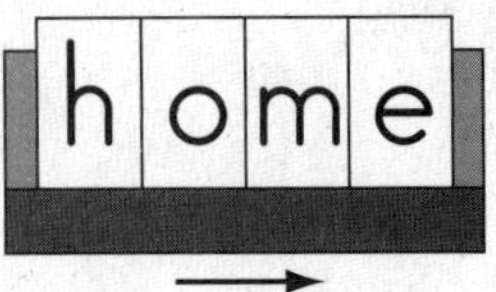

RETEACH Put the letters *h*, *o*, *m*, and *e* in a Word Builder and have children do the same. Slide your hand under the letters as you blend the sounds—/hhōōmm/. Then read the word naturally—*home*. Have children repeat after you. Then have children build and read new words.

Change the *m* to *p*. What word did you make? *(hope)*

Change the *p* to *s*. What word did you make? *(hose)*

Add *c* in front of *hose*. What word did you make? *(chose)*

Change the *c* to *t*. What word did you make? *(those)*

Change the *th* to *r* and the *s* to *b*. What word did you make? *(robe)*

Change the *r* to *gl*. What word did you make? *(globe)*

Distribute *Intervention Practice Book* page 78 to children.

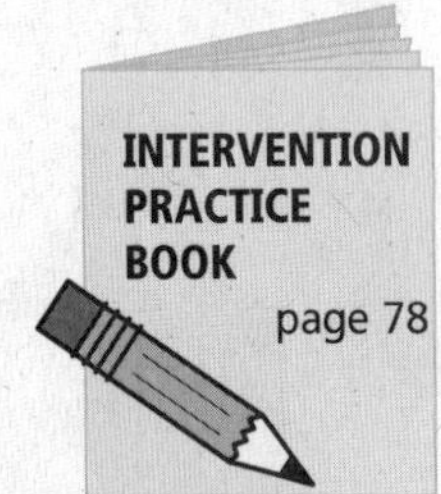

High-Frequency Words

another

change

again

blue

RETEACH ***another, change, again, blue*** Distribute word cards with the words listed above. Have partners take turns displaying the words for each other and reading them. After they read each word, have children spell it and then repeat the word. Then have them spell the word again and write it on a sheet of paper.

Read: *What a Bee Can See*

What a Bee Can See

Focus Skill **Cause/Effect** Remind children that understanding a story is easier when they think about what happens in a story and why it happens. Have children reread *What a Bee Can See* one page at a time and think about what causes certain things to happen. Ask: **How do bees find nectar? Why doesn't the bee stop at fields that have green or red flowers?** (*The bee can't see those colors*) **Why does the bee go home? What will it do there?** Have children decide on answers and compare their ideas.

Phonics: Blends with l

PRETEACH Write the word *ice* at the top of a sheet of chart paper. Ask children what they would need to do to change *ice* into *slice*. Write *slice* next to *ice*. Follow the same procedure for turning *am* into *clam*, *at* into *flat*, and *ink* into *blink*. End the activity by pointing to words at random and having children read the words.

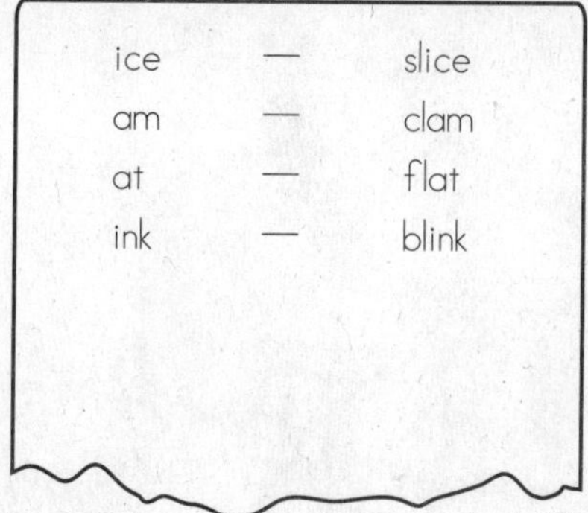

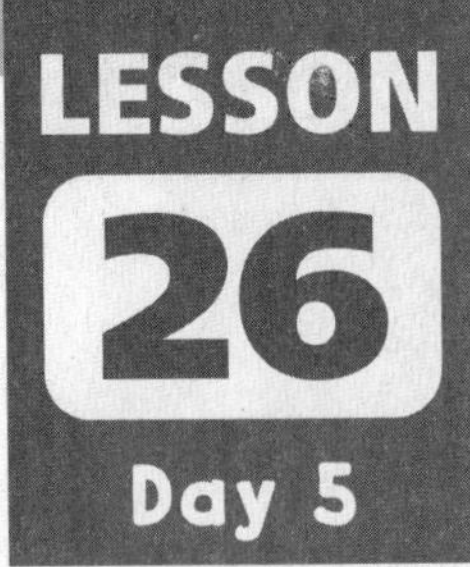

MATERIALS

Write-on/Wipe-off Boards

Word Cards again, another, blue, change, high, love

Word Builder

Word Builder Cards g, h, i, l, n, r, s, t

another

change

again

blue

high

love

Warm-Up: Phonemic Awareness

Phoneme Blending Tell children that together you are going to play a game of "Fix It." Say that you are going to say some words that are all broken and they should listen to see if they can put the sounds together to figure out the word. Listen: **/ch/-/ō/-/z/. What word does /ch/-/ō/-/z/ say?** (*chose*) Continue with the following words:

/n/-/ō/-/t/ *(note)*	**/h/-/ō/-/p/** *(hope)*	**/l/-/ī/-/t/** *(light)*
/s/-/l/-/ī/ *(sly)*	**/r/-/ī/-/t/** *(right)*	**/s/-/p/-/ō/-/k/** *(spoke)*

Phonics: Blends with l

RETEACH Write the word *cap* on a Write-on/Wipe-off Board and have children do the same. Then have them read the word. Ask: **What letter should we add if we want to change *cap* to *clap*?** (*l*) **Where should we add it?** (*after the first letter*) **Let's do that.** Continue the activity with the following sets of words: *fame/flame*, *side/slide*, *pan/plan*.

High-Frequency Words

Cumulative Review *another, change, again, blue, high, love* Place the words in a pocket chart. Say one of the words aloud and use it in a sentence. Have a volunteer find and point to the word. Have children clap and say the spelling of the word. Then have them write it. Have children read aloud their list of words.

Read: Self-Selected Reading

Have children select a book to read from their browsing boxes. After they have completed their reading, suggest that they point out a word, such as a long o word, that they successfully figured out on their own.

Phonics: Long Vowel /ī/igh

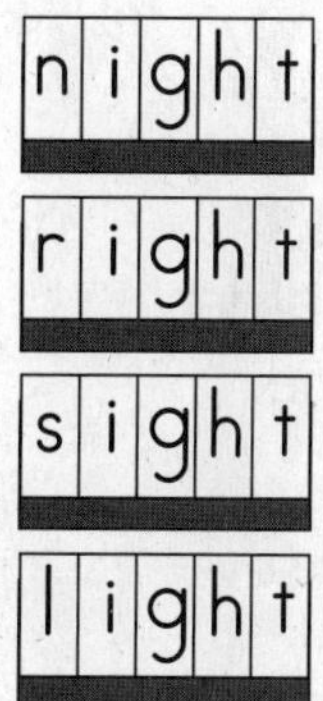

PRETEACH Use the Word Builder and Word Builder Cards to model blending words. Place the Word Builder Cards *n, i, g, h,* and *t* in the Word Builder. Tell children that *igh* can stand for /ī/, the sound in the middle of the word *light*.

Point to the *n* and say /n/. Point to the letters *igh* and say /ī/. Push the letters together and blend the sounds, elongating them /nnīī/. Have children repeat after you.

Point to *t* and say /t/. Slide the *t* next to *nigh*. Move your hand under the letters and blend the sounds, elongating them /nnīītt/. Have children repeat.

Then have children read the word *night* along with you.

Follow the same procedure for the words *right*, *sight*, and *light*.

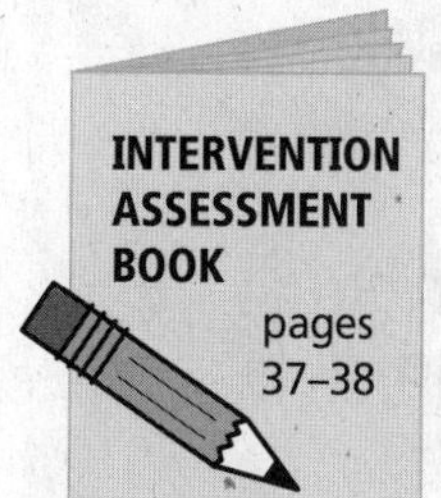

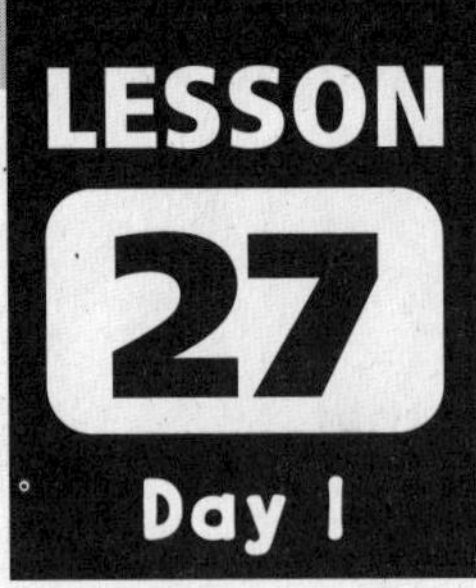

MATERIALS

Word Cards nothing, thought

Word Builder

Word Builder Cards b, g, h, h, i, m, n, r, s, t

Flying High

Warm-Up: Phonemic Awareness

Onset and Rime Tell children that you are going to say some words, but you are going to say them in parts. Have children listen to see if they can figure out the word. Demonstrate by saying: **/s/-igh—What word did I say?** (*sigh*)

/t/-ight	**/br/-ight**	**/h/-igh**	**/fr/-ight**
/s/-ight	**/m/-ight**	**/fl/-ight**	**/n/-ight**

Phonics: Long Vowel /ī/igh

PRETEACH **Blending** Write the letters *igh* on the board. These letters are *i*, *g*, and *h*. When they appear in that order, the letters *igh* can stand for /ī/, the long sound of *i* in the middle of words such as *night*, *right*, and *tight*.

Have children repeat the sound as you touch the letters several times.

Use the Word Builder Cards and a pocket chart to model blending words.

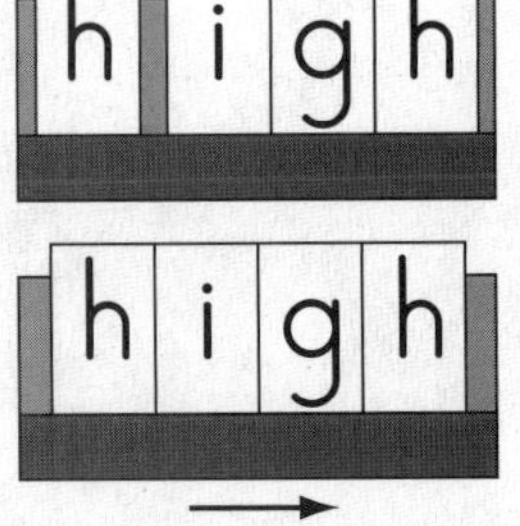

Place the Word Builder Cards *h*, *i*, *g*, and *h* in the Word Builder. Slide the *igh* together. Point to the *h* and say /h/. Point to the *igh* and say /ī/.

Slide the *igh* next to the *h*. Move your hands under the letters and blend the sounds, elongating them /hhīī/. Have children repeat after you.

Then have children read the word *high* along with you.

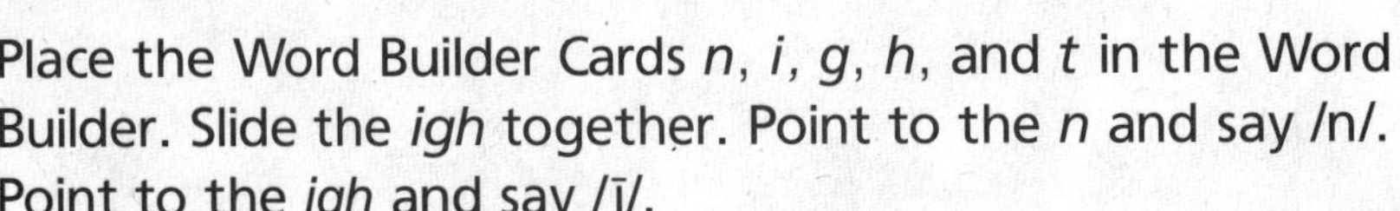

Place the Word Builder Cards *n*, *i*, *g*, *h*, and *t* in the Word Builder. Slide the *igh* together. Point to the *n* and say /n/. Point to the *igh* and say /ī/.

Slide the *igh* next to the *n*. Move your hands under the letters and blend the sounds, elongating them /nnīī/. Have children repeat after you.

Point to the *t* and say /t/. Slide the *t* next to *nigh*. Move your hands under the letters and blend the sounds, elongating them /nnīītt/. Have children repeat. Then have children read the word *night* with you.

High-Frequency Words

PRETEACH ***nothing, thought*** Display the word card *nothing*. **This word is *nothing*. There is nothing in my hand. Read the word with me—*nothing*. Spell the word with me—**

nothing

thought

n-o-t-h-i-n-g. Read the word with me. What is this word? (*nothing*)
Follow the same procedure for the word *thought*.

> ***thought*—I thought it might rain today.**

Then place the two words in a pocket chart and have volunteers read the words, as you randomly point to them.

Flying High

Read: *Flying High*

Story Words/Vocabulary Write the words *three, learn, afraid,* and *join* on the board. Say the words aloud and have children repeat them. Then point to each word, say it again, and have children repeat it. Be sure to assist children in reading these words as they proceed with the story.

Distribute copies of the book and have children put their finger on the title. Read the title aloud while children follow along. Ask them to touch the word *Flying*, then the word *High*. Ask which word was just spelled using the Word Builder (*High*). Echo read the book with children. Read page 2 aloud and then have children read it to you. Follow this procedure throughout the book.

Phonics: Word Building with /ī/igh

PRETEACH Place the letters *s, i, g,* and *h* in a Word Builder and have children do the same. Model how to blend the word *sigh*. Slide your hand under the letters as you slowly elongate the sounds /ssīī/. Have children do the same. Then read the word naturally—*sigh*. Have children do the same.

Have children blend and read new words by telling them:

Add *t* to the end of the word. What word did you make? *(sight)*

Change *s* to *m*. What word did you make? *(might)*

Change *m* to an *n*. What word did you make? *(night)*

Change the *n* to *r*. What word did you make? *(right)*

Add *b* in front of *r*. What word did you make? *(bright)*

Distribute *Intervention Practice Book* page 79 to children.

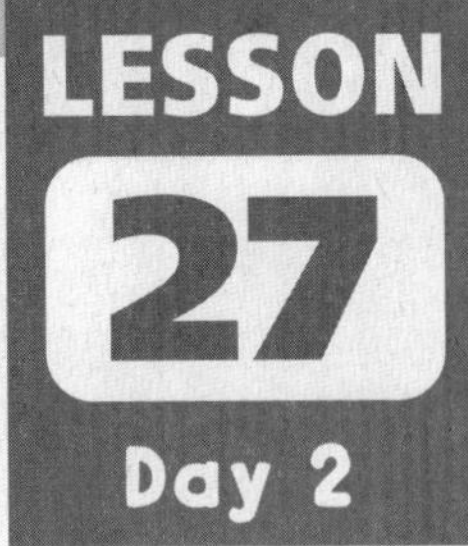

MATERIALS

Word Builder

Word Builder Cards b, f, g, h, i, l, r, s, t, t

Flying High

Warm-Up: Phonemic Awareness

Phoneme Isolation Say the word *sight* and have children repeat it.

Tell children to listen to the /ī/ sound in the middle of *sight*. Then say the words *rose* and *light* and have children repeat both words. Ask: **Which of these words has the /ī/ sound you hear in *sight*?** (*light*) Continue with the words *slight, might, loud; high, whale, sigh; bright, tight, home*.

Phonics: Word Building with /ī/igh

RETEACH Place the letters *l*, *i*, *g*, *h*, and *t* in a Word Builder and have children do the same. Model how to blend the word *light*. Slide your hand under the letters as you slowly elongate the sounds /llīītt/. Have children do the same. Then read the word naturally—*light*. Have children do the same.

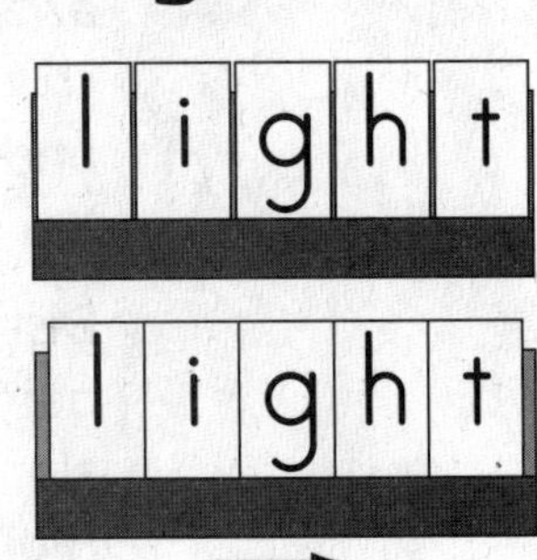

Have children blend and read new words by telling them:

Add *f* in front of *l*. What word did you make? *(flight)*

Change *l* to *r*. What word did you make? *(fright)*

Change *f* to *b*. What word did you make? *(bright)*

Drop *b*. What word did you make? *(right)*

Change *r* to *t*. What word did you make? *(tight)*

Change the first *t* to *s*. What word did you make? *(sight)*

Drop the *t* in *sight*. What word did you make? *(sigh)*

High-Frequency Words

RETEACH ***nothing, thought*** Write the word *nothing* on the board or on chart paper and have children read it. Show them that *nothing* is made up of two words—*no* and *thing*. **If you have no thing, then you have nothing.**

Write the word *thought* on the board or chart paper and have children read it. Outline the letters, paying attention to the letters that extend up and down from the base line. Write *those*, *they*, and *there* on the board and outline them too. **What makes these words alike? What makes them different?**

nothing **thought**

Read: *Flying High*

Distribute copies of the book to children. Read page 2 with them. Tell children that the first page of the book includes words with three different ways to spell the long /ē/ sound. Challenge children to find the three ways. They should find and frame the letters and then read the words. (*tree*, *leafy*) Be sure to point out to children that there are two long /ē/ sounds in *leafy*, one made by the *ea* and the other by the *y*. Tell them to be on the lookout for different ways of spelling the long /ī/ sound in the story, too. Then choral read the book with children. Let your voice fade if children start to gain control of the text.

Phonics: Reading Sentences with /ī/igh

PRETEACH Distribute *Intervention Practice Book* page 80 to children. Point to the first sentence and have children read it aloud. Ask them to find the word *light*, frame it with their fingers, and circle the word. Then work with children to complete the page.

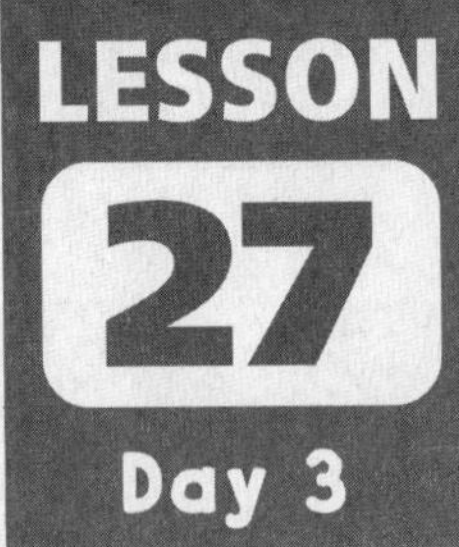

Warm-Up: Phonemic Awareness

Phoneme Blending Tell children that they are going to be detectives and find the word you are thinking about. Say: **I'm thinking of a word that means the opposite of *day*. When the sun sets it is ________. The word is /n/-/ī/-/t/. What's my word?** (*night*) Continue with the following words: /h/-/ī/ (*high*), /l/-/ī/-/t/ (*light*), /b/-/r/-/ī/-/t/ (*bright*), /t/-/ī/-/t/ (*tight*), /f/-/l/-/ī/-/t/ (*flight*).

MATERIALS

Picture Cards: ax, bed, box, bug, can, clam, fish, hat, map, red, ship, zebra

Word Builder

Word Builder Cards a, b, g, h, i, m, r, s, t, t

Flying High

Phonics: Reading Sentences with /ī/ igh

Help children blend and read new words and sentences shown. Have them read the sentence, blending each word in sequence. The high-frequency words are underlined; children should read these as a unit, not blending the sounds.

mighty **lights** **slight** **midnight**

<u>I</u> might see a ball game.

<u>Go</u> right <u>to</u> <u>the</u> shop.

Did <u>you</u> get on <u>the</u> flight?

<u>She</u> will sigh all night.

High-Frequency Words

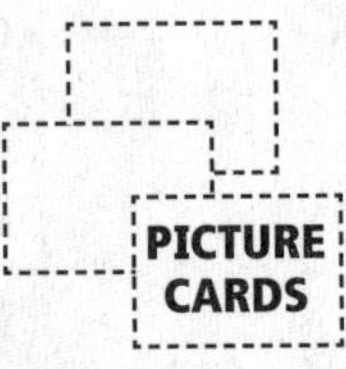

RETEACH ***nothing, thought*** Write the following sentence on tag board and display it in a pocket chart along with the Picture Cards *box, bed, can, hat, six, map*. Call on children to choose a Picture Card to complete the sentence and read it aloud. Then ask: **Could you really have something to eat in your ________?**

There is nothing to eat in this ________.

Do the same for the following sentence and Picture Cards *ax, clam, fish, red, ship, zebra*.

I thought I had a pet ________.

Read: *Flying High*

Distribute copies of the book and have children read aloud the title. Then guide children through the book as they read.

Pages 2–5: Have children read the pages to find what is in the tree.

Where is the tree? (*by the house*) **Find and read the words that tell about the tree.** (*tall, leafy, green*) **What is in the tree?** (*a nest*) **What is in the nest?** (*three white eggs*) **What happens after the shells crack? Find and read the words that tell.** (*Now there are three young birds in the small nest.*)

Pages 6–7: Have children read to learn what happens to the baby birds.

What do the little birds do when they are hungry? Find and frame the sentence that tells. (*They cry for food.*) **Who helps them?** (*the mama bird*) **What does she do to help? Find and read the words that tell.** (*She finds food for them to eat.*)

Pages 8–9: Have children read to find out what the birds have to learn to do.

What are the birds going to learn now? Find and read the words that tell. (*It is time for them to learn to fly.*) **Are they afraid?** (*no*)

Pages 10-12: Have children read to find out what happens to the three birds.

Where does the first bird fly? (*above the house and the tree*) **What do the other two birds do?** (*join him*) **What do all three birds do together?** (*fly up into the sky, into the light of the sun*)

Ask children to use the pictures to help summarize the book.

Phonics: Building Words

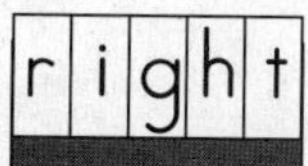

PRETEACH Put the letters *r, i, g, h, t* in a Word Builder and have children do the same. Slide your hand under the letters as you blend the sounds—/rrīītt/. Then read the word naturally—*right*. Have children repeat after you. Then have children build and read new words.

Add *b* in front of *r*. What word did you make? (*bright*)

Change *br* to *m*. What word did you make? (*might*)

Change *m* to *t*. What word did you make? (*tight*)

Change the first *t* to *s*. What word did you make? (*sight*)

Drop the final *t*. What word did you make? (*sigh*)

LESSON 27
Day 4

MATERIALS

Picture Cards: cup, fish, net, nine, pen, thumb

Write-on/Wipe-off Boards with disks

Word Cards for another, change, nothing, thought

Word Builder

Word Builder Cards b, f, g, h, i, l, n, r, s, s, t

Flying High

Warm-Up: Phonemic Awareness

PICTURE CARDS

Phoneme Segmentation Have children use the three boxes on the Write-on/Wipe-off Boards. Remind children that the boxes stand for the sounds in words. Show the Picture Card *net* and ask: **What is the first sound you hear in *net*?** (/n/) Have children place a disk in the first box. Then have children name the second sound in *net* (/e/) and place a disk in the second box. Then have them identify the third sound in *net* (/t/) and place a disk in the third box. Point to each box in sequence as children say the word. **How many sounds do you hear in *net*?** (*three*) Repeat this procedure with the Picture Cards *nine*, *pen*, *fish*, *thumb*, and *cup*.

Phonics: Building Words

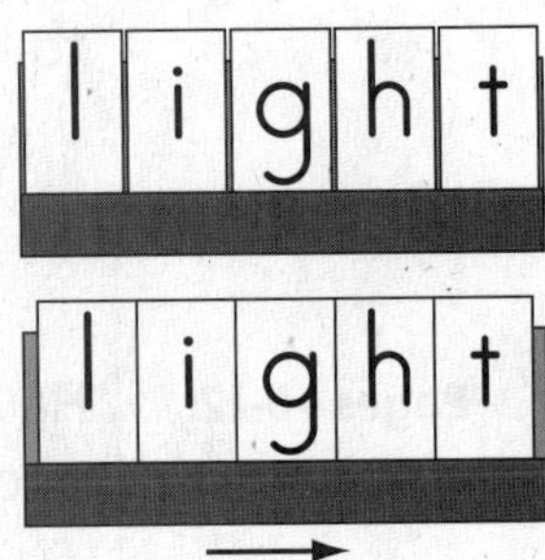

RETEACH Put the letters *l, i, g, h, t* in a Word Builder and have children do the same. Slide your hand under the letters as you blend the sounds—/llīītt/. Then read the word naturally—*light*. Have children repeat after you. Then have children build and read new words.

Add *s* after *t*. What word did you make? (*lights*)

Change *l* to *n*. What word did you make? (*nights*)

Change *n* to *s*. What word did you make? (*sights*)

Drop the last *s*. What word did you make? (*sight*)

Change *s* to *r*. What word did you make? (*right*)

Add *b* in front of *r*. What word did you make? (*bright*)

Change *b* to *f*. What word did you make? (*fright*)

Distribute *Intervention Practice Book* page 81 to children.

High-Frequency Words

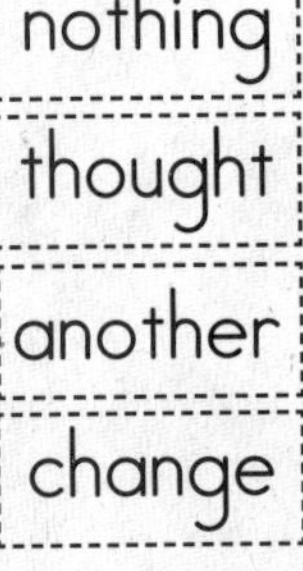

RETEACH ***nothing, thought, another, change***. Distribute word cards with the words listed above. Have partners take turns displaying the words for each other and reading them. After they read each word, have children spell it and then repeat the word. Then have them spell the word again and write it on a sheet of paper.

Read: *Flying High*

Plot Explain that the plot is what happens in a story. Then remind children that they will understand a story better if they think about its plot as they read. Have children reread *Flying Hig*h one page at a time and think about the story's plot. Ask questions like these: **What happens to the eggs after they are laid? What do the birds need to have when they have just hatched? How will they get it? What do the birds need to learn how to do? Is it easy for them, or is it hard?** Have children decide on answers and compare their ideas.

Phonics: Inflections -ed, -ing

PRETEACH Write the word *race* on the board and have children read it. Say: **Today I will *race*. Yesterday I *raced*.** Write *raced* next to *race*. **When a word ends with *e*, you have to drop the *e* before you put on the *-ed* ending.** Write *racing* next to *raced*. **Today I was *racing*. You also drop the *e* when you add the *–ing* ending.** Write *like* on the board and show how it is turned into *liked* and then *liking*. Repeat with *shave/shaved/shaving*, *hope/hoped/hoping*, and *bake/baked/baking*.

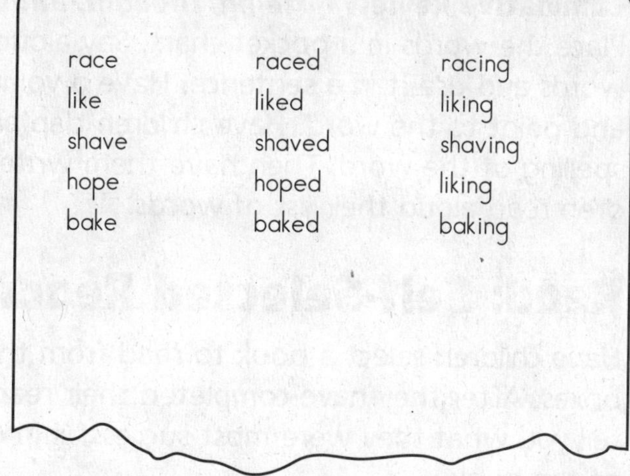

race raced racing
like liked liking
shave shaved shaving
hope hoped liking
bake baked baking

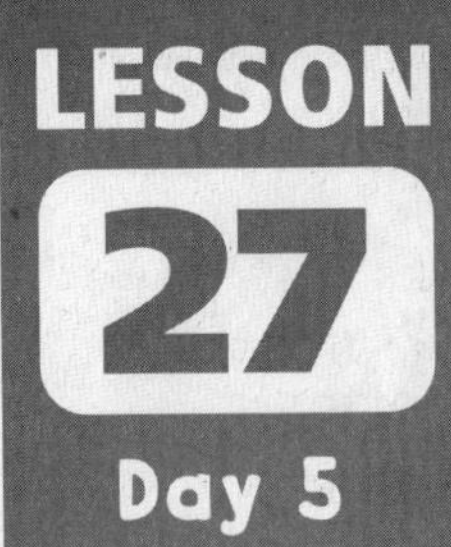

MATERIALS

Write-on/Wipe off Boards

Word Cards another, change, nothing, thought

Word Builder

Word Builder Cards a, i, l, p, s, y

Warm-Up: Phonemic Awareness

Phoneme Blending Tell children that together you are going to play a put together game. Tell them that you are going to say some words sound by sound and they should listen to see if they can put the sounds together to figure out the word. Listen: **/s/-/ī/-/t/. What word does /s/-/ī/-/t/ say?** (*sight*) Continue with the following words:

/n/-/ī/-/t/ *(night)*	**/m/-/ī/-/t/** *(might)*	**/l/-/ou/-/d/** *(loud)*
/s/-/t/-/ā/ *(stay)*	**/th/-/ō/-/z/** *(those)*	**/m/-/ā/-/l/** *(mail)*

Phonics: Inflections -ed, -ing

RETEACH Write the word *hike* on a Write-on/Wipe-off Board and have children do the same. Then have them read the word. Ask: **What should we do if we want to change *hike* to *hiked*?** (Drop the *-e,* add *-ed*) **Let's do that.** Continue the activity with the following words: *wade, waded; poke, poked; smile, smiled; skate, skated*. Then ask **What should we do if we want to change *hike* to *hiking*?** (Drop the -e, add *-ing*) **Let's do that.** Repeat with the same words: *wade, wading; poke, poking; smile, smiling; skate, skating*.

High-Frequency Words

Cumulative Review *nothing, thought, another, change* Place the words in a pocket chart. Say aloud one of the words and use it in a sentence. Have a volunteer find and point to the word. Have children clap and say the spelling of the word. Then have them write it. Have children read aloud their list of words.

nothing

thought

another

change

Read: Self-Selected Reading

Have children select a book to read from their browsing boxes. After they have completed their reading, have them tell you what they were most successful in during the reading of the book.

Phonics: Long Vowel /ā/ai, ay

PRETEACH Write the letters *ai* and *ay* on the board on or chart paper. **The letters *ai* and *ay* can stand for the /ā/ sound in such words as *rain* and *say*.** Point to the letters *ai* and *ay* and say /ā/. Have children repeat the sound as you touch the letters *ai* and *ay* several times.

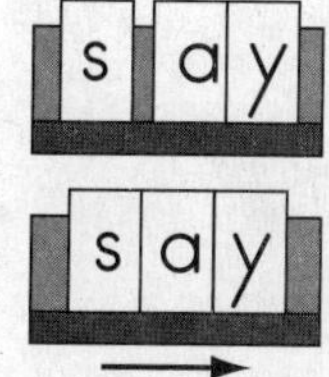

Use the Word Builder and Word Builder Cards to model blending words. Place the Word Builder Cards *s*, *a*, and *y* in the Word Builder. Tell children that *ay* at the end of the word can stand for /ā/, the long sound of *a* at the end of the word *pay*.

Point to the letter *s*. Say /s/. Point to the *ay*. Say /ā/. Slide the *ay* next to the *s*. Move your hand under the letters and blend the sounds, elongating them /ssāā/. Then read the word *say* naturally and have children read the word along with you.

Use the Word Builder Cards *p*, *a*, *i*, and *l*. Place them in the Word Builder, keeping *ai* together. Tell children that *ai* can also stand for /ā/. Point to *p*. Say /p/. Point to *ai*. Say /ā/. Slide *ai* next to *p*. Slide your hand under the letters and blend the sounds, elongating them /ppāā/.

Point to *l*. Say /l/. Slide *l* next to *pai*. Slide your hand under the letters and blend the sounds, elongating them /ppāall/. Have children repeat. Then read the word *pail* naturally and have children read the word along with you.

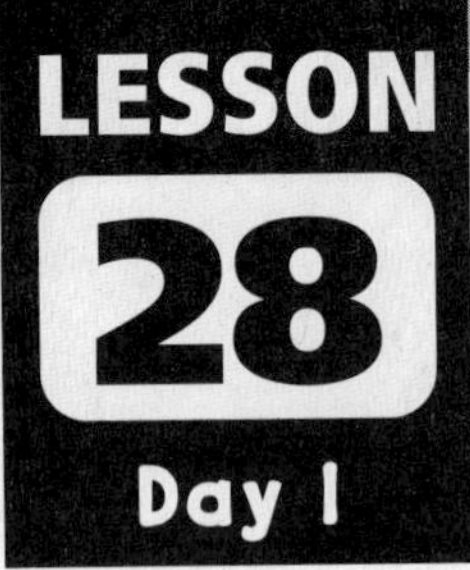

Warm-Up: Phonemic Awareness

Onset and Rime Tell children that you are going to say some words, but you are going to say them in parts. Have children listen to see if they can figure out the word. Demonstrate by saying: **/d/-ay—What word did I say?** (*day*)

/tr/-ay	**/br/-aid**	**/h/-ay**	**/tr/-ail**
/s/-ail	**/m/-ail**	**/spr/-ay**	**/gr/-ay**

MATERIALS

Word Cards cold, sure

Word Builder

Word Builder Cards a, c, d, h, l, m, p, s, y

Rainy Day Friends

Phonics: Long Vowel /ā/ai, ay

RETEACH **Blending** Write *ai* on the board. **These letters are *a* and *i*. When they appear together, the letters *ai* can stand for /ā/, the long sound of *a* in words such as *aim*, *pain*, and *sail*.** Have children repeat the sound as you touch the letters several times.

Use the Word Builder Cards and a pocket chart to model blending words.

Place the Word Builder Cards *s, a, i,* and *l* in the Word Builder. Slide the *ai* together. Point to the *s* and say /s/. Point to the *ai* and say /ā/.

Slide the *ai* next to the *s*. Move your hand under the letters and blend the sounds, elongating them /ssā/. Have children repeat after you.

Point to the *l* and say /l/. Slide the *l* next to *sai*. Move your hand under the letters and blend the sounds, elongating them /ssāāll/. Have children repeat. Then say the word naturally—*sail*. Have children do the same.

s a i l

s a i l

s a i l

s a i l

Write *ay* on the board. **These letters are *a* and *y*. When they appear together, the letters *ay* can also stand for /ā/, the long sound of *a* at the end of words such as *say*, *day*, and *play*.** Have children repeat the sound as you touch the letters several times.

Place the Word Builder cards *p, a,* and *y* in the Word Builder. Slide the *ay* together. Point to the *p* and say /p/. Point to the *ay* and say /ā/.

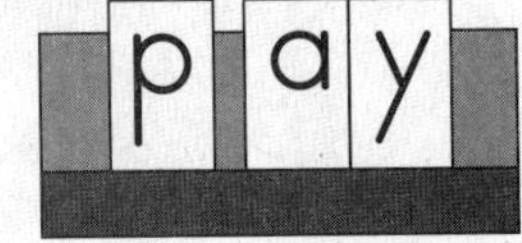

Slide the *ay* next to the *p*. Move your hands under the letters and blend the sounds, elongating them /ppāā/. Have children repeat. Then have children read the word *pay* along with you.

High-Frequency Words

cold

sure

PRETEACH ***cold, sure*** Display the word card *cold*. **This word is *cold*. I need a jacket because it is cold outside. Read the word with me—*cold*. Spell the word with me—c-o-l-d. Read the word with me. What is this word?** (*cold*)

Follow the same procedure for the word sure.

sure—**I am *sure* I can do this work.**

Then place the two words in a pocket chart and have volunteers read the words, as you randomly point to them.

Read: *Rainy Day Friends*

Story words/Vocabulary Write the words *hurried*, *both*, and *caught*. Read the words and have children repeat them after you. Help children as necessary with these words as they read. Distribute copies of the book and have children put their finger on the title. Read the title aloud while children follow along. Ask them to touch the word *Rainy*, then the words *Day* and *Friends*. Have volunteers choose a word in the title to read aloud. Ask children what they think the story will be about. Echo read the book with children. Read page 2 aloud and then have children read it to you. Follow this procedure throughout the book.

Phonics: Word Building with /ā/ai, ay

PRETEACH Place the letters *m*, *a*, and *y* in a Word Builder and have children do the same. Model how to blend the word may. Slide your hand under the letters as you slowly elongate the sounds /mmāā/. Have children do the same. Then read the word naturally—*may*. Have children do the same.

Have children blend and read new words by telling them:

Change the *m* to *d*. What word did you make? (*day*)

Change *d* to *h*. What word did you make? (*hay*)

Change *h* to *s*. What word did you make? (*say*)

Change *s* to *p*. What word did you make? (*pay*)

Add an *l* in front of *ay*. What word did you make? (*play*)

Change the *y* to *i*. Put the *l* at the end. What word did you make? (*clay*)

Distribute *Intervention Practice Book* page 82 to children.

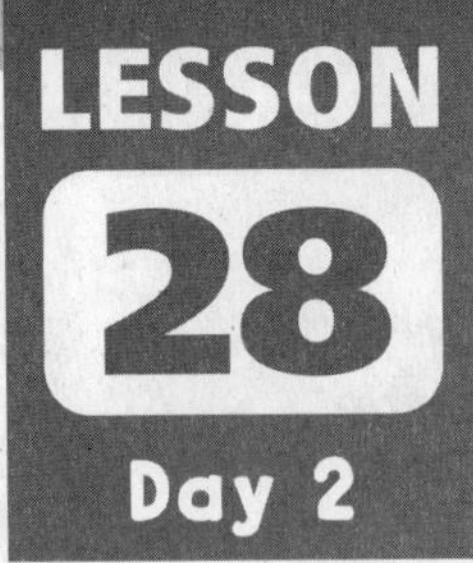

MATERIALS

Word Builder

Word Builder Cards
a, i, l, n, p, r, t, y

Rainy Day Friends

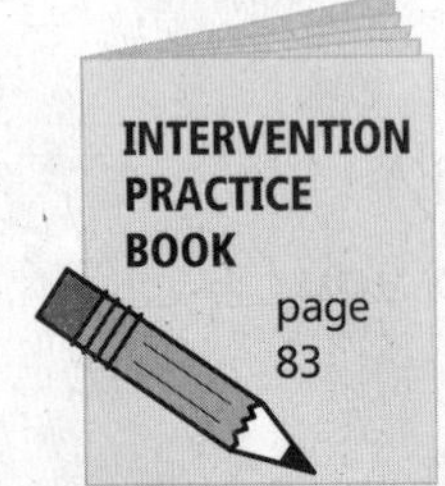

Warm-Up: Phonemic Awareness

Phoneme Isolation Say the word *nail* and have children repeat it. Tell children to listen to the /ā/ sound in the middle of nail. Then say the words *chain* and *bright* and have children repeat both words. Ask: **Which of these words has the /ā/ sound you hear in nail?** (*chain*)

Continue with the words *braid, rain, broke; stay, gray, stand; tray, fly, bay*.

Phonics: Word Building with /ā/ai, ay

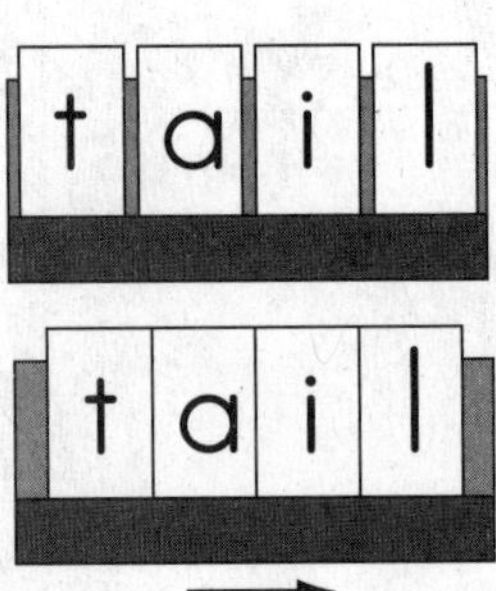

RETEACH Place the letters *t, a, i,* and *l* in a Word Builder and have children do the same. Model how to blend the word *tail*. Slide your hand under the letters as you slowly elongate the sounds /ttāāll/. Have children do the same. Then read the word naturally—*tail*. Have children do the same.

Have children blend and read new words by telling them:

Change the *t* to *p*. What word did you make? (*pail*)

Change the *l* to *n*. What word did you make? (*pain*)

Change the *p* to *r*. What word did you make? (*rain*)

Add a *t* in front of *rain*. What word did you make? (*train*)

Take away the *n*. Change the *i* to *y*. What word did you make? (*tray*)

Take away the *t*. What word did you make? (*ray*)

High-Frequency Words

RETEACH ***cold, sure*** Write the word *old* and have children read it. Then write the word *cold* next to *old* and have children read the word. **How are these words the same? How are they different? Let's read them again: old cold.** Repeat the procedure with *sir/sure.*

cold old

Rainy Day Friends

Read: *Rainy Day Friends*

Distribute copies of the book to children. Read page 2 with them. Point out the quotation marks that surround Anna's words. Tell children that these are called quotation marks. **Quotation marks come in pairs. One set shows when a person begins to talk, and the other set shows when the person stops talking.** Have children be on the lookout for quotation marks as they read. Then choral read the book with children. Let your voice fade if children start to gain control of the text.

Phonics: Reading Sentences with /ā/ai, ay

PRE15TEACH Distribute *Intervention Practice Book* page 83 to children. Point to the first sentence and have children read it aloud. Ask them to find the word *rain*, frame it with their fingers, and circle the word. Then work with children to complete the page.

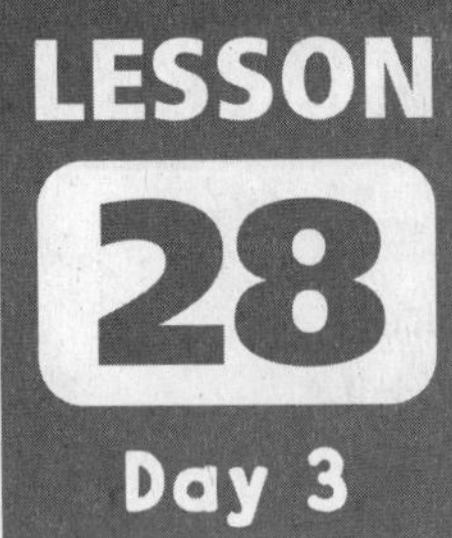

Warm-Up: Phonemic Awareness

Phoneme Blending Tell children that they are going to be detectives and find the word you are thinking about. Say: **I'm thinking of a word that can sometimes be found in wood. You can hammer it. The word is /n/-/ā/-/l/. What's my word?** (*nail*) Continue with the following words: /d/-/ā/ (*day*), /m/-/ā/-/l/ (*mail*), /s/-/t/-/ā/-/n/ (*stain*), /p/-/l/-/ā/ (*play*), /b/-/r/-/ā/-/d/ (*braid*).

MATERIALS

Picture Cards box, cat, fan, fox, hat, lock, pig, quilt, sock, thumb, vest

Word Builder

Word Builder Cards a, b, e, f, i, l, m, n, s, t

Rainy Day Friends

Phonics: Reading Sentences with /ā/ai, ay

RETEACH Help children blend and read new words and sentences shown. Have them read the sentence, blending each word in sequence. The high-frequency words are underlined; they should read these as a unit, not blending the sounds.

bay **trail** **stay** **drain**

This is <u>a</u> gray day.

Tie <u>the</u> chain <u>to</u> <u>the</u> pail.

Her braid has <u>a</u> clip.

Stack <u>the</u> mail <u>on</u> <u>the</u> tray.

High-Frequency Words

RETEACH ***cold, sure*** Write the following sentence on tag board and display it in a pocket chart along with the Picture Cards *hat, sock, thumb, quilt, lock, fan*. Call on children to choose a Picture Card to complete the sentence and read it aloud. Then ask: **If you were cold, would you really put on a ______?**

PICTURE CARDS

It is cold, so I put on a ______.

Do the same for the following sentence and Picture Cards *pig, hat, sock, cat, vest, box, fox*.

I am sure I see a blue ______.

Read: *Rainy Day Friends*

Distribute copies of the book and have children put their finger on the title. Then guide children through the book as they read.

Pages 2–5: Have children read the pages to find how the story begins.

> **Who are the characters in the story?** (*Nick and Anna*) **What kind of a day is it?** (*wet and cold*) **What can't Nick and Anna do?** (*go to the lake together*) **What does Nick love to do?** (*go fishing*) **What does Anna say they can do? Find and read the sentence that tells.** (*We will fish in my house.*)

Pages 6–9: Have children read to find out how they will fish in the house.

> **They only have one fishing pole. What will they do?** (*take turns*) **What did Anna catch?** (*a blue boot*) **Find and read the words that tell.** (*I caught a big blue one!*) **What did Nick catch?** (*a big red boot*) **How do you know Nick is having a good time?** (*He says, "This sure is fun."*)

Pages 10–12: Have children read to find out what happens next.

> **What has Anna's mama done?** (*made food*) **Find and frame the words that tell.** (*Mama has made us something to eat.*) **What does Nick like to eat?** (*fish*) **Does he like to eat boots?** (*no*) **Find and read the sentence that tells.** (*I'm glad your mama didn't cook those boots!*) **Is Nick sad and cold now?** (*no*) **How does he feel?** (*happy and warm*) **What kinds of friends are the best?** (*rainy day friends*)

Ask children to use the pictures to help summarize the book.

Phonics: Building Words

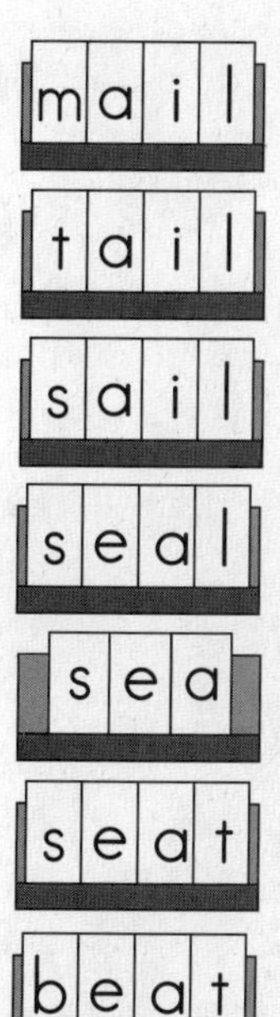

PRETEACH Place the letters *m*, *a*, *i*, and *l* in a Word Builder and have children do the same. Slide your hand under the letters as you blend the sounds—/mmāāll/. Then read the word naturally—*mail*. Have children repeat after you. Then have children build and read new words.

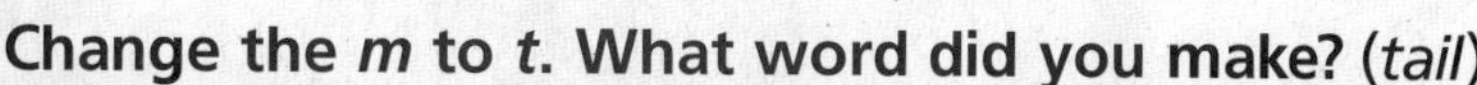

Change the *m* to *t*. What word did you make? (*tail*)

Change *t* to *s*. What word did you make? (*sail*)

Change *ai* to *ea*. What word did you make? (*seal*)

Take away the *l*. What word did you make? (*sea*)

Add *t* after the sea. What word did you make? (*seat*)

Change *s* to *b*. What word did you make? (*beat*)

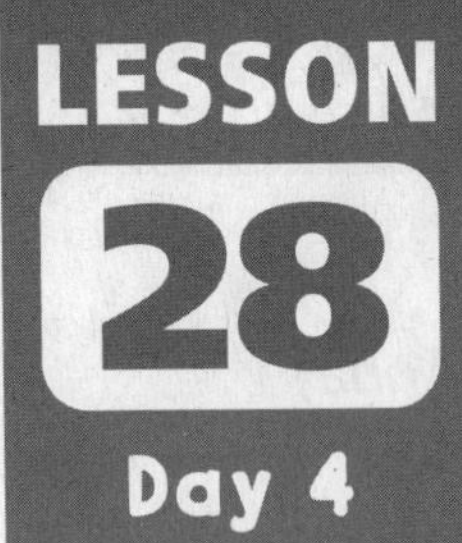

MATERIALS

Picture Cards: lamp, nest, plum, sled, smile, train

Papers with four boxes side by side, plus disks

Word Cards cold, sure, nothing, thought

Word Builder

Word Builder Cards a, c, d, g, l, m, p, r, s, t, y

Rainy Day Friends

Warm-Up: Phonemic Awareness

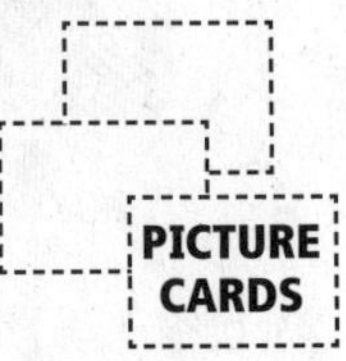

Phoneme Segmentation Distribute the four-box paper to children. Tell them that the boxes stand for sounds in words. Show the Picture Card *train* and ask: **What is the first sound you hear in *train*?** (/t/) Have children place a disk in the first box to represent this sound. Then have them name the second sound in *train* (/r/) and place a second disk on the paper. Then have them identify the third and fourth sounds in train (/ā/ and /n/) and place a disk on the paper for each sound. Point to the disks in sequence as children say the word. **How many sounds do you hear in *train*?** (*four*) Repeat this procedure with the Picture Cards *smile*, *lamp*, *plum*, *sled*, and *nest*.

Phonics: Building Words

RETEACH Put the letters *t, r, a, y* in a Word Builder and have children do the same. Slide your hand under the letters as you blend the sounds—/ttrraa/. Then read the word naturally—*tray*. Have children repeat after you. Then have children build and read new words.

Change the *t* to *g*. What word did you make? (*gray*)

Change the *gr* to *pl*. What word did you make? (*play*)

Take away the *l*. What word did you make? (*pay*)

Change the *p* to *d*. What word did you make? (*day*)

Change the *d* to *s*. What word did you make? (*say*)

Change the *s* to *m*. What word did you make? (*may*)

Change the *m* to *cl*. What word did you make? (*clay*)

Distribute *Intervention Practice Book* page 84 to children.

High-Frequency Words

RETEACH ***cold, sure, nothing, thought*** Distribute word cards with the words listed above. Have partners take turns displaying the words for each other and reading them. After they read each word, have children spell it and then repeat the word. Then have them spell the word again and write it on a sheet of paper.

Read: *Rainy Day Friends*

Rainy Day Friends

Focus Skill **Cause/Effect** Remind children that reading can become easier when they think about why certain things happen in a story. This is called understanding cause and effect. Have children reread *Rainy Day Friends* one page at a time and think about why certain things happened. Ask: **What did Nick want to do? Why couldn't he do it? What did they imagine the boots were? Why? Why didn't Anna and Nick want to eat what they caught?** Have children decide on answers and compare their ideas. Encourage children to write at least one "because" sentence.

> Nick couldn't fish at the lake *because* it was raining.

Phonograms: -ail, -ain

PREteach Write the letters *ail* and *ain* at the top of a sheet of chart paper. Have children suggest words that end with *-ail* and say what letters they would need to write the words. Then write the words underneath the heading *ail*. Use the same procedure for *-ain*. Then have children read each column of words. End the activity by pointing to words at random and having children read the words.

ail	ain
sail, pail, rail, tail, trail, hail, quail, snail, mail, nail, jail, fail	rain, train, main, brain, drain, grain, pain, stain, strain, plain, gain, chain

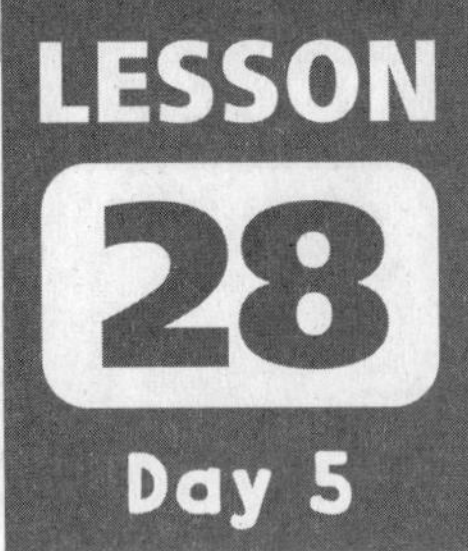

Warm-Up: Phonemic Awareness

Phoneme Blending Tell children that they will be builders and that they will put together sounds to figure out words. **Listen: /t/-/ā/-/l /. What word does /t/-/ā/-/l/ say?** (*tail*) Continue with the following words:

/r/-/ā/-/z/ (*raise*)
/l/-/ī/-/t/ (*light*)
/ch/-/ī/-/l/-/d/ (*child*)
/k/-/ī/-/n/-/d/ (*kind*)
/s/-/p/-/r/-/ā/ (*spray*)
/d/-/r/-/ā/-/n/ (*drain*)

MATERIALS

Write-on/Wipe-off Boards

Word Cards cold, sure, nothing, thought

Word Builder

Word Builder Cards k, i, n, d

Phonics: Phonograms: -ail, -ain

RETEACH Write the word *rail* on a Write-on/Wipe-off Board and have children do the same. Then have them read the word. Ask: **What letter should we write if we want to change rail to pail?** (*p*) **Let's do that.** Continue the activity with the words *mail*, *sail*, *jail*, and *trail*. Repeat the activity, using the words *train*, *brain*, *grain*, and *chain*.

High-Frequency Words

Cumulative Review *cold, sure, nothing, thought* Place the words in a pocket chart. Say one of the words aloud and use it in a sentence. Have a volunteer find and point to the word. Have children clap and say the spelling of the word. Then have them write it. Have children read aloud their list of words.

Read: Self-Selected Reading

Have children select a book to read from their browsing boxes. After they have completed their reading, have them show you one or more words they successfully figured out on their own.

Phonics: Phonics: Long Vowel /ī/i

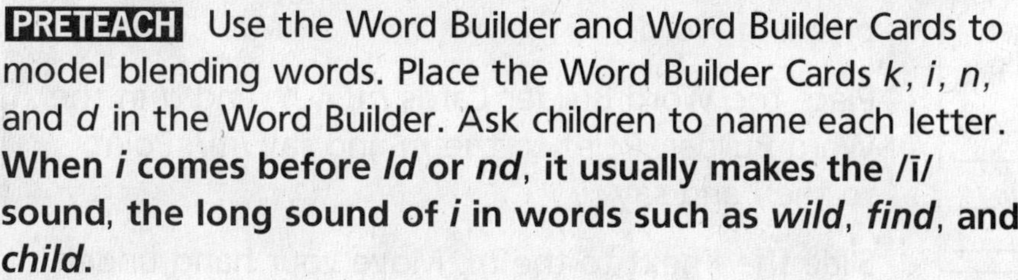

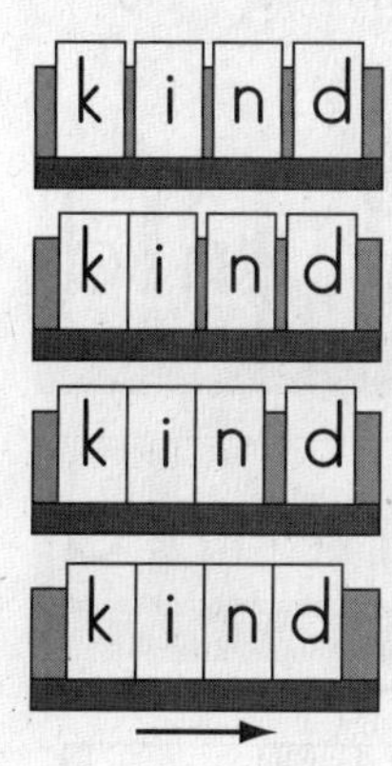

PRETEACH Use the Word Builder and Word Builder Cards to model blending words. Place the Word Builder Cards *k*, *i*, *n*, and *d* in the Word Builder. Ask children to name each letter. **When *i* comes before *ld* or *nd*, it usually makes the /ī/ sound, the long sound of *i* in words such as *wild*, *find*, and *child*.**

Point to the letter *k* and say /k/. Point to the *i* and say /ī/.

Slide the *i* next to the *k*. Move your hand under the letters and blend the sounds, elongating them /kkīī/. Have children repeat after you.

Point to *n* and say /n/. Slide the *n* next to *ki*. Slide your hand under the letters and blend the sounds, elongating them /kkīīnn/. Have children repeat.

Point to *d* and say /d/. Slide the *d* next to *kin*. Slide your hand under the letters and blend the sounds, elongating them /kkīīnndd/. Then have children read the word kind along with you.

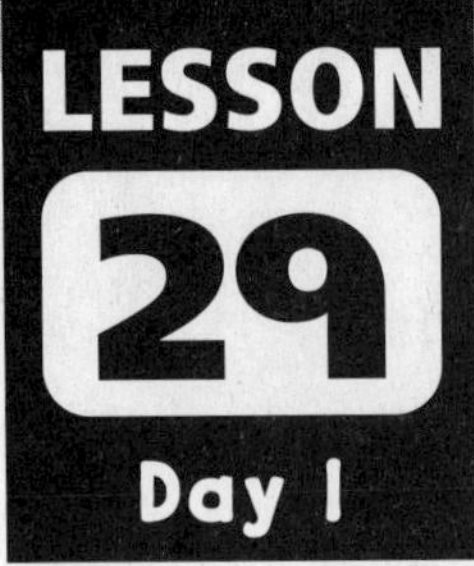

Warm-Up: Phonemic Awareness

Onset and Rime Tell children that you are going to say some words, but you are going to say them in parts. Have children listen to see if they can figure out the word. Demonstrate by saying: **/w/-ild—What word did I say?** (*wild*)

/ch/-ild	**/m/-ind**	**/m/-ild**	**/f/-ind**
/bl/-ind	**/k/-ind**	**/gr/-ind**	**/w/-ind**

MATERIALS

Word Card both

Word Builder

Word Builder Cards c, d, f, h, i, k, l, m, n, w

Alphabet Masters Ii

Young Animals

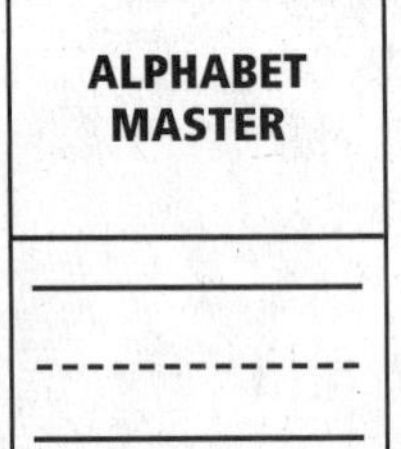

Phonics: Long Vowel /ī/i

RETEACH Blending Display Alphabet Master *Ii*. **This letter is *i*. The letter *i* can stand for the /ī/ sound, the long sound of the letter *i* in words such as *wild*, *grind*, and *find*.** Have children repeat the sound as you touch the letter *i* several times.

Use the Word Builder Cards and a pocket chart to model blending words.

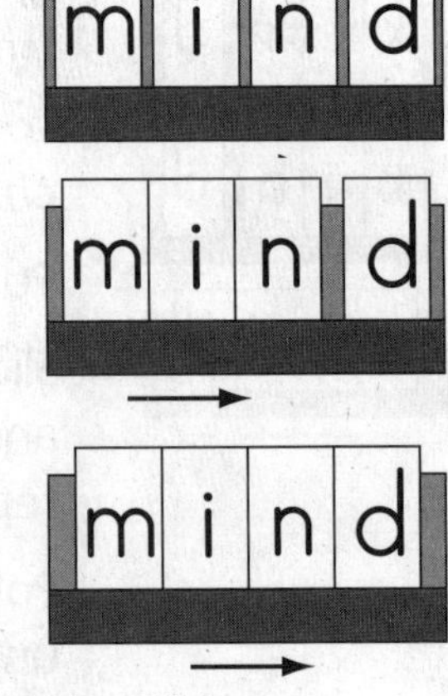

Place the Word Builder Cards *m, i, n,* and *d* in the Word Builder. Point to the *m* and say /m/. Point to the *i* and say /ī/.

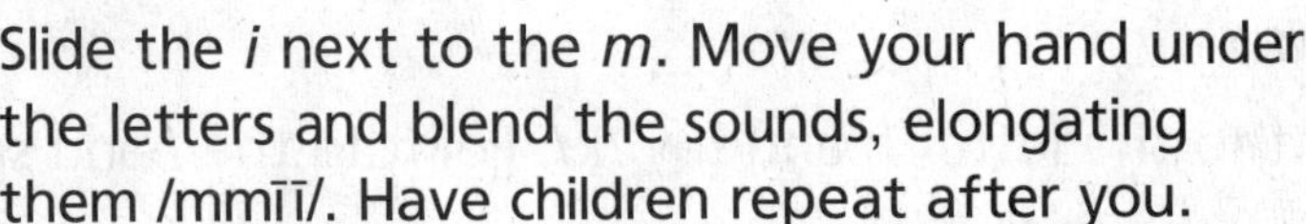

Slide the *i* next to the *m*. Move your hand under the letters and blend the sounds, elongating them /mmīī/. Have children repeat after you.

Point to the letter *n* and say /n/. Have children say /n/ as you point to *n*.

Slide *n* next to *mi*. Slide your hand under *min* and blend by elongating the sounds—/mmīīnn/. Have children repeat. Point to *d*. Say /d/. Slide *d* next to *min*. Slide your hand under the letters and blend the sounds, elongating them /mmīīnndd/. Then have children read the word *mind* along with you.

High-Frequency Words

PREACH

both

PRETEACH *both* Display the word card *both*. **This word is *both*. We both have red shirts on. Read the word with me—*both*. Spell the word with me—*b-o-t-h*. Read the word with me. What is this word?** (*both*)

Read: *Young Animals*

Story Words/Vocabulary Write the words *young*, *during*, *spring*, and *ready* on the board. Point to each word, say it aloud, and have children repeat it after you. Provide help with these words to any child who needs it during the reading of the story.

Distribute copies of the book and have children put their finger on the title. Read the title aloud while children follow along. Ask them to touch the word *Young*, then the word *Animals*. Have volunteers point to a word in the title and read it aloud. Echo read the book with children. Read page 2 aloud and then have children read it to you. Follow this procedure throughout the book.

Phonics: Word Building with /ī/i

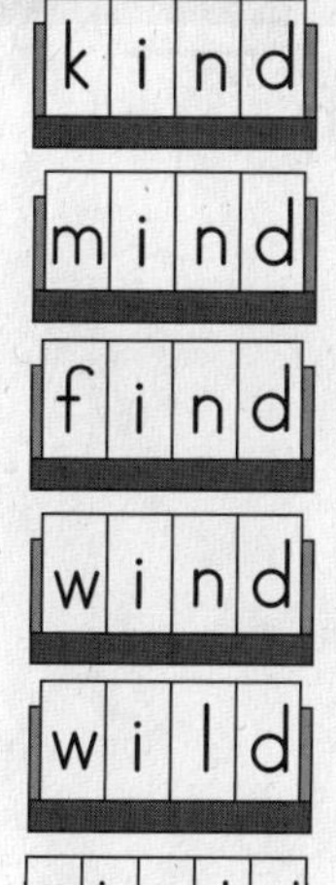

PRETEACH Place the letters *k*, *i*, *n*, and *d* in a Word Builder and have children do the same. Model how to blend the word *kind*. Slide your hand under the letters as you slowly elongate the sounds /kkīīnndd/. Have children do the same. Then read the word naturally—*kind*. Have children do the same.

Have children blend and read new words by telling them:

Change the *k* to *m*. What word did you make? *(mind)*

Change the *m* to *f*. What word did you make? *(find)*

Change the *f* to *w*. What word did you make? *(wind)*

Change the *n* to *l*. What word did you make? *(wild)*

Change the *w* to *ch*. What word did you make? *(child)*

Distribute *Intervention Practice Book* page 85 to children.

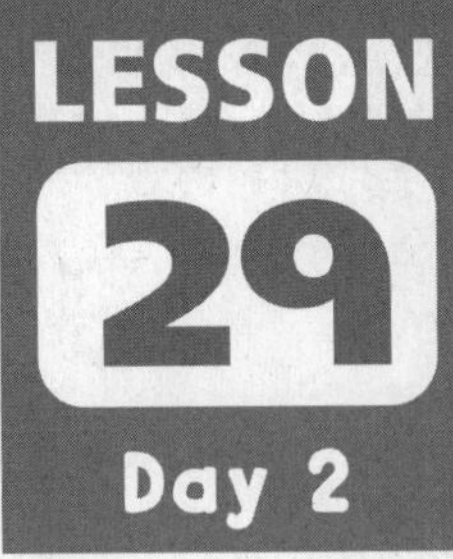

MATERIALS

Word Builder

Word Builder Cards b, c, d, f, h, i, k, l, m, n, w

Young Animals

Warm-Up: Phonemic Awareness

Phoneme Isolation Say the word *kind*. Tell children to listen to the /ī/ sound in the middle of the word *kind*. Then say the words *mild* and *sail*. Have them repeat the words aloud. Ask: **Which of these words has the /ī/ sound you hear in *kind*?** (*mild*) Continue with the words *child, grind, hand; wild, blind, bone; kind, whale, child.*

Phonics: Word Building with /ī/i

RETEACH Place the letters *w*, *i*, *l*, and *d* in a Word Builder and have children do the same. Model how to blend the word *wild*. Slide your hand under the letters as you slowly elongate the sounds /wwīllldd/. Have children do the same. Then read the word naturally—*wild*. Have children do the same.

Have children blend and read new words by telling them:

Change the *w* to *ch*. What word did you make? *(child)*

Change the *ch* to *m*. What word did you make? *(mild)*

Change the *l* to *n*. What word did you make? *(mind)*

Change the *m* to *f*. What word did you make? *(find)*

Change the *f* to *k*. What word did you make? *(kind)*

Change the *k* to *bl*. What word did you make? *(blind)*

High-Frequency Words

RETEACH ***both*** On the board, write the sentence **Both the *o* and the *a* took a bath.** Have children read it. Point to the words *both* and *bath*. Ask: **How are these words alike? How are they different? Let's read them again.** Have children read the sentence again. Then have volunteers read all the words in the sentence as you point to them one by one.

Read: *Young Animals*

Distribute copies of the book to children. Read page 2 with them. Write the words *are* and *care*. Have volunteers read the words. Point out that although the letters *–are* are the same, the letters are not pronounced the same way. Read each word and have children repeat them. Choral read the book with children. Let your voice fade if children start to gain control of the text. When you read page 6, point out that the word *live* here is pronounced /līv/, not /liv/.

Phonics: Reading Sentences with /ī/i

PRETEACH Distribute *Intervention Practice Book* page 86 to children. Point to the first sentence and have children read it aloud. Ask them to find the word *find*, frame it with their fingers, and circle the word. Then work with children to complete the page.

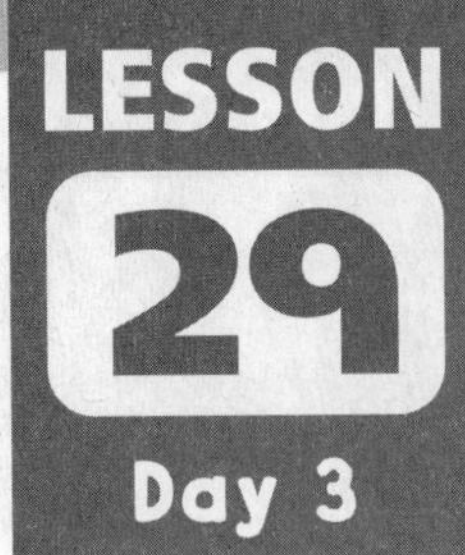

Warm-Up: Phonemic Awareness

Phoneme Blending Tell children that they are going to play a guessing game. Then say: **I'm thinking of a word that tells about some kinds of animals. Animals like lions and tigers are not tame. Instead they are /w/-/ī/-/l/-/d/. What's my word?** (*wild*) Continue with the following words: /m/-/ī/-/n/-/d/ (*mind*), /f/-/ī/-/n/-/d/ (*find*), /m/-/ī/-/l/-/d/ (mild), /b/-/l/-/ī/-/n/-/d/ (*blind*), /ch/-/ī/-/l/-/d/ (*child*)

MATERIALS

Picture Cards: box, fish, jeep, mule, nine, zebra

Word Builder

Word Builder Cards d, e, f, i, k, l, m, n, o, p,

Young Animals

Phonics: Reading Sentences with /ī/i

RETEACH Help children blend and read new words and sentences shown. Have them read the sentence, blending each word in sequence. The high-frequency words are underlined; they should read these as a unit, not blending the sounds.

rind **wilder** **hind** **finding**

I will find <u>the</u> child.

Did <u>you</u> wind <u>the</u> clock?

It is a nice, mild day.

<u>He</u> <u>was</u> <u>very</u> kind to <u>us</u>.

High-Frequency Words

RETEACH ***both*** Write the following sentence on tag board and display it in a pocket chart along with the Picture Cards *box*, *fish*, *jeep*, *nine*, *zebra*, *mule*. Call on children to choose a Picture Card to complete the sentence and read it aloud. Then ask: **Can you really sit on a ________?**

PICTURE CARDS

Both of us sat on a ________.

Read: *Young Animals*

Young Animals

Distribute copies of the book and have children read the title. Then guide children through reading the book.

Have children read to find out about newborn animals.

Pages 2–5: **When are some animals born?** (*during the spring*) **Do wild animals care for their babies?** (*yes*) **Who do some baby animals stay with for a long time?** (*their mothers*) **Do all mother animals care for their newborns?** (*no*)

Pages 6–9: Have children read to learn about different ways that animals are born.

How are some animals born? (*They are born live.*) **How are other animals born?** (*They hatch from eggs.*) **What does the book say about father animals?** (*Some fathers take care of their eggs.*) **What do animals do the most?** (*They wait.*)

Pages 10–11: Have children read to find out what newborn animals need.

What do animals need? (*to learn about the world*) **What else do they need?** (*to learn to take care of themselves*). **What will the animals do when they are ready?** (*They will live on their own.*) **What word means a young bear? Find and read it.** (*cub*)

Review the names of the baby animals on page 12. Then ask children to use the pictures to help summarize the book.

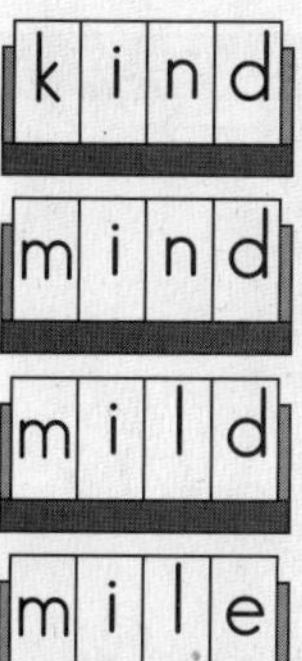

Phonics: Building Words

PRETEACH Put the letters *k*, *i*, *n*, *d* in a Word Builder and have children do the same. Slide your hand under the letters as you blend the sounds—/kkīīnndd/. Then read the word naturally—*kind*. Have children repeat after you. Then have children build and read new words.

Change *k* to *m*. What word did you make? (*mind*)
Change *n* to *l*. What word did you make? (*mild*)
Change *d* to e. What word did you make? (*mile*)
Change *i* to *o*. What word did you make? (*mole*)
Change *m* to *p*. What word did you make? (*pole*)
Change *p* to *i*. What word did you make? (*pile*)
Change *l* to *n*. What word did you make? (*pine*)
Change *p* to *f*. What word did you make? (*fine*)
Change *e* to *d*. What word did you make? (*find*)

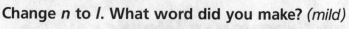

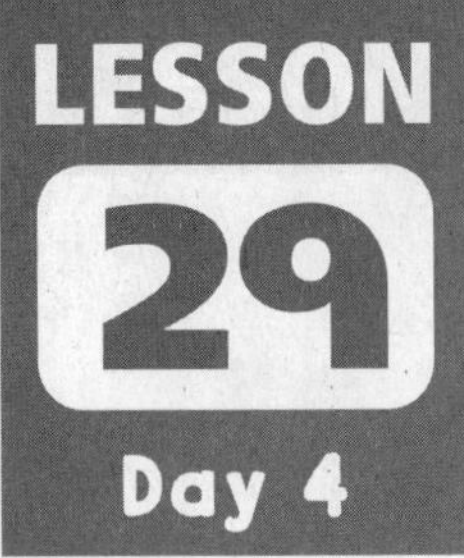

MATERIALS

Picture Cards clock, flag, mask, plum, smile, vest

Papers with four boxes side by side, plus disks

Word Cards for both, cold, sure

Word Builder

Word Builder Cards c, d, f, g, h, i, l, m, n, r, w

Young Animals

Warm-Up: Phonemic Awareness

PICTURE CARDS

Phoneme Segmentation Distribute the four-box papers to children. Tell them that the boxes stand for sounds in words. Show the Picture Card *plum* and ask: **What is the first sound you hear in *plum*?** (/p/) Have children place a disk in the first box. Then have children name the second sound in *plum* (/l/) and place a second disk on the paper. Then have them identify the third sound (/u/) and the last sound (/m/) in *plum* and place the third and fourth disks on the paper. Point to the disks in sequence as children say the word. **How many sounds do you hear in *plum*?** (*four*) Repeat this procedure with the following Picture Cards: *clock, vest, mask, flag, smile*.

Phonics: Building Words

RETEACH Put the letters *g, r, i, n, d* in a Word Builder and have children do the same. Slide your hand under the letters as you blend the sounds—/ggrrīīnndd/. Then read the word naturally—*grind*. Have children repeat after you. Then have children build and read new words.

Take away the *g*. What word did you make? *(rind)*

Change *r* to *w*. What word did you make? *(wind)*

Change *n* to *l*. What word did you make? *(wild)*

Change *w* to *ch*. What word did you make? *(child)*

Change *ch* to *m*. What word did you make? *(mild)*

Change *l* to *n*. What word did you make? *(mind)*

Change *m* to *f*. What word did you make? *(find)*

Distribute *Intervention Practice Book* page 87 to children.

High-Frequency Words

RETEACH ***both, sure, cold*** Distribute word cards with the words listed above. Have partners take turns displaying the words for each other and reading them. After they read each word, have children spell it and then repeat the word. Then have them spell the word again and write it on a sheet of paper.

Young Animals

Read: *Young Animals*

Main Idea Remind children that knowing the main idea of a story can help them understand what they read. Have children reread *Young Animals*, considering the main idea. Ask: **What is the most important idea on pages 2 through 7? What is the most important idea the rest of the book tells us?** Help children write the most important things they learned.

Animals are born in different ways.

Animals need to learn about the world

Phonics: Inflections -ed, -ing

PRETEACH Write the word *stop* at the top of a sheet of chart paper. Say: **Today I will stop at the grocery store.** Then write the word *stopped* next to *stop*. Say: **Yesterday I *stopped* at the grocery store.** Ask children to find the differences between the two words. Tell children that when a short word ends with a short vowel and one consonant, the consonant usually needs to be doubled before adding *-ed*. Help children turn *rub* into *rubbed*. Then repeat with the words *grin*, *wag*, and *pin*.

Return to the top of the paper. Write *stopping* next to *stop*. Say: **I feel like stopping at the grocery store.** Point out that the same words also double the final consonant when *-ing* is added. Repeat, adding *-ing* to *rub*, *grin*, *wag*, and *pin*. Then have children read each column of words. End the activity by pointing to words at random and having children read the words.

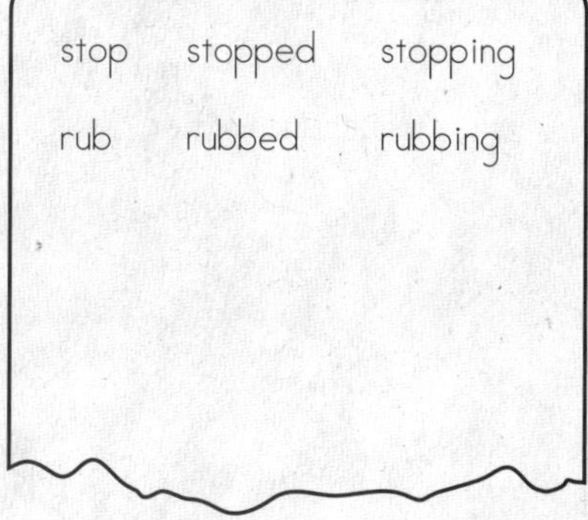

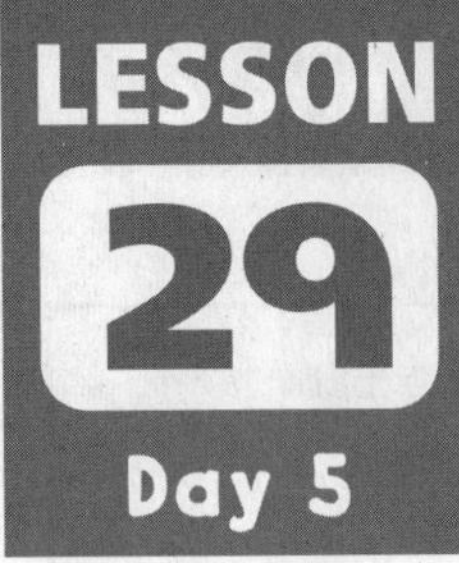

MATERIALS

Write-on/Wipe off Boards

Word Cards for cold, sure, both

Word Builder

Word Builder Cards d, f, g, l, m, o, p, s, t

Warm-Up: Phonemic Awareness

Phoneme Blending Tell children that together you are going to play a game of "Fix It." Tell them that you are going to say some words that are all broken and they should listen to see if they can put the sounds together to figure out the word. **Listen: /f/-/ī/-/n/-/d/. What word does /f/-/ī/-/n/-/d/ say?** (*find*) Continue with the following words:

/s/-/l/-/ī/-/d/ *(slide)*	**/ch/-/ī/-/l/-/d/** *(child)*	**/m/-/ō/-/s/-/t/** *(most)*
/p/-/ā/-/l/ *(pail)*	**/h/-/ō/-/l/-/d/** *(hold)*	**/m/-/ī/-/n/-/d/** *(mind)*

Phonics: Inflections -ed, -ing

RETEACH Write the word *hop* on a Write-on/ Wipe-off Board and have children do the same. Then have them read the word. Ask: **What should we do if we want to change *hop* to *hopped*?** (*double the consonant, add -ed*) **Let's do that. What should we do if we want to change *hop* to *hopping*?** (double the consonant, add *–ing*) **Let's do that.** Continue the activity with the following words: *pat*, *tug*, *slam*, and *skid*.

High-Frequency Words

cold

sure

both

Cumulative Review *cold, sure, both* Place the words in a pocket chart. Say aloud one of the words and use it in a sentence. Have a volunteer find and point to the word. Have children clap and say the spelling of the word. Then have them write it. Have children read aloud their list of words.

Read: Self-Selected Reading

Have children select a book to read from their browsing boxes. After they have completed their reading, have them tell you what they were most successful in during the reading of the book.

Phonics: Long Vowel /ō/o

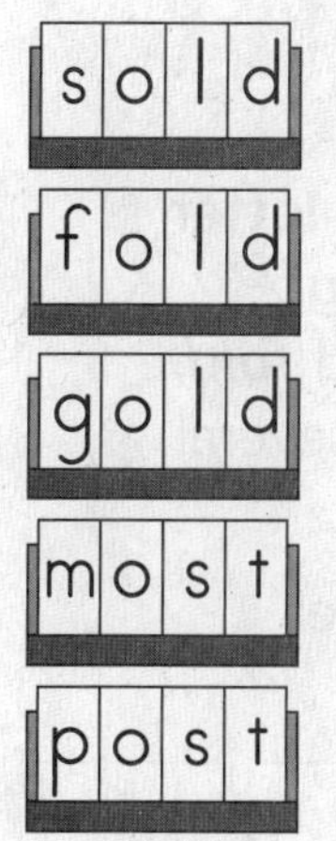

PRETEACH Use the Word Builder and Word Builder Cards to model blending words. Place the Word Builder Cards *s, o, l,* and *d* in the Word Builder. Point to the *s* and say /s/. Point to *o* and say /o/.

Slide the *o* next to the *s*. Move your hand under the letters and blend the sounds, elongating them /ssōō/. Have children repeat after you. Point to the letter *l*. Say /l/. Slide the *l* next to *so*. Slide your hand under *sol* and blend by elongating the sounds /ssōōll/. Have children repeat. Point to *d*. Say /d/. Slide the *d* next to *sol*. Slide your hand under the letters and blend, elongating the sounds /ssōōlldd/.

Then have children read the word *sold* along with you.

Follow the same procedure for the words *fold*, *gold*, *most*, and *post*.

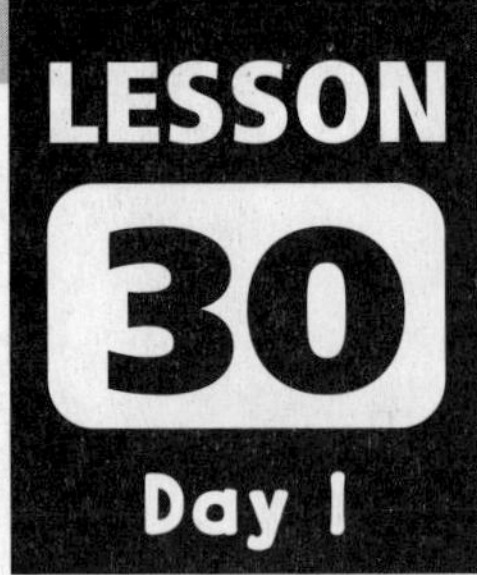

Warm-Up: Phonemic Awareness

Onset and Rime Tell children that you are going to say some words, but you are going to say them in parts. Have children listen to see if they can figure out the word. Demonstrate by saying: **/s/-old—What word did I say?** (*sold*)

/p/-ost	**/m/-ost**	**/r/-oll**	**/f/-old**
/k/-old	**/tr/-oll**	**/g/-old**	**/sk/-old**

MATERIALS

Word Cards for about, because, our, said

Word Builder

Word Builder Cards c, d, f, l, m, o, p, s, t

Alphabet Masters Oo

The Thing that Visited Our Camp

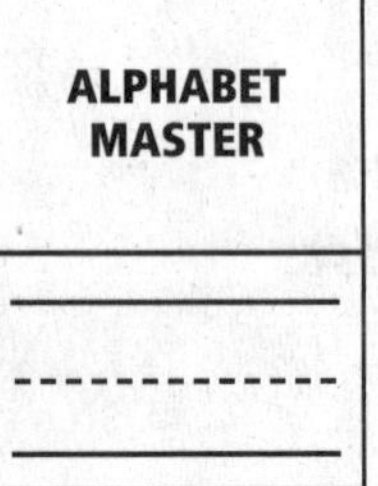

Phonics: : Long Vowel /ō/o

RETEACH **Blending** Display Alphabet Master *Oo*. **This letter is *o*. The letter *o* can stand for the /ō/ sound, the long sound of the letter *o* in words such as *most*, *colt*, and *fold*.** Have children repeat the sound as you touch the card several times.

Use the Word Builder Cards and a pocket chart to model blending words.

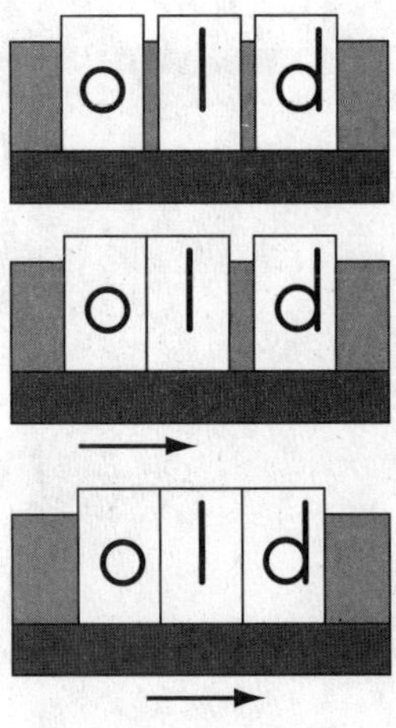

Place the Word Builder Cards *o*, *l*, and *d* in the Word Builder. Point to the *o* and say /ō/. Point to the l and say /l/.

Slide the *l* next to the *o*. Move your hand under the letters and blend the sounds, elongating them /ōōll/. Have children repeat after you.

Point to the letter *d* and say /d/. Have children say /d/ as you point to *d*.

Slide *d* next to *ol*. Slide your hand under old and blend by elongating the sounds—/ōōlldd/. Have children repeat.

Place the Word Builder Cards *m*, *o*, *s*, and *t* in the Word Builder. Point to *m*. Say /m/. Point to *o*. Say /ō/. Slide *o* next to *m*. Slide your hand under the letters and blend the sounds, elongating them /mmōō/. Have children repeat after you.

Point to *s*. Say /s/. Slide *s* next to *mo*. Slide your hand under the letters and blend, elongating the sounds: /mmōōss/. Point to t. Say /t/. Slide *t* next to *mos*. Slide your hand under the letters and blend the sounds, elongating them /mmōōsstt/.

Then have children read the word *most* along with you.

High-Frequency Words

about
because
our
said

RETEACH ***about, because, our, said*** Display the word card *about*. **This word is *about*. I am about to go to sleep. Read the word with me—*about*. Spell the word with me—*a-b-o-u-t*. Read the word with me. What is this word?** (*about*)

Repeat with the words *because*, *our*, and *said*, using the following sentences:

because—**I liked the movie *because* it was funny.**

our—**Did you see *our* pet dog?**

said—**She *said* she wanted to come to my house.**

Read: *The Thing that Visited Our Camp*

The Thing that Visited Our Camp

Story Words/Vocabulary Write the words *floor*, *nature*, *detective, clues, claw, visitor, piece*, and *special*. Tell children they will see these words in the book "The Thing that Visited Our Camp." Read the words to children and have them repeat the words. Provide help with the words as children read.

Distribute copies of the book and have children put their fingers on the title. Read the title aloud while children follow along. Ask them to find the high-frequency word they just practiced (*our*). Echo read the book with children. Read page 2 aloud and then have children read it to you. Follow this procedure throughout the book.

Phonics: Word Building with /ō/o

PRETEACH Place the letters *c, o, l,* and *t* in a Word Builder and have children do the same. Model how to blend the word *colt*. Slide your hand under the letters as you slowly elongate the sounds /kkōōlltt/. Have children do the same. Then read the word naturally—*colt*. Have children do the same.

Have children blend and read new words by telling them:

Change the *t* to *d*. What word did you make? (*cold*)
Change the *c* to *f*. What word did you make? (*fold*)
Change the *f* to *t*. What word did you make? (*told*)
Change the *t* to *m*. What word did you make? (*mold*)
Change the *ld* to *st*. What word did you make? (*most*)
Change the *m* to *p*. What word did you make? (*post*)

Distribute *Intervention Practice Book* page 88 to children.

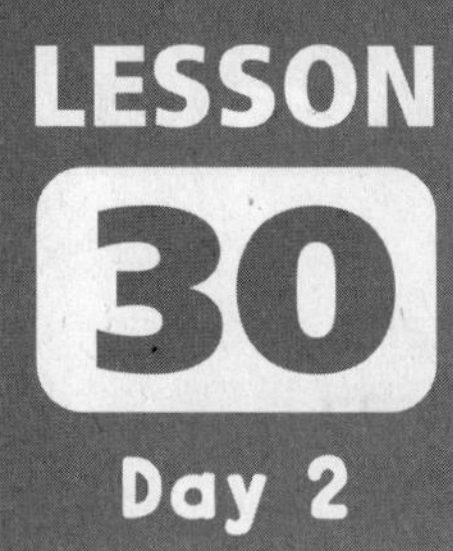

MATERIALS

Word Builder

Word Builder Cards
f, g, h, l, o, s, t

The Thing that Visited Our Camp

Warm-Up: Phonemic Awareness

Phoneme Isolation Say the word *post*. Tell children to listen to the /ō/ sound in the middle of the word *post*. Then say the words *mind* and *colt*. Have them repeat the words aloud. Ask: **Which of these words also has the /ō/ sound you hear in *post*?** (*colt*)

Continue with the words *fold, troll, drop; most, mile, hold; scold, grind, bolt.*

Phonics: Word Building with /ō/o

RETEACH Place the letters *g, o, l,* and *d* in a Word Builder and have children do the same. Model how to blend the word *gold*. Slide your hand under the letters as you slowly elongate the sounds /ggōōllldd/ . Have children do the same. Then read the word naturally—*gold*. Have children do the same.

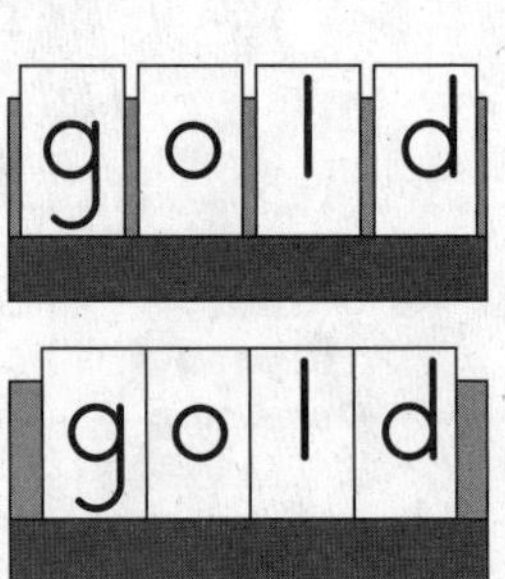

Have children blend and read new words by telling them:

Change the *g* to *s*. What word did you make? (*sold*)

Drop the *s*. What word did you make? (*old*)

Add *t* in front of *o*. What word did you make? (*told*)

Change the *t* to *f*. What word did you make? (*fold*)

Add s after *d*. What word did you make? (*folds*)

Change the *f* to *h*. What word did you make? (*holds*)

High-Frequency Words

RETEACH ***about, because, our, said*** Write the words *above* and *about* on the board and have children read them. Outline the words. Ask: **How are these words alike? How are they different? Let's read them again: *above about*.**

above about

Repeat the procedure with *because/brought*, *our/out*, *said/sad*.

Read: *The Thing that Visited Our Camp*

The Thing that Visited Our Camp

Distribute copies of the book to children. Read page 2 with them. Have children find two words that have long vowels and end with the letter combination *ke*. (*woke, hike*) Tell children that the /k/ sound at the end of a word is most often spelled with *ck* or *k*. **When there is a long vowel sound in a word, the spelling of the /k/ sound after the long vowel is almost always *k*.** Then choral read the book with children. Let your voice fade if children start to gain control of the text.

Phonics: Reading Sentences with /ō/o

PRETEACH Distribute *Intervention Practice Book* page 89 to children. Point to the first sentence and have children read it aloud. Ask them to find the word *roll*, frame it with their fingers, and circle the word. Then work with children to complete the page.

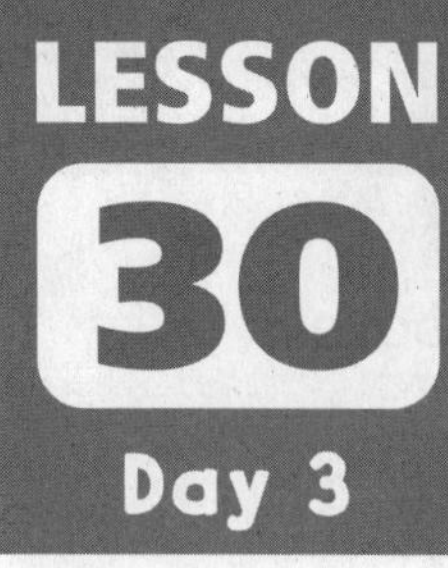

MATERIALS

Picture Cards desk, flag, jeep, kite, octopus, pen, plum, quilt, six, ship, sock, wagon

Word Builder

Word Builder Cards c, d, e, h, l, m, o, p, r, s, t

The Thing that Visited Our Camp

Warm-Up: Phonemic Awareness

Phoneme Blending Tell children that they are going to play a guessing game. Then say: **I'm thinking of a word that means a very valuable metal. People sometimes dig in the ground to find it, and its name is /g/-/ō/-/l/-/d/ . What's my word?** (*gold*) Continue with the following words: /m/-/ō/-/s/-/t/ (*most*), /f/-/ō/-/l/-/d/ (*fold*), /b/-/ō/-/l/-/t/ (*bolt*), /t/-/r/-/ō/-/l/ (*troll*), /h/-/ō/-/l/-/d/-/s/ (*holds*).

Phonics: Reading Sentences with /ō/o

RETEACH Help children blend and read new words and sentences shown. Have them read the sentence, blending each word in sequence. The high-frequency words are underlined; they should read these as a unit, not blending the sounds.

scold **host** **folder** **stroller**

I told my dog to sit.

Can you fold this map?

Hold tight to the post.

The colt runs very far.

High-Frequency Words

RETEACH ***about, because, our, said*** Write the following sentence on tag board and display it in a pocket chart along with the Picture Cards *jeep*, *quilt*, *plum*, *wagon*, *desk*, *ship*. Call on children to choose a Picture Card to complete the sentence and read it aloud. Then ask: **Can you really be bigger than a ______?**

PICTURE CARDS

She said she was bigger than our ______.

Repeat, using the following sentence and Picture Cards *kite*, *pen*, *octopus*, *six*, *flag*, *sock*:

I am about to cry because my dog ate my ______.

Read: *The Thing that Visited Our Camp*

The Thing that Visited Our Camp

Distribute copies of the book and have children read aloud the title. Then guide children through the book as they read.

Pages 2–3: Have children read the pages to find out what the mystery is.

Who is telling the story? (*the boy*) **Why did the boy have to get up?** (*We planned to go for a nature hike*) **What did he see when he stepped out of his tent?** (*a bag of rolls*) **What was the boy wondering?** (*Where did this come from?*)

Pages 4–7: Have children read to find out more about the mystery.

What happened to the camp? (*It was a mess.*) **What did the family start to do?** (*clean up*) **What did the boy have to do?** (*some detective work*) **How did the boy know the visitor was an animal? Find and read the words that tell.** (*First I found some claw marks.*)

Pages 8–9: Have children read to find out more about the detective work.

What did he notice about the food boxes? (*some were open and some were not; some were on the ground*) **Did the boxes on the ground have food in them?** (*no*) **Find and read the first question that the boy asks.** (*What kind of animal can open food boxes?*)

Pages 10–12: Have children read to find out the answer to the mystery.

What animal does the boy think it was? (*a bear*) **What did his sister do?** (*She ran back into the tent.*) **Where did the family put their food? Read the words that tell.** (*in a special locker that keeps out bears*)

Ask children to use the pictures to help summarize the book.

Phonics: Building Words

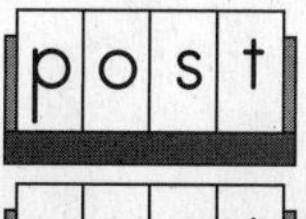

PRETEACH Put the letters *p, o, s, t* in a Word Builder and have children do the same. Slide your hand under the letters as you blend the sounds—/ppōōsstt/. Then read the word naturally—*post*. Have children repeat after you. Then have children build and read new words.

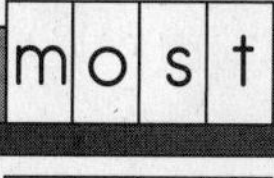

Change *p* to *m*. What word did you make? (*most*)

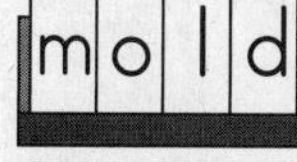

Change *st* to *ld*. What word did you make? (*mold*)

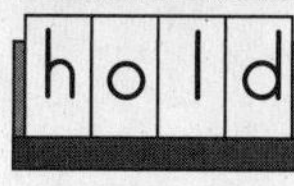

Change *m* to *h*. What word did you make? (*hold*)

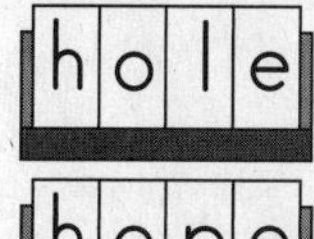

Change *d* to *e*. What word did you make? (*hole*)

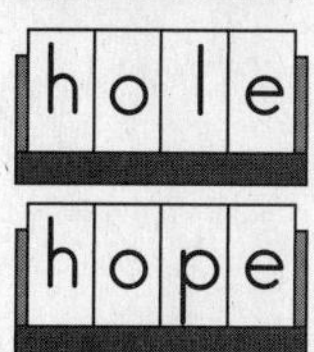

Change *l* to *p*. What word did you make? (*hope*)

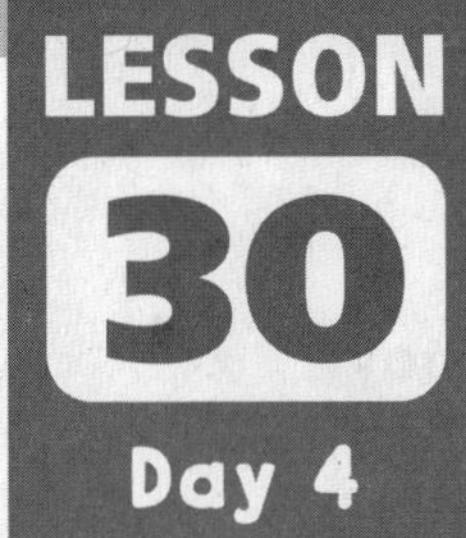

MATERIALS

Picture Cards clam, lamp, nest, sled, smile

Papers with four boxes side-by-side, plus disks

Word Cards about, because, our, said

Word Builder

Word Builder Cards c, d, f, h, l, o, p, s, t

The Thing that Visited Our Camp

Warm-Up: Phonemic Awareness

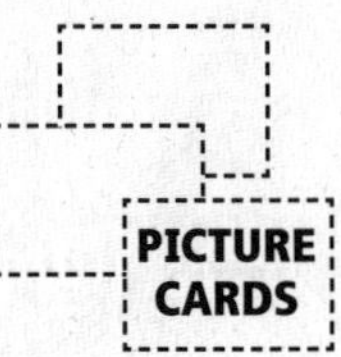

Phoneme Segmentation Distribute the four-box papers to children. Tell them that the boxes stand for sounds in words. Say: **Listen carefully as I say this word: *fold*. What is the first sound you hear in *fold*?** (/f/) Have children place a disk in the first box to represent this sound. Then have children name the second sound in *fold* (/ō/) and place a second disk on the paper. Then have them identify the third sound (/l/) in *fold* and the last sound /d/ as well, and then place the third and fourth disks on the paper. Point to the disks in sequence as children say the word. **How many sounds do you hear in fold?** (*four*) Repeat this procedure with the following Picture Cards: *clam*, *lamp*, *nest*, *sled*, *smile*.

Phonics: Building Words

RETEACH Put the letters *f, o, l, d* in a Word Builder and have children do the same. Slide your hand under the letters as you blend the sounds—/ffōōlldd/. Then read the word naturally—*fold*. Have children repeat after you. Then have children build and read new words.

Take away the *f*. What word did you make? (*old*)

Add *t* in front of *o*. What word did you make? (*told*)

Change *t* to *c*. What word did you make? (*cold*)

Add *s* in front of *c*. What word did you make? (*scold*)

Drop *c*. What word did you make? (*sold*)

Change *s* to *h*. What word did you make? (*hold*)

Change *ld* to *st*. What word did you make? (*host*)

Change *h* to *p*. What word did you make? (*post*)

Distribute *Intervention Practice Book* page 90 to children.

about

because

our

said

High-Frequency Words

RETEACH ***about, because, our, said*** Distribute word cards with the words listed above. Have partners take turns displaying the words for each other and reading them. After they read each word, have children spell it and then repeat the word. Then have them spell the word again and write it on a sheet of paper.

The Thing that Visited Our Camp

Read: *The Thing that Visited Our Camp*

Focus Skill **Main Idea** Remind children that knowing the main idea of a story can help them understand what they read. Have children reread *The Thing that Visited Our Camp*, thinking about the main idea. Ask: **What is the most important thing we learn about on the first four pages? What is the most important clue the boy finds? How does the boy decide that a bear was in the camp?** Help children list the most important ideas in the book.

1. the camp was a mess
2. the boy found claw marks
3.

Phonics: Contractions 've, 'd, 're

PRETEACH Write the words *you have* at the top of a sheet of chart paper. Say: **We can use an apostrophe to make *you have* into one word.** Write *you've* next to *you have*. **This word is *you've*. The *ha* in *have* becomes an apostrophe, and the words are pushed together.** Write *we have* on the board and explain that it can be written as *we've* for short. Repeat with *I have/I've* and *they have/they've*.

Write the words *I would* on the board and have children read them. Say: **We can use an apostrophe to write the word *would* in a shorter way, too.** Write *I'd* next to *I would*. **The *woul* in would becomes an apostrophe, and the words are pushed together.** Write *he would* on the board and explain that it can be written as *he'd* for short. Repeat with *she would/she'd*, *we would/we'd*, and *you would/you'd*.

Write *we are* on the board. Have children read the words. Say: **We can also use an apostrophe to make the word *are* shorter.** Write *we're* next to *we are*. Have children read the word. **The *a* in *are* becomes an apostrophe this time.** Repeat with *you are/you're* and *they are/they're*.

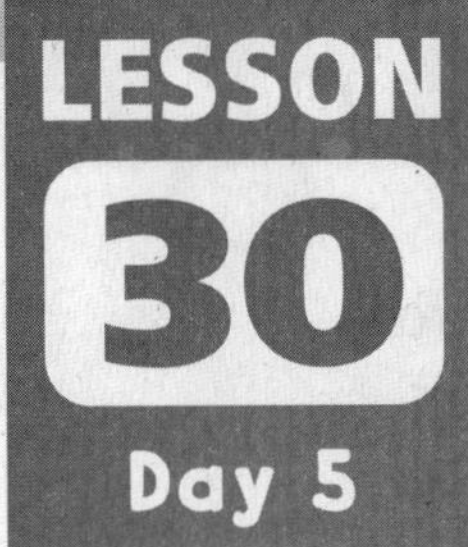

MATERIALS

Paper for each child

Word Cards about, because, both, could, our, said, sure

Word Builder

Word Builder Cards a, b, d, e, g, p

Warm-Up: Phonemic Awareness

Phoneme Blending Tell children that together you are going to play a building sound by sound game. Tell them that you are going to say some words and they should listen to see if they can put the sounds together to figure out the word. **Listen: /f/-/ō/-/l/-/d/. What word does /f/-/ō/-/l/-/d/ say?** (*fold*) Continue with the following words:

/k/-/ō/-/l/-/t/ (*colt*)	**/b/-/a/-/j/** (*badge*)
/p/-/ō/-/s/-/t/ (*post*)	**/l/-/ī/-/t/-/s/** (*lights*)
/w/-/ī/-/l/-/d/ (*wild*)	**/s/-/t/-/ā/-/j/** (*stage*)

Phonics: Contractions 've, 'd, 're

RETEACH Write the words *we have*, *we would*, and *we are* in three columns on chart paper and have children do the same on their own paper. Then have them read the words. Ask: **What should we do if we want to change *we have* to *we've* for short?** (*put the words together and replace* ha *with an apostrophe*) **Let's do that. What should we do if we want to change *we would* to *we'd*?** (*put the words together and replace* woul *with an apostrophe*) **Let's do that. What should we do if we want to change *we are* to *we're*?** (*put the words together and replace a with an apostrophe*) **Let's do that.** Continue the activity with the following sets of words: *you have, you would, you are; they have, they would, they are.* Suggest that children keep their paper to help them remember the contractions they just wrote.

High-Frequency Words

about

because

our

said

both

sure

could

Cumulative Review *about, because, our, said, both, sure, could* Place the words in a pocket chart. Say aloud one of the words and use it in a sentence. Have a volunteer find and point to the word. Have children clap and say the spelling of the word. Then have them write it. Have children read aloud their list of words.

Read: Self-Selected Reading

Have children select a book to read from their browsing boxes. After they have completed their reading, have them tell you what they were most successful in during the reading of the book.

Phonics: Short Vowel /j/g, dge

PRETEACH Use the Word Builder and Word Builder Cards to model blending words. Place the Word Builder Cards *p, a, g,* and *e* in the Word Builder. Ask children to name each letter. Tell children that *g* and *dge* can stand for /j/ as in *stage* and *fudge*. Point to the *p* and say /p/. Point to *a* and *e* at the same time and say /ā/.

Slide the *a* next to the *p*. Move your hand under the letters and blend the sounds, elongating them /ppāā/. Have children repeat after you.

Point to the letter *g*. Say /j/. Slide the *ge* next to *pa*. Slide your hand under *page* and blend by elongating the sounds /ppāājj/. Have children repeat.

Then have children read the word *page* along with you.

Place the Word Builder Cards *b, a, d, g,* and *e* in the Word Builder. Point to *b* and say /b/. Point to *a* and say /a/. Slide the *a* next to *b*. Slide your hand under the letters and blend by elongating the sounds /bbaa/.

Point to *dge*. Say /j/. Slide *dge* next to *ba*. Slide your hand under the letters and blend the sounds, elongating them /bbaajj/. Have children repeat. Then have children read the word badge along with you.

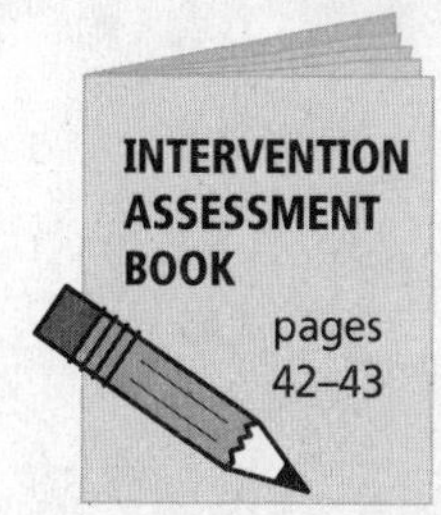

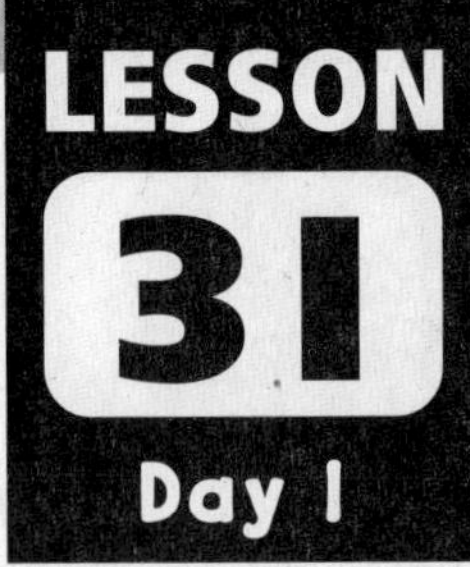

Warm-Up: Phonemic Awareness

Onset and Rime Tell children that you are going to say some words, but you are going to say them in parts. Have children listen to see if they can figure out the word. Demonstrate by saying: **/k/ -age—What word did I say?** *(cage)*

/p/-age	**/br/-idge**	**/d/-odge**	**/j/-udge**
/st/-age	**/sm/-udge**	**/l/-edge**	**/b/-adge**

MATERIALS

Word Cards another, change, love, sure

Word Builder

Word Builder Cards a, b, c, d, e, e, g, p, r, s, t, w

Alphabet Master Gg

Storm Watch

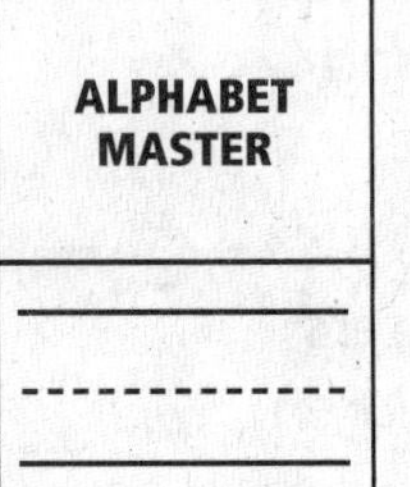

Phonics: Consonant /j/g, dge

RETEACH **Blending** Display Alphabet Master *Gg*. **This letter is *g*. The letter *g* can stand for the sound /j/ you hear at the end of such words as *page, cage,* and *stage*.** Have children repeat the sound as you touch the letter several times.

Use the Word Builder Cards and a pocket chart to model blending words.

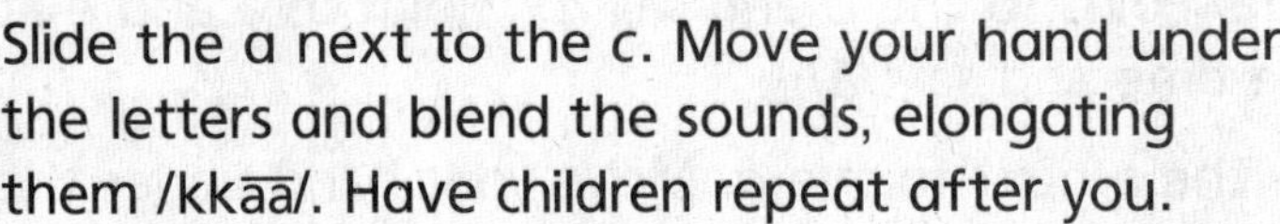

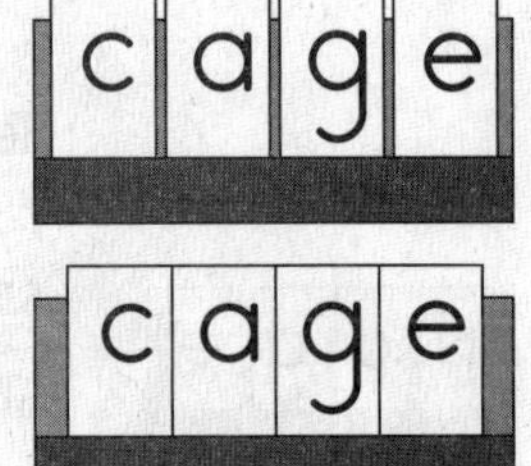

Place the Word Builder Cards *c, a, g,* and *e* in the Word Builder. Point to the *c* and say /k/. Point to the *a* and say /ā/.

Slide the *a* next to the *c*. Move your hand under the letters and blend the sounds, elongating them /kkāā/. Have children repeat after you.

Point to the *g* and say /j/.

Slide the *ge* next to the *a*. Move your hand under the letters and blend the sounds, elongating them /kkāājj/. Have children repeat after you.

Write *dge* on the board. **The letter combination *dge* can also stand for the sound /j/, as in the words *smudge, ridge,* and *dodge*.** Place the Word Builder Cards *e, d, g,* and *e* in the Word Builder. Point to the first *e*. Say /e/. Point to *dge*. Say /j/. Slide *dge* next to *e*. Slide your hand under the letters and blend the sounds, elongating them /eejj/. Then have children read the word *edge* along with you.

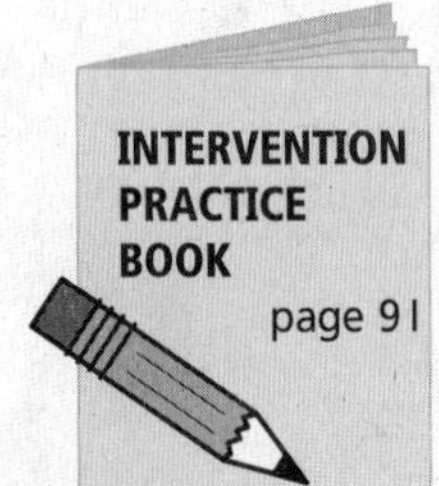

another

change

love

sure

High-Frequency Words

PRETEACH ***another, change, love, sure*** Display the word card *another*. **This word is *another*. May I have *another* glass of water? Read the word with me—*another*. Spell the word with me—*a-n-o-t-h-e-r*. Read the word with me. What is this word?** *(another)*

Repeat with the words *change, love,* and *sure,* using the following sentences:

change—**I should change my shirt.**

love—**I love to visit my grandparents.**

sure—**Are you sure you want to play a game?**

Read: *Storm Watch*

Story Words/Vocabulary Write on the board the words *angry, weather, radar, sorry, hurricanes,* and *nearly*. Read the words and have children repeat them.

Distribute copies of the book and have children put their finger on the title. Read the title aloud while children follow along. Have them touch the word *Storm*, then the word *Watch*. Have volunteers point to a word in the title and read it aloud. Echo read the book with children. Read page 2 aloud and then have children read it to you. Follow this procedure throughout the book.

Phonics: Word Building with /j/g, dge

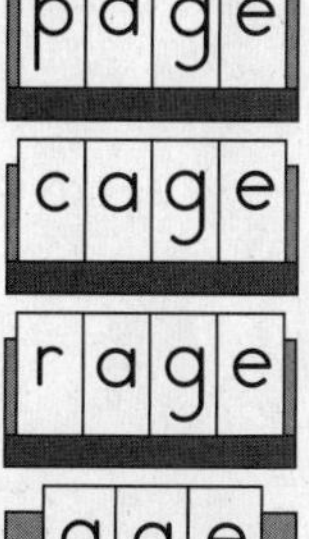

stage

edge

PRETEACH Place the letters *p, a, g,* and *e* in a Word Builder and have children do the same. Model how to blend *page*. Slide your hand under the letters as you slowly elongate the sounds /ppāājj/. Have children do the same. Then read the word naturally—*page*. Have children do the same.

Have children blend and read new words by telling them:

Change the *p* to *c*. What word did you make? *(cage)*

Change the *c* to *r*. What word did you make? *(rage)*

Drop the *r*. What word did you make? *(age)*

Add *st* in front of *a*. What word did you make? *(stage)*

Change *sta* to *ed*. What word did you make? *(edge)*

Distribute *Intervention Practice Book* page 91 to children.

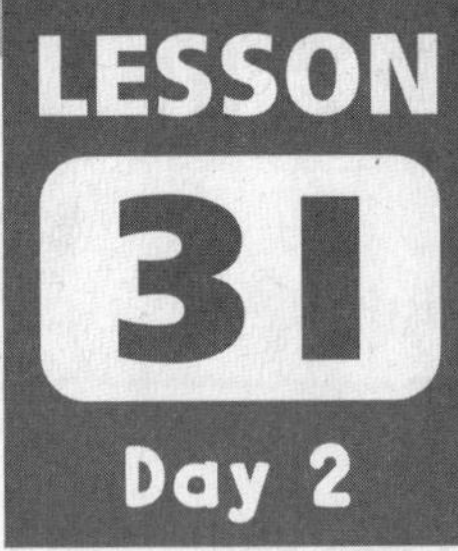

Warm-Up: Phonemic Awareness

Phoneme Isolation Say the word *cage*. Tell children to listen to the /j/ sound at the end of the word *cage*. Then say the words *track* and *fudge*. Have them repeat the words aloud. Ask: **Which of these wordshas the /j/ sound you hear in *cage*?** *(fudge)*

Continue with the words *stage, ridge, night; dodge, page, frog; badge, smudge, small.*

MATERIALS

Word Builder

Word Builder Cards a, b, d, e, e, f, g, i, j, p, r, w

Storm Watch

Phonics: Word Building with /j/g, dge

RETEACH Place the letters *r, i, d, g,* and *e* in a Word Builder and have children do the same. Model how to blend the word *ridge*. Slide your hand under the letters as you slowly elongate the sounds /rriijj/. Have children do the same. Then read the word naturally—*ridge*. Have children do the same.

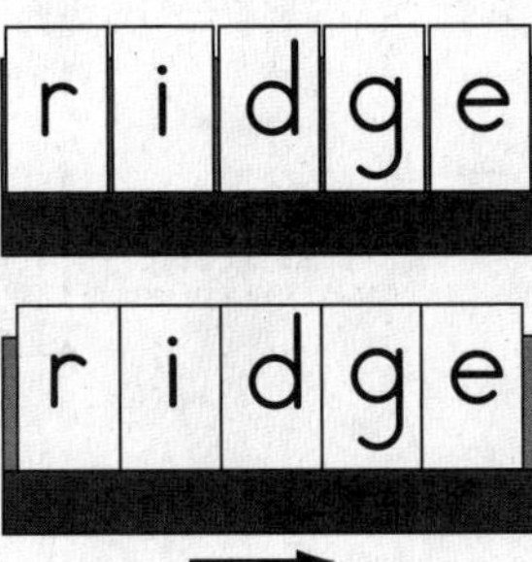

Have children blend and read new words by telling them:

Add *b* in front of *r*. What word did you make? *(bridge)*

Change the *ri* to *a*. What word did you make? *(badge)*

Change the *b* to *p*. Drop the *d*. What word did you make? *(page)*

Change the *p* to *fw*. What word did you make? *(wage)*

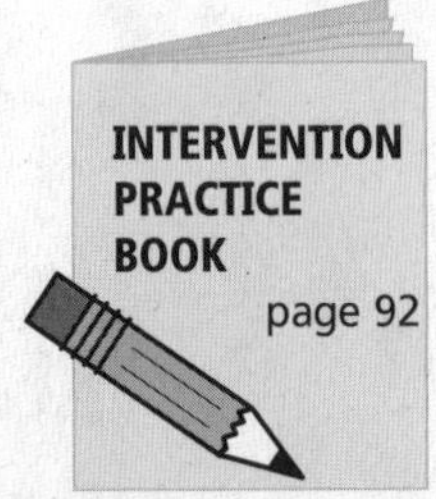

High-Frequency Words

RETEACH ***another, change, love, sure*** Write the words *another* and *animals* on the board and have children read them. Outline the words. Ask: **How are these words alike? How are they different? Let's read them again: another animals.** Repeat with the following word pairs: *change/chain, love/late, sure/said.*

Then have volunteers read all the words as you point to them one by one.

another   animals

Read: *Storm Watch*

Storm Watch

Distribute copies of the book to children. Read page 2 with them. Have children find the three words that end with the letter *y*. (*sky, angry, may*) Remind children that the *y* at the end of a word can represent different sounds. **If a word ends with *ay*, the two letters represent the sound /ā/ as in *may*. If a *y* ends a one-syllable word, it usually represents the sound /ī/ as in *sky*. If *y* ends a word of more than one syllable, it usually represents the sound /e/ as in *angry*.** Then choral read the book with children. Let your voice fade if children start to gain control of the text.

Phonics: Reading Sentences with /j/g, dge

PRETEACH Distribute *Intervention Practice Book* page 92 to children. Point to the first sentence and have children read it aloud. Ask them to find the word *badge*, frame it with their fingers, and circle the word. Then work with children to complete the page.

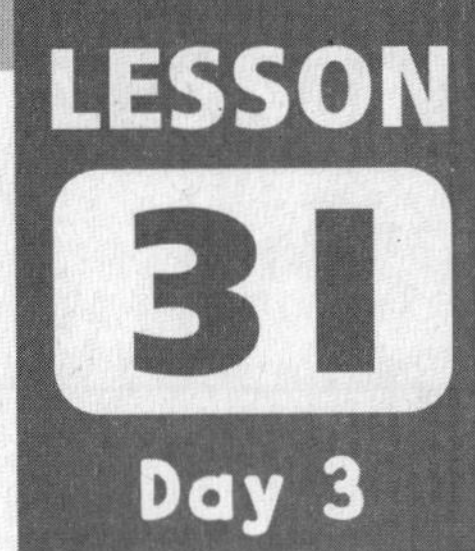

LESSON 31 Day 3

MATERIALS

Picture Cards: clam, fish, hat, mask, nine, nut, plum, ship, smile, sock, yarn

Word Builder

Word Builder Cards a, b, c, d, e, g, h, i, k, l, r

Storm Watch

Warm-Up: Phonemic Awareness

Phoneme Blending Tell children that they are going to be detectives and use clues to find the word you have in mind. Then say: **I'm thinking of a word that means something a sheriff or a police officer might wear. It shows that the person wearing it belongs to the police force, and its name is /b/-/a/-/j/. What's my word?** (*badge*) Continue with the following words: /s/-/t/-/ā/-/j/ (*stage*), /f/-/u/-/j/ (*fudge*), /b/-/r/-/i/-/j/ (*bridge*), /l/-/är/-/j/ (*large*), /h/-/e/-/j/ (*hedge*)

Phonics: Reading Sentences with /j/g, dge

RETEACH Help children blend and read new words and sentences shown. Have them read the sentence, blending each word in sequence. The high-frequency words are underlined; they should read these as a unit, not blending the sounds.

nudge **barge** **lodge** **large**

<u>The</u> judge is in charge.

A smudge <u>was</u> <u>on</u> <u>her</u> face.

<u>Read</u> <u>the</u> last page.

<u>They</u> all ran <u>up</u> <u>on</u> <u>the</u> stage.

High-Frequency Words

RETEACH ***another, change, love, sure*** Write the following sentence on tag board and display it in a pocket chart along with the Picture Cards *plum, fish, clam, yarn, ship, nut.* Call on children to choose a Picture Card to complete the sentence and read it aloud. Then ask: **Can you really eat a _____?**

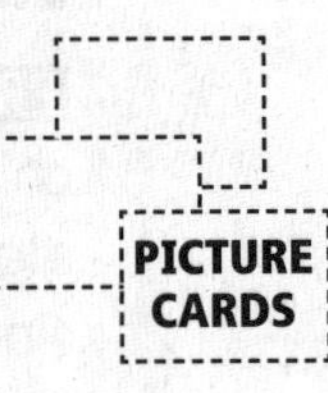

I would love to eat another _____.

Repeat, using the following sentence and Picture Cards *yarn, nine, smile, sock, hat, mask:*

Are you sure you want to change your _____?

Read: *Storm Watch*

Storm Watch

Distribute copies of the book and have children read aloud the title. Then guide children through the book as they read.

Page 2–3: Have children read the pages to find out what the story will be about.

Which people use lots of different maps? (*weather watchers*) **What do the maps tell them about? Read the words that tell.** (*the winds, the clouds, warm and cold air*)

Pages 4–7: Have children read to find out about thunderstorms.

What kind of picture is on page 4? (*a radar picture*) **What does the weather forecaster predict?** (*strong wind and thunderstorms*) **What makes a thunderstorm happen?** (*warm air and cool air meet*) **Do thunder and lightning harm you?** (*lightning can, but thunder will not*)

Pages 8–9: Have children read to find out about other storms.

When do hurricanes happen? (*during the summer*) **Are hurricanes small or large?** (*large*) **How much area can a hurricane cover?** (*hundreds of miles*)

Pages 10–12: Have children read to find out how to keep themselves safe.

What do hurricanes bring? (*strong winds and lots of rain*) **Why should people listen to warnings about storms?** (*Hurricanes can do a lot of harm.*)

Ask children to use the pictures to help summarize the book.

Phonics: Building Words

PRETEACH Put the letters *l, a, r, g, e* in a Word Builder and have children do the same. Slide your hand under the letters as you blend the sounds—/lläärjj/. Then read the word naturally—*large*. Have children repeat after you. Then have children build and read new words.

Change *l* to *ch*. What word did you make? *(charge)*

Change *ch* to *b*. What word did you make? *(barge)*

Change *r* to *d*. What word did you make? *(badge)*

Change *dg* to *k*. What word did you make? *(bake)*

Change *a* to *i*. What word did you make? *(bike)*

Change *b* to *l*. What word did you make? *(like)*

Change *i* to *a*. What word did you make? (*lake*)

Change *l* to *c*. What word did you make? (*cake*)

large

charge

barge

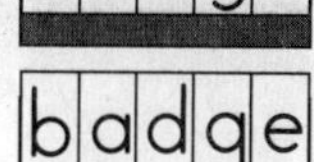

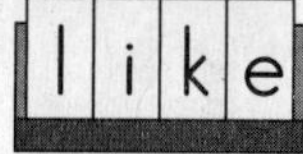

lake

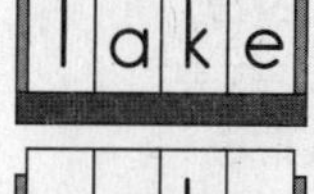

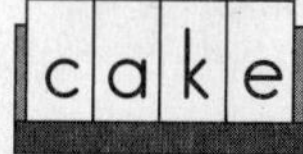

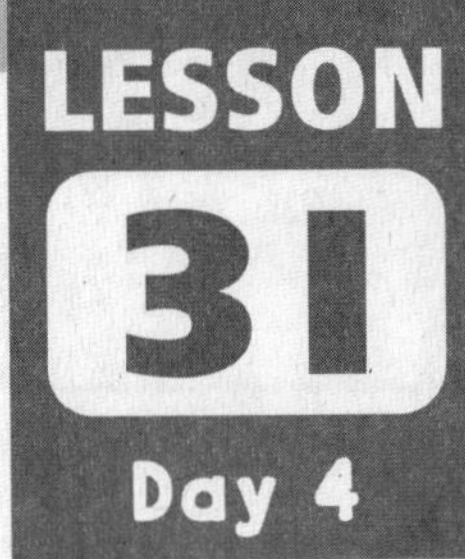

MATERIALS

Picture Cards: cup, fish, mule, sock, ten

Write-on/Wipe-off Boards with disks

Word Cards another, change, love, sure

Word Builder

Word Builder Cards a, c, d, d, e, e, g, h, l, o, s, t, w

Storm Watch

Warm-Up: Phonemic Awareness

Phoneme Segmentation Have children use the three boxes on the Write-on/Wipe-off Boards. Say: **Listen carefully as I say this word: *badge*. What is the first sound you hear in *badge*?** (/b/) Have children place a disk in the first box. Then have children name the second sound in *badge* (/a/) and place a disk in the second box. Then have them identify the third sound (/j/) and place a disk in the third box. Point to each box in sequence as children say the word. **How many sounds do you hear in *badge*?** (*three*) Repeat this procedure with the following Picture Cards: *ten, sock, mule, cup.*

Phonics: Building Words

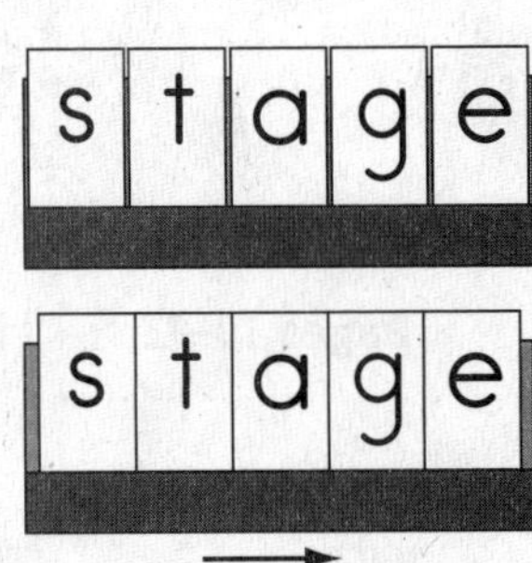

RETEACH Put the letters *s, t, a, g, e* in a Word Builder and have children do the same. Slide your hand under the letters as you blend the sounds —/ssttāajj/. Then read the word naturally—*stage.* Have children repeat after you. Then have children build and read new words.

Change st to c. What word did you make? (*cage*)

Change c to w. What word did you make? (*wage*)

Change a to ed. What word did you make? (*wedge*)

Change w to h. What word did you make? (*hedge*)

Take away the h. What word did you make? (*edge*)

Add l in front of the first e. What word did you make? (*ledge*)

Change the first e to o. What word did you make? (*lodge*)

Change l to d. What word did you make? (*dodge*)

Distribute *Intervention Practice Book* page 93 to children.

High-Frequency Words

RETEACH ***another, change, love, sure*** Distribute word cards with the words listed above. Have partners take turns displaying the words for each other and reading them. After they read each word, have children spell it and then repeat the word. Then have them spell the word again and write it on a sheet of paper.

Storm Watch

Read: *Storm Watch*

Plot Remind children that the plot of a story is what happens in the story. Have children reread *Storm Watch*, thinking about the plot. Ask: **What happens first in the book? What does the book tell about after that? How do the ideas in the book fit together?** Help children make a chart to show the order of the things described in the book.

1. about dark clouds
2. about rain
3. about big storms

Phonics: Contractions ’ve, ’d, ’re

PRETEACH Write the words *I have* at the top of a sheet of chart paper. Say **We can use an apostrophe to make *I have* into one word.** Write *I've* next to *I have*. **This word is *I've*. The *ha* in *have* becomes an apostrophe, and the words are pushed together.** Write they have on the board and explain that it can be written as they've for short. Repeat with you *have/you've* and *we have/we've.*

Write the words *he would* on the board and have children read them. Say **We can use an apostrophe to write the word *would* in a shorter way, too.** Write *he'd* next to *he would*. **The *woul* in *would* becomes an apostrophe, and the words are pushed together.** Write *they would* on the board and explain that it can be written as *they'd* for short. Repeat with *she would/she'd, I would/I'd,* and *you would/you'd*.

Write *they are* on the board. Have children read the words. Say **We can also use an apostrophe to make the word *are* shorter.** Write *they're* next to *they are*. Have children read the word. **The *a* in *are* becomes an apostrophe this time.** Repeat with *you are/you're* and *we are/we're.*

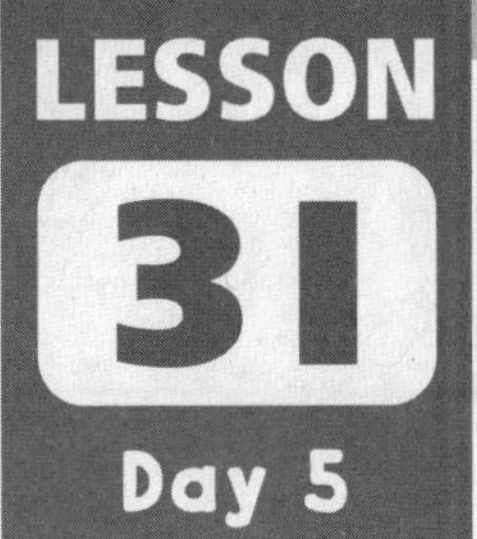

MATERIALS

Write-on/Wipe off Boards

Word Cards another, change, love, sure, both

Word Builder

Word Builder Cards b, d, e, l, r, t, u

Warm-Up: Phonemic Awareness

Phoneme Blending Tell children that together you are going to play a game of "Fix It." Tell them that you are going to say some words that are all broken and they should listen to see if they can put the sounds together to figure out the word. **Listen: /j/-/u/-/j/. What word does /j/-/u/-/j/ say?** (*judge*) Continue with the following words:

/k/-/ā/-/j/ (*cage*)	**/h/-/yōō/-/j/** (*huge*)	**/m/-/ō/-/s/-/t/** (*most*)
/r/-/ī/-/t/-/er/ (*writer*)	**/k/-/yōō/-/b/** (*cube*)	**/s/-/m/-/u/-/j/** (*smudge*)

Phonics: Contractions 've, 'd, 're

RETEACH Write the words *you have, you would,* and *you are* in three columns on a *Write-on/Wipe-off Board* and have children do the same. Then have them read the words. Ask: **What should we do if we want to change *you have* to *you've* for short?** (*put the words together, replace* ha *with an apostrophe*) **Let's do that. What should we do if we want to change you would to *you'd*?** (*put the words together, replace* woul *with an apostrophe*) **Let's do that. What should we do if we want to change *you are* to *you're*?** (*put the words together, replace a with an apostrophe*) **Let's do that.** Continue the activity with the following sets of words: *we have, we would, we are; they have, they would, they are.*

High-Frequency Words

Cumulative Review *another, change, love, sure, both* Place the words in a pocket chart. Say aloud one of the words and use it in a sentence. Have a volunteer find and point to the word. Have children clap and say the spelling of the word. Then have them write it. Have children read aloud their list of words.

another

change

love

sure

both

Read: Self-Selected Reading

Have children select a book to read from their browsing boxes. After they have completed their reading, have them tell you what they were most successful in during the reading of the book.

Phonics: Long Vowel /(y)o͞o/u-e

Use the Word Builder and Word Builder Cards to model blending words. Place the Word Builder Cards *r, u, l*, and *e* in the Word Builder. Ask children to name each letter. Tell children that *u* followed by *e* can stand for /(y)o͞o/ as in *cute* and *tube*. Point to the *r* and say /r/. Point to *u* and *e* together and say /o͞o/.

Slide the *u* next to the *r*. Move your hand under the letters and blend the sounds, elongating them /rro͞oo͞o/. Have children repeat after you.

Point to the letter l. Say /l/. Slide the *le* next to *ru*. Slide your hand under *rule* and blend by elongating the sounds /rro͞oo͞oll/. Have children repeat.

Then have children read the word *rule* along with you.

Repeat with the words *tube* and *rude*.

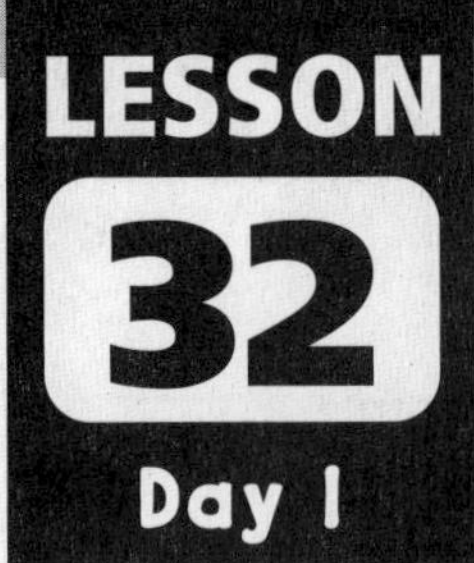

Warm-Up: Phonemic Awareness

Onset and Rime Tell children that you are going to say some words, but you are going to say them in parts. Have children listen to see if they can figure out the word. Demonstrate by saying: **/k/-ute—What word did I say?** (*cute*)

/t/-ube	**/t/-une**	**/d/-uke**	**/h/-uge**
/k/-ube	**/r/-ule**	**/d/-ude**	**/m/-ule**

MATERIALS

Word Cards boy, head, read

Word Builder

Word Builder Cards b, c, d, e, g, h, k, n, r, s, t, u

Alphabet Masters Ee, Uu,

Goldy and the Three Bears

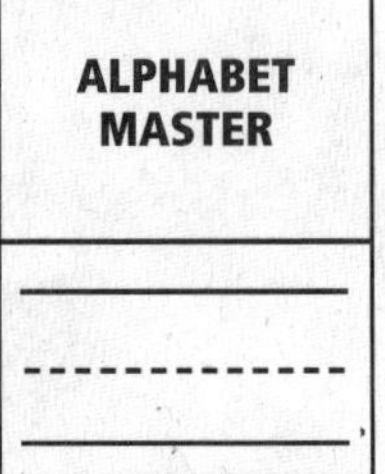

Phonics: Long Vowel /(y)o͞o/u-e

RETEACH **blending** Display Alphabet Masters *Uu* and *Ee*. **These letters are *u* and *e*. When *e* comes at the end of a word with *u*, the letter *u* can stand for /(y)o͞o/, the long sound of the vowel *u* in the middle of words such as *cube*, *rude*, and *June*.** Have children repeat the sound as you touch the letter *u* several times.

Use the Word Builder Cards and a pocket chart to model blending words.

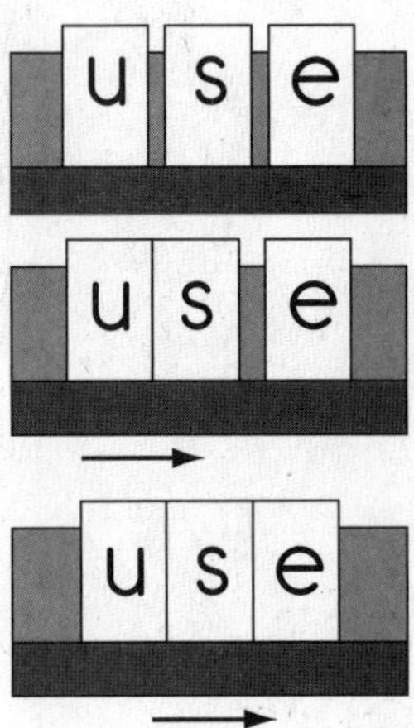

Place the Word Builder Cards *u*, *s*, and *e* in the Word Builder. Point to the *u* and *e* together and say /yo͞o/. Point to the *s* and say /z/.

Slide the *se* next to the *u*. Move your hand under the letters and blend the sounds, elongating them /yyo͞oo͞ozz/. Have children repeat after you.

Place the Word Builder Cards *h*, *u*, *g*, and *e* in the Word Builder. Point to the *h*. Say /h/. Point to *u* and e together. Say /yo͞o/. Slide *u* next to *h*. Slide your hand under the letters and blend the sounds, elongating them /hhyyo͞oo͞o/. Have children repeat after you.

Point to *g*. Say /j/. Slide *ge* next to *hu*. Slide your hand under the letters and blend the sounds, elongating them /hhyyo͞oo͞ojj/. Then have children read the word huge along with you.

High-Frequency Words

boy

head

read

PRETEACH ***boy, head, read*** Display the word card *boy*. **This word is boy. I saw a *boy* playing in the park today. Read the word with me—*boy*. Spell the word with me—*b-o-y*. Read the word with me. What is this word?** (*boy*)

Repeat with the words *head* and *read*.

Read: *Goldy and the Three Bears*

Goldy and the Three Bears

Story Words/Vocabulary Write the words *brought* and *few* on the board. Read them to children and have children repeat them. Point out that the word *few* has the /yōō/ sound.

Distribute copies of the book and have children put their fingers on the title. Read the title aloud while children follow along. Have them touch the word *Goldy*, then the words *Three* and *Bears*. Have volunteers point to a word in the title and read it aloud. Echo read the book with children. Read page 2 aloud and then have children read it to you. Follow this procedure throughout the book.

Phonics: Word Building with /(y)ōō/u-e

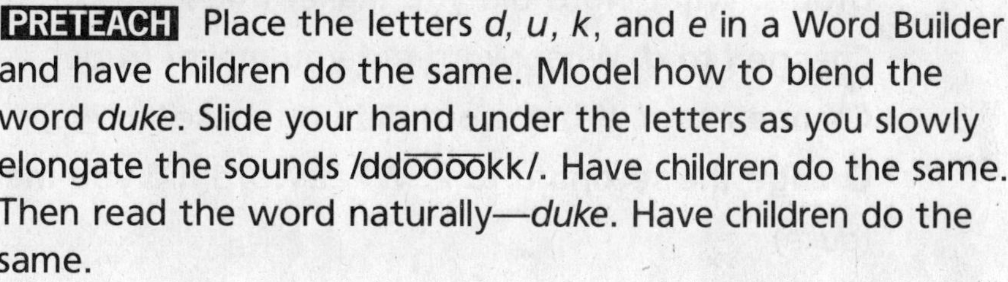

PRETEACH Place the letters *d*, *u*, *k*, and *e* in a Word Builder and have children do the same. Model how to blend the word *duke*. Slide your hand under the letters as you slowly elongate the sounds /ddōōōōkk/. Have children do the same. Then read the word naturally—*duke*. Have children do the same.

Have children blend and read new words by telling them:

Change *k* to *n*. What word did you make? (*dune*)

Change *d* to *t*. What word did you make? (*tune*)

Change *n* to *b*. What word did you make? (*tube*)

Change *t* to *c*. What word did you make? (*cube*)

Change *b* to *t*. What word did you make? (*cute*)

Distribute *Intervention Practice Book* page 94 to children.

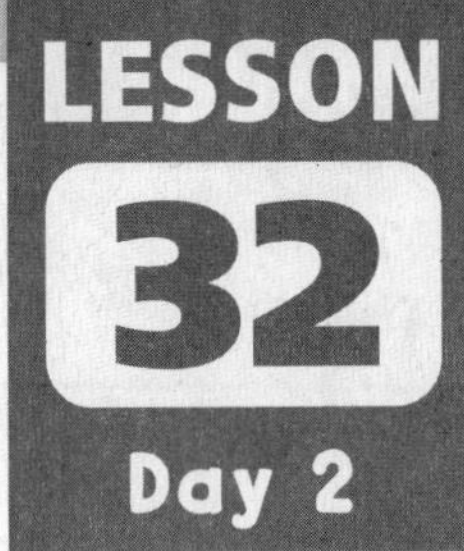

MATERIALS

Word Builder

Word Builder Cards d, d, e, k, l, m, r, s, u

Goldy and the Three Bears

Warm-Up: Phonemic Awareness

Phoneme Isolation Say the word *mule*. Tell children to listen to the /yōō/ sound in the middle of the word *mule*. Then say the words *cage* and *cute*. Have them repeat the words aloud. Ask: **Which of these words has the /yōō/ sound you hear in *mule*?** (*cute*) Continue with the words *cube*, *huge*, *yarn*; *Luke*, *dune*, *sky;* *brute*, *June*, *fudge*.

Phonics: Word Building with /(y)ōō/u-e

RETEACH Place the letters *m*, *u*, *l*, and *e* in a Word Builder and have children do the same. Model how to blend the word *mule*. Slide your hand under the letters as you slowly elongate the sounds /mmyyōōōōll/. Have children do the same. Then read the word naturally—*mule*. Have children do the same.

Have children blend and read new words by telling them:

Add *s* at the end of the word. What word did you make? (*mules*)

Change *m* to *r*. What word did you make? (*rules*)

Drop *s*. What word did you make? (*rule*)

Change *l* to *d*. What word did you make? (*rude*)

Change *r* to *d*. What word did you make? (*dude*)

Change the second *d* to *k*. What word did you make? (*duke*)

High-Frequency Words

RETEACH ***boy, head, read*** Write the words *boy* and *box* on the board and have children read them. Outline the words. Ask **How are these words alike? How are they different? Let's read them again: boy box.** Repeat with the following word pairs: *head/help*, *read/red*.

box

Read: *Goldy and the Three Bears*

Goldy and the Three Bears

Distribute copies of the book to children. Read page 2 with them. Have children find the words that include the sound /(y)oo/. (*you, June, use, new*) Remind children that /(y)$\overline{oo}$/ can be spelled in several different ways. Point out the different spellings of the /(y)$\overline{oo}$/ sound in the words *you*, *June/use*, and *new*. Then choral read the book with children. Let your voice fade if children start to gain control of the text.

Phonics: Reading Sentences with /(y)$\overline{oo}$/u-e

PRETEACH Distribute *Intervention Practice Book* page 95 to children. Point to the first sentence and have children read it aloud. Ask them to find the word tune, frame it with their fingers, and circle the word. Then work with children to complete the page.

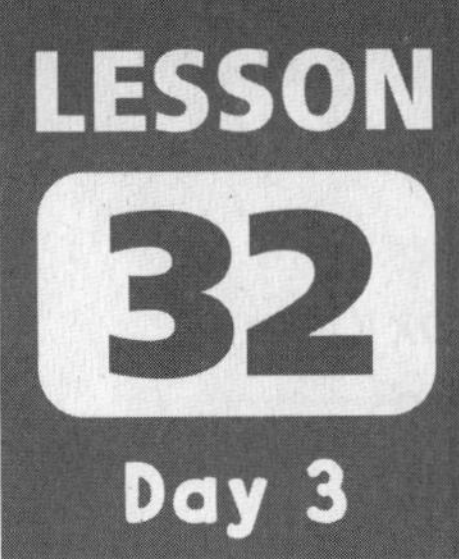

MATERIALS

Picture Cards: bat, bed, box, desk, fan, goat, lamp, leaf, octopus, pig, sock, wagon, octopus, zebra

Word Builder

Word Builder Cards b, c, e, n, t, u

Goldy and the Three Bears

Warm-Up: Phonemic Awareness

Phoneme Blending Tell children that they are going to play a guessing game and use clues to find the word you have in mind. Then say: **I'm thinking of a word that means something very large. An elephant is big, but a whale is /h/-/yōō/-/j/. What's my word?** (*huge*) Continue with the following words: /k/-/yōō/-/t/ (*cute*), /d/-/ōō/-/n/ (*dune*), /r/-/ōō/-/d/ (*rude*), /yōō/-/z/-/d/ (*used*)

Phonics: Reading Sentences with /(y)ōō/u-e

RETEACH Help children blend and read new words and sentences shown. Have them read the sentence, blending each word in sequence. The high-frequency words are underlined; they should read these as a unit, not blending the sounds.

fuse **spruce** **cube** **Bruce**

<u>My</u> mule is quite silly.

I <u>like</u> June <u>the</u> best.

It is rude <u>to</u> yell.

Bow down <u>to</u> <u>the</u> duke!

High-Frequency Words

RETEACH ***boy, head, read*** Write the following sentence on tagboard and display it in a pocket chart along with the Picture Cards *lamp*, *bed*, *pig*, *leaf*, *desk*, *bat*. Call on children to choose a Picture Card to complete the sentence and read it aloud. Then ask: **Can you really read at a _____?**

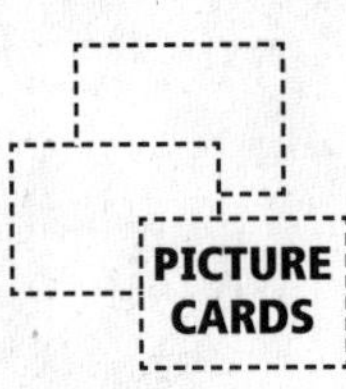

The boy read at the _____.

Repeat, using the following sentence and Picture Cards *box*, *sock*, *fan*, *goat*, *octopus*, *zebra*:

I patted the _____ on the head.

Read: *Goldy and the Three Bears*

Goldy and the Three Bears

Distribute copies of the book and have children read aloud the title. Then guide children through the book as they read.

Pages 2–3: Have children read to find out what Little Bear needs.

> **What did Mama Bear say to Little Bear?** (*"You could use a new bed."*) **Where did the bear family go then?** (*to the store*)

Pages 4–7: Have children read to find out what Little Bear thinks about the beds he sees.

> **What was Little Bear singing to himself?** (*"I'm getting a new bed! I have this tune in my head!"*) **What did Little Bear do to try out the first bed?** (*He took out his book and read.*) **Did he like the new bed after he tried it? Find and read the sentence that tells.** (*The bed was not right.*)

Pages 8–9: Have children read to find out about the next bed Little Bear saw.

> **How did Little Bear test the bunkbed?** (*he cuddled his teddy*) **Was the bunkbed right?** (*no*) **Did Little Bear like the racecar bed?** (*yes*) **What was the problem with the racecar bed?** (*Someone was sleeping in the bed.*)

Pages 10–12: Have children read to find out how the problem is solved.

> **What does Little Bear say when he sees Goldy?** (*"Someone is sleeping in MY bed! Wake up!"*) **What did Goldy tell Little Bear?** (*I picked this bed for you.*) **Where did they all go with the new bed?** (*home*) **What did they find at home?** (*a little boy in Little Bear's old bed*)

Ask children to use the pictures to help summarize the book.

Phonics: Building Words

PRETEACH Put the letters *c*, *u*, *t*, *e* in a Word Builder and have children do the same. Slide your hand under the letters as you blend the sounds—/kkyyo͞oo͞ott/. Then read the word naturally—*cute*. Have children repeat after you. Then have children build and read new words.

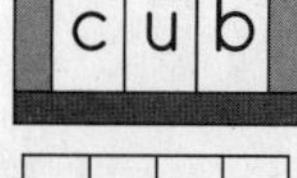

Drop the e. What word did you make? (*cut*)

Change *t* to *b*. What word did you make? (*cub*)

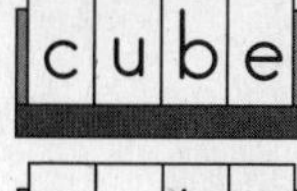

Add *e* after *b*. What word did you make? (*cube*)

Change *c* to *t*. What word did you make? (*tube*)

Change *b* to *n*. What word did you make? (*tune*)

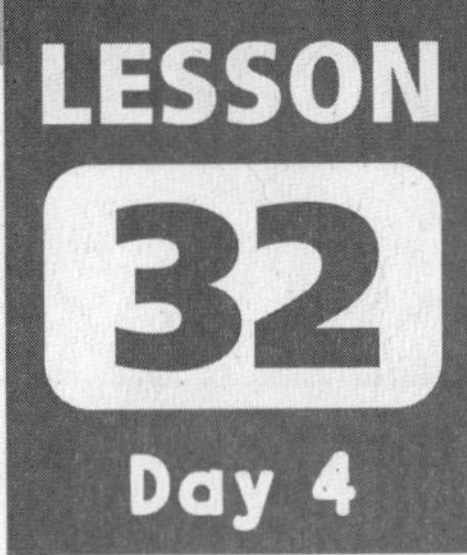

MATERIALS

Picture Cards hat, mule, nine, rake, sock

Write-on/Wipe-off Boards with disks

Word Cards boy, head, read, any, again

Word Builder

Word Builder Cards b, c, d, d, e, n, r, t, u

Goldy and the Three Bears

Warm-Up: Phonemic Awareness

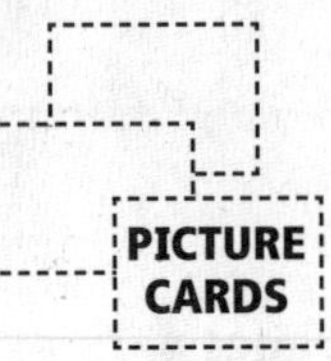

Phoneme Segmentation Have children use the three boxes on the Write-on/Wipe-off Boards. Remind children that the boxes stand for the sounds in words. Show the Picture Card *mule* and ask: **What is the first sound you hear in *mule*?** (/m/) Have children place a disk in the first box. Then have children name the second sound in *mule* (/yo͞o/) and place a disk in the second box. Then have them identify the third sound (/l/) and place a disk in the third box. Point to each box in sequence as children say the word. How many sounds do you hear in *mule*? (*three*) Repeat this procedure with the following Picture Cards: *hat*, *nine*, *sock*, *rake*.

Phonics: Building Words

RETEACH Put the letters *c*, *u*, *t*, *e* in a Word Builder and have children do the same. Slide your hand under the letters as you blend the sounds— /kkyyo͞oo͞ott/. Then read the word naturally— *cute*. Have children repeat after you. Then have children build and read new words.

Change *t* to *b*. What word did you make? (*cube*)

Change *c* to *t*. What word did you make? (*tube*)

Change *b* to *n*. What word did you make? (*tune*)

Change *t* to *d*. What word did you make? (*dune*)

Change *n* to *d*. What word did you make? (*dude*)

Change *d* to *r*. What word did you make? (*rude*)

Add *c* before *r*. What word did you make? (*crude*)

Distribute *Intervention Practice Book* page 96 to children.

boy

head

read

any

again

High-Frequency Words

RETEACH ***boy, head, read, any, again*** Distribute word cards with the words listed above. Have partners take turns displaying the words for each other and reading them. After they read each word, have children spell it and then repeat the word. Then have them spell the word again and write it on a sheet of paper.

Goldy and the Three Bears

Read: *Goldy and the Three Bears*

Focus Skill **Predict Outcomes** Remind children that thinking about what may happen next in a story can help them better understand the stories they read. Have children reread *Goldy and the Three Bears*, predicting what might happen next. Ask: **What could the family do the next time Little Bear needs a new bed? Do you think Little Bear will like his bed just as much when he gets home? What could happen to the little boy?** Suggest that children write at least one prediction.

Inflections -ed, -ing

PRETEACH Write the word *rub* at the top of a sheet of chart paper and have children read it. Say: **Today I will *rub* my elbow. Yesterday I *rubbed* my elbow.** Write *rubbed* next to *rub*. **This word is rubbed. In a little word which ends with *one* short vowel and *one* consonant, we have to double the final consonant before adding the *–ed* ending.** Write *pat* and *patted* on the board and explain that *pat* becomes *patted*, doubling the *t*, when the word describes something done in the past. Repeat with *drum/drummed* and *pin/pinned*.

Now write *rubbing* next to *rubbed*. Say: **We need to double the consonant to form the word *rubbing*, too.** Write *pat* and *patting* on the board and explain that the same doubling rule applies for this word as well. Repeat with *drumming* and *pinned*.

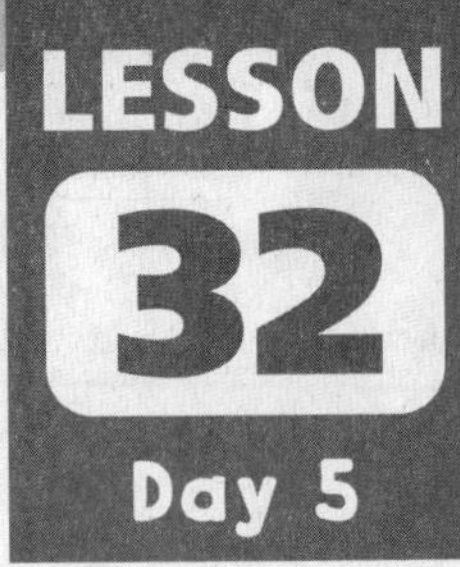

Warm-Up: Phonemic Awareness

Phoneme Blending Tell children that together you are going to play a word game. Tell them that you are going to say some words sound by sound and they should listen to see if they can put the sounds together to figure out the word. **Listen: /r/-/o͞o/-/l/. What word does /r/-/o͞o/-/l/ say?** (*rule*) Continue with the following words:

/k/-/yo͞o/-/b/ (*cube*)	**/h/-/e/-/j/** (*hedge*)
/b/-/r/-/e/-/d/ (*bread*)	**/b/-/r/-/o͞o/-/t/** (*brute*)
/k/-/yo͞o/-/t/ (*cute*)	**/h/-/e/-/v/-/ē/** (*heavy*)

Phonics: Inflections -ed, -ing

RETEACH Write the word *trap* on a Write-on/Wipe-off Board and have children do the same. Then have them read the word. Ask: **What should we do if we want to change *trap* to *trapped*?** (*double the consonant, add -ed*) **Let's do that. What should we do if we want to change *trap* to *trapping*?** (*double the consonant, add -ing*) Let's do that. Continue the activity with the following words: *fan*, *rob*, *slam*, *tag*.

MATERIALS

Write-on/Wipe off Boards

Word Cards because, boy, head, most, read

Word Builder

Word Builder Cards a, d, e, h, r, l

High-Frequency Words

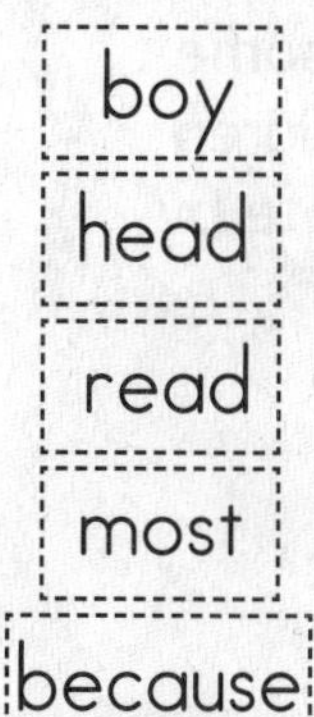

Cumulative Review *boy, head, read, most, because* Place the words in a pocket chart. Say aloud one of the words and use it in a sentence. Have a volunteer find and point to the word. Have children clap and say the spelling of the word. Then have them write it. Have children read aloud their list of words.

Read: Self-Selected Reading

Have children select a book to read from their browsing boxes. After they have completed their reading, have them tell you what they were most successful in during the reading of the book.

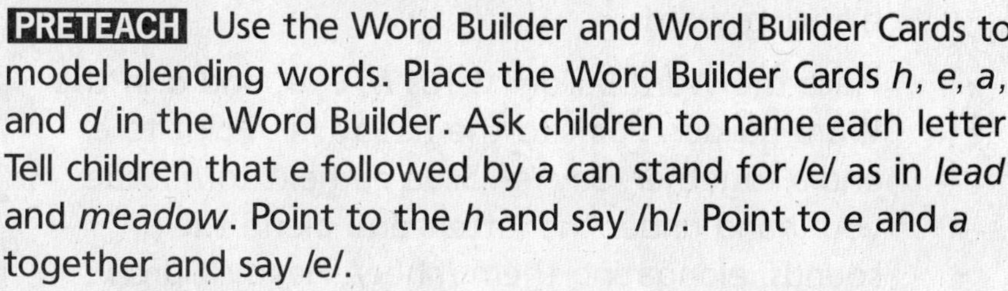

Phonics: Short Vowel /e/ea

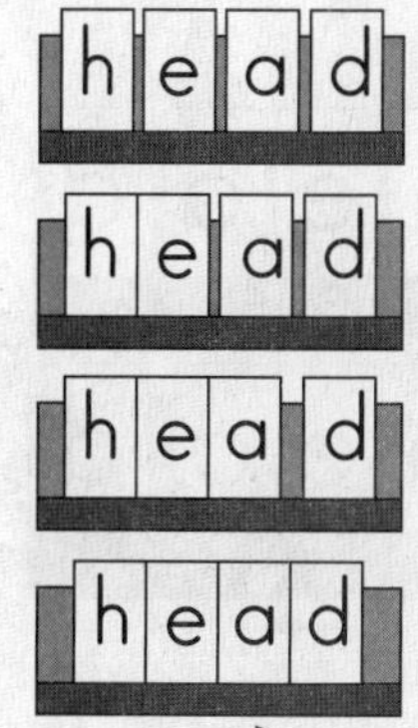

PRETEACH Use the Word Builder and Word Builder Cards to model blending words. Place the Word Builder Cards *h*, *e*, *a*, and *d* in the Word Builder. Ask children to name each letter. Tell children that e followed by *a* can stand for /e/ as in *lead* and *meadow*. Point to the *h* and say /h/. Point to e and *a* together and say /e/.

Slide the *ea* next to the *h*. Move your hand under the letters and blend the sounds, elongating them /hhee/. Have children repeat after you.

Point to the letter *d*. Say /d/. Slide the *d* next to *hea*. Slide your hand under head and blend by elongating the sounds /head/. Have children repeat.

Then have children read the word *head* along with you.

Repeat with the words *lead* and *read*.

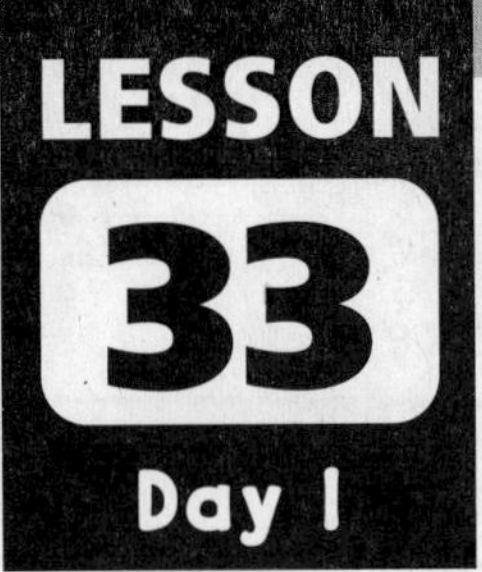

MATERIALS

Word Cards also, boy, read, thought

Word Builder

Word Builder Cards a, b, d, e, h, l, r, t

An Afternoon Nap

Warm-Up: Phonemic Awareness

Onset and Rime Tell children that you are going to say some words, but you are going to say them in parts. Have children listen to see if they can figure out the word. Demonstrate by saying: **/h/-ead—What word did I say?** (*head*)

/r/-eady	**/thr/-ead**	**/br/-ead**	**/h/-eavy**
/r/-ead	**/w/-ealthy**	**/f/-eather**	**/br/-eath**

Phonics: Short Vowel /e/ea

RETEACH **Blending** Write *ea* on the board. **These letters are *e* and *a*. Sometimes *ea* can stand for /e/, the short sound of the vowel *e* in the middle of words such as *head*, *lead*, and *breath*.** Have children repeat the sound as you touch the letters *ea* several times.

Use the Word Builder Cards and a pocket chart to model blending words.

Place the Word Builder Cards *h*, *e*, *a*, and *d* in the Word Builder. Point to the *h*. Say /h/. Point to *e* and *a* together. Say /e/. Slide *ea* next to *h*. Slide your hand under the letters and blend the sounds, elongating them /hhee/. Have children repeat after you.

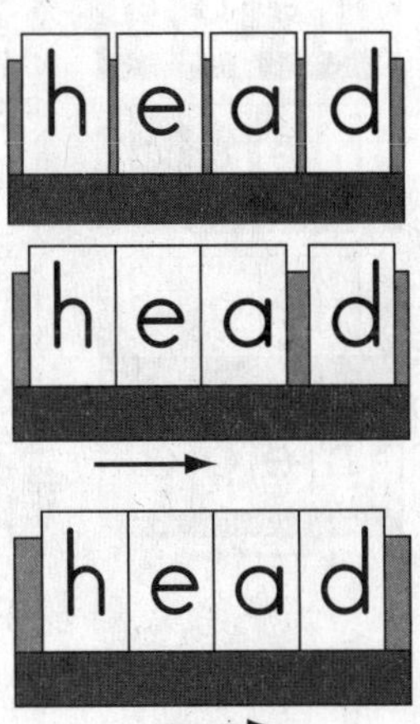

Point to *d*. Say /d/. Slide *d* next to *hea*. Slide your hand under the letters and blend the sounds, elongating them /hheedd/. Then have children read the word *head* along with you.

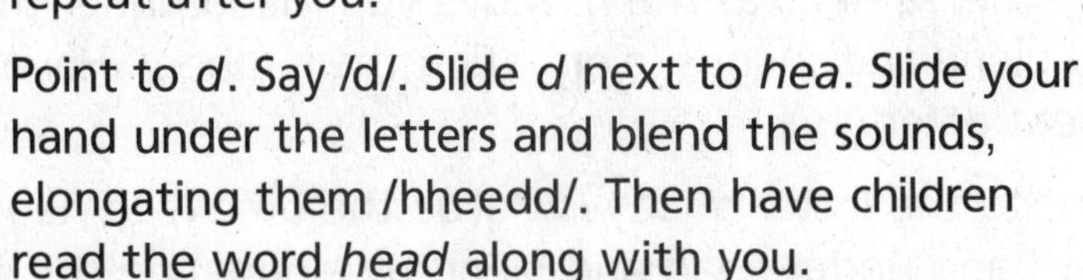

High-Frequency Words

PRETEACH ***read, boy, thought, also*** Display the word card *read*. **This word is *read*. I *read* a good story last week. Read the word with me—*read*. Spell the word with me—*r-e-a-d*. Read the word with me. What is this word?** (*read*)

read

boy

thought

also

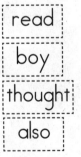

Repeat with the words *boy*, *thought*, and *also*. Then place the four words in a pocket chart and have volunteers read the words, as you randomly point to them.

An Afternoon Nap

Read: *An Afternoon Nap*

Story Words/Vocabulary Write the words *afternoon, carry, wander, bicycle, hours, often, parents,* and *yawn*. Read each word and have children repeat it. Tell children that they will see these words in the book "An Afternoon Nap."

Distribute copies of the book and have children put their fingers on the title. Read the title aloud while children follow along. Have them touch the word *Afternoon*, then the word *Nap*. Echo read the book with children. Read page 2 aloud and then have children read it to you. Follow this procedure throughout the book.

Phonics: Word Building with /e/ea

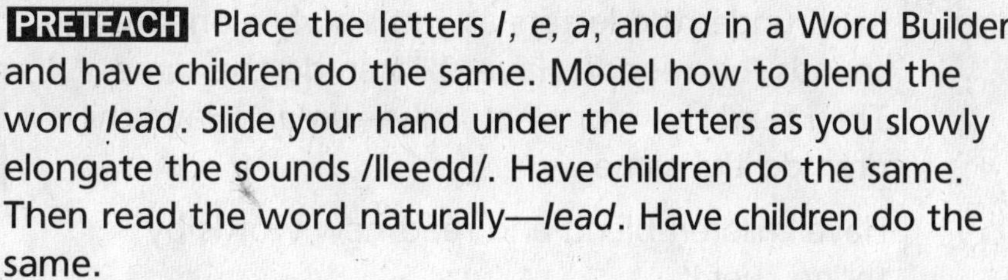

PRETEACH Place the letters *l*, *e*, *a*, and *d* in a Word Builder and have children do the same. Model how to blend the word *lead*. Slide your hand under the letters as you slowly elongate the sounds /lleedd/. Have children do the same. Then read the word naturally—*lead*. Have children do the same.

Have children blend and read new words by telling them:

Change *l* to *h*. What word did you make? *(head)*

Change *h* to *r*. What word did you make? *(read)*

Add *th* in front of *r*. What word did you make? *(thread)*

Change *th* to *b*. What word did you make? *(bread)*

Change *d* to *th*. What word did you make? *(breath)*

Distribute *Intervention Practice Book* page 97 to children.

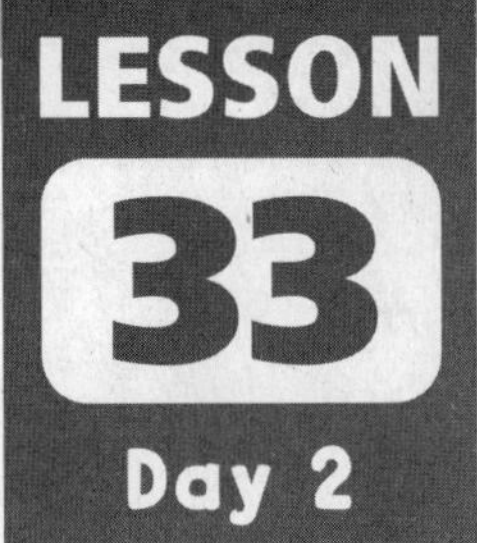

Warm-up: Phonemic Awareness

Phoneme Isolation Say the word *health*. Tell children to listen to the /e/ sound in the middle of the word *health*. Then say the words *dealt* and *rude*. Have them repeat the words aloud. Ask: **Which of these words also has the /e/ sound?** (*dealt*)

Continue with the words *tread*, *budge*, *wealth*; *steady*, *fried*, *heavy*; *leather*, *weather*, *wider*.

MATERIALS

Word Builder

Word Builder Cards a, b, d, e, h, l, r, t, y

An Afternoon Nap

Phonics: Word Building with /e/ea

RETEACH Place the letters *b, r, e, a*, and *d* in a Word Builder and have children do the same. Model how to blend the word *bread*. Slide your hand under the letters as you slowly elongate the sounds /bbrreedd/. Have children do the same. Then read the word naturally—*bread*. Have children do the same.

Have children blend and read new words by telling them:

Change b to th. What word did you make? (*thread*)

Drop *h*. What word did you make? (*tread*)

Change *tr* to *l*. What word did you make? (*lead*)

Change *l* to *h*. What word did you make? (*head*)

Change *h* to *r*. What word did you make? (*read*)

Add *y* after *d*. What word did you make? (*ready*)

High-Frequency Words

RETEACH ***read, boy, thought, also*** Write the words read and red on the board and have children read them. Outline the words. Ask **How are these words alike? How are they different? Let's read them again: read red.** Repeat with the following word pairs: *boy/box*, *thought/thing*, *also/always*.

read red

Repeat the procedure with *turn/picture* and *who/why*.

Read: *An Afternoon Nap*

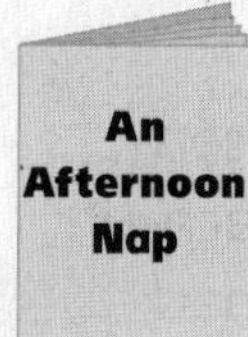

Distribute copies of the book to children. Read page 2 with them. Have children find and frame the word *shops*. **The *s* at the end of *shops* tells us that there is more than one shop. What other word on this page has *s* at the end to mean "more than one"?** (*streets*) Then choral read the book with children. Let your voice fade if children start to gain control of the text.

Phonics: Reading Sentences with /e/ea

PRETEACH Distribute *Intervention Practice Book* page 98 to children. Point to the first sentence and have children read it aloud. Ask them to find the word *heavy*, frame it with their fingers, and circle the word. Then work with children to complete the page.

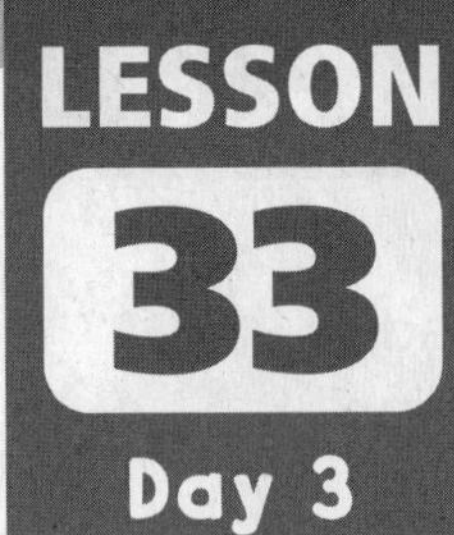
LESSON 33 Day 3

MATERIALS

Picture Cards: boat, box, fish, jeep, mule, nine, quilt, ship, six

Word Builder

Word Builder Cards a, b, d, d, e, f, h, l, r

An Afternoon Nap

Warm-up: Phonemic Awareness

Phoneme Blending Tell children that they are going to be detectives and use clues to find the word you have in mind. Then say: **I'm thinking of a word that means a part of your body. It sits on your neck, and it is called a /h/-/e/-/d/. What's my word?** (*head*) Continue with the following words: /b/-/r/-/e/-/d/ (*bread*), /r/-/e/-/d/-/ē/ (*ready*), /th/-/r/-/e/-/d/ (*thread*), /w/-/e/-/th/-/er/ (*weather*), /h/-/e/-/l/-/th/-/ē/ (*healthy*)

Phonics: Reading Sentences with /e/ea

RETEACH Help children blend and read new words and sentences shown. Have them read the sentence, blending each word in sequence. The high-frequency words are underlined; they should read these as a unit, not blending the sounds.

dealt **leather** **dread** **instead**

We read a funny book.

A feather is not heavy.

This thread is very thin

The weather is cold today.

High-Frequency Words

RETEACH ***read, boy, thought, also*** Write the following sentence on tagboard and display it in a pocket chart along with the Picture Cards *box*, *fish*, *jeep*, *mule*, *ship*, *nine*. Call on children to choose a Picture Card to complete the sentence and read it aloud. Then ask: **Can you really ride on a ______?**

PICTURE CARDS

The boy thought he rode on a ______.

Repeat, using the following sentence and Picture Cards *fish*, *boat*, *quilt*, *jeep*, six:

I also read a book about how to fix a ______.

Read: *An Afternoon Nap*

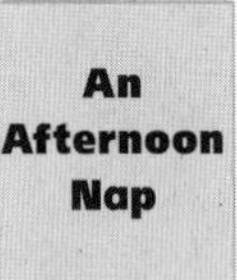

Distribute copies of the book and have children read aloud the title. Then guide children through the book as they read.

Pages 2–5: Have children read the pages to find out what is happening on the street.

What time of day is it? (*morning*) **What word describes the streets?** (*busy*) **What are the workers bringing outside?** (*baskets and boxes*) **What is the baker doing?** (*checking the bread she baked*) **Why are the trucks stopping?** (*to unload more boxes*)

Pages 6–7: Have children read to find out what happens in the afternoon.

How do the people get around in this town? (*walk, bicycles, skates*) **What happens in the afternoon?** (*The city slows down.*) **What do many shops do?** (*close for two hours*)

Pages 8–9: Have children read to find out what people do in the afternoon.

What do the shop owners do? (*pull down the blinds and close the doors*) **What do families do?** (*visit and eat*) **Why is this meal so important? Read the words that tell.** (*This is their biggest meal of the day*)

Pages 10–12: Have children read to find out what happens after people eat.

What do people do? (*watch the news, check the weather, take a nap*) **Where do people nap?** (*on cots or in a hammock*) **What happens when the afternoon nap ends? Read the words that tell.** (*they go back to work*)

Ask children to use the pictures to help summarize the book.

Phonics: Building Words

PRETEACH Put the letters *h, e, a, d* in a Word Builder and have children do the same. Slide your hand under the letters as you blend the sounds—/hheedd/. Then read the word naturally—*head*. Have children repeat after you. Then have children build and read new words.

Change *h* to *l*. What word did you make? (*lead*)

Change *l* to *r*. What word did you make? (*read*)

Add *b* in front of *r*. What word did you make? (*bread*)

Change *br* to *d*. What word did you make? (*dead*)

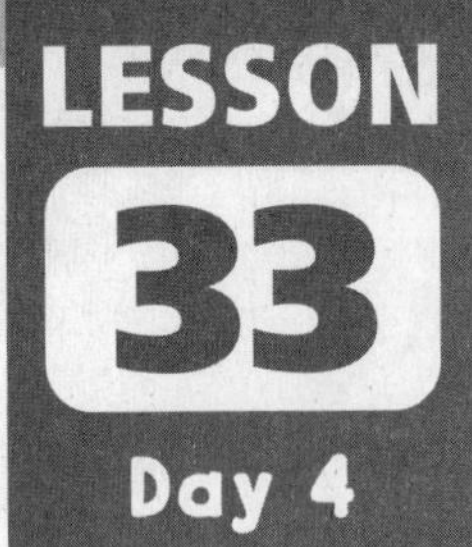

MATERIALS

Picture Cards: bed, boat, lock, nine, ship, yarn

Write-on/Wipe-off Boards with disks

Word Cards also, boy, read, thought

Word Builder

Word Builder Cards a, b, d, e, h, l, r, t, v, y

An Afternoon Nap

Warm-Up: Phonemic Awareness

Phoneme Segmentation Have children use the three boxes on the Write-on/Wipe-off Boards. Remind children that the boxes stand for the sounds in words. Show the Picture Card ship and ask: **What is the first sound you hear in *ship*?** (/*sh*/) Have children place a disk in the first box. Then have children name the second sound in *ship* (/*i*/) and place a disk in the second box. Then have them identify the third sound (/*p*/) and place a disk in the third box. Point to each box in sequence as children say the word. **How many sounds do you hear in ship?** (*three*) Repeat this procedure with the following Picture Cards: *nine, lock, boat, bed.*

PICTURE CARDS

Phonics: Building Words

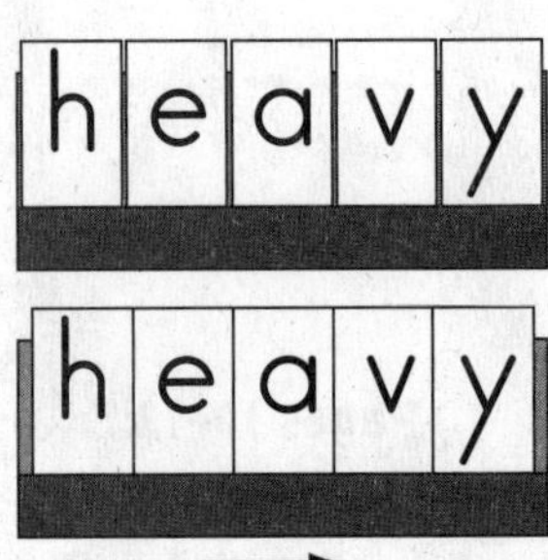

RETEACH Put the letters *h, e, a, v, y* in a Word Builder and have children do the same. Slide your hand under the letters as you blend the sounds—/hheevvēē/. Then read the word naturally—*heavy*. Have children repeat after you. Then have children build and read new words.

Change *vy* to *d*. What word did you make? (*head*)

Change *h* to *l*. What word did you make? (*lead*)

Change *l* to *br*. What word did you make? (*bread*)

Change *b* to *t*. What word did you make? (*tread*)

Add *h* after *t*. What word did you make? (*thread*)

Drop *th*. What word did you make? (*read*)

Add *y* after *d*. What word did you make? (*ready*)

Distribute *Intervention Practice Book* page 99 to children.

High-Frequency Words

read

boy

thought

also

RETEACH ***read, boy, thought, also*** Distribute word cards with the words listed above. Have partners take turns displaying the words for each other and reading them. After they read each word, have children spell it and then repeat the word. Then have them spell the word again and write it on a sheet of paper.

Read: *An Afternoon Nap*

An Afternoon Nap

Focus Skill **Main Idea** Remind children that finding the main idea of a story can help them understand what they read. Have children reread *An Afternoon Nap*, looking for the most important ideas. Ask: **What important things do you learn about life in this town? If you could tell a friend one thing you learned from this book, what would it be, and why?** (*Possible responses: Many people work and shop at the market. In the afternoon, people stop to rest.*) Encourage children to write a sentence about one important thing they learned from the story.

Inflections -er, -est

PRETEACH Write the word *tall* at the top of a sheet of chart paper and have children read it. Draw three tall stick figures of different heights. Point to the shortest and say **This person is *tall*.** Point to the second and third figures. **This person is *taller*, and this one is *tallest*.** Write *taller* and *tallest* on the board and explain that the *-er* and *-est* endings help compare how tall the people are. Continue, without making pictures, with the words *quick/quicker/quickest* and *light/lighter/lightest*.

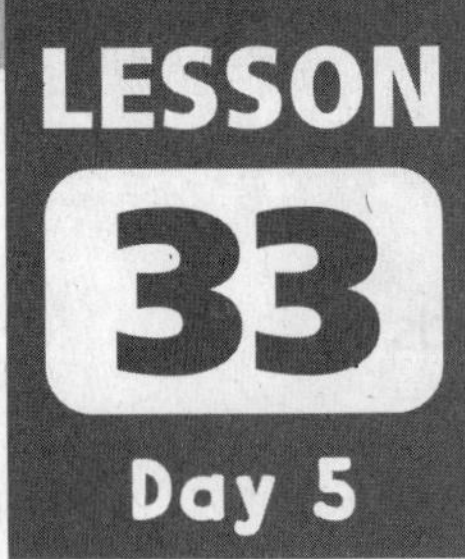

LESSON 33

Day 5

MATERIALS

Write-on/Wipe off Boards

Word Cards also, boy, only, read, thought

Word Builder

Word Builder Cards h, l, m, n, o, p, c

Warm-up: Phonemic Awareness

Phoneme Blending Tell children that together you are going to play a puzzle game. Tell them that you are going to say some words in pieces like a puzzle and they should put the puzzle pieces together to figure out the word. Listen: **/f/-/e/-/th/-/ûr/. What word does /f/-/e/-/th/-/ûr/ say?** (*feather*) Continue with the following words:

/s/-/p/-/oo/-/n/ *(spoon)*	**/h/-/e/-/v/-/ē/** *(heavy)*
/b/-/r/-/e/-/d/ *(bread)*	**/b/-/r/-/e/-/th/** *(breath)*
/f/-/u/-/j/ *(fudge)*	**/t/-/oo/-/th/** *(tooth)*

Phonics: Inflections -er, -est

RETEACH Write the word *short* on a Write-on/ Wipe-off Board and have children do the same. Then have them read the word. Ask: **What should we do if we want to change *short* to *shorter*?** (*add -er*) **Let's do that. What should we do if we want to change *short* to *shortest*?** (*add -est*) **Let's do that.** Continue the activity with the following words: *small*, *dark*, and *old*.

High-Frequency Words

Cumulative Review read, boy, thought, also, only Place the words in a pocket chart. Say aloud one of the words and use it in a sentence. Have a volunteer find and point to the word. Have children clap and say the spelling of the word. Then have them write it. Have children read aloud their list of words.

read

boy

thought

also

Read: Self-Selected Reading

Have children select a book to read from their browsing boxes. After they have completed their reading, have them tell you what they were most successful in during the reading of the book.

Phonics: Vowel Digraph /o͞o/oo

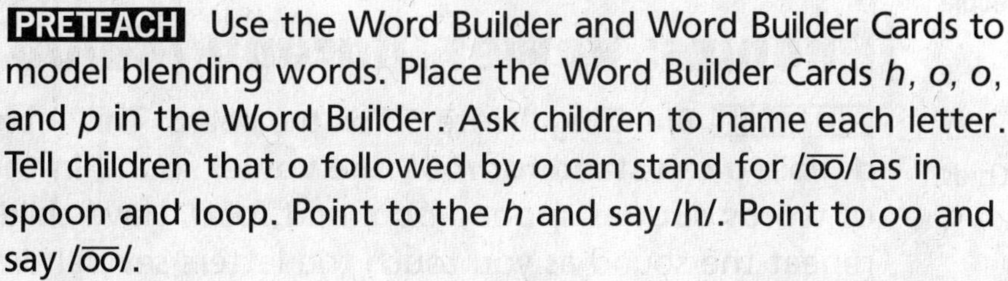

PRETEACH Use the Word Builder and Word Builder Cards to model blending words. Place the Word Builder Cards *h, o, o,* and *p* in the Word Builder. Ask children to name each letter. Tell children that *o* followed by *o* can stand for /o͞o/ as in spoon and loop. Point to the *h* and say /h/. Point to *oo* and say /o͞o/.

Slide the *oo* next to the *h*. Move your hand under the letters and blend the sounds, elongating them /hho͞oo͞o/. Have children repeat after you.

Point to the letter *p*. Say /p/. Slide the *p* next to *hoo*. Slide your hand under *hoop* and blend by elongating the sounds /hho͞oo͞opp/. Have children repeat.

Then have children read the word *hoop* along with you.

Repeat with the words *moon* and *cool*.

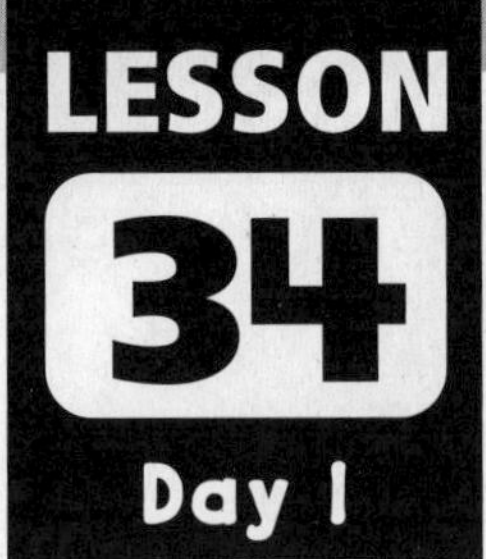

Warm-Up: Phonemic Awareness

Onset and Rime Tell children that you are going to say some words, but you are going to say them in parts. Have children listen to see if they can figure out the word. Demonstrate by saying: **/h/ -oop—What word did I say?** (*hoop*)

/f/-ood	**/b/-oost**	**/br/-oom**	**/l/-oop**
/r/-oom	**/f/-oolish**	**/sp/-oon**	**/r/-ooster**

MATERIALS

Word Cards people, most, why

Word Builder

Word Builder Cards b, c, h, l, m, n, o, o, r, t, t

Baboon's Park

Phonics: Vowel Digraph /o͞o/oo

RETEACH **Blending** Write o͞o on the board. **This letter is *o*. A double *o* can stand for /o͞o/, the vowel sound in the middle of words such as *spoon, loop,* and *food*.** Have children repeat the sound as you touch the letters several times.

Use the Word Builder Cards and a pocket chart to model blending words.

Place the Word Builder Cards *m, o, o,* and *n* in the Word Builder. Point to the *m*. Say /m/. Point to *oo*. Say /o͞o/. Slide *oo* next to *m*. Slide your hand under the letters and blend the sounds, elongating them /mmo͞oo͞o/. Have children repeat after you.

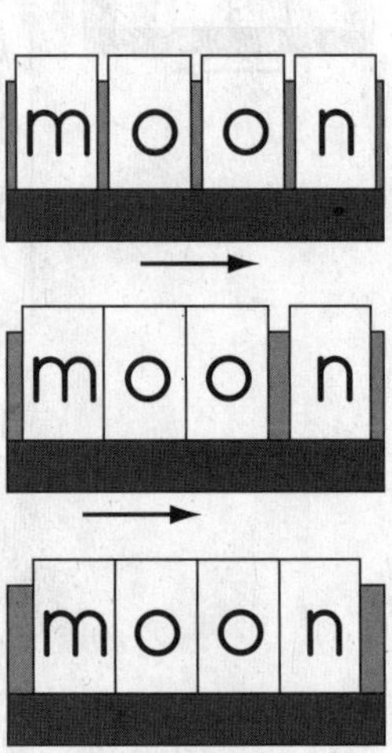

Point to *n*. Say /n/. Slide *n* next to *moo*. Slide your hand under the letters and blend the sounds, elongating them /mmo͞oo͞onn/. Then have children read the word *moon* along with you.

High-Frequency Words

PRETEACH ***people, why, most*** Display the word card *people*. **This word is *people*. The *people* had a good time at the zoo. Read the word with me—*people*. Spell the word with me—*p-e-o-p-l-e*. Read the word with me. What is this word?** (*people*)

Repeat with the words *why* and *most*, using the following sentences:

why—**I know *why* the stars come out at night.**

most—**Most *people* like animals.**

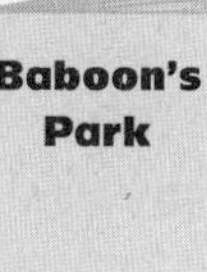

Read: *Baboon's Park*

Story Words/Vocabulary Print the words *fire, quietly, against, shook, rhinoceros, careful*, and *disappear*. Read the words aloud to children. Have children repeat each word after you. Provide help as needed with these words as children read the story.

Distribute copies of the book and have children put their fingers on the title. Read the title aloud while children follow along. Have them touch the word *Baboon's*, then the word *Park*. Point out that the *'s* at the end of the word *Baboon* tells that the park belongs to the baboon. Have volunteers point to a word in the title and read it aloud. Echo read the book with children. Read page 2 aloud and then have children read it to you. Follow this procedure throughout the book.

Phonics: Word Building with /oo/oo

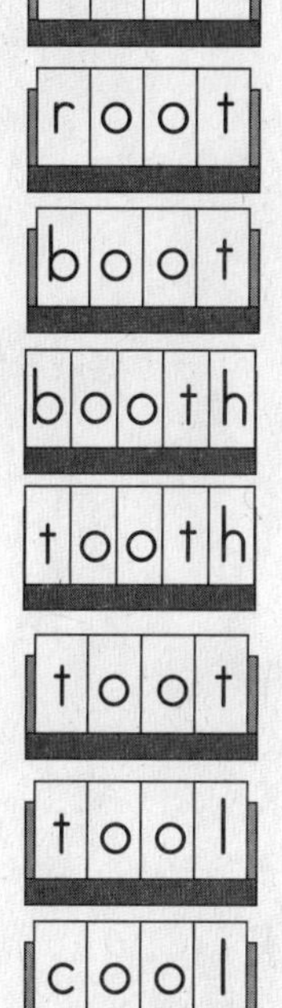

PRETEACH Place the letters *r, o, o,* and *m* in a Word Builder and have children do the same. Model how to blend the word *room*. Slide your hand under the letters as you slowly elongate the sounds /rrōōōōmm/. Have children do the same. Then read the word naturally—*room*. Have children do the same.

Have children blend and read new words by telling them:

Change *m* to *t*. What word did you make? (*root*)

Change *r* to *b*. What word did you make? (*boot*)

Add an *h* after *t*. What word did you make? (*booth*)

Change *b* to *t*. What word did you make? (*tooth*)

Drop *h*. What word did you make? (*toot*)

Change the second *t* to *l*. What word did you make? (*tool*)

Change *t* to *c*. What word did you make? (*cool*)

Distribute *Intervention Practice Book* page 100 to children.

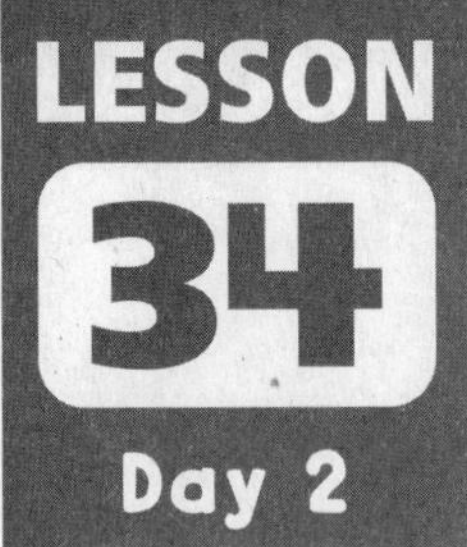

MATERIALS

Word Builder

Word Builder Cards c, d, f, l, m, n, o, o, p, t

Baboon's Park

Warm-Up: Phonemic Awareness

Phoneme Isolation Say the word *soon*. Tell children to listen to the /o͞o/ sound in the middle of the word *soon*. Then say the words *bread* and *boot*. Have them repeat the words aloud. Ask: **Which of these words has the /o͞o/ sound you hear in *soon*?** (*boot*) Continue with the words *tooth, zoom, badge; spool, piece, broom; spoon, brood, gold*.

Phonics: Word Building with /o͞o/oo

RETEACH Place the letters *p, o, o,* and *l* in a Word Builder and have children do the same. Model how to blend the word *pool*. Slide your hand under the letters as you slowly elongate the sounds /ppo͞oo͞oll/. Have children do the same. Then read the word naturally—*pool*. Have children do the same.

Have children blend and read new words by telling them:

Change *p* to *c*. What word did you make? (*cool*)

Change *c* to *t*. What word did you make? (*tool*)

Change *t* to *f*. What word did you make? (*fool*)

Change *l* to *d*. What word did you make? (*food*)

Change *f* to *m*. What word did you make? (*mood*)

Change *d* to *n*. What word did you make? (*moon*)

Drop the *d*. What word did you make? (*moo*)

High-Frequency Words

RETEACH ***people, why, most*** Write the words people and plum on the board and have children read them. Outline the words. Ask **How are these words alike? How are they different? Let's read them again:** *people plum.* Repeat with the following word pairs: *why/way, most/made.*

people plum

Read: *Baboon's Park*

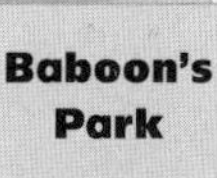

Baboon's Park

Distribute copies of the book to children. Read pages 2 and 3 with them. **The words on page 3 are a letter from Tiger to Baboon. The letter begins with the word *Hello* and then says the name of the person who is getting the letter. Who is getting the letter?** (*Baboon*) **The letter ends with the words *Love, Tiger.* Who is the letter from?** (*Tiger*) Then choral read the book with children. Let your voice fade if children start to gain control of the text.

Phonics: Reading Sentences with /o͞o/oo

PRETEACH Distribute *Intervention Practice Book* page 101 to children. Point to the first sentence and have children read it aloud. Ask them to find the word food, frame it with their fingers, and circle the word. Then work with children to complete the page.

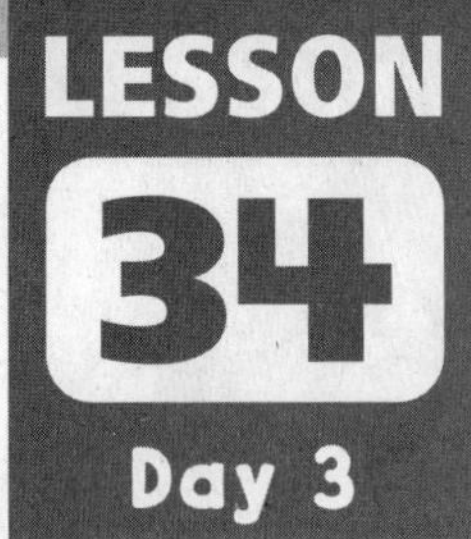

MATERIALS

Picture Cards: clock, cup, drum, fish, flag, jet, kite, lamp, leaf, nut, octopus, sled

Word Builder

Word Builder Cards a, b, e, e, f, h, i, l, o, o, t, t, u

Baboon's Park

Warm-Up: Phonemic Awareness

Phoneme Blending Tell children that they are going to play a guessing game and find the word you have in mind. Then say: **I'm thinking of a word that means something you can use to clean a floor. You use it to sweep things into a dustpan, and it is called a /b/-/r/-/o͞o/-/m/. What's my word?** (*broom*) Continue with the following words: /s/-/p/-/o͞o/-/n/ (*spoon*), /l/-/o͞o/-/p/-/s/ (*loops*), /t/-/o͞o/-/th/ (*tooth*), /k/-/o͞o/-/l/-/ûr/ (*cooler*), /b/-/l/-/o͞o/-/m/ (*bloom*)

Phonics: Reading Sentences with /o͞o/oo

RETEACH Help children blend and read new words and sentences shown. Have them read the sentence, blending each word in sequence. The high-frequency words are underlined; they should read these as a unit, not blending the sounds.

shoot **tool** **stool** **sooner**

<u>Here's</u> <u>a</u> spool <u>of</u> thread.

Eat with <u>a</u> spoon.

Did <u>you</u> brush that tooth?

<u>A</u> mushroom can <u>be</u> food.

High-Frequency Words

RETEACH ***people, why, most*** Write the following sentence on tag board and display it in a pocket chart along with the Picture Cards *kite, flag, jet, nut, sled, drum.* Call on children to choose a Picture Card to complete the sentence and read it aloud. Then ask: **Can you really fly a ________?**

PICTURE CARDS

Most people like to fly a ________.

Repeat, using the following sentence and Picture Cards *fish, clock, cup, leaf, lamp, octopus:*

Why is that ________ so fast?

Read: *Baboon's Park*

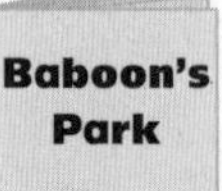

Distribute copies of the book and have children read aloud the title. Then guide children through the book as they read.

Page 2–5: Have children read the pages to find out how Baboon is feeling.

What did Baboon get from Tiger? (*a card and a picture*) **What did Tiger do today?** (*played at the park*) **Why doesn't Baboon want to play tag with Ape? Read the sentence that tells.** (*I am not in the mood)*

Pages 6–7: Have children read to find out what Baboon would like to have.

What does Baboon wish for? (*a park*) **What would Baboon like to do in a park?** (*slide and swing*) **What did Mama do?** *(put her arms around Baboon)*

Pages 8–9: Have children read to find out about the surprise Baboon gets.

Who said he had a surprise for Baboon? (*Ape*) **What kind of animal is Spot?** (*a giraffe*) **What did Ape and Baboon do? Read the words that tell.** (*Ape and Baboon slid down Spot's long, smooth neck*)

Pages 10–12: Have children read to find out how the story ends.

Who pretended to be a swing? (*a snake*) **What did Ape say about the park?** (*"This is a great park!"*) **What does Baboon write to Tiger?** (*We have a new park. We can play in it together!*)

Ask children to use the pictures to help summarize the book.

Phonics: Building Words

PRETEACH Put the letters *t*, *o*, *o*, *t* in a Word Builder and have children do the same. Slide your hand under the letters as you blend the sounds—/ttōōōott/. Then read the word naturally—*toot*. Have children repeat after you. Then have children build and read new words.

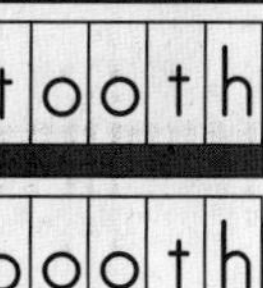

Add *h* after the second *t*. What word did you make? (*tooth*)

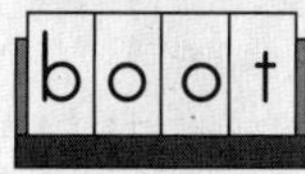

Change the first *t* to *b*. What word did you make? (*booth*)

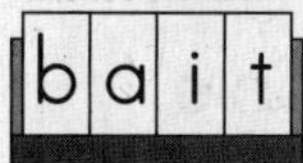

Drop the *h*. What word did you make? (*boot*)

Change *oo* to *ai*. What word did you make? (*bait*)

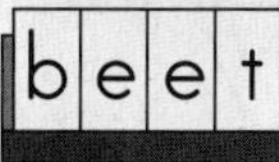

Change *ai* to *ee*. What word did you make? (*beet*)

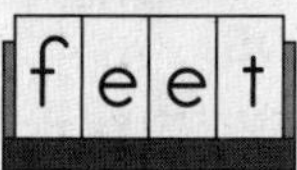

Change *b* to *f*. What word did you make? (*feet*)

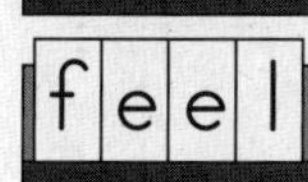

Change *t* to *l*. What word did you make? (*feel*)

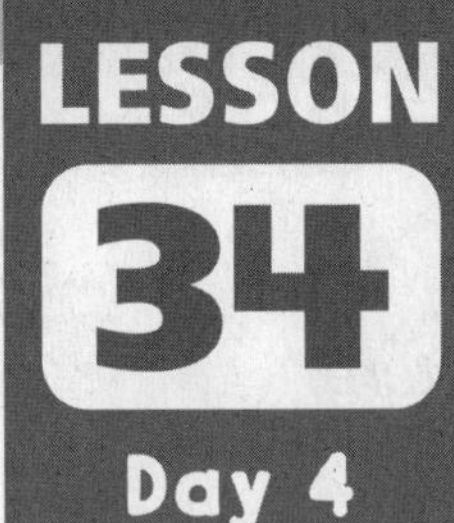

MATERIALS

Picture Cards clam, igloo, smile, lamp

Papers with four boxes, plus disks

Word Cards people, most, why

Word Builder

Word Builder Cards d, f, l, m, n, o, o, p, s

Baboon's Park

Warm-Up: Phonemic Awareness

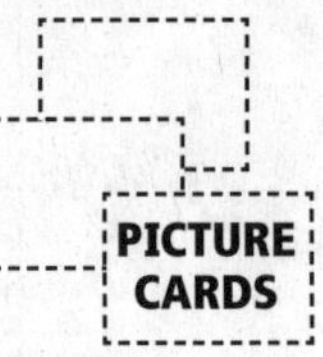

Phoneme Segmentation Distribute the four-box papers to children. Tell them that the boxes stand for sounds in words. Show the Picture Card *igloo* and ask: **What is the first sound you hear in igloo?** (/i/) Have children place a disk in the first box to represent this sound. Then have them name the second sound in *igloo* (/g/) and place a second disk on the paper. Then have them identify the third and fourth sounds in *igloo* (/l/ and /o͞o/) and place a disk on the paper for each sound. Point to the disks in sequence as children say the word. **How many sounds do you hear in *igloo*?** (*four*) Repeat this procedure with the Picture Cards *clam, smile, lamp*.

Phonics: Building Words

RETEACH Put the letters *s, o, o, n* in a Word Builder and have children do the same. Slide your hand under the letters as you blend the sounds —/sso͞oo͞onn/. Then read the word naturally—*soon*. Have children repeat after you. Then have children build and read new words.

Change *s* to *m*. What word did you make? (*moon*)

Change *n* to *d*. What word did you make? (*mood*)

Change *m* to *f*. What word did you make? (*food*)

Change *d* to *l*. What word did you make? (*fool*)

Change *f* to *p*. What word did you make? (*pool*)

Add *s* before *p*. What word did you make? (*spool*)

Distribute *Intervention Practice Book* page 102 to children.

High-Frequency Words

RETEACH ***people, why, most*** Distribute word cards with the words listed above. Have partners take turns displaying the words for each other and reading them. After they read each word, have children spell it and then repeat the word. Then have them spell the word again and write it on a sheet of paper.

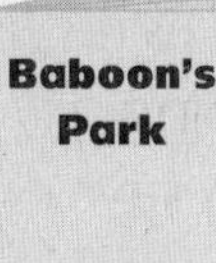

Read: *Baboon's Park*

Focus Skill **Plot** Remind children that the plot is what happens in a story and that thinking about the plot can help them better understand the stories they read. Have children reread *Baboon's Park*, thinking about the plot. Ask: **What is making Baboon unhappy? What does he wish he had? Who helps him get what he wants? How does he feel at the end of the story?** Help children make a chart to show the plot of the story.

1. Tiger writes a letter.
2. Baboon wishes he had a playground.
3. Other animals help Baboon have a park to play in.

Phonics: Phonograms -oom, -oot

PRETEACH Write the letters *oom* and *oot* at the top of a sheet of chart paper. Have children suggest words that end with *-oom* and say what letters they would need to write the words. Then write the words underneath the heading *-oom.* Use the same procedure for *-oot.* Then have children read each column of words. End the activity by pointing to words at random and having children read the words.

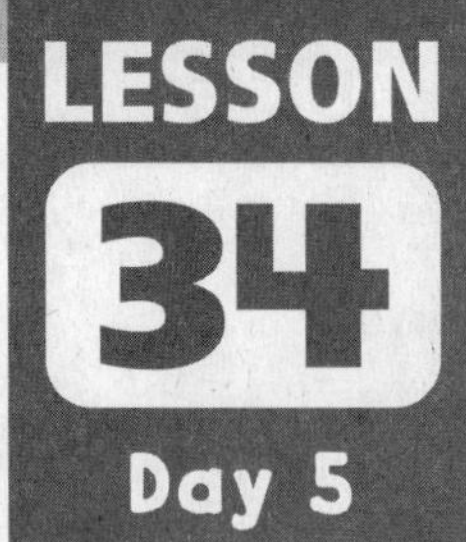

LESSON 34 Day 5

Warm-Up: Phonemic Awareness

Phoneme Blending Tell children that together you are going to play a game of "Fix It." Tell them that you are going to say some words that are all broken and they should listen to see if they can put the sounds together to figure out the word. **Listen: /f/-/o͞o/-/l/. What word does /f/-/o͞o/-/l/ say?** (*fool*) Continue with the following words:

/s/-/t/-/o͞o/-/l/ *(stool)*	**/r/-/e/-/d/-/ē/** *(ready)*	**/b/-/r/-/o͞o/-/m/** *(broom)*
/b/-/ō/-/th/ *(both)*	**/k/-/ā/-/j/** *(cage)*	**/m/-/o͞o/-/n/** *(moon)*

MATERIALS

Write-on/Wipe off Boards

Word Cards boy, head, most, why

Phonics: Phonograms -oom, -oot

RETEACH Write the word *zoom* on a Write-on/Wipe-off Board and have children do the same. Then have them read the word. Ask: **What letter should we write if we want to change *zoom* to *boom*?** (*b*) **Let's do that.** Continue the activity with the following words: *room*, *loom*, and *doom.* Repeat the activity, starting with the word *root* and continuing with the words *hoot, boot,* and *toot*.

High-Frequency Words

boy

head

why

most

Cumulative Review *boy, head, why, most* Place the words in a pocket chart. Say aloud one of the words and use it in a sentence. Have a volunteer find and point to the word. Have children clap and say the spelling of the word. Then have them write it. Have children read aloud their list of words.

Read: Self-Selected Reading

Have children select a book to read from their browsing boxes. After they have completed their reading, have them tell you what they were most successful in during the reading of the book.

Trophies Correlation Chart

Intervention Teacher's Guide	Intervention Lesson	Use With Theme/Week	PE Selection
2	Lesson 1	I Am Your Friend, Week 1	The Hat
12	Lesson 2	I Am Your Friend, Week 2	Sam and the Bag
22	Lesson 3	I Am Your Friend, Week 3	Ants
32	Lesson 4	Just for Fun, Week 1	Jack and Rick
42	Lesson 5	Just for Fun, Week 2	Todd's Box
52	Lesson 6	Just for Fun, Week 3	All That Corn
62	Lesson 7	It's My Turn Now, Week 1	Dan's Pet
72	Lesson 8	It's My Turn Now, Week 2	Boots for Beth
82	Lesson 9	It's My Turn Now, Week 3	Space Pup
92	Lesson 10	It's My Turn Now, Week 4	Where Do Frogs Come From?
102	Lesson 11	It's My Turn Now, Week 5	Try Your Best
112	Lesson 12	It's My Turn Now, Week 6	Fun with Fish
122	Lesson 13	I Think I Can! Week 1	I Am a Butterfly
132	Lesson 14	I Think I Can! Week 2	Did You See Chip?
142	Lesson 15	I Think I Can! Week 3	Tomás Rivera
152	Lesson 16	I Think I Can! Week 4	On the Way to the Pond

Intervention Teacher's Guide	Intervention Lesson	Use With Theme/Week	PE Selection
162	Lesson 17	I Think I Can! Week 5	Friends Forever
172	Lesson 18	I Think I Can! Week 6	The Fox and the Stork
182	Lesson 19	Hello, Neighbor, Week 1	A Bed Full of Cats
192	Lesson 20	Hello, Neighbor, Week 2	Me On the Map
202	Lesson 21	Hello, Neighbor, Week 3	At Home Around the World
212	Lesson 22	Hello, Neighbor, Week 4	Tell Me a Story
222	Lesson 23	Hello, Neighbor, Week 5	My Robot
232	Lesson 24	Hello, Neighbor, Week 6	On the Job with Dr. Martha Smith
242	Lesson 25	Hello, Neighbor, Week 7	Little Bear's Friend
252	Lesson 26	Hello, Neighbor, Week 8	Busy Buzzy Bee
262	Lesson 27	Going Places, Week 1	The Story of a Blue Bird
272	Lesson 28	Going Places, Week 2	Frog and Toad All Year
282	Lesson 29	Going Places, Week 3	Fishing Bears
292	Lesson 30	Going Places, Week 4	How to Be a Nature Detective
302	Lesson 31	Going Places, Week 5	The Puddle
312	Lesson 32	Going Places, Week 6	Poppleton Everyday
322	Lesson 33	Going Places, Week 7	Sleep Is for Everyone
332	Lesson 34	Going Places, Week 8	Baboon